Conceptions of Inquiry

Conceptions of Inquiry

A READER EDITED BY

Stuart Brown, John Fauvel and Ruth Finnegan

AT THE OPEN UNIVERSITY

R

ROUTLEDGE

in association with

THE OPEN UNIVERSITY PRESS

First published in 1981 by
Methuen & Co. Ltd
in association with
The Open University Press

Reprinted 1989 by
Routledge
11 New Fetter Lane, London EC4P 4EE

Typeset by Scarborough Typesetting Services
and printed in Great Britain by
Richard Clay Ltd, Bungay, Suffolk

British Library Cataloguing in Publication Data

Conceptions of inquiry.
1. Inquiry (Theory of knowledge) – Addresses,
essays, lectures
I. Brown, Stuart, b. 1938   II. Fauvel, John
III. Finnegan, Ruth   IV. Open University
V. Series
001   BD183   80–41100

ISBN 0–416–3021–6
ISBN 0–415–04565–7 Pbk   (University paperbacks)

Acknowledgements

The editors and publishers wish to thank the following individuals, companies and institutions for kind permission to reproduce copyright © material: George Allen & Unwin Ltd for extracts 1.4, 2.2 and 6.3; The Editor, The Aristotelian Society, 7.2; Cambridge University Press, 1.5, 2.3, 9.2 and 10.3; The Courant Institute, 2.5; Professor David Easton, 6.2; Editions Gallimard, 8.4; Harvard University Press, 2.1; The Harvester Press Ltd, 1.3; Hutchinson Educational Books Ltd, 3.2; Methuen & Co Ltd, 2.4; The Open Court Publishing Company, La Salle, Illinois, 4.4; The Open University, 4.5; Oxford University Press, 5.1 and 8.1; Penguin Books Ltd, 1.1; Sir Karl Popper, 5.4; Radical Science Journal, 1.7; Routledge & Kegan Paul Ltd, 1.6, 4.3, 7.1, 7.3, 8.2 and 8.3; Professor Israel Scheffler, 9.1; Society for the Study of Social Problems, 10.2; Tavistock Publications, 8.4; Unesco Courier, 3.3 and The University of Chicago Press, 5.2, 5.3 and 9.3.

Contents

PART THREE: CONCEPTIONS OF
SOCIAL INQUIRY

PART FOUR: CONCEPTIONS OF INQUIRY

Introduction

The materials collected in this volume articulate contrasting or competing conceptions of inquiry. The final part is directed to general questions about inquiry or which are applicable to several areas, but particular attention is given in the earlier parts to inquiry in mathematics, science, history and social science. The volume is designed for use in an Open University course on *Inquiry* whose students are not expected to have already studied any particular area in any depth. The materials we have selected are, therefore, largely suitable for a general readership.

The *Inquiry* course aims to introduce students to the nature of inquiry both through studying examples or case studies and through a critical examination of unifying conceptions of a mainly philosophical character. Our assumption, shared by many of the contributors to this volume, is that conceptions of inquiry need, in the last analysis, to be judged by reference to actual cases.

This assumption seems to have been borne out by the history of such conceptions. Mathematics, for example, long enjoyed pride of place amongst the sciences. It had been developed to a high level by the ancient Greeks. At a time when forms of inquiry we should now classify as natural sciences seemed fraught with obscurity and controversy, mathematical inquiry stood out as clear in its methods and certain in its conclusions. Philosophers in the seventeenth century, such as René Descartes, tried to articulate a vision of what science generally should be like, taking the example of mathematics, and geometry in particular, to heart. The prescribed mode of inquiry, whether in physics, metaphysics, ethics, jurisprudence or any other 'science', was to be modelled on this example of conspicuously successful science. Any system of scientific knowledge was to be derived from first principles which, like the axioms of Euclidean geometry, were themselves to be beyond doubt. A system thus would consist of a series of proofs and expand so as to encompass, at least ideally, everything which required explanation or justification.

Although conceptions of inquiry always have a prescriptive dimension, they are not produced out of nothing. On the contrary, they must accurately reflect those kinds and cases of inquiry they take to be exemplary. No one now accepts the conception of inquiry just sketched, and for this reason we have not included here any extract to represent it. The downfall of that conception of inquiry which makes geometrical inquiry the paradigm of all scientific inquiry into the world illustrates, however, the way in which even the most general conceptions of inquiry are answerable, in the end, to examples of their practice — for the possibility of constructing geometries with assumptions different from those of Euclid immediately brings in question the assumption that there is a single system of geometry which proves the necessary structure of space. Such developments, once understood, raise the question as to which kind of geometry best fits the world we actually inhabit. That question in turn calls for a different conception of geometry and a separation of pure mathematics from natural science.

The first major part of this volume is concerned with the nature of inquiry in mathematics and with how mathematics relates to the world. Even if the conception of science which saw in mathematics the key to the mysteries of the universe proved, in the long run, to be unacceptable, it was not without its practical successes, particularly in optics and astronomy. The fact that so many of the exemplary achievements of scientific inquiry have represented nature in fundamentally mathematical terms continues to pose questions which are addressed in several extracts in chapter 2.

Most of the materials included in this volume are from works written in recent decades. We have, however, included one or two classics, such as an extract from Plato's *Meno* in which is articulated a view of mathematics that still has some persuasive force two millennia later. There is also a short extract from Newton's *Principia*, a work which, although laid out in the geometrical form expected of scientific works in the seventeenth century, broke the rules then accepted for a proper scientific system. Newton put forward universal gravitational attraction as a fundamental principle governing the behaviour of bodies throughout the universe and he gave it a sharp mathematical expression in his inverse square law. But he ought, according to the expectation of many contemporaries, to have explained the cause of gravitational attraction. His failure to do so or, at any rate, his refusal to offer a 'hypothesis' as to the cause of gravity, was seen as a failure to put his system on a clear and certain foundation. Newton's work confounded those critics and became, in the eighteenth century, the example on which conceptions of inquiry were to be modelled. The 'experimental' or, as it was later known, the 'inductive' philosophy became the orthodox view of natural science and remained so until relatively recently.

Part Two of this volume includes two extracts from John Stuart Mill's *A System of Logic*, a classic nineteenth-century defence of the 'inductive' conception of natural science. Most of the extracts in this part, however, reflect a post-inductivist view of science. The picture of the steady accumulation of theoretical knowledge – generalization built carefully on experiment and observation and theory built on carefully established hypotheses – was rudely shattered by the revolutionary rejection of the very theory which had for so long been held up as an example of a scientific demonstration, namely, Newton's mechanics. Extracts by Popper (4.3) and Bondi (5.1) illustrate how the acceptance of Einstein's theory in preference to Newton's called for changes in how science was conceived as progressing. The discussions in this part reflect the search for a conception of science which can admit revolutionary changes in theory without denying that the history of science is a history of progress.

Just as the natural sciences were at one time conceived on the model of mathematics, their establishment made them in turn the exemplars for the emergence of a less-established area of inquiry. The extracts in Part Three by Mill (6.1) and Hempel (6.3) exemplify ways in which social science and history have been conceived as modelled on the natural sciences. The aptness of natural-science models for explaining human behaviour has, however, been widely disputed. The extract (7.1) from Winch's *The Idea of a Social Science* articulates a very different view which has itself been the focus for much controversy. Yet Winch's critics, including MacIntyre (7.2), agree with him that a society must first be understood 'in its own terms'. To the extent that the social anthropologist, for example, needs to enter into other people's ways of thought, as Beattie stresses (7.3), his explanations are unlikely to take the reductive form characteristic of the natural sciences.

These questions have not always seemed particularly pressing for many of the subjects within the humanities tradition – the study, for example, of literature, art or music. But they are a matter of constant and even anxious debate within the disciplines which in one way or another take some interest in generalizing in relation to social life and in defining themselves as involved in empirical inquiry. In the 'social sciences' above all – a heading under which history is not infrequently included – there is continuing controversy, both explicit and implicit, about the aims and methodology of inquiry and how these are related to those of the natural sciences.

The accounts of inquiry in Part Three are all, as it were, internal ones. In other words they direct themselves to elucidating the logic of the aims and procedures within social and natural science inquiries, but do not raise questions about the social context and constraints within which the practitioners conduct their research. Though certain assumptions are made about 'progress' in science, especially by the empiricist writers, there is no consideration of the wider questions of how radical changes in outlook or 'paradigms' may come about, as discussed by Kuhn for instance (5.2, 5.3), or of the social and economic pressures which direct us to one mode of inquiry rather than another (see Hodgkin, 1.7; Foucault, 8.4), or of the part which may or may not be played by the researcher's own values (see chs 9 and 10). All these aspects are indeed important ones for the question of how social (and natural) science inquiries are actually delimited and carried out in practice. But from the point of view of the controversies exemplified in Part Three, as in the philosophy of social science generally, concentration is placed rather on the internal logic of the methodology which is, or arguably should be, followed in social inquiry, and its relation to that in the natural sciences.

Included in Part Four are two interrelated chapters which have a bearing on this debate. The chapter on objectivity includes a statement by Israel Scheffler of a conception of objectivity which he holds to be common to all inquiry. There are criticisms in other extracts of that view of objectivity as a tenable one for the natural sciences. As well as the dispute whether the so-called 'hard' sciences are quite so objective as is commonly supposed, it is a matter of controversy whether physics *is* objective in a way the humanities are not. Passmore (9.4) claims that, so far as history is concerned, there is no relevant sense in which it fails, where physics succeeds, in being objective.

The natural sciences are commonly represented as being 'value-free'. This has been disputed by Kuhn (9.3) and others. But it has commonly been assumed and is argued, e.g. by Max Weber (10.1), that the social sciences should be equally value-free. Against this it has been argued, e.g. by Gouldner (10.2), that value-freedom in the social sciences can never be more than a pretence beneath which a commitment to the existing order is hidden. This is one point on which Marxist social scientists have challenged the natural-science-oriented view prevailing in their subjects.

Many conceptions of inquiry accord a special status to the natural sciences. This is true of Hume (8.1) as much as it is of his intellectual heirs, such as Mill and Hempel. Hume divides knowledge up in such a way as to make the distinction between inquiry into general facts (e.g. politics and physics) and inquiry into particular facts (e.g. history and astronomy) more fundamental than the distinction between the science of man and the science of nature. Hume indeed aspired to be the Newton of the science of man. Within his hierarchical structure the social sciences are just one area of the 'experimental philosophy'.

Against such a hierarchical conception of inquiry it has more recently been maintained, by Hirst, that there are a number of quite autonomous 'forms of knowledge' which are not reducible to one another (8.2, 8.3). Foucault (8.4) rejects the assumption, common to Hume, Hirst and indeed to much Anglo-Saxon writing on inquiry, that distinctions can be drawn between forms of inquiry in a timeless way. If Foucault is right, different disciplines of inquiry have a historical and therefore changing identity as well as an institutional basis. A study of the nature of botany or mathematics would need to include the social basis of its discourse — there are, for Foucault, no timeless forms of knowledge. The extract included here is from a book appropriately entitled, in translation, *The Archaeology of Knowledge*.

The intellectual commerce about the nature of various areas of inquiry is no longer one simply between philosophers and practitioners. It has become a many-way traffic in ideas — between philosophers and social anthropologists, mathematicians and physicists, sociologists and historians — to mention but some of the exchanges reflected in this volume. There is competition for colonial preference, especially perhaps between philosophers and sociologists of knowledge, but by and large the trade is freer than it was a few decades ago. Whether inquiry into inquiry will prosper in such conditions remains to be seen, but the free trade has one advantage from the point of view of the non-specialist. It is that a practitioner of one discipline who wants to communicate with students of other disciplines must write in terms which those who are not specialized in his own discipline can understand.

None of the extracts included in this volume was specially written for it. The selection has been made by various members of the *Inquiry* course team. Noel Parker also advised on and provided the editorial introduction to the extract from Foucault. John Fauvel has been responsible for editing Part One, I (Stuart Brown) for Part Two and chapters 8 and 9 and Ruth Finnegan for Part Three and chapter 10.

Stuart Brown

Part One
Conceptions of Mathematics

1 Mathematical inquiry

The question of what someone is doing in carrying out a mathematical inquiry is one of those simple-looking questions the answer to which can rapidly become rather complicated both philosophically and procedurally. Philosophically, it depends on one's conception of what mathematics *is*, even down to the language used in describing mathematical inquiry: to speak of *discovering* mathematics generally implies a belief that mathematical truths exist independently of our minds, while *inventing* mathematics carries the suggestion that it is a human construction. This problem is not unique to mathematics – photographers have been arguing for a century about whether a photograph is *taken* or *made* – but an awareness of the issues is particularly important in understanding the place of mathematics in other kinds of inquiry. The aim of this chapter is to provide a number of contrasting views of mathematical activity, in which it may be seen how each is related to a particular conception not only of what mathematics *is* but also of what *value* or purpose it has.

1.1 MATHEMATICS AS ETERNAL TRUTH

PLATO (*c*.427–*c*.347 B.C.), *from his dialogue* Meno, *81E–86C, Guthrie, W. K. C., trans., Harmondsworth, Penguin, 1956*

The conception of mathematical inquiry made explicit in this passage may take the modern reader by surprise; that inquiry should be considered a bringing back into the memory of truths forgotten from a previous existence is now probably felt rather unlikely. Indeed, at the end of this extract even Socrates sounds a little doubtful ('I shouldn't like to take my oath on the whole story'). This serves to highlight the several layers of meaning that Plato is communicating. On one level, this is a classic statement of the view that mathematics exists independently of human beings, and that mathematical inquiry is therefore a (re)discovery of real mathematical truths. On another level, Socrates' procedure in reminding the slave boy of mathematical truth is presented as a paradigm of how to conduct an inquiry; Socrates' asides to Meno provide a running commentary on the Socratic method in action. On a third level, this experiment is a demonstration of the value of inquiry itself − it is this which Socrates says 'I am ready to fight for as long as I can'. Previously Meno had raised the objection that inquiry itself is a futile activity, on the grounds that either we know the answer, in which case there is no point in inquiry, or we do not, in which case we would not recognize an answer if we found it, so inquiry is again pointless. Before embarking on a book, or a course, on inquiry it is as well to have some reason for believing that inquiry is worthwhile; Plato here provides it. A further implication which could be drawn from the discussion is that the only kind of inquiry which is worth pursuing, the only kind of knowledge that we can be certain of, is mathematical, or shares with mathematics the attributes of being eternally true and independent of the empirical world. This extract is thus an important text at the head of the long western tradition that inquiries are better and more reliable the closer they approach to the forms and methods of mathematical inquiry.

MENO. What do you mean when you say that we don't learn anything, but that what we call learning is recollection? Can you teach me that it is so?

SOCRATES. I have just said that you're a rascal, and now you ask me if I can teach you, when I say there is no such thing as teaching, only recollection. Evidently you want to catch me contradicting myself straight away.

MENO. No, honestly, Socrates, I wasn't thinking of that. It was just habit. If you can in any way make clear to me that what you say is true, please do.

SOCRATES. It isn't an easy thing, but still I should like to do what I can since you ask me. I see you have a large number of retainers here. Call one of them, anyone you like, and I will use him to demonstrate it to you.

MENO. Certainly. *(To a slave-boy.)* Come here.

SOCRATES. He is a Greek and speaks our language?

MENO. Indeed yes — born and bred in the house.

SOCRATES. Listen carefully then, and see whether it seems to you that he is learning from me or simply being reminded.

MENO. I will.

SOCRATES. Now boy, you know that a square is a figure like this?
(Socrates begins to draw figures in the sand at his feet. He points to the square ABCD.*)*

BOY. Yes.

SOCRATES. It has all these four sides equal?

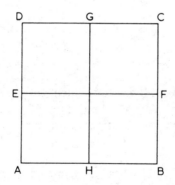

BOY. Yes.

SOCRATES. And these lines which go through the middle of it are also equal? *(The lines* EF, GH.*)*

BOY. Yes.

SOCRATES. Such a figure could be either larger or smaller, could it not?

BOY. Yes.

SOCRATES. Now if this side is two feet long, and this side the same, how many feet will the whole be? Put it this way. If it were two feet in this direction and only one in that, must not the area be two feet taken once?

BOY. Yes.

SOCRATES. But since it is two feet this way also, does it not become twice two feet?

BOY. Yes.

SOCRATES. And how many feet is twice two? Work it out and tell me.

BOY. Four.

SOCRATES. Now could one draw another figure double the size of this, but similar, that is, with all its sides equal like this one?

BOY. Yes.

SOCRATES. How many feet will its area be?

BOY. Eight.

SOCRATES. Now then, try to tell me how long each of its sides will be. The present figure has a side of two feet. What will be the side of the double-sized one?

BOY. It will be double, Socrates, obviously.

SOCRATES. You see, Meno, that I am not teaching him anything, only asking. Now he thinks he knows the length of the side of the eight-feet square.

MENO. Yes.

SOCRATES. But does he?

MENO. Certainly not.

SOCRATES. He thinks it is twice the length of the other.

MENO. Yes.

SOCRATES. Now watch how he recollects things in order — the proper way to recollect.

You say that the side of double length produces the double-sized figure? Like this I mean, not long this way and short that. It must be equal on all sides like the first figure, only twice its size, that is eight feet. Think a moment whether you still expect to get it from doubling the side.

BOY. Yes, I do.

SOCRATES. Well now, shall we have a line double the length of this (AB) if we add another the same length at this end (BJ)?

BOY. Yes.

SOCRATES. It is on this line then, according to you, that we shall make the eight-feet square, by taking four of the same length?

BOY. Yes.

SOCRATES. Let us draw in four equal lines (*i.e. counting* AJ, *and adding* JK, KL, *and* LA *made complete by drawing in its second half* LD), using the first as a base. Does this not give us what you call the eight-feet figure?

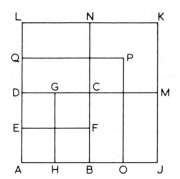

BOY. Certainly.

SOCRATES. But does it contain these four squares, each equal to the original four-feet one?

(Socrates has drawn in the lines CM, CN *to complete the squares that he wishes to point out.)*

BOY. Yes.

SOCRATES. How big is it then? Won't it be four times as big?

BOY. Of course.

SOCRATES. And is four times the same as twice?

BOY. Of course not.

SOCRATES. So doubling the side has given us not a double but a four-fold figure?

BOY. True.

SOCRATES. And four times four are sixteen, are they not?

BOY. Yes.

SOCRATES. Then how big is the side of the eight-feet figure? This one has given us four times the original area, hasn't it?

BOY. Yes.

SOCRATES. And a side half the length gave us a square of four feet?

BOY. Yes.

SOCRATES. Good. And isn't a square of eight feet double this one and half that?

BOY. Yes.

SOCRATES. Will it not have a side greater than this one but less than that?

BOY. I think it will.

SOCRATES. Right. Always answer what you think. Now tell me: was not this side two feet long, and this one four?

BOY. Yes.

SOCRATES. Then the side of the eight-feet figure must be longer than two feet but shorter than four?

BOY. It must.

SOCRATES. Try to say how long you think it is.

BOY. Three feet.

SOCRATES. If so, shall we add half of this bit (BO, *half of* BJ) and make it three feet? Here are two, and this is one, and on this side similarly we have two plus one; and here is the figure you want.

(*Socrates completes the square* AOPQ.)

BOY. Yes.

SOCRATES. If it is three feet this way and three that, will the whole area be three times three feet?

BOY. It looks like it.

SOCRATES. And that is how many?

BOY. Nine.

SOCRATES. Whereas the square double our first square had to be how many?

BOY. Eight.

SOCRATES. But we haven't yet got the square of eight feet even from a three-feet side?

BOY. No.

SOCRATES. Then what length will give it? Try to tell us exactly. If you don't want to count it up, just show us on the diagram.

BOY. It's no use, Socrates, I just don't know.

SOCRATES. Observe, Meno, the stage he has reached on the path of recollection. At the beginning he did not know the side of the square of eight feet. Nor indeed does he know it now, but then he thought he knew it and answered boldly, as was appropriate — he felt no perplexity. Now however he does feel perplexed. Not only does he not know the answer; he doesn't even think he knows.

MENO. Quite true.

SOCRATES. Isn't he in a better position now in relation to what he didn't know?

MENO. I admit that too.

SOCRATES. So in perplexing him and numbing him like the sting-ray, have we done him any harm?

MENO. I think not.

SOCRATES. In fact we have helped him to some extent towards finding out the right answer, for now not only is he ignorant of it but he will be quite glad to look for it. Up to now, he thought he could speak well and fluently, on many occasions and before large audiences, on the subject of a square double the size of a given square, maintaining that it must have a side of double the length.

MENO. No doubt.

SOCRATES. Do you suppose then that he would have attempted to look for, or learn, what he thought he knew (though he did not), before he was thrown into perplexity, became aware of his ignorance, and felt a desire to know?

MENO. No.

SOCRATES. Then the numbing process was good for him?

MENO. I agree.

SOCRATES. Now notice what, starting from this state of perplexity, he will discover by seeking the truth in company with me, though I simply ask him questions without teaching him. Be ready to catch me if I give him any instruction or explanation instead of simply interrogating him on his own opinions.

(Socrates here rubs out the previous figures and starts again.)
Tell me, boy, is not this our square of four feet? (ABCD.) You understand?

BOY. Yes.

SOCRATES. Now we can add another equal to it like this? (BCEF.)

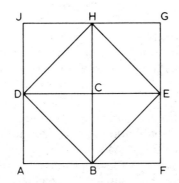

BOY. Yes.

SOCRATES. And a third here, equal to each of the others? (CEGH.)

BOY. Yes.

SOCRATES. And then we can fill in this one in the corner? (DCHJ.)

BOY. Yes.

SOCRATES. Then here we have four equal squares?

BOY. Yes.

SOCRATES. And how many times the size of the first square is the whole?

BOY. Four times.

SOCRATES. And we want one double the size. You remember?

BOY. Yes.

SOCRATES. Now does this line going from corner to corner cut each of these squares in half?

BOY. Yes.

SOCRATES. And these are four equal lines enclosing this area? (BEHD.)

BOY. They are.

SOCRATES. Now think. How big is this area?

BOY. I don't understand.

SOCRATES. Here are four squares. Has not each line cut off the inner half of each of them?

BOY. Yes.

SOCRATES. And how many such halves are there in this figure? (BEHD.)

BOY. Four.

SOCRATES. And how many in this one? (ABCD.)

BOY. Two.

SOCRATES. And what is the relation of four to two?

BOY. Double.

SOCRATES. How big is this figure then?

BOY. Eight feet.

SOCRATES. On what base?

BOY. This one.

SOCRATES. The line which goes from corner to corner of the square of four feet?

BOY. Yes.

SOCRATES. The technical name for it is 'diagonal'; so if we use that name, it is your personal opinion that the square on the diagonal of the original square is double its area.

BOY. That is so, Socrates.

SOCRATES. What do you think, Meno? Has he answered with any opinions that were not his own?

MENO. No, they were all his.

SOCRATES. Yet he did not know, as we agreed a few minutes ago.

MENO. True.

SOCRATES. But these opinions were somewhere in him, were they not?

MENO. Yes.

SOCRATES. So a man who does not know has in himself true opinions on a subject without having knowledge.

MENO. It would appear so.

SOCRATES. At present these opinions, being newly aroused, have a dream-like quality. But if the same questions are put to him on many occasions and in different ways, you can see that in the end he will have a knowledge on the subject as accurate as anybody's.

MENO. Probably.

SOCRATES. This knowledge will not come from teaching but from questioning. He will recover it for himself.

MENO. Yes.

SOCRATES. And the spontaneous recovery of knowledge that is in him is recollection, isn't it?

MENO. Yes.

SOCRATES. Either then he has at some time acquired the knowledge which he now has, or he has always possessed it. If he always possessed it, he must always have known; if on the other hand he acquired it at some previous time, it cannot have been in this life, unless somebody has taught him geometry. He will behave in the same way with all geometrical knowledge, and every other subject. Has anyone taught him all these? You ought to know, especially as he has been brought up in your household.

MENO. Yes, I know that no one ever taught him.

SOCRATES. And has he these opinions, or hasn't he?

MENO. It seems we can't deny it.

SOCRATES. Then if he did not acquire them in this life, isn't it immediately clear that he possessed and had learned them during some other period?

MENO. It seems so.

SOCRATES. When he was not in human shape?

MENO. Yes.

SOCRATES. If then there are going to exist in him, both while he is and while he is not a man, true opinions which can be aroused by questioning and turned into knowledge, may we say that his soul has been for ever in a state of knowledge? Clearly he always either is or is not a man.

MENO. Clearly.

SOCRATES. And if the truth about reality is always in our soul, the soul must be immortal, and one must take courage and try to discover — that is, to recollect — what one doesn't happen to know, or (more correctly) remember, at the moment.

MENO. Somehow or other I believe you are right.

SOCRATES. I think I am. I shouldn't like to take my oath on the whole story, but one thing I am ready to fight for as long as I can, in word and act: that is, that we shall be better, braver and more active men if we believe it right to look for what we don't know than if we believe there is no point in looking because what we don't know we can never discover.

MENO. There too I am sure you are right.

1.2   MATHEMATICS AS AESTHETIC CREATION

HENRI POINCARÉ (1854–1912), *a slightly shortened version of his lecture on 'Mathematical discovery', from his collection of essays* Science and Method, *Maitland, Francis, trans., London, Thomas Nelson & Sons, 1914*

This is the most detailed account by a mathematician of Poincaré's distinction of 'what happens in the very soul of the mathematician' (as he describes it). Just because Poincaré was mathematically so uncommonly gifted, though, his account should not be taken as necessarily typical of all mathematical inquiries. But it is worth noting the judgement of the contemporary mathematician Jean Dieudonné:[1] 'His well-known description of the process of mathematical discovery remains unsurpassed and has been on the whole corroborated by many mathematicians, despite the fact that Poincaré's imagination was completely atypical'.[2] In any event, one purpose of including this essay here is not to assert some particular model for mathematical inquiry but to draw attention to what mathematical inquiry is not. The point may be made by comparing Poincaré's experience with that of his contemporary Sigmund Freud, whose biographer wrote:

> Of how far removed Freud's mode of working was from *purely intellectual activity such as takes place in much of mathematics and physics* one gets a vivid impression from his own descriptions. They make it plain that, especially in those formative years, he was being moved forward almost entirely by unconscious forces and was very much at the mercy of them. He oscillated greatly between moods in which ideas came readily into his mind, when there would be a clear view of the conceptions he was building up, and on the other hand moods when he was evidently inhibited, with no flow of ideas, and when his mind was quite sluggish and dull.[3]

It is clear from Poincaré's essay, however, that Ernest Jones's description of Freud's mode of working would not be inapplicable to him. It follows that wherever the difference between mathematical and other forms of inquiry may lie, it is not in the feelings attendant on the creative experience.

As with Plato's story, a particular view of the nature of mathematics (and also of the human mind) is presupposed in Poincaré's discussion, though he lays more emphasis on the beauty and harmony in mathematics. It may be noted how the presuppositions determine even the terms of the inquiry, in that Poincaré's distinction between understanding and discovering mathematics could not have arisen within Plato's analysis. And Poincaré's view of the mind — which is like Freud's in having both a conscious and an active unconscious, but dissimilar in other respects — entails a greater degree of biological determinism, in respect of mathematical ability, than does Plato's. Whereas mathematics is for Plato latent in everyone's mind, Poincaré's aesthetic sieve appears to be something which, if you have it, you are a mathematician; and if not, not. But — as in reading Plato — it is not necessary to take one's oath on the whole story to perceive the importance of the concerns and observations which Poincaré here brings to light.

Notes

1. Dieudonné, J. (1975) Article on Poincaré in *Dictionary of Scientific Biography*, New York, Charles Scribner's Sons, vol. 11, p. 60.
2. No significance should be attached to the translator's use of 'discovery' here; another well-known translation uses 'creation' throughout.
3. Jones, Ernest (1953) *Sigmund Freud: Life and Work*, London, Hogarth, vol. I, pp. 377–8, emphasis added.

1 The genesis of mathematical discovery is a problem which must inspire the psychologist with the keenest interest. For this is the process in which the human mind seems to borrow least from the exterior world, in which it acts, or appears to act, only by itself and on itself, so that by studying the process of geometric thought we may hope to arrive at what is most essential in the human mind.

2   One first fact must astonish us, or rather would astonish us if we were not too much accustomed to it. How does it happen that there are people who do not understand mathematics? If the science invokes only the rules of logic, those accepted by all well-formed minds, if its evidence is founded on principles that are common to all men, and that none but a madman would attempt to deny, how does it happen that there are so many people who are entirely impervious to it?

3   There is nothing mysterious in the fact that every one is not capable of discovery. That every one should not be able to retain a demonstration he has once learnt is still comprehensible. But what does seem most surprising, when we consider it, is that any one should be unable to understand a mathematical argument at the very moment it is stated to him. And yet those who can only follow the argument with difficulty are in a majority; this is incontestable, and the experience of teachers of secondary education will certainly not contradict me.

4   And still further, how is error possible in mathematics? A healthy intellect should not be guilty of any error in logic, and yet there are very keen minds which will not make a false step in a short argument such as those we have to make in the ordinary actions of life, which yet are incapable of following or repeating without error the demonstrations of mathematics which are longer, but which are, after all, only accumulations of short arguments exactly analogous to those they make so easily. Is it necessary to add that mathematicians themselves are not infallible?

5   The answer appears to me obvious. Imagine a long series of syllogisms in which the conclusions of those that precede form the premises of those that follow. We shall be capable of grasping each of the syllogisms, and it is not in the passage from premises to conclusion that we are in danger of going astray. But between the moment when we meet a proposition for the first time as the conclusion of one syllogism, and the moment when we find it once more as the premise of another syllogism, much time will sometimes have elapsed, and we shall have unfolded many links of the chain; accordingly it may well happen that we shall have forgotten it, or, what is more serious, forgotten its meaning. So we may chance to replace it by a somewhat different proposition, or to preserve the same statement but give it a slightly different meaning, and thus we are in danger of falling into error.

6   A mathematician must often use a rule, and, naturally, he begins by demonstrating the rule. At the moment the demonstration is quite fresh in his memory he understands perfectly its meaning and significance, and he is in no danger of changing it. But later on he commits it to memory, and only applies it in a mechanical way, and then, if his

memory fails him, he may apply it wrongly. It is thus, to take a simple and almost vulgar example, that we sometimes make mistakes in calculation, because we have forgotten our multiplication table.

7   On this view special aptitude for mathematics would be due to nothing but a very certain memory or a tremendous power of attention. It would be a quality analogous to that of the whist player who can remember the cards played, or, to rise a step higher, to that of the chess player who can picture a very great number of combinations and retain them in his memory. Every good mathematician should also be a good chess player and vice versa, and similarly he should be a good numerical calculator. Certainly this sometimes happens, and thus Gauss was at once a geometrician of genius and a very precocious and very certain calculator.

8   But there are exceptions, or rather I am wrong, for I cannot call them exceptions, otherwise the exceptions would be more numerous than the cases of conformity with the rule. On the contrary, it was Gauss who was an exception. As for myself, I must confess I am absolutely incapable of doing an addition sum without a mistake. Similarly I should be a very bad chess player. I could easily calculate that by playing in a certain way I should be exposed to such and such a danger; I should then review many other moves, which I should reject for other reasons, and I should end by making the move I first examined, having forgotten in the interval the danger I had foreseen.

9   In a word, my memory is not bad, but it would be insufficient to make me a good chess player. Why, then, does it not fail me in a difficult mathematical argument in which the majority of chess players would be lost? Clearly because it is guided by the general trend of the argument. A mathematical demonstration is not a simple juxtaposition of syllogisms; it consists of syllogisms *placed in a certain order*, and the order in which these elements are placed is much more important than the elements themselves. If I have the feeling, so to speak the intuition, of this order, so that I can perceive the whole of the argument at a glance, I need no longer be afraid of forgetting one of the elements; each of them will place itself naturally in the position prepared for it, without my having to make any effort of memory.

10   It seems to me, then, as I repeat an argument I have learnt, that I could have discovered it. This is often only an illusion; but even then, even if I am not clever enough to create for myself, I rediscover it myself as I repeat it.

11   We can understand that this feeling, this intuition of mathematical order, which enables us to guess hidden harmonies and relations, cannot belong to every one. Some have neither this delicate feeling that

is difficult to define, nor a power of memory and attention above the common, and so they are absolutely incapable of understanding even the first steps of higher mathematics. This applies to the majority of people. Others have the feeling only in a slight degree, but they are gifted with an uncommon memory and a great capacity for attention. They learn the details one after the other by heart, they can understand mathematics and sometimes apply them, but they are not in a condition to create. Lastly, others possess the special intuition I have spoken of more or less highly developed, and they can not only understand mathematics, even though their memory is in no way extraordinary, but they can become creators, and seek to make discovery with more or less chance of success, according as their intuition is more or less developed.

12   What, in fact, is mathematical discovery? It does not consist in making new combinations with mathematical entities that are already known. That can be done by any one, and the combinations that could be so formed would be infinite in number, and the greater part of them would be absolutely devoid of interest. Discovery consists precisely in not constructing useless combinations, but in constructing those that are useful, which are an infinitely small minority. Discovery is discernment, selection.

13   How this selection is to be made I have explained above. Mathematical facts worthy of being studied are those which, by their analogy with other facts, are capable of conducting us to the knowledge of a mathematical law, in the same way that experimental facts conduct us to the knowledge of a physical law. They are those which reveal unsuspected relations between other facts, long since known, but wrongly believed to be unrelated to each other.

14   Among the combinations we choose, the most fruitful are often those which are formed of elements borrowed from widely separated domains. I do not mean to say that for discovery it is sufficient to bring together objects that are as incongruous as possible. The greater part of the combinations so formed would be entirely fruitless, but some among them, though very rare, are the most fruitful of all.

15   Discovery, as I have said, is selection. But this is perhaps not quite the right word. It suggests a purchaser who has been shown a large number of samples, and examines them one after the other in order to make his selection. In our case the samples would be so numerous that a whole life would not give sufficient time to examine them. Things do not happen in this way. Unfruitful combinations do not so much as present themselves to the mind of the discoverer. In the field of his consciousness there never appear any but really useful combinations, and some that he rejects, which, however, partake to some extent of the character of

useful combinations. Everything happens as if the discoverer were a secondary examiner who had only to interrogate candidates declared eligible after passing a preliminary test.

16   But what I have said up to now is only what can be observed or inferred by reading the works of geometricians, provided they are read with some reflection.

17   It is time to penetrate further, and to see what happens in the very soul of the mathematician. For this purpose I think I cannot do better than recount my personal recollections. Only I am going to confine myself to relating how I wrote my first treatise on Fuchsian functions. I must apologize, for I am going to introduce some technical expressions, but they need not alarm the reader, for he has no need to understand them. I shall say, for instance, that I found the demonstration of such and such a theorem under such and such circumstances; the theorem will have a barbarous name that many will not know, but that is of no importance. What is interesting for the psychologist is not the theorem but the circumstances.

18   For a fortnight I had been attempting to prove that there could not be any function analogous to what I have since called Fuchsian functions. I was at that time very ignorant. Every day I sat down at my table and spent an hour or two trying a great number of combinations, and I arrived at no result. One night I took some black coffee, contrary to my custom, and was unable to sleep. A host of ideas kept surging in my head; I could almost feel them jostling one another, until two of them coalesced, so to speak, to form a stable combination. When morning came, I had established the existence of one class of Fuchsian functions, those that are derived from the hypergeometric series. I had only to verify the results, which only took a few hours.

19   Then I wished to represent these functions by the quotient of two series. This idea was perfectly conscious and deliberate; I was guided by the analogy with elliptical functions. I asked myself what must be the properties of these series, if they existed, and I succeeded without difficulty in forming the series that I have called Theta-Fuchsian.

20   At this moment I left Caen, where I was then living, to take part in a geological conference arranged by the School of Mines. The incidents of the journey made me forget my mathematical work. When we arrived at Coutances, we got into a break to go for a drive, and, just as I put my foot on the step, the idea came to me, though nothing in my former thoughts seemed to have prepared me for it, that the transformations I had used to define Fuchsian functions were identical with those of non-Euclidian geometry. I made no verification, and had no time to do so, since I took up the conversation again as soon as I had sat down in the

break, but I felt absolute certainty at once. When I got back to Caen I verified the result at my leisure to satisfy my conscience.

21   I then began to study arithmetical questions without any great apparent result, and without suspecting that they could have the least connexion with my previous researches. Disgusted at my want of success, I went away to spend a few days at the seaside, and thought of entirely different things. One day, as I was walking on the cliff, the idea came to me, again with the same characteristics of conciseness, suddenness, and immediate certainty, that arithmetical transformations of indefinite ternary quadratic forms are identical with those of non-Euclidian geometry.

22   Returning to Caen, I reflected on this result and deduced its consequences. The example of quadratic forms showed me that there are Fuchsian groups other than those which correspond with the hypergeometric series; I saw that I could apply to them the theory of the Theta-Fuchsian series, and that, consequently, there are Fuchsian functions other than those which are derived from the hypergeometric series, the only ones I knew up to that time. Naturally, I proposed to form all these functions. I laid siege to them systematically and captured all the outworks one after the other. There was one, however, which still held out, whose fall would carry with it that of the central fortress. But all my efforts were of no avail at first, except to make me better understand the difficulty, which was already something. All this work was perfectly conscious.

23   Thereupon I left for Mont-Valérien, where I had to serve my time in the army, and so my mind was preoccupied with very different matters. One day, as I was crossing the street, the solution of the difficulty which had brought me to a standstill came to me all at once. I did not try to fathom it immediately, and it was only after my service was finished that I returned to the question. I had all the elements, and had only to assemble and arrange them. Accordingly I composed my definitive treatise at a sitting and without any difficulty.

24   One is at once struck by these appearances of sudden illumination, obvious indications of a long course of previous unconscious work. The part played by this unconscious work in mathematical discovery seems to me indisputable, and we shall find traces of it in other cases where it is less evident. Often when a man is working at a difficult question, he accomplishes nothing the first time he sets to work. Then he takes more or less of a rest, and sits down again at his table. During the first half-hour he still finds nothing, and then all at once the decisive idea presents itself to his mind. We might say that the conscious work proved more fruitful because it was interrupted and the rest restored force and

freshness to the mind. But it is more probable that the rest was occupied with unconscious work, and that the result of this work was afterwards revealed to the geometrician exactly as in the cases I have quoted, except that the revelation, instead of coming to light during a walk or a journey, came during a period of conscious work, but independently of that work, which at most only performs the unlocking process, as if it were the spur that excited into conscious form the results already acquired during the rest, which till then remained unconscious.

25   There is another remark to be made regarding the conditions of this unconscious work, which is, that it is not possible, or in any case not fruitful, unless it is first preceded and then followed by a period of conscious work. These sudden inspirations are never produced (and this is sufficiently proved already by the examples I have quoted) except after some days of voluntary efforts which appeared absolutely fruitless, in which one thought one had accomplished nothing, and seemed to be on a totally wrong track. These efforts, however, were not as barren as one thought; they set the unconscious machine in motion, and without them it would not have worked at all, and would not have produced anything.

26   The necessity for the second period of conscious work can be even more readily understood. It is necessary to work out the results of the inspiration, to deduce the immediate consequences and put them in order and to set out the demonstrations; but, above all, it is necessary to verify them. I have spoken of the feeling of absolute certainty which accompanies the inspiration; in the cases quoted this feeling was not deceptive, and more often than not this will be the case. But we must beware of thinking that this is a rule without exceptions. Often the feeling deceives us without being any less distinct on that account, and we only detect it when we attempt to establish the demonstration. I have observed this fact most notably with regard to ideas that have come to me in the morning or at night when I have been in bed in a semi-somnolent condition.

27   Such are the facts of the case, and they suggest the following reflections. The result of all that precedes is to show that the unconscious ego, or, as it is called, the subliminal ego, plays a most important part in mathematical discovery. But the subliminal ego is generally thought of as purely automatic. Now we have seen that mathematical work is not a simple mechanical work, and that it could not be entrusted to any machine, whatever the degree of perfection we suppose it to have been brought to. It is not merely a question of applying certain rules, of manufacturing as many combinations as possible according to certain fixed laws. The combinations so obtained

would be extremely numerous, useless, and encumbering. The real work of the discoverer consists in choosing between these combinations with a view to eliminating those that are useless, or rather not giving himself the trouble of making them at all. The rules which must guide this choice are extremely subtle and delicate, and it is practically impossible to state them in precise language; they must be felt rather than formulated. Under these conditions, how can we imagine a sieve capable of applying them mechanically?

28   How can we explain the fact that, of the thousand products of our unconscious activity, some are invited to cross the threshold, while others remain outside? Is it mere chance that gives them this privilege? Evidently not. For instance, of all the excitements of our senses, it is only the most intense that retain our attention, unless it has been directed upon them by other causes. More commonly the privileged unconscious phenomena, those that are capable of becoming conscious, are those which, directly or indirectly, most deeply affect our sensibility.

29   It may appear surprising that sensibility should be introduced in connexion with mathematical demonstrations, which, it would seem, can only interest the intellect. But not if we bear in mind the feeling of mathematical beauty, of the harmony of numbers and forms and of geometric elegance. It is a real aesthetic feeling that all true mathematicians recognize, and this is truly sensibility.

30   Now, what are the mathematical entities to which we attribute this character of beauty and elegance, which are capable of developing in us a kind of aesthetic emotion? Those whose elements are harmoniously arranged so that the mind can, without effort, take in the whole without neglecting the details. This harmony is at once a satisfaction to our aesthetic requirements, and an assistance to the mind which it supports and guides. At the same time, by setting before our eyes a well-ordered whole, it gives us a presentiment of a mathematical law. Now, as I have said above, the only mathematical facts worthy of retaining our attention and capable of being useful are those which can make us acquainted with a mathematical law. Accordingly we arrive at the following conclusion. The useful combinations are precisely the most beautiful, I mean those that can most charm that special sensibility that all mathematicians know, but of which laymen are so ignorant that they are often tempted to smile at it.

31   What follows, then? Of the very large number of combinations which the subliminal ego blindly forms, almost all are without interest and without utility. But, for that very reason, they are without action on the aesthetic sensibility; the consciousness will never know them. A few only are harmonious, and consequently at once useful and beautiful, and

they will be capable of affecting the geometrician's special sensibility I have been speaking of; which, once aroused, will direct our attention upon them, and will thus give them the opportunity of becoming conscious.

32 This is only a hypothesis, and yet there is an observation which tends to confirm it. When a sudden illumination invades the mathematician's mind, it most frequently happens that it does not mislead him. But it also happens sometimes, as I have said, that it will not stand the test of verification. Well, it is to be observed almost always that this false idea, if it had been correct, would have flattered our natural instinct for mathematical elegance.

33 Thus it is this special aesthetic sensibility that plays the part of the delicate sieve of which I spoke above, and this makes it sufficiently clear why the man who has it not will never be a real discoverer.

1.3 MATHEMATICS AS LOGIC

DOUGLAS R. HOFSTADTER (1915–   ), *extract from* Gödel, Escher, Bach: An Eternal Golden Braid, *Brighton, Harvester Press, 1979, pp. 19–24*

This extract, a more historically directed account than the other views in this chapter, is notable for its clear exposition of the logical problems and hopes which reached their turning point in Gödel's Theorem. It describes why mathematics had come to be seen by some mathematicians as, essentially, logic, and how this belief could no longer be so fully and optimistically sustained after 1931.

Two further points may be made to place this discussion in context. Firstly, not all mathematicians were persuaded, even before Gödel's work, of the usefulness of considering mathematics as reducible to logic. Poincaré, for instance, was scornful of the whole approach, satirizing Hilbert's attitude in these words:

Thus it will be readily understood that, in order to demonstrate a theorem, it is not necessary or even useful to know what it means. We might . . . imagine a machine where we should put in axioms at one end and take out theorems at another, like that legendary machine in Chicago where pigs go in alive and come out transformed into hams and sausages. It is no more necessary for the mathematician than it is for these machines to know what he is doing.[1]

Secondly, although Gödel's Theorem signalled the passing of one programme of mathematical inquiry, the ingenious and subtle techniques he utilized for his proof have developed into a flourishing branch of mathematics, allied to the growth of computers.

Note

1. Poincaré, Henri (1908) 'Mathematics and logic', in *Science and Method*, Maitland, Francis, trans., New York, Dover (1952 ed.), p. 147.

Mathematical logic: a synopsis

A proper appreciation of Gödel's Theorem requires a setting of context. Therefore, I will now attempt to summarize in a short space the history of mathematical logic prior to 1931 — an impossible task. . . . It all began with the attempts to mechanize the thought processes of reasoning. Now our ability to reason has often been claimed to be what distinguishes us from other species; so it seems somewhat paradoxical, on first thought, to mechanize that which is most human. Yet even the ancient Greeks knew that reasoning is a patterned process, and is at least partially governed by statable laws. Aristotle codified syllogisms, and Euclid codified geometry; but thereafter, many centuries had to pass before progress in the study of axiomatic reasoning would take place again. . . .

    Later in the nineteenth century, the English logicians George Boole and Augustus De Morgan went considerably further than Aristotle in codifying strictly deductive reasoning patterns. Boole even called his book[1] *The Laws of Thought* — surely an exaggeration, but it was an important contribution. Lewis Carroll was fascinated by these mechanized reasoning methods, and invented many puzzles which could be solved with them. Gottlob Frege in Jena and Giuseppe Peano in Turin worked on combining formal reasoning with the study of sets and numbers. David Hilbert in Göttingen worked on stricter formalizations of geometry than Euclid's. All of these efforts were directed towards clarifying what one means by 'proof'.

In the meantime, interesting developments were taking place in classical mathematics. A theory of different types of infinities, known as the *theory of sets*, was developed by Georg Cantor in the 1880s. The theory was powerful and beautiful, but intuition-defying. Before long, a variety of set-theoretical paradoxes had been unearthed. The situation was very disturbing, because just as mathematics seemed to be recovering from one set of paradoxes — those related to the theory of limits, in the calculus — along came a whole new set, which looked worse!

The most famous is Russell's paradox. Most sets, it would seem, are not members of themselves — for example, the set of walruses is not a walrus, the set containing only Joan of Arc is not Joan of Arc (a set is not a person) — and so on. In this respect, most sets are rather 'run-of-the-mill'. However, some 'self-swallowing' sets *do* contain themselves as members, such as the set of all sets, or the set of all things except Joan of Arc, and so on. Clearly, every set is either run-of-the-mill or self-swallowing, and no set can be both. Now nothing prevents us from inventing R: *the set of all run-of-the-mill sets*. At first, R might seem a rather run-of-the-mill invention — but that opinion must be revised when you ask yourself, 'Is R itself a run-of-the-mill set or a self-swallowing set?' You will find that the answer is: 'R is neither run-of-the-mill nor self-swallowing, for either choice leads to paradox.' Try it!

But if R is neither run-of-the-mill nor self-swallowing, then what is it? At the very least, pathological. But no one was satisfied with evasive answers of that sort. And so people began to dig more deeply into the foundations of set theory. The crucial questions seemed to be: 'What is wrong with our intuitive concept of "set"? Can we make a rigorous theory of sets which corresponds closely with our intuitions, but which skirts the paradoxes?' Here, as in number theory and geometry, the problem is in trying to line up intuition with formalized, or axiomatized, reasoning systems.

A startling variant of Russell's paradox, called 'Grelling's paradox', can be made using adjectives instead of sets. Divide the adjectives in English into two categories: those which are self-descriptive, such as 'pentasyllabic', 'awkwardnessful', and 'recherché', and those which are not, such as 'edible', 'incomplete', and 'bisyllabic'. Now if we admit 'non-self-descriptive' as an adjective, to which class does it belong? If it seems questionable to include hyphenated words, we can use two terms invented specially for this paradox: *autological* (= 'self-descriptive'), and *heterological* (= 'non-self-descriptive'). The question then becomes: 'Is "heterological" heterological?' Try it!

There seems to be one common culprit in these paradoxes, namely self-reference, or 'Strange Loopiness'. So if the goal is to ban all paradoxes, why not try banning self-reference and anything that allows it to arise? This is not so easy as it might seem, because it can be hard to figure out just where self-reference is occurring. It may be spread out over a whole Strange Loop with several steps, as in this 'expanded' version of Epimenides, reminiscent of *Drawing Hands*:

> The following sentence is false.
> The preceding sentence is true.

Taken together, these sentences have the same effect as the original Epimenides paradox; yet separately, they are harmless and even potentially useful sentences. The 'blame' for this Strange Loop can't be pinned on either sentence − only on the way they 'point' at each other. In the same way, each local region of *Ascending and Descending* is quite legitimate; it is only the way they are globally put together that creates an impossibility. Since there are indirect as well as direct ways of achieving self-reference, one must figure out how to ban both types at once − if one sees self-reference as the root of all evil.

Banishing Strange Loops

Russell and Whitehead did subscribe to this view, and accordingly, *Principia Mathematica*[2] was a mammoth exercise in exorcising Strange Loops from logic, set theory, and number theory. The idea of their system was basically this. A set of the lowest 'type' could contain only 'objects' as members − not sets. A set of the next type up could only contain objects, or sets of the lowest type. In general, a set of a given type could only contain sets of lower type, or objects. Every set would belong to a specific type. Clearly, no set could contain itself because it would have to belong to a type higher than its own type. Only 'run-of-the-mill' sets exist in such a system; furthermore, old R − the set of all run-of-the-mill sets − no longer is considered a set at all, because it does not belong to any finite type. To all appearances, then, this *theory of types*, which we might also call the 'theory of the abolition of Strange Loops', successfully rids set theory of its paradoxes, but only at the cost of introducing an artificial-seeming hierarchy, and of disallowing the formation of certain kinds of sets − such as the set of all run-of-the-mill sets. Intuitively, this is not the way we imagine sets.

The theory of types handled Russell's paradox, but it did nothing about the Epimenides paradox or Grelling's paradox. For people whose interest went no further than set theory, this was quite adequate − but for people interested in the elimination of paradoxes generally, some similar 'hierarchization' seemed necessary, to forbid looping back inside language. At the bottom of such a hierarchy would be an *object language*. Here, reference could be made only to a specific domain – not to aspects of the object language itself (such as its grammatical rules, or specific sentences in it). For that purpose there would be a *metalanguage*. This experience of two linguistic levels is familiar to all learners of foreign languages. Then there would be a metameta-language for discussing the metalanguage, and so on. It would be required that every sentence should belong to some precise level of the hierarchy. Therefore, if one could find no level in which a given utterance fit, then the utterance would be deemed meaningless, and forgotten.

An analysis can be attempted on the two-step Epimenides loop given above. The first sentence, since it speaks of the second, must be on a higher level than the second. But by the same token, the second sentence must be on a higher level than the first. Since this is impossible, the two sentences are 'meaningless'. More precisely, such sentences simply cannot be formulated at all in a system based on a strict hierarchy of languages. This prevents all versions of the Epimenides paradox as well as Grelling's paradox. (To what language level could 'heterological' belong?)

Now in set theory, which deals with abstractions that we don't use all the time, a stratification like the theory of types seems acceptable, even if a little strange – but when it comes to language, an all-pervading part of life, such stratification appears absurd. We don't think of ourselves as jumping up and down a hierarchy of languages when we speak about various things. A rather matter-of-fact sentence such as, 'In this book, I criticize the theory of types' would be doubly forbidden in the system we are discussing. Firstly, it mentions 'this book', which should only be mentionable in a 'metabook' – and secondly, it mentions *me* – a person whom I should not be allowed to speak of at all! This example points out how silly the theory of types seems, when you import it into a familiar context. The remedy it adopts for paradoxes – total banishment of self-reference in any form – is a real case of over-kill, branding many perfectly good constructions as meaningless. The adjective 'meaningless', by the way, would have to apply to all discussions of the theory of linguistic types (such as that of this very paragraph) for they clearly could not occur on any of the levels – neither object language, nor metalanguage, nor metametalanguage, etc. So the very act of discussing the theory would be the most blatant possible violation of it!

Now one could defend such theories by saying that they were only intended to deal with formal languages – not with ordinary, informal language. This may be so, but then it shows that such theories are extremely academic and have little to say about paradoxes except when they crop up in special tailor-made systems. Besides, the drive to eliminate paradoxes at any cost, especially when it requires the creation of highly artificial formalisms, puts too much stress on bland consistency, and too little on the quirky and bizarre, which make life and mathematics interesting. It is of course important to try to maintain consistency, but when this effort forces you into a stupendously ugly theory, you know something is wrong.

These types of issues in the foundations of mathematics were responsible for the high interest in codifying human reasoning methods which was present in the early part of this century. Mathematicians and philosophers had begun to have serious doubts about whether even the most concrete of theories, such as the study of whole numbers (number theory), were built on solid foundations. If paradoxes could pop up so easily in set theory – a theory whose basic concept, that of a set, is surely very intuitively appealing – then might they not also exist in other branches of mathematics? Another related worry was that the paradoxes of logic, such as the Epimenides paradox, might turn out to be internal to mathematics, and thereby cast in doubt all of mathematics. This was especially worrisome to those – and there were a good number – who firmly believed that mathematics is simply a branch of logic (or conversely, that logic is simply a branch of mathematics). In fact, this very question – 'Are mathematics and logic distinct, or separate?' – was the source of much controversy.

This study of mathematics itself became known as *metamathematics* – or occasionally, *metalogic*, since mathematics and logic are so intertwined. The most urgent priority of metamathematicians was to determine the true nature of mathematical reasoning. What is a legal method of procedure, and what is an illegal one? Since mathematical reasoning had always been done in 'natural language' (e.g. French or Latin or some language for normal communication), there was always a lot of possible ambiguity. Words had different meanings to different people, conjured up different images, and so forth. It seemed reasonable and even important to establish a single uniform notation in which all mathematical work could be done, and with the aid of which any two mathematicians could resolve disputes over whether a suggested proof was valid or not. This would require a complete codification of the universally acceptable modes of human reasoning, at least as far as they applied to mathematics.

Consistency, completeness, Hilbert's program

This was the goal of *Principia Mathematica*, which purported to derive all of mathematics from logic, and, to be sure, without contradictions! It was widely admired, but no one was sure if (1) all of mathematics really was contained in the methods delineated by Russell and White-head, or (2) the methods given were even self-consistent. Was it absolutely clear that contradictory results could *never* be derived, by any mathematicians whatsoever, following the methods of Russell and Whitehead?

This question particularly bothered the distinguished German mathematician (and metamathematician) David Hilbert, who set before the world community of mathematicians (and metamathe-maticians) this challenge: to demonstrate rigorously – perhaps following the very methods outlined by Russell and Whitehead – that the system defined in *Principia Mathematica* was both *consistent* (contradiction-free), and *complete* (i.e. that every 'true statement of number theory could be derived within the framework drawn up in *P.M.*). This was a tall order, and one could criticize it on the grounds that it was somewhat circular: how can you justify your methods of reasoning on the basis of those same methods of reasoning? It is like lifting yourself up by your own bootstraps. (We just don't seem to be able to get away from these Strange Loops!)

Hilbert was fully aware of this dilemma, of course, and therefore expressed the hope that a demonstration of consistency or completeness could be found which depended only on 'finitistic' modes of reasoning. These were a small set of reasoning methods usually accepted by mathe-maticians. In this way, Hilbert hoped that mathematicians could partially lift themselves by their own bootstraps: the sum total of mathematical methods might be proved sound, by invoking only a smaller set of methods. This goal may sound rather esoteric, but it occupied the minds of many of the greatest mathematicians in the world during the first thirty years of this century.

In the thirty-first year, however, Gödel published his paper, which in some ways utterly demolished Hilbert's program. This paper revealed not only that there were irreparable 'holes' in the axiomatic system proposed by Russell and Whitehead, but more generally, that no axiomatic system whatsoever could produce all number-theoretical truths, unless it were an inconsistent system! And finally, the hope of proving the consistency of a system such as that presented in *P.M.* was shown to be vain: if such a proof could be found using only methods inside *P.M.*, then – and this is one of the most mystifying consequences of Gödel's work – *P.M.* itself would be inconsistent!

The final irony of it all is that the proof of Gödel's Incompleteness Theorem involved importing the Epimenides paradox right into the heart of *Principia Mathematica*, a bastion supposedly invulnerable to the attacks of Strange Loops! Although Gödel's Strange Loop did not destroy *Principia Mathematica*, it made it far less interesting to mathematicians, for it showed that Russell and Whitehead's original aims were illusory.

Notes

1. Boole, George (1854) *An Investigation into the Laws of Thought*, London, Walton & Maberly.
2. Whitehead, A. N. and Russell, B. A. W. (1910) *Principia Mathematica*, Cambridge, Cambridge University Press.

1.4 MATHEMATICS AS LANGUAGE

LANCELOT HOGBEN (1895–1975), *from* Mathematics for the Million, *London, George Allen & Unwin, 1936, pp. 26–8*

To describe mathematics as a language is sometimes just a way of speaking, with no further implications for mathematical inquiry. When Galileo, for example, said in quite a detailed metaphor:

> Philosophy is written in this grand book, the universe, which stands continually open to our gaze. But the book cannot be understood unless one first learns to comprehend the language and read the letters in which it is composed. It is written in the language of mathematics.[1]

he was advocating a view of how inquiries into the world ought to proceed, not asserting mathematics to be a language rather than something else. But in this extract Hogben claims mathematics as a language to provide an alternative to, in particular, Plato's views (see 1.1). His reasons for adopting this view become evident in the extract, and are both educational (the subtitle of his book is *A Popular Self Educator*) and social. The latter motivation is even more explicit elsewhere; Hogben writes, for example (recall it was first published in 1936):

Maybe the Western world is about to be plunged

irrevocably into barbarism. If it escapes this fate, the men and women of the leisure state which is now within our grasp will regard the democratization of mathematics as a decisive step in the advance of civilization. . . .

Without a knowledge of mathematics, the grammar of size and order, we cannot plan the rational society in which there will be leisure for all and poverty for none. . . . Neither as children nor as adults are we told how the knowledge of this grammar has been used again and again throughout history to assist in the liberation of mankind from superstition.[2]

In Hogben's conception, then, mathematics is inseparable from its social purpose.

The other view Hogben criticizes, that mathematics is a game, is an attitude sometimes held to describe the approach of David Hilbert discussed at the end of the Hofstadter extract (1.3).

Notes

1. Drake, Stillman, ed. and trans. (1957) *Discoveries and Opinions of Galileo*, New York, p. 237.
2. Op. cit., pp. 20–1.

This book will narrate how the grammar of measurement and counting has evolved under the pressure of man's changing social achievements, how in successive stages it has been held in check by the barriers of custom, how it has been used in charting a universe which can be commanded when its laws are obeyed, but can never be propitiated by ceremonial and sacrifice. As the outline of the story develops, one difficulty which many people experience will become less formidable. The expert in mathematics is essentially a technician. So his chief concern in teaching is to make other technicians. Mathematical books are largely packed with exercises which are designed to give proficiency in workmanship. This makes us discouraged because of the immense territory which we have to traverse before we can get insight into the kind of mathematics which is used in modern science and social statistics. The fact is that modern mathematics does not borrow so very much from antiquity. To be sure, every useful development in mathematics rests on the historical foundation of some earlier branch. At the same time every new branch liquidates the usefulness of clumsier tools which preceded it. Although algebra, trigonometry, the use of graphs, the calculus all depend on the rules of Greek geometry, scarcely more than a dozen from the two hundred propositions of Euclid's elements are essential to help us in understanding how to use them. The remainder are complicated ways of doing things which can be done more simply when we know later branches of mathematics. For the mathematical technician these complications may provide a useful discipline. The person who wants to understand the place of mathematics in modern civilization is merely distracted and disheartened by them. What follows is for those who have been already disheartened and distracted, and have consequently forgotten what they may have learned already or fail to see the meaning or usefulness of what they remember. So we shall begin at the very beginning.

Two views are commonly held about mathematics. One comes from Plato. This is that mathematical statements represent eternal truths. Plato's doctrine was used by the German philosopher, Kant, as a stick with which to beat the materialists of his time, when revolutionary writings like those of Diderot were challenging priestcraft. Kant thought that the principles of geometry were eternal, and that they were totally independent of our sense organs. It happened that Kant wrote just before biologists discovered that we have a sense organ, part of what is called the internal ear, sensitive to the pull of gravitation. Since that discovery, the significance of which was first fully recognized by the German physicist, Ernst Mach, the geometry which Kant knew has been brought down to earth by Einstein. It no longer dwells in the sky where Plato put it. We know that geometrical statements when applied to the real world are only approximate truths. The theory of Relativity has been very unsettling to mathematicians, and it has now become a fashion to say that mathematics is only a game. Of course, this does not tell us anything about mathematics. It only tells us something about the cultural limitations of some mathematicians. When a man says that mathematics is a game, he is making a private statement. He is telling us something about himself, his own attitude to mathematics. He is not telling us anything about the public meaning of a mathematical statement.

If mathematics is a game, there is no reason why people should play it if they do not want to. With football, it belongs to those amusements without which life would be endurable. The view which we shall explore is that mathematics is the language of size, and that it is an essential part of the equipment of an intelligent citizen to understand this language.

If the rules of mathematics are rules of grammar, there is no stupidity involved when we fail to see that a mathematical truth is obvious. The rules of ordinary grammar are not obvious. They have to be learned. They are not eternal truths. They are conveniences without whose aid truths about the sorts of things in the world cannot be communicated from one person to another. In Cobbett's memorable words, Mr Prynne would not have been able to impeach Archbishop Laud if his command of grammar had been insufficient to make himself understood. So it is with mathematics, the grammar of size. The rules of mathematics are rules to be learned. If they are formidable, they are formidable because they are unfamiliar when you first meet them − like gerunds or nominative absolutes. They are also formidable because in all languages there are so many rules and words to memorize before we can read newspapers or pick up radio news from foreign stations. Everybody knows that being able to chatter in several foreign languages is not a sign of great social intelligence. Neither is being able to chatter in the language of size. Real social intelligence lies in the use of a language, in applying the right words in the right context. It is important to know the language of size, because entrusting the laws of human society, social statistics, population, man's hereditary make-up, the balance of trade, to the isolated mathematician without checking his conclusions is like letting a committee of philologists manufacture the truths of human, animal, or plant anatomy from the resources of their own imaginations.

1.5 MATHEMATICS AS ART

G. H. HARDY (1877−1947), A Mathematician's Apology, Cambridge, Cambridge University Press, 1940, sections 10−11

G. H. Hardy was 'generally recognized as the leading English mathematician of his time'.[1] A Mathematician's Apology is one of the most notable − for some, notorious − of books about mathematics, for the beautiful exposition of views which sometimes seem (especially to non-mathematicians) to verge on the deliberately eccentric. Thus the friendly reference in this extract to the great chemist (and Nobel laureate) Frederick Soddy (1877−1956) did not prevent the latter from reviewing Hardy's book in the words 'From such cloistral clowning the world sickens'.[2] An example of what Soddy refers to can be found in this extract: 'if a chess problem is, in the crude sense, "useless", then that is equally true of most of the best mathematics'. From this it can be seen why Hardy conducts his defence of mathematics as art here partly through a discussion on the views of Lancelot Hogben (see reading 1.4).

Of all the conceptions of mathematics in this chapter, Hardy's views — which are further described in reading 2.3 — come closest to Plato's, as to what mathematics is inquiring into. But he stresses even more than Poincaré the aesthetic criteria necessary to mathematics, emphasizing its seriousness by contrast with games such as chess.

The apparent play on the word *serious* in the final paragraph is characteristic of Hardy's playfulness and subtlety, leaving a lingering impression of yet another jibe at Hogben — just as Hardy disclaims any qualifications in aesthetics, so Hogben, by qualification a biologist, should show less temerity in criticizing Hardy's type of mathematics.

Notes

1. Titchmarsh, E. C., entry on Hardy in *Dictionary of National Biography*.
2. *Nature*, 147, 4 January 1941, p. 3.

10

A mathematician, like a painter or a poet, is a maker of patterns. If his patterns are more permanent than theirs, it is because they are made with *ideas*. A painter makes patterns with shapes and colours, a poet with words. A painting may embody an 'idea', but the idea is usually commonplace and unimportant. In poetry, ideas count for a good deal more; but, as Housman insisted, the importance of ideas in poetry is habitually exaggerated: 'I cannot satisfy myself that there are any such things as poetical ideas. . . . Poetry is not the thing said but a way of saying it.'

> Not all the water in the rough rude sea
> Can wash the balm from an anointed King.

Could lines be better, and could ideas be at once more trite and more false? The poverty of the ideas seems hardly to affect the beauty of the verbal pattern. A mathematician, on the other hand, has no material to work with but ideas, and so his patterns are likely to last longer, since ideas wear less with time than words.

The mathematician's patterns, like the painter's or the poet's, must be *beautiful*; the ideas, like the colours or the words, must fit together in a harmonious way. Beauty is the first test: there is no permanent place in the world for ugly mathematics. And here I must deal with a misconception which is still widespread (though probably much less so now than it was twenty years ago), what Whitehead has called the 'literary superstition' that love of and aesthetic appreciation of mathematics is 'a monomania confined to a few eccentrics in each generation'.

It would be difficult now to find an educated man quite insensitive to the aesthetic appeal of mathematics. It may be very hard to *define* mathematical beauty, but that is just as true of beauty of any kind − we may not know quite what we mean by a beautiful poem, but that does not prevent us from recognizing one when we read it. Even Professor Hogben, who is out to minimize at all costs the importance of the aesthetic element in mathematics, does not venture to deny its reality. 'There are, to be sure, individuals for whom mathematics exercises a coldly impersonal attraction. . . . The aesthetic appeal of mathematics may be very real for a chosen few.' But they are 'few', he suggests, and they feel 'coldly' (and are really rather ridiculous people, who live in silly little university towns sheltered from the fresh breezes of the wide open spaces). In this he is merely echoing Whitehead's 'literary superstition'.

The fact is that there are few more 'popular' subjects than mathematics. Most people have some appreciation of mathematics, just as most people can enjoy a pleasant tune; and there are probably more people really interested in mathematics than in music. Appearances may suggest the contrary, but there are easy explanations. Music can be used to stimulate mass emotion, while mathematics cannot; and musical incapacity is recognized (no doubt rightly) as mildly discreditable, whereas most people are so frightened of the name of mathematics that they are ready, quite unaffectedly, to exaggerate their own mathematical stupidity.

A very little reflection is enough to expose the absurdity of the 'literary superstition'. There are masses of chess-players in every civilized country − in Russia, almost the whole educated population; and every chess-player can recognize and appreciate a 'beautiful' game or problem. Yet a chess problem is *simply* an exercise in pure mathematics (a game not entirely, since psychology also plays a part), and everyone who calls a problem 'beautiful' is applauding mathematical beauty, even if it is beauty of a comparatively lowly kind. Chess problems are the hymn-tunes of mathematics.

We may learn the same lesson, at a lower level but for a wider public, from bridge, or descending further, from the puzzle columns of the popular newspapers. Nearly all their immense popularity is a tribute to the drawing power of rudimentary mathematics, and the better makers of puzzles, such as Dudeney or 'Caliban', use very little else. They know their business; what the public wants is a little intellectual 'kick', and nothing else has quite the kick of mathematics.

I might add that there is nothing in the world which pleases even famous men (and men who have used disparaging language about mathematics) quite so much as to discover, or rediscover, a genuine mathematical theorem. Herbert Spencer republished in his auto-biography a theorem about circles which he proved when he was twenty (not knowing that it had been proved over two thousand years before by Plato). Professor Soddy is a more recent and a more striking example (but *his* theorem really is his own).

11

A chess problem is genuine mathematics, but it is in some way 'trivial' mathematics. However ingenious and intricate, however original and surprising the moves, there is something essential lacking. Chess problems are *unimportant*. The best mathematics is *serious* as well as beautiful — 'important' if you like, but the word is very ambiguous, and 'serious' expresses what I mean much better.

I am not thinking of the 'practical' consequences of mathematics. I have to return to that point later: at present I will say only that if a chess problem is, in the crude sense, 'useless', then that is equally true of most of the best mathematics; that very little of mathematics is useful practically, and that that little is comparatively dull. The 'seriousness' of a mathematical theorem lies, not in its practical consequences, which are usually negligible, but in the *significance* of the mathematical ideas which it connects. We may say, roughly, that a mathematical idea is 'significant' if it can be connected, in a natural and illuminating way, with a large complex of other mathematical ideas. Thus a serious mathematical theorem, a theorem which connects significant ideas, is likely to lead to important advances in mathematics itself and even in other sciences. No chess problem has ever affected the general development of scientific thought; Pythagoras, Newton, Einstein have in their times changed its whole direction.

The seriousness of a theorem, of course, does not *lie in* its consequences, which are merely the *evidence* for its seriousness. Shakespeare had an enormous influence on the development of the English language, Otway next to none, but that is not why Shakespeare was the better poet. He was the better poet because he wrote much better poetry. The inferiority of the chess problem, like that of Otway's poetry, lies not in its consequences but in its content.

There is one more point which I shall dismiss very shortly, not because it is uninteresting but because it is difficult, and because I have no qualifications for any serious discussion in aesthetics. The beauty of a mathematical theorem *depends* a great deal on its seriousness, as even in poetry the beauty of a line may depend to some extent on the significance of the ideas which it contains. I quoted two lines of Shakespeare as an example of the sheer beauty of a verbal pattern; but

<blockquote>After life's fitful fever he sleeps well</blockquote>

seems still more beautiful. The pattern is just as fine, and in this case the ideas have significance and the thesis is sound, so that our emotions are stirred much more deeply. The ideas do matter to the pattern, even in poetry, and much more, naturally, in mathematics; but I must not try to argue the question seriously.

1.6 MATHEMATICS AS INTELLECTUAL PASSION

MICHAEL POLANYI (1891–1976), Personal Knowledge: Towards a Post-Critical Philosophy, *London, Routledge & Kegan Paul, 1958, extracts from pp. 186–93*

Michael Polanyi, born in Hungary, was teaching in Berlin when Hitler's rise to power led to his coming to Britain in 1933, where he was successively Professor of Physical Chemistry and Professor of Social Studies at the University of Manchester. (A not dissimilar life experience informs the contributions, later in this volume, of Karl Popper and Imre Lakatos.) Polanyi's affirmation of the truth and beauty of mathematics, therefore, while owing something to G. H. Hardy's position (reading 1.5), shows a greater awareness of the dependence of intellectual constructs and values on people continuing to share this passion.

This extract is part of the discussion of mathematics within the much larger inquiry which Polanyi set himself, into the nature and justification of knowledge, of which he says:

> I regard knowing as an active comprehension of the things known, an action that requires skill. . . . Such is the *personal participation* of the knower in all acts of understanding. But this does not make our understanding *subjective*. Comprehension is neither an arbitrary act nor a passive experience, but a responsible act claiming universal validity. Such knowing is indeed *objective* in the sense of establishing contact with a hidden reality; . . . I have shown that into every act of knowing there enters a passionate contribution of the person knowing what is being known, and that this co-efficient is no mere imperfection but a vital component of his knowledge.[1]

This position therefore attempts to transcend the familiar dichotomy between mathematical inquiry as creation, and as discovery of objective truth.

Polanyi's description of mathematics as 'the continued invention of a game in the very course of playing the game' is very apposite to Gödel's Theorem and its consequences (see 1.3), as well as to other 'radical conceptual innovations' such as the work of Georg Cantor which he discusses later in the extract. In this light, Hogben's dismissal of the view that mathematics can be interpreted as a game (reading 1.4) may rely in part on too conventional a notion of 'game'.

Note

1. Op. cit., pp. vii–viii.

No sharp distinction can be drawn between mathematical theories which apply to external objects, and mathematical inventions which are interesting only in themselves, for there is always a possibility that a mathematical theorem may prove applicable to experience some time. Yet the fact that this is not necessarily true, and indeed appears very unlikely for the far greater part of mathematics, is a distinctive feature of this science. Not being primarily concerned with foretelling what is going to happen, or with contriving what anyone wished to happen, but merely with understanding exactly how alternative aspects of a certain set of conceptions are logically connected, mathematics can extend its subject matter indefinitely by conceiving new problems of this sort, without any reference to experience. New conceptions are thus consolidated, as their wider implications and more extensive operability come into view, and this pursuit perpetuates itself by throwing up ever new opportunities for further conceptual innovations.

It now appears that the logical structure of this process is not quite that of inventing a game, but rather that of the continued invention of a game in the very course of playing the game. This kind of game-inventing is akin to the writing of a novel, and the parallel is indeed quite close up to a point. . . . Mathematics is a much freer creation than either natural science or technology. While its early primitive conceptions and operations were no doubt originally suggested by experience and have served to control the manipulation of material things, these empirical and practical contacts do not enter effectively into its present appreciation.

What, then, is mathematics? . . . Mathematics cannot be defined without acknowledging its most obvious feature: namely, that it is interesting. Nowhere is intellectual beauty so deeply felt and fastidiously appreciated in its various grades and qualities as in mathematics, and only the informal appreciation of mathematical value can distinguish what is mathematics from a welter of formally similar, yet altogether trivial statements and operations. And we shall see that this emotional colour of mathematics also justifies its acceptance as true. It is by satisfying his intellectual passions that mathematics fascinates the mathematician and compels him to pursue it in his thoughts and give it his assent. . . .

It is on account of its intellectual beauty, which his own passion proclaims as revealing a universal truth, that the mathematician feels compelled to accept mathematics as true, even though he is today deprived of the belief in its logical necessity and doomed to admit forever the conceivable possibility that its whole fabric may suddenly collapse by revealing a decisive self-contradiction. And it is the same urge to see sense and make sense that supports his tacit bridging of the logical gaps internal to every formal proof.

There is in fact ample evidence that such intellectual passions are intrinsic to the affirmation of mathematics. Modern mathematics has emerged from a long series of conceptual reforms tending towards greater generality and rigour, as well as from more radical conceptual inventions opening up altogether new perspectives. The acceptance of such conceptual innovations is a self-modifying mental act in search of a truer intellectual life. It has been authoritatively stated that 'the moments of greatest creative advancement in science frequently coincide with the introduction of new notions by means of a definition'.[1] This can be true only because the acceptance of a new conception, even when it is specified by a definition, is ultimately an informal act: a transformation of the framework on which we rely in the process of formal reasoning. It is the crossing of a logical gap to another shore, where we shall never again see things as we did before. . . .

Since the convincing power of a mathematical proof operates through our tacit understanding of it, the acceptance of a proof may also involve radical conceptual innovations. 'There are beautiful theorems in the "theory of aggregates" (*Mengenlehre*) such as Cantor's theorem of the "non enumerability" of the continuum', writes G. H. Hardy, 'the proof [of which] is easy enough once the language has been mastered, but considerable explanation is necessary before the meaning of the theorem becomes clear.'[2] Cantor's proofs traversed a logical gap across which only those willing to enter into their meaning and capable of grasping it could follow him. Reluctance or incapacity to do so caused divisions among mathematicians, similar to those which arose between Van't Hoff and Kolbe on the subject of the asymmetric carbon atom, or between Pasteur and Liebig on that of fermentation as a vital function of yeast. Hadamard describes how he and the great Lebesgue, finding themselves on opposite sides of this dispute, were compelled to recognise the impossibility of understanding each other. 'We could not avoid the conclusion that what is evident — the very starting point of certitude in every domain of thought — had not the same meaning for him and for me.'[3] The fundamental conceptual changes involved in Cantor's work were so repulsive to Kroneker, who dominated German mathematics in the 1880s, that he barred Cantor from promotion in all German universities and even from having his papers published in any German mathematical journal. . . .

We should declare candidly that we dwell on mathematics and affirm its statements for the sake of its intellectual beauty, which betokens the reality of its conceptions and the truth of its assertions. For if this passion were extinct, we would cease to understand mathematics; its conceptions would dissolve and its proofs carry no conviction. Mathematics would become pointless and would lose itself in a welter of insignificant tautologies and of Heath Robinson operations, from which it could no longer be distinguished.

Mathematics has once already fallen into oblivion by becoming incomprehensible. After the death of Apollonius in 205 B.C. there occurred a break in the oral tradition which alone made the mathematical texts of the Greeks intelligible to students. This was probably due in part to a growing distrust of mathematics, owing to its conflict with the conception of number at the point where it led to magnitudes like $\sqrt{2}$ which could not be expressed in terms of integers. In our own time Gödel's theorem of uncertainty might conceivably erode confidence, likewise, in our own mathematics. And other influences might deepen this distrust. Ideological utilitarianism censures Archimedes today for speaking lightly of his own practical inventions and his passion for intellectual beauty, which he expressed by desiring his grave to be marked by his most brilliant geometrical theorem, is dismissed as an aberration. This movement would discredit the core of mathematics, which is its intellectual beauty. The transmission of mathematics has today been rendered more precarious than ever by the fact that no single mathematician can fully understand any longer more than a tiny fraction of mathematics. Modern mathematics can be kept alive only by a large number of mathematicians cultivating different parts of the same system of values: a community which can be kept coherent only by the passionate vigilance of universities, journals and meetings, fostering these values and imposing the same respect for them on all mathematicians. Such a far-flung structure is highly vulnerable and, once broken, impossible to restore. Its ruins would bury modern mathematics in an oblivion more complete and lasting than that which enveloped Greek mathematics twenty-two centuries ago.

Notes

1. Tarski, A. (1944) 'The semantic conception of truth and the foundations of semantics', *Philosophy and Phenomenological Research*, 4, 359.
2. Hardy, G. H. (1940) *A Mathematician's Apology*, Cambridge, Cambridge University Press, p. 38.
3. Hadamard, J. (1945) *The Psychology of Invention in the Mathematical Field*, Princeton, p. 92. (I [Polanyi] have taken the liberty of revising the text slightly in the sense which I believe to have been intended.)

1.7 MATHEMATICS AS SOCIAL PRACTICE

LUKE HODGKIN (1938–   ), *from his paper 'Politics and physical sciences'*, Radical Science Journal 4 (1976), 29–60

This extract shows how discussion of mathematical

inquiry can be placed in a quite different framework. As Poincaré and Hardy were, Hodgkin is a professional mathematician drawing upon his own experience to reflect on how mathematical discovery takes place; but there the resemblance ends. The result is an explicit denial of Hardy's position ('From a materialist point of view the knowledge produced by scientists has no existence except insofar as it is learnt') as well as, implicitly, an alternative view to Poincaré's. For where Poincaré asserts at the start that 'The genesis of mathematical discovery . . . is the process in which the human mind seems to borrow least from the exterior world', Hodgkin emphasizes the social bases of mathematical activity as well as of mathematical truth.

There is beginning to grow up an increasingly critical reflective viewpoint on the practice of mathematics itself. And the people who work in the field are the first to see that this viewpoint makes sense[1] and that mathematics is not so much a hard crystalline mountain of truth painstakingly built up by successive generalizations as a field for error, for the conflict of ideas, for vagueness, for continual approximation and conjecture as the means of progress. So it's recognized among mathematicians, if not outside, that we do mathematics one way, but we might well do it another. For example, we were allowed to talk of 'infinitesimal quantities' from the time of Leibniz (1680) to the late nineteenth century. Then it became ridiculous, contradictory, inadmissible. Now since 1965 or so the work of Abraham Robinson[2] has made it scientifically 'respectable' to do just what Leibniz and his successors were doing. And this is only one example among several. But even among those who grant this, the idea that the changes and conflicts which exist in mathematics should have social determinants may seem far-fetched. . . .

We now have *two* problems − to examine the social nature of scientific practice and of scientific knowledge. Taking scientific practice first, however much we may want to argue about the past, it's clear that *today* the social context plays an overwhelming role in structuring scientific work. The subsistence of the mathematician Bloggs while he works on his thesis, his 'choice' of a problem and of how to approach it, his decision that he has done enough work and can write it down as a thesis and submit it − these are not part of an isolated struggle between himself and 'nature' or 'the literature'. Rather, they form part of a social progress — his construction, subject to constraints, of a product called 'Bloggs' Thesis' in which his supervisor, his fellow graduates, contacts in the field met at seminars or conferences (patrons, advisers, rivals), and at a different level the Science Research Council, IBM, NATO and other potential sources of money, may all intervene. . . . Bloggs' Thesis may, when/if published, become 'Bloggs' Theorem', exchangeable (for some years) for jobs, recognition, invitations. It may be recognized as a special case of someone else's much more important work. It may turn out to have important applications in cosmology or soil chemistry, and Bloggs may suddenly find himself with a completely different group of colleagues, different interests, different work prospects. It may be proved wrong or go out of fashion. All these are effects of the interaction of Bloggs's work with the totality of scientific knowledge. They are unpredictable and external in the same way as (much more obviously) the changing state of the job market for scientists due to slumps, wars, cycles of capitalist expansion and contraction in general and 'events' like the space race. As with other production processes, it is the product, scientific knowledge, which 'society' needs, and the particular producers are in the long run dispensable.

But although the scientific knowledge which we construct becomes a 'power above ourselves', it is *not* a power above society any more than capital (which is produced in an analogous way) is; I think this is a crucial mistake of those who have tried to separate 'science' in the sense of scientific knowledge from the society in which it is produced and consumed. From a materialist point of view the knowledge produced by scientists has no existence except insofar as it is learnt, understood, applied, transformed in the practice of other scientists (for we know that in general scientific truths such as the laws of physics are *relative* in the sense that they are always ready to be superseded by new ones or incorporated in them); or, more generally, by people who need, for whatever reason, to use them. It is tempting to extend the analogy with capital further; for science, like capital, must circulate to grow and, one might almost say, must grow to exist.[3]

Finally, the very process by which scientific knowledge is accepted as true is a social one. . . . Our ideas of scientific truth, of the tests and evidences for it, are acquired and transmitted in institutions, usually teaching institutions; and these institutions vary greatly from one society to another. Even the two most elementary verifications that we have of our rightness in a piece of scientific work (themselves very different) — 'It works' and 'I got full marks for it' — are socially defined in those institutions where we learn to say them. A 'solution' of a differential equation will mean one thing to a mathematician; another to an engineering student who is trying to relate what the mathematician is telling her to other things she's learning; another again to a working engineer. Because of differences in teaching approach, it may mean something different to an engineering student in France and in England. Admittedly students are only taught partial results (who isn't?) but they use them, and their use is part of the social practice of mathematics. Hence we have important ways in which scientific knowledge changes character, even locally, with changing culture. And this determining character of social institutions on the knowledge acquired is even *well-known* among scientists; X was at Princeton, at Grenoble, at Warwick, *and so* he/she sees a differential equation in a particular way, even has a particular idea of 'proof'. But this knowledge is not spread outside the restricted community of scientists, so that outsiders still believe in a universal agreement on an abstract 'rightness', which is something they themselves have been *taught* to believe in – at school, and in mathematics in particular. As Wittgenstein said: 'Our children are not only given practice in calculation, but are trained to adopt a particular attitude towards a mistake in calculating.'[4] We must learn to live with this kind of insight and to build it into our view of scientific knowledge: learning is socialization.

Notes

1. Here the early work of I. Lakatos has been fundamental, because it's both readable, scientifically respectable in that he clearly knew what he was describing, and convincing. See Worrall, J. and Zahar, E. (eds) (1976) *Proofs and Refutations: the Logic of Mathematical Discovery*, Cambridge, Cambridge University Press.
2. Robinson proved that the free use of infinitesimal quantities like dx does not lead to contradictions, as it did in classical mechanics.
3. There are counter examples of 'stagnant' science (circulation without accumulation) – science taught by rote and transmitted from teacher to student over a long period. The analogy breaks down here, and more investigation is needed. But it certainly isn't applicable to science since 1800.
4. Wittgenstein, L. J. F., *Remarks on the Foundations of Mathematics*, von Wright, G. H., Rhees, R., Anscombe, G. E. M., eds, Anscombe, G. E. M., trans., Oxford, Basil Blackwell, 1956, pp. v–40.

2 Mathematics and the world

While most readings in the previous chapter contained, or derived from, some view of the relation between mathematics and the world, this chapter emphasizes more strongly that *conceptions of the world* are of equal importance in seeking to understand this relationship. What 'understanding' in this context consists in is variously interpreted: 2.3 (Hardy) and 2.4 (Einstein) can be seen as containing answers to the question 'How is mathematics applied to the world?', 2.5 (Wigner) poses the question 'Why does applied mathematics work?' All three arise through considering mathematics and the world to be quite distinct. Why this conception is that most commonly held today is described by Kline in 2.2; and why the relation of mathematics and the world was once felt to be so much more intimate is discussed by Ivins in the opening reading.

2.1 GEOMETRY AND PERCEPTION

WILLIAM M. IVINS Jr. (1881–1961), Art and Geometry: A Study in Space Intuitions, *New York, Dover, 1964, introduction and ch. 1, pp. ix–x, 1–9. Copyright 1946 the President and Fellows of Harvard College*; © *1974 by Barbara Ivins.*

The book of which this is the introduction and opening chapter is of interest as a clearly described example of an inquiry of which the author says 'By its very nature this task can only be done by the amateur, for no man can possibly be expert in the length and breadth of such a field'. Perhaps because of his lack of preconceptions (through having no qualifications, in Hardy's sense, in the areas he discusses) Ivins approaches the relation between mathematics and the world from an unusual direction. What he is fundamentally concerned with is how people's perceptions of the world influence the type of mathematics they produce. In this extract Ivins is laying the ground by distinguishing the intuitions derived from tactile and from visual perceptions. His claim is that different cultures lay greater emphasis on aspects of one or the other, and that the 'basic sensuous intuition' of the Greeks, as evidenced in their geometry and their art, was tactile.

To give an example expanding on the brief mention of *congruence* in Ivins's third paragraph, proposition 4 in Euclid's Book 1 states that if two triangles have each of two sides and the angle between them equal, then the triangles are equal; his proof of this amounts to picking one triangle up and placing it on the other.[1] Implicit in this procedure, therefore, is a conception of mathematical objects as things which can be moved about and superimposed on one another. Ivins takes the fact that Euclid does not recognize this as an assumption, as evidence that it was too deeply embedded in Greek modes of thinking to be perceived from within the culture. It is instructive to compare Ivins's attitude with Bertrand Russell's; Russell took a more severe view of this Euclidean proof, which he said

> strikes every intelligent [late Victorian, British,] child as a juggle. In the first place, to speak of motion implies that our triangles are not spatial, but material. For a point of space *is* a position, and can no more change its position than the leopard can change his spots. . . . Hence motion, in the ordinary sense, is only possible to matter, not to space. But in this case superposition proves no geometrical property.[2]

The different uses Russell and Ivins make of this proof reflect their different purposes: Russell was showing the inadequacy of Euclidean logic (as compared with his own), Ivins wishes to explain the cultural relativism of the relation between the mathematics of a culture and its world. Ivins stresses, too, the deep correspondences between mathematical, artistic and other forms of inquiry:

> Unlike the world of the Greeks, the world we live in is not static and neither is it discontinuous. What we know and study is forms of transition. Three atomic bombs that exploded during the writing of this essay were more incompatible with ancient ideas than with the places where they exploded. There has thus been a complete change in the basic postulates of thought, and with that change the fundamental Greek notions, from mathematics to art and all that lies in between, have become only another variety, albeit an exceedingly suggestive and interesting one, in the great historical collection of such things.[3]

Notes

1. The precise wording of the proposition is: 'If two triangles have the two sides equal to two sides respectively, and have the angles contained by the equal straight lines equal, they will also have the base equal to the base, the triangle will be equal to the triangle, and the remaining angles will be equal to the remaining angles respectively, namely those which the equal sides subtend.' Euclid, *Elements*, Heath, T. L. (trans.), New York, 1925. An extract from the proof, relevant to the point at issue, reads: 'if the triangle ABC *be applied to* the triangle DEF, and if the point A *be placed on* the point D and the straight line AB on DE, then the point B will also *coincide with* E' (emphasis added).
2. Russell, Bertrand (1903) *The Philosophy of Mathematics*, London, George Allen & Unwin (2nd ed. 1937), p. 405.
3. Ivins, op. cit., pp. 111–12.

Introduction

Some years ago the queer perspective in Dürer's prints led me to a superficial but painful acquaintance with a number of books about geometry, old and new. Among them was Federigo Enriques's *The Problems of Science.* . . . I was much interested by his remarks[1] . . . to the effect that the differences between metrical and perspective geometry could be traced back to the differences between the tactile-muscular and the visual intuitions of space. It occurred to me that, as metrical geometry was Greek and perspective geometry is modern, the same thing was, perhaps, true of the differences between Greek and modern art, and that it would be worth while to look into the matter.

Thanks to the plan and lay-out of the Metropolitan Museum, it had for many years been necessary for me to walk through its galleries of classical art on the way to and from my office in the department of prints. Thus, while I had no technical or book knowledge of Greek art, I was more or less accustomed to it and was not afraid to look at it for myself just as if it were any other kind of art. I began to look harder than ever at the classical objects, among which for a while there were arranged a group of casts of the more important and famous ancient statues, and I even read a few books and articles that dealt with them and especially with some other things.

It seems to me that the basic intuitional assumptions of any group of people must be sought among the things they take so much for granted that they are unaware of them. The easiest way to discover such unphrased basic assumptions is by approach from the point of view of a very different group of people with very different habits and ideas. To give a concrete example of this: the Greeks never mentioned among the axioms and postulates of their geometry their basic assumption of congruence, and yet if we come to their geometry from a geometry which is careful not to make that assumption, it is obvious that it is among the most fundamental things in Greek geometry, and plays a determining role in its form, its power, and its limitations.

The following essay is an account of part of my adventure in search of understanding. I hope that it may be of interest as an attempt, however amateurish and in spite of all the errors it undoubtedly contains, to deal with some long-range problems that are usually overlooked in the historical study of art.

Eye and hand

My adventure began with some simple homemade experiments with my hands and eyes as the respective organs of the tactile-muscular and visual intuitions. Obvious and unexciting as their results may appear to be, their implications are of remarkable interest.

Unless the eye moves rather quickly, it is conscious of no breaks in the continuity of its awarenesses, although, of course, as seeing is a selective volitional activity, such breaks are many and great. Things emerge into full consciousness very gradually as they come into the field of vision. If, while looking straight ahead, we hold a hand out at full arm's length sideways behind the line of the two shoulders, we cannot see it nor are we visually aware of it. However, if we slowly swing the arm forward, we discover that long before we can see the hand we are visually aware of it. There are positions early in the swing of the arm from the side to the front in which we are not visually aware of the hand as long as it remains still but are aware of it as soon as it begins to wiggle or move. As the hand is swung forward from this range it slowly assumes shape and color, but the whole hand never attains its fullness of both for the unmoving eye. The smallness of the angle of sharp vision can be tested by looking fixedly at a short word in a line of text and noticing how quickly the type in the words to its right and left loses definition, and that there are no points at which this loss either begins or finally culminates in a complete failure of awareness.[2] Because we can and do continually move our eyes without being aware that we are doing it, we are not usually conscious of this fading in and out, but we act on it continuously every time we walk down a crowded street.

If in a darkened room a red-point light is slowly swung from behind the shoulder line into the position of sharp vision for the unmoving forward-looking eye, it makes its coming into awareness in several different ways. It comes into awareness not suddenly but gradually, so gradually that it is difficult to say just when in its swing it does come into awareness. As it swings forward it gradually becomes more brilliant. Somewhere in the course of this swing a remarkable thing happens. When the eye is first aware of the dim luminous spot, the spot has a neutral grayish color. As it moves further forward it enters a region in which it changes color and becomes a full red.

To phenomena of this kind we must add the 'after images'. If we look fixedly at a pattern in bright red and then look at a piece of white paper we continue to be aware of the pattern, but as a pattern in green. If we look at a pattern of black squares separated by lanes of white, the lanes have flickering cores of gray. These things have much to do with the fact that our awareness of the hue of any particular portion of a surface depends in large measure upon its area and upon the areas and the hues of the neighboring portions and the comparative brilliance of their illumination.

In addition to things of these kinds there is the long series of visual effects that take place with changes in position. Objects get smaller and less brilliant as they get further away from us. Very distant objects are mere shapeless nubbins. Near objects continuously change their shapes as we move about them. A pine wood close to us is a mixture of deep greens and browns, but at a distance it becomes a diaphanous light blue. In the course of the day the whole landscape drastically changes its color. As the light decreases, the different colors disappear from view at different times. Parallel lines as they recede from us tend to come together.

Now, as against all this fading in and out, this shifting, varying, unbroken continuity of quite different visual effects, what do we discover when we examine the tactile-muscular sense returns given by the exploring hand? Doubtless these returns are extremely complex in themselves, but as compared with the visual returns they are definite, simple, and very restricted in gamut. To begin with, as we all know from our experiences in finding our ways about in completely dark rooms, tactile awareness for practical purposes is not accomplished by a gradual fading in and out of consciousness, but by catastrophic contacts and breaking of contacts. My hand either touches something or it does not. My hand tells me that something is light or heavy, hot or cold, smooth or rough. I can measure an object that is simple in form against a phalange of my thumb or a stick, and by counting my motions I can tell how many phalanges or sticks high or wide it is. Short of accident, my muscles tell me that these measurements always require the same number of movements, i.e. that the object does not change in size or shape. If the object is a molding, I can run my fingers or a stick along it and determine that within the reach of my hand its lines are always the same distance apart and do not come together, i.e. that the lines are parallel. Furthermore, the fact that I can touch an object, hold it, push it, pull it, gives me a sense that there is really something there, that I am not the sport of a trick or illusion, and that this something remains the same no matter what its heaviness or lightness, its hotness or coldness, its smoothness or roughness. Moreover, the shapes of objects as known by the hand do not change with shifts in position as do the shapes known by the eye.

The hand, however, as compared to the eye works only within the short limits of reachable and touchable form. When detail gets small, the finger tips are unable to read it. When a form is large the hand cannot read it unless it is very simple in shape, and if it is very large the hand can only read limited portions of it. The hand is unable to correlate a series of simultaneous movements of different elements, and can gain little or no idea of the simultaneity of change in the shapes of the muscles and the limbs and body of an animal in motion. If a form in decoration is very simple and is repeated, like the egg and dart or the wave fret, the hand can follow and recognize it, but if it is complex and constantly changing without repeat, as in a rinceau or on a Gothic capital, the hand is at a very great disadvantage. In any continuous pattern the hand needs simple and static forms and it likes repeated ones. It knows objects separately, one after another, and unlike the eye it has no way of getting a practically simultaneous view or acquaintance with a group of objects as a single awareness. Unlike the eye, the unaided hand is unable to discover whether three or more objects are on a line.

Because of the fact that we frequently see objects at the same time that we touch them, we are apt to associate two different groups of sensations, so that we say that something looks heavy or dry or cold, although the eye in fact is unable to know these sensations. But, it is important to notice that we never say anything feels red. Thus we are constantly giving visual expression to tactile qualities, but rarely or never reverse the process. The result of this is that, although the presence of a drawing on a sheet of paper escapes tactile detection, we can look at the drawing and say that it is composed in largest measure not of visual but of tactile awarenesses. Where an object visually overlaps another of the same hue and illumination its outlines are actually lost to sight, but our tactile intuition forces us to indicate its visually lost outline in our drawing.

As a result of all this I believe the tactile mind is very apt to be aware of and to think of things without any feeling of necessary relationship between them, except such perhaps as results from memory of an invariant time order of repeated but distinct and separate awarenesses.

Tactually, things exist in a series of *heres* in space, but where there are no things, space, even though 'empty', continues to exist, because the exploring hand knows that it is in space even when it is in contact with nothing. The eye, contrariwise, can only see *things*, and where there are no things there is nothing, not even empty space, for that cannot be seen. There is no sense of contact in vision, but tactile awareness exists only as conscious contact. The hand, moving among the things it feels, is always literally 'here', and while it has three dimensional coördinates it has no point of view and in consequence no vanishing point; the eye, having two dimensional coördinates, has a point of view and a vanishing point, and it sees 'there', where it is not. The result is that visually things are not located in an independently existing space, but that space, rather, is a quality or relationship of things and has no existence without them.

From what has been said it is obvious that there repeatedly come crises when the visual and tactile-muscular returns are in conflict.[3] When this happens it is necessary that we elect for one or the other as the test of 'reality'. As we habitually elect for one or the other so we make assumptions on which we base our philosophies and our accounts of the world. I believe that the ancient Greeks provide an unusually clear example of this.

As nearly as I can discover, the Greek idea of a primary substance, or matter, having extension and located in an independently existing space, but set off against a lot of mirage-like secondary, attributable, qualities, may be regarded as the reduction of the tactile-muscular intuitions to a sort of basic philosophical principle. In many ways it would seem that such a central idea is destructive of any sense of necessary unity or continuity between things. It seems to me that running through most of what the Greeks did I perceive qualities that are difficult to explain on any grounds other than that intuitionally the Greeks were tactile minded, and that whenever they were given the choice between a tactile or a visual way of thought they instinctively chose the tactile one.[4] I can imagine nothing more antithetical to Greek thought than Nicod's remark that 'the order of views thus becomes the only fundamental space of nature'.[5]

Greek philosophers used the analogies of imitative art to illustrate their teaching about the unreliability of sensuous, and particularly of visual, apprehension and knowledge. Visual art was imitative and as such was a falsehood, and Socrates—Plato even went so far as to take a moral stand against it on that basis.[6] If I read the *Republic*, the *Sophist*, and the *Timaeus*, and Professor Cornford's commentary on the last of them, correctly, Greek painters and sculptors, and for that matter poets and dramatists too, were but imitations of Platonic ideas making imitations of imitations of Platonic ideas.[7] I suppose Plato, from his extreme realist point of view, would have called one of the Roman copies that today do duty in our museums for so much of Greek sculpture the imitation of an imitation of an imitation by the imitation of an imitation − the cube of an imitation multiplied by the square of an imitation, or imitation raised to its fifth power or dimension of falsity.[8] I hesitate to think how many powers of falsity Plato would have needed for a so-called restoration of a Roman copy by a German professor. Whatever one may think of rigmaroles such as that which I have just perpetrated, they are more serious than they may seem, and they account very satisfactorily for the abstract lack of personality, the composite group-photograph quality, of much of Greek art.[9]

In view of Plato's attitude towards art, little can be more interesting than the fact that over the door of his school there was an inscription which said 'Let no one destitute of geometry enter my doors.' In the *Republic*, 527, he says of geometry that it is 'pursued for the sake of the knowledge of what eternally exists, and not of what comes for a moment into existence, and then perishes', and that it 'must tend to draw the soul towards truth, and to give the finishing touch to the philosophic spirit'.

The contrast drawn by Plato between the falsity of art and the truth of geometry was seemingly a commonplace, and so long as that dichotomy existed there was little chance that the similarities between the two would be recognized. Today, however, the situation has vastly changed. In the eighteenth century Berkeley made his destructive criticism of the distinction between the primary and secondary qualities or characteristics. In the nineteenth century and in this one, study of the relationships between logic and mathematics has brought about a much deeper understanding of what mathematics is. Today geometry has ceased to be The Truth and become a form of art marked by lack of contradiction above rather a superficial level. Thus, G. H. Hardy refers to 'the real mathematics, which must be justified as art if it can be justified at all'.[10] We know that the number of possible geometries is very large, and that any of them as a form of mathematics is only 'true in virtue of its form'.[11] Just what 'true in virtue of its form' may mean seems not to be definitely known, but short of some very unforeseen implications it is probable that it applies equally well to both geometry and representational art.

Notes

1. Enriques, Federigo (1914) *The Problems of Science*, Chicago, pp. 205ff.
2. It is said that at a point two and a half degrees from the point of greatest sharpness of vision there is a 50 per cent decrease in acuity, and that at forty-five degrees the acuity has fallen to $2\frac{1}{2}$ per cent. See Duke-Elder, W. S. (1933) 'Wertheim's curve' in *Text Book of Ophthalmology*, St Louis, p. 924.
3. A familiar example is the return from the crossed finger tips that there are two peas although the eye says there is only one. A more dramatic instance, as dealing with motion and not number, is afforded by the following trick. Make a pin hole in a piece of dark paper or thin cardboard. Hold the paper close to the eye in a position such that the light strikes through the hole to the eye. Then, between the paper and the eye, pass the head of a pin slowly up and down across the hole. When we push the pin head up, our eye tells us that it is going down, and vice versa. The scientific explanation of this contradiction in sense returns does not change them.
4. We are apt to forget that in many ways the Greeks, even of the 'great period', were a primitive people. For a bibliography of studies of the visual awarenesses of primitive peoples see Duke-Elder, op. cit., p. 886.
5. Nicod, Jean (1930) *Foundations of Geometry and Induction*, New York, Harcourt Brace, p. 182.
6. See e.g. Plato (1852) *Republic*, 603, Davies, J. L. and Vaughan, D. J., trans., Cambridge, Cambridge University Press, where Plato writes:

   Did we not assert the impossibility of entertaining, at the same time and with the same part of us, contradictory opinions with reference to the same things?

Yes, and we were right in asserting it.

Then that part of the soul, whose opinion runs counter to the measurements, cannot be identical with that part which agrees with them.

Certainly not.

But surely that part, which relies on measurement and calculation, must be the best part of the soul.

Doubtless it must.

Hence, that which contradicts this part must be one of the inferior elements of our nature.

Necessarily so.

This was the point which I wished to settle between us, when I said that painting, or to speak generally, the whole art of imitation, is busy about a work which is far removed from truth; and that it associates moreover with that part of us, which is far removed from wisdom, and is its mistress and friend for no wholesome or true purpose.

Unquestionably.

Thus the art of imitation is the worthless mistress of a worthless friend, and the parent of a worthless progeny.

7. Cornford, F. M. (1937) *Plato's Cosmology*, New York, Harcourt Brace, p. 28: 'The world, then, is a copy, an image, of the real. It is not, indeed, like an artist's painting at the third remove from reality; . . .'

8. The results of 'a copy of a copy of a copy', etc., are among the most familiar qualities of much of the older book illustration. To any one who desires to check this I can recommend a comparative study of the illustrations in the early herbals, e.g. as reproduced in the pages of Agnes Arber's *Herbals, Their Origin and Evolution*, Cambridge, 1938.

9. A recent rereading has left me as much in the dark about Aristotle's theory of art as I was when, more than forty years ago, I first read S. H. Butcher's *Aristotle's Theory of Poetry and Fine Art*, London, Macmillan, 1902. If Professor Butcher was right in saying (at p. 150): 'If we may expand Aristotle's idea in the light of his own system, – fine art eliminates what is transient and particular and reveals the permanent and essential features of the original,' it would seem to be a theory of imitation based on a theoretical difference between primary and secondary qualities. Thus, aside from Plato's personal moral stand, there seems to be little difference between the basic assumptions of the two philosophers.

10. Hardy, G. H. (1940) *A Mathematician's Apology*, Cambridge, Cambridge University Press, p. 79.

11. The phrase is Bertrand Russell's. See his *Principles of Mathematics*, 2nd ed., New York, W. W. Norton, 1937, p. xii. In the preface to that edition he briefly points out some of the paradoxes or contradictions that infest the logical foundations of mathematics, and he deals with more of them in his text, notably in chapter 42, where he discusses Zeno's 'paradoxes'.

2.2   GEOMETRY AND TRUTH

MORRIS KLINE (1908–   ), *an extract from* Mathematics in Western Culture, *Harmondsworth, Penguin, 1972, pp. 478–82 (originally published 1953)*

Having seen in the previous reading how perceptions
of the world have influenced mathematics, we see
here how mathematical developments have influenced conceptions of inquiry into the world. Non-
Euclidean geometry was the most prominent of a
number of nineteenth-century developments in
mathematics — others are the investigation of
alternative arithmetical systems, and the consequences of set theory described in reading 1.3 —
which changed people's views on the relation
between mathematical and empirical truth.

The importance of non-Euclidean geometry in the general history of
thought cannot be exaggerated. Like Copernicus' heliocentric theory,
Newton's law of gravitation, and Darwin's theory of evolution, non-
Euclidean geometry has radically affected science, philosophy, and
religion. It is fair to say that no more cataclysmic event has ever taken
place in the history of all thought.

First, the creation of non-Euclidean geometry brought into clear light
a distinction that had always been implicit but never recognized — the
distinction between a mathematical space and physical space. The
original identification of the two was due to a misunderstanding.
Fleeting visitors to our minds, sensations of sight and touch, suggested
that the axioms of Euclidean geometry were true of physical space. The
theorems deduced from these axioms were checked with further
sensations of sight and touch and, behold, they checked perfectly — at
least as far as these sensations could reveal. Euclidean geometry was
therefore held to be an exact description of physical space. This habit of
thought became so well established over hundreds of years that the very
notion of a new geometry failed to make sense. Geometry meant the
geometry of physical space and that geometry was Euclid's. With the
creation of non-Euclidean geometry, however, mathematicians, scientists, and laymen were ultimately compelled to appreciate the fact that
*systems of thought based on statements about physical space are
different from that physical space.*

This distinction is vital to an understanding of the developments in
mathematics and science since 1880. We must say now that a mathematical space takes on the nature of a scientific theory. It is applied to
the study of physical space as long as it fits the facts of experience and
serves the needs of science. However, if one mathematical space can be
replaced by another in closer agreement with the expanding results of

scientific work, then it will be replaced just as the Ptolemaic theory of the motion of the heavenly bodies was replaced by the Copernican theory. Nor should the reader be surprised if he discovers that this possibility has materialized by the time he reaches the next chapter.

We should regard any theory about physical space, then, as a purely subjective construction and not impute to it objective reality. Man constructs a geometry, Euclidean or non-Euclidean, and decides to view space in those terms. The advantages in doing so, even though he cannot be sure space possesses any of the characteristics of the structure he has built up in his own mind, are that he can then think about space and use his theory in scientific work. This view of space and of nature generally does not deny that there is such a thing as an objective physical world. It merely recognizes the fact that man's judgements and conclusions about space are purely of his own making.

The creation of non-Euclidean geometry cut a devastating swath through the realm of truth. Like religion in ancient societies mathematics occupied a revered and unchallenged position in Western thought. In the temple of mathematics reposed all truth, and Euclid was its high priest. But the cult, its high priest, and all its attendants were stripped of divine sanction by the work of the unholy three: Bolyai, Lobatchevsky, and Riemann. It is true that in undertaking their research these audacious intellects had in mind only the logical problem of investigating the consequences of a new parallel axiom. It certainly did not occur to them at the outset that they were challenging Truth itself. And as long as their work was regarded merely as an ingenious bit of mathematical hocus-pocus, no serious questions were raised. The moment men realized, however, that the non-Euclidean geometries could be valid descriptions of physical space, an inescapable problem presented itself. How could mathematics, which had always claimed to present the truth about quantity and space, now offer several contradictory geometries? No more than one of these could be the truth. Indeed, and even more disturbing, perhaps the truth was different from all these geometries. The creation of the new geometries, therefore, forced recognition of the fact that there could be an 'if' about all mathematical axioms. *If* the axioms of Euclidean geometry are truths about the physical world then the theorems are. But, unfortunately, we cannot decide on *a priori* grounds that the axioms of Euclid, or of any other geometry, are truths.

In depriving mathematics of its status as a collection of truths, the creation of non-Euclidean geometries robbed man of his most respected truths and perhaps even of the hope of ever attaining certainty about anything. Before 1800 every age had believed in the existence of absolute truth; men differed only in their choice of sources. Aristotle, the fathers of the Church, the Bible, philosophy, and science all had their day as arbiters of objective, eternal truths. In the eighteenth century human reason alone was upheld, and this because of what it had produced in mathematics and in the mathematical domains of science. The possession of mathematical truths had been especially comforting because they held out hope of more to come. Alas, the hope was blasted. The end of the dominance of Euclidean geometry was the end of the dominance of all such absolute standards. The philosopher may still claim the conviction of profound thought; the artist may passionately insist on the validity of the insight which his technical skill makes manifest; the religionist may fill the largest cathedral with the echoes of divine inspiration; and the romantic poet may lull our intellects into drowsy numbness and induce uncritical acceptance of his alluring composition. Perhaps these are all sources of truth. Perhaps there are others. But the rational person who has grasped the lesson of non-Euclidean geometry is at least wary of snares, and, if he accepts any truths, he does so tentatively, expecting at any moment to be disillusioned. Paradoxically, although the new geometries impugned man's ability to attain truths, they provide the best example of the power of the human mind, for the mind had to defy and overcome habit, intuition, and sense perceptions to produce these geometries.

The loss of the sanctity of truth appears to dispose of an age-old question concerning the nature of mathematics itself. Does mathematics exist independently of man, as do the mountains and seas, or is it entirely a human creation? In other words, is the mathematician in his labours unearthing diamonds that have been hidden in the darkness for centuries or is he manufacturing a synthetic stone? Even in the latter part of the nineteenth century, with the story of non-Euclidean geometry before him, the illustrious physicist, Heinrich Hertz, could say, 'One cannot escape the feeling that these mathematical formulas have an independent existence and an intelligence of their own, that they are wiser than we are, wiser even than their discoverers, that we get more out of them than was originally put into them.' Despite this opinion, mathematics does appear to be the product of human, fallible minds rather than the everlasting substance of a world independent of man. It is not a structure of steel resting on the bedrock of objective reality but gossamer floating with other speculations in the partially explored regions of the human mind.

If the creation of non-Euclidean geometry rudely thrust mathematics off the pedestal of truth it also set it free to roam. The work of Lobatchevsky, Riemann, and Bolyai, in effect, gave mathematicians carte blanche to wander wherever they wanted. Because the non-Euclidean geometries, which were investigated originally for the sake of what seemed to be an interesting logical nicety, proved to have incomparable importance, it now seems clear that mathematicians should explore the possibilities in *any* question and in *any* set of axioms as long as the investigation is of some interest; application to the physical world, a leading motive for mathematical investigation, might still follow. At this stage in its history mathematics scrubbed the clay of earth from its feet and separated itself from science, just as science had broken from philosophy, philosophy from religion, and religion from animism and magic. It is possible now to say with Georg Cantor that 'The essence of mathematics is its freedom.'

The position of the mathematician before 1830 can be compared with that of an artist whose driving force is the sheer love of his art but who is compelled by the dictates of necessity to confine himself to drawing magazine covers. Freed from such a restriction the artist might give unlimited rein to his imagination and activities and produce memorable works. Non-Euclidean geometry had just this liberating effect. The tremendous expansion in mathematical activities as well as the increasing emphasis on aesthetic quality in the work of mathematicians since the middle of the last century bears witness to the influence of the new geometry.

Non-Euclidean geometry with its unparalleled importance in the history of thought was the culmination of two thousand years of dabbling in 'useless', logic questions. Mathematics thus provided one more example of the wisdom of abstract, logical thinking unmotivated by utilitarian considerations, and one more example of the wisdom of occasionally rejecting the evidence of the senses, as Copernicus asked us to do in his heliocentric theory, for the sake of what the mind might produce.

2.3 TWO REALITIES

G. H. HARDY (1877–1947), A Mathematician's Apology, *Cambridge, Cambridge University Press, 1940, sections 22–4*

Here Hardy describes his conceptions of mathematical and of physical reality, which interestingly counter Kline's suggestion (reading 2.2) that mathematics now seems, in the aftermath of non-Euclidean geometry, 'not a structure of steel resting on the bedrock of objective reality but gossamer floating with other speculations'. For Hardy, on the contrary, the more different geometries are discovered, the more we know about mathematical reality, 'a reality far more intense and far more rigid than the dubious and elusive reality of physics'.[1]

Hardy's enjoyment in physicist-baiting shows through even more clearly in the 1922 address to which he refers in this extract. He said then − recall that in 1919 Eddington had provided the first experimental support for Einstein's General Theory of Relativity:

> The present is a particularly happy moment for a pure mathematician, since it has been marked by one of the greatest recorded triumphs of pure mathematics. This triumph is the work, as it happens, of a man who would probably not describe himself as a mathematician, but who has done more than any mathematician to vindicate the dignity of mathematics, and to put that obscure and perplexing construction, commonly described as 'physical reality', in its proper place.[2]

Einstein's own views on the relation between mathematics and the world are to be found in reading 2.4.

Notes

1. Address by G. H. Hardy in *Report of the British Association for the Advancement of Science, 1922*, London, John Murray, 1923, p. 17.
2. ibid.

22

There is another misconception against which we must guard. It is quite natural to suppose that there is a great difference in utility between 'pure' and 'applied' mathematics. This is a delusion: there is a sharp distinction between the two kinds of mathematics, which I will explain in a moment, but it hardly affects their utility.

How do pure and applied mathematics differ from one another? This is a question which can be answered definitely and about which there is general agreement among mathematicians. There will be nothing in the least unorthodox about my answer, but it needs a little preface.

My next two sections will have a mildly philosophical flavour. The philosophy will not cut deep, or be in any way vital to my main theses; but I shall use words which are used very frequently with definite philosophical implications, and a reader might well become confused if I did not explain how I shall use them.

I have often used the adjective 'real', and as we use it commonly in conversation. I have spoken of 'real mathematics' and 'real mathematicians', as I might have spoken of 'real poetry' or 'real poets', and I shall continue to do so. But I shall also use the word 'reality', and with two different connotations.

In the first place, I shall speak of 'physical reality', and here again I shall be using the word in the ordinary sense. By physical reality I mean the material world, the world of day and night, earthquakes and eclipses, the world which physical science tries to describe.

I hardly suppose that, up to this point, any reader is likely to find trouble with my language, but now I am near to more difficult ground. For me, and I suppose for most mathematicians, there is another reality, which I will call 'mathematical reality'; and there is no sort of agreement about the nature of mathematical reality among either mathematicians or philosophers. Some hold that it is 'mental' and that in some sense we construct it, others that it is outside and independent of us. A man who could give a convincing account of mathematical reality would have solved very many of the most difficult problems of metaphysics. If he could include physical reality in his account, he would have solved them all.

I should not wish to argue any of these questions here even if I were competent to do so, but I will state my own position dogmatically in order to avoid minor misapprehensions. I believe that mathematical reality lies outside us, that our function is to discover or *observe* it, and that the theorems which we prove, and which we describe grandiloquently as our 'creations', are simply our notes of our observations. This view has been held, in one form or another, by many philosophers of high reputation from Plato onwards, and I shall use the language which is natural to a man who holds it. A reader who does not like the philosophy can alter the language: it will make very little difference to my conclusions.

23

The contrast between pure and applied mathematics stands out most clearly, perhaps, in geometry. There is the science of pure geometry, in which there are many geometries, projective geometry, Euclidean geometry, non-Euclidean geometry, and so forth. Each of these geometries is a *model*, a pattern of ideas, and is to be judged by the interest and beauty of its particular pattern. It is a *map* or *picture*, the joint product of many hands, a partial and imperfect copy (yet exact so far as it extends) of a section of mathematical reality. But the point which is important to us now is this, that there is one thing at any rate of which pure geometries are *not* pictures, and that is the spatio-temporal reality of the physical world. It is obvious, surely, that they cannot be, since earthquakes and eclipses are not mathematical concepts.

This may sound a little paradoxical to an outsider, but it is a truism to a geometer; and I may perhaps be able to make it clearer by an illustration. Let us suppose that I am giving a lecture on some system of geometry, such as ordinary Euclidean geometry, and that I draw figures on the blackboard to stimulate the imagination of my audience, rough drawings of straight lines or circles or ellipses. It is plain, first, that the truth of the theorems which I prove is in no way affected by the quality of my drawings. Their function is merely to bring home my meaning to my hearers, and, if I can do that, there would be no gain in having them redrawn by the most skilful draughtsman. They are pedagogical illustrations, not part of the real subject-matter of the lecture.

Now let us go a stage further. The room in which I am lecturing is part of the physical world, and has itself a certain pattern. The study of that pattern, and of the general pattern of physical reality, is a science in itself, which we may call 'physical geometry'. Suppose now that a violent dynamo, or a massive gravitating body, is introduced into the room. Then the physicists tell us that the geometry of the room is changed, its whole physical pattern slightly but definitely distorted. Do the theorems which I have proved become false? Surely it would be nonsense to suppose that the proofs of them which I have given are affected in any way. It would be like supposing that a play of Shakespeare is changed when a reader spills his tea over a page. The play is independent of the pages on which it is printed, and 'pure geometries' are independent of lecture rooms, or of any other detail of the physical world.

This is the point of view of a pure mathematician. Applied mathematicians, mathematical physicists, naturally take a different view, since they are preoccupied with the physical world itself, which also has its structure or pattern. We cannot describe this pattern exactly, as we can that of a pure geometry, but we can say something significant about it. We can describe, sometimes fairly accurately, sometimes very roughly, the relations which hold between some of its constituents, and compare them with the exact relations holding between constituents of some system of pure geometry. We may be able to trace a certain resemblance between the two sets of relations, and then the pure geometry will become interesting to physicists; it will give us, to that extent, a map which 'fits the facts' of the physical world. The geometer offers to the physicist a whole set of maps from which to choose. One map, perhaps, will fit the facts better than others, and then the geometry which provides that particular map will be the geometry most important for applied mathematics. I may add that even a pure mathematician may find his appreciation of this geometry quickened, since there is no mathematician so pure that he feels no interest at all in the physical world; but, in so far as he succumbs to this temptation, he will be abandoning his purely mathematical position.

24

There is another remark which suggests itself here and which physicists may find paradoxical, though the paradox will probably seem a good deal less than it did eighteen years ago. I will express it in much the same words which I used in 1922 in an address to Section A of the British Association. My audience then was composed almost entirely of physicists, and I may have spoken a little provocatively on that account; but I would still stand by the substance of what I said.

I began by saying that there is probably less difference between the positions of a mathematician and of a physicist than is generally supposed, and that the most important seems to me to be this, that the mathematician is in much more direct contact with reality. This may seem a paradox, since it is the physicist who deals with the subject-matter usually described as 'real'; but a very little reflection is enough to show that the physicist's reality, whatever it may be, has few or none of the attributes which common sense ascribes instinctively to reality. A chair may be a collection of whirling electrons, or an idea in the mind of God: each of these accounts of it may have its merits, but neither conforms at all closely to the suggestions of common sense.

I went on to say that neither physicists nor philosophers have ever given any convincing account of what 'physical reality' is, or of how the physicist passes, from the confused mass of fact or sensation with which he starts, to the construction of the objects which he calls 'real'. Thus we cannot be said to know what the subject-matter of physics is; but this need not prevent us from understanding roughly what a physicist is trying to do. It is plain that he is trying to correlate the incoherent body of crude fact confronting him with some definite and orderly scheme of abstract relations, the kind of scheme which he can borrow only from mathematics.

A mathematician, on the other hand, is working with his own mathematical reality. Of this reality, as I explained in section 22, I take a 'realistic' and not an 'idealistic' view. At any rate (and this was my main point) this realistic view is much more plausible of mathematical than of physical reality, because mathematical objects are so much more what they seem. A chair or a star is not in the least like what it seems to be; the more we think of it, the fuzzier its outlines become in the haze of sensation which surrounds it; but '2' or '317' has nothing to do with sensation, and its properties stand out the more clearly the more closely we scrutinize it. It may be that modern physics fits best into some framework of an idealistic philosophy — I do not believe it, but there are eminent physicists who say so. Pure mathematics, on the other hand, seems to me a rock on which all idealism founders: 317 is a prime, not because we think so, or because our minds are shaped in one way rather than another, but *because it is so*, because mathematical reality is built that way.

2.4 GEOMETRY AND EXPERIENCE

ALBERT EINSTEIN (1879–1955), *extract from 'Geometry and experience', in* Sidelights on Relativity, *London, Methuen, 1922*

Einstein gave the lecture of which this is the opening part in 1921. It will be seen that his view of the *relation* between mathematics and the world is not unlike Hardy's (previous reading), though without sharing Hardy's conception of 'mathematical reality' — indeed, Einstein's reference to 'axiomatics', and his statement 'These axioms are free creations of the human mind', show that his conception of mathematics was very different from Hardy's.

Some indication of the role Einstein's discussion here has played in philosophical controversies — focused centrally on conceptions of valid inquiry — may be gathered from the use made of it by Einstein's friend Philipp Frank, who described this lecture as

> a historic landmark in the long and tortuous approach to philosophical clarity. The relation

between experience and logic in geometry, and in science altogether, was presented, the first time, in a satisfactory way. Einstein did it with great simplicity and directness leaving no dark angle where remnants of truth could take a hiding. . . . Einstein's theory was a clear example which showed that the axioms of geometry are either purely analytical and do not say anything about reality or are not different from the statements of physics, biology or economics. The scientific basis of a great many philosophical doctrines was destroyed radically. There was no longer any scientific foundation for the contention that the human mind can make valid statements by other than the scientific method. . . . The belief that there is any 'philosophical method' besides the empirical−logical method had lost its most scientific foundation.[1]

Whether or not this fairly describes even Einstein's own views − on which a further perspective is provided by Paul Dirac's lecture reproduced as reading 3.3 − Frank's enlisting of Einstein under the banner of logical positivism demonstrates yet again how critical, for conceptions of inquiry down the ages, has been the view taken of the relationship between mathematics and the world.

Note

1. Frank, Philipp (1949) 'Einstein's philosophy of science', *Reviews of Modern Physics*, 21, 351−2.

One reason why mathematics enjoys special esteem, above all other sciences, is that its laws are absolutely certain and indisputable, while those of all other sciences are to some extent debatable and in constant danger of being overthrown by newly discovered facts. In spite of this, the investigator in another department of science would not need to envy the mathematician if the laws of mathematics referred to objects of our mere imagination, and not to objects of reality. For it cannot occasion surprise that different persons should arrive at the same logical conclusions when they have already agreed upon the fundamental laws (axioms), as well as the methods by which other laws are to be deduced therefrom. But there is another reason for the high repute of mathematics, in that it is mathematics which affords the exact natural sciences a certain measure of security, to which without mathematics they could not attain.

At this point an enigma presents itself which in all ages has agitated inquiring minds. How can it be that mathematics, being after all a product of human thought which is independent of experience, is so admirably appropriate to the objects of reality? Is human reason, then, without experience, merely by taking thought, able to fathom the properties of real things?

In my opinion the answer to this question is, briefly, this: – As far as the laws of mathematics refer to reality, they are not certain; and as far as they are certain, they do not refer to reality. It seems to me that complete clearness as to this state of things first became common property through that new departure in mathematics which is known by the name of mathematical logic or 'Axiomatics'. The progress achieved by axiomatics consists in its having neatly separated the logical–formal from its objective or intuitive content; according to axiomatics the logical–formal alone forms the subject-matter of mathematics, which is not concerned with the intuitive or other content associated with the logical–formal.

Let us for a moment consider from this point of view any axiom of geometry, for instance, the following: – Through two points in space there always passes one and only one straight line. How is this axiom to be interpreted in the older sense and in the more modern sense?

The older interpretation: – Every one knows what a straight line is, and what a point is. Whether this knowledge springs from an ability of the human mind or from experience, from some collaboration of the two or from some other source, is not for the mathematician to decide. He leaves the question to the philosopher. Being based upon this knowledge, which precedes all mathematics, the axiom stated above is, like all other axioms, self-evident, that is, it is the expression of a part of this *a priori* knowledge.

The more modern interpretation: – Geometry treats of entities which are denoted by the words straight line, point, etc. These entities do not take for granted any knowledge or intuition whatever, but they presuppose only the validity of the axioms, such as the one stated above, which are to be taken in a purely formal sense, i.e. as void of all content of intuition or experience. These axioms are free creations of the human mind. All other propositions of geometry are logical inferences from the axioms (which are to be taken in the nominalistic sense only). The matter of which geometry treats is first defined by the axioms. Schlick in his book on epistemology has therefore characterized axioms very aptly as 'implicit definitions'.

This view of axioms, advocated by modern axiomatics, purges mathematics of all extraneous elements, and thus dispels the mystic obscurity which formerly surrounded the principles of mathematics. But a presentation of its principles thus clarified makes it also evident that mathematics as such cannot predicate anything about perceptual objects or real objects. In axiomatic geometry the words 'point', 'straight line', etc., stand only for empty conceptual schemata. That which gives them substance is not relevant to mathematics.

Yet on the other hand it is certain that mathematics generally, and particularly geometry, owes its existence to the need which was felt of learning something about the relations of real things to one another. The very word geometry, which, of course, means earth-measuring, proves this. For earth-measuring has to do with the possibilities of the disposition of certain natural objects with respect to one another, namely, with parts of the earth, measuring-lines, measuring-wands, etc. It is clear that the system of concepts of axiomatic geometry alone cannot make any assertions as to the relations of real objects of this kind, which we will call practically-rigid bodies. To be able to make such assertions, geometry must be stripped of its merely logical–formal character by the coordination of real objects of experience with the empty conceptual framework of axiomatic geometry. To accomplish this we need only add the proposition: – Solid bodies are related, with respect to their possible dispositions, as are bodies in Euclidean geometry of three dimensions. Then the propositions of Euclid contain affirmations as to the relations of practically-rigid bodies.

Geometry thus completed is evidently a natural science; we may in fact regard it as the most ancient branch of physics. Its affirmations rest essentially on induction from experience, but not on logical inferences only. We will call this completed geometry 'practical geometry', and shall distinguish it in what follows from 'purely axiomatic geometry'. The question whether the practical geometry of the universe is Euclidean or not has a clear meaning, and its answer can only be furnished by experience. All linear measurement in physics is practical geometry in this sense, so too is geodetic and astronomical linear measurement, if we call to our help the law of experience that light is propagated in a straight line, and indeed in a straight line in the sense of practical geometry.

I attach special importance to the view of geometry which I have just set forth, because without it I should have been unable to formulate the theory of relativity.

2.5 MATHEMATICS AND SCIENTIFIC INQUIRY

E. P. WIGNER (1902–   ), The Unreasonable Effectiveness of Mathematics in the Natural Sciences, *Richard Courant Lecture in Mathematical Sciences delivered at New York University, 11 May 1959, abridged*

This lecture by the distinguished nuclear physicist Eugene Wigner – he received the 1963 Nobel physics prize – raises a question leading on from the positions discussed in the previous readings: given a relationship between mathematics and the world such as conceived by Hardy or Einstein, why *does* it apply to the world so well? It should be noted that this is a comment on the world's behaviour rather more than on mathematics. Its significance may be seen by applying the question to, for example, Hardy's view (reading 2.3) that 'The geometer offers to the physicist a whole set of maps from which to choose. One map, perhaps, will fit the facts better than others.' What this leaves unexplained is how it is that any geometrical map does 'fit the facts' so well as to be unaltered by fresh geometric deductions, or by more accurate empirical measurements. It is not immediately clear even what an explanation of this phenomenon – a prerequisite of scientific inquiry – would look like. On a view of mathematics such as Hogben's (reading 1.4), it might be claimed that the applicability of mathematics is unsurprising, on the grounds that mathematical language is just a way of talking about the world as we perceive it; but this cannot sensibly be said of the type of mathematics used by nuclear physicists (and other scientists).

Wigner finally raises an important question about inquiries: when the world is investigated by different modes of inquiry – for example, by the methods of physics and of biology – can we have any expectation that their results will be even consistent?

While this question is not readily answerable, the very posing of it makes us aware of the kind of assumption we may be bringing to the study of different conceptions of inquiry.

There is a story about two friends, who were classmates in high school, talking about their jobs. One of them became a statistician and was working on population trends. He showed a reprint to his former classmate. The reprint started, as usual, with the Gaussian distribution and the statistician explained to his former classmate the meaning of the symbols for the actual population, for the average population, and so on. His classmate was a bit incredulous and was not quite sure whether the statistician was pulling his leg. 'How can you know that?' was his query. 'And what is this symbol here?' 'Oh,' said the statistician, 'this is π.' 'What is that?' 'The ratio of the circumference of the circle to its diameter.' 'Well, now you are pushing your joke too far,' said the classmate, 'surely the population has nothing to do with the circumference of the circle.'

Naturally, we are inclined to smile about the simplicity of the classmate's approach. Nevertheless, when I heard this story, I had to admit to an eerie feeling because, surely, the reaction of the classmate betrayed only plain common sense. I was even more confused when, not many days later, someone came to me and expressed his bewilderment with the fact that we make a rather narrow selection when choosing the data on which we test our theories. 'How do we know that, if we made a theory which focuses its attention on phenomena we disregard and disregards some of the phenomena now commanding our attention, that we could not build another theory which has little in common with the present one but which, nevertheless, explains just as many phenomena as the present theory?' It has to be admitted that we have no definite evidence that there is no such theory.

The preceding two stories illustrate the two main points which are the subjects of the present discourse. The first point is that mathematical concepts turn up in entirely unexpected connections. Moreover, they often permit an unexpectedly close and accurate description of the phenomena in these connections. Secondly, just because of this circumstance, and because we do not understand the reasons of their usefulness, we cannot know whether a theory formulated in terms of mathematical concepts is uniquely appropriate. We are in a position similar to that of a man who was provided with a bunch of keys and who, having to open several doors in succession, always hit on the right key on the first or second trial. He became sceptical concerning the uniqueness of the coordination between keys and doors.

Most of what will be said on these questions will not be new; it has probably occurred to most scientists in one form or another. My principal aim is to illuminate it from several sides. The first point is that the enormous usefulness of mathematics in the natural sciences is something bordering on the mysterious and that there is no rational explanation for it. Second, it is just this uncanny usefulness of mathematical concepts that raises the question of the uniqueness of our physical theories. . . .

The physicist is interested in discovering the laws of inanimate nature. In order to understand this statement, it is necessary to analyze the concept, 'law of nature'.

The world around us is of baffling complexity and the most obvious fact about it is that we cannot predict the future. Although the joke attributes only to the optimist the view that the future is uncertain, the optimist is right in this case: the future is unpredictable. It is, as Schrödinger has remarked, a miracle that in spite of the baffling complexity of the world, certain regularities in the events could be discovered.[1] One such regularity, discovered by Galileo, is that two rocks, dropped at the same time from the same height, reach the ground at the same time. The laws of nature are concerned with such regularities. Galileo's regularity is a prototype of a large class of regularities. It is a surprising regularity for three reasons.

The first reason that it is surprising is that it is true not only in Pisa, and in Galileo's time, it is true everywhere on the Earth, was always true, and will always be true. This property of the regularity is a recognized invariance property and, as I had occasion to point out some time ago,[2] without invariance principles similar to those implied in the preceding generalization of Galileo's observation, physics would not be possible. The second surprising feature is that the regularity which we are discussing is independent of so many conditions which could have an effect on it. It is valid no matter whether it rains or not, whether the experiment is carried out in a room or from the Leaning Tower, no matter whether the person who drops the rocks is a man or a woman. It is valid even if the two rocks are dropped, simultaneously and from the same height, by two different people. There are, obviously, innumerable other conditions which are all immaterial from the point of view of the validity of Galileo's regularity. The irrelevancy of so many circumstances which *could* play a role in the phenomenon observed has also been called an invariance. However, this invariance is of a different character from the preceding one since it cannot be formulated as a general principle. The exploration of the conditions which do, and which do not, influence a phenomenon is part of the early experimental exploration of a field. It is the skill and ingenuity of the experimenter which show him phenomena which depend on a relatively narrow set of relatively easily realizable and reproducible conditions.[3] In the present case, Galileo's restriction of his observations to relatively heavy bodies was the most important step in this regard. Again, it is true that if there were no phenomena which are independent of all but a manageably small set of conditions, physics would be impossible.

The preceding two points, though highly significant from the point of view of the philosopher, are not the ones which surprised Galileo most, nor do they contain a specific law of nature. The law of nature is contained in the statement that the length of time which it takes for a heavy object to fall from a given height is independent of the size, material, and shape of the body which drops. In the framework of Newton's second 'law', this amounts to the statement that the gravitational force which acts on the falling body is proportional to its mass but independent of the size, material, and shape of the body which falls.

The preceding discussion is intended to remind us, first, that it is not at all natural that 'laws of nature' exist, much less that man is able to discover them. . . .[4]

Naturally, we do use mathematics in everyday physics to evaluate the results of the laws of nature, to apply the conditional statements to the particular conditions which happen to prevail or happen to interest us. In order that this be possible, the laws of nature must already be formulated in mathematical language. However, the role of evaluating the consequences of already established theories is not the most important role of mathematics in physics. Mathematics, or, rather, applied mathematics, is not so much the master of the situation in this function: it is merely serving as a tool.

Mathematics does play, however, also a more sovereign role in physics. This was already implied in the statement, made when discussing the role of applied mathematics, that the laws of nature must have been formulated in the language of mathematics to be an object for the use of applied mathematics. The statement that the laws of nature are written in the language of mathematics was properly made three hundred years ago;[5] it is now more true than ever before. In order to show the importance which mathematical concepts possess in the formulation of the laws of physics, let us recall, as an example, the axioms of quantum mechanics as formulated, explicitly, by the great mathematician, von Neumann,[6] or, implicitly, by the great physicist, Dirac.[7] There are two basic concepts in quantum mechanics: states and observables. The states are vectors in Hilbert space, the observables self-adjoint operators on these vectors. The possible values of the observations are the characteristic values of the operators — but we had better stop here lest we engage in a listing of the mathematical concepts developed in the theory of linear operators.

It is true, of course, that physics chooses certain mathematical concepts for the formulation of the laws of nature, and surely only a fraction of all mathematical concepts is used in physics. It is true also that the concepts which were chosen were not selected arbitrarily from a listing of mathematical terms but were developed, in many if not most cases, independently by the physicist and recognized then as having been conceived before by the mathematician. It is not true, however, as is so often stated, that this had to happen because mathematics uses the simplest possible concepts and these were bound to occur in any formalism. As we saw before, the concepts of mathematics are not chosen for their conceptual simplicity — even sequences of pairs of numbers are far from being the simplest concepts — but for their amenability to clever manipulations and to striking brilliant arguments. Let us not forget that the Hilbert space of quantum mechanics is the complex Hilbert space, with a Hermitean scalar product. Surely to the unpreoccupied mind, complex numbers are far from natural or simple and they cannot be suggested by physical observations. Furthermore, the use of complex numbers is in this case not a calculational trick of applied mathematics but comes close to being a necessity in the formulation of the laws of quantum mechanics. Finally, it now begins to appear that not only complex numbers but so-called analytic functions are destined to play a decisive role in the formulation of quantum theory. I am referring to the rapidly developing theory of dispersion relations.

It is difficult to avoid the impression that a miracle confronts us here, quite comparable in its striking nature to the miracle that the human mind can string a thousand arguments together without getting itself into contradictions, or to the two miracles of the existence of laws of nature and of the human mind's capacity to divine them. The observation which comes closest to an explanation for the mathematical concepts' cropping up in physics which I know is Einstein's statement that the only physical theories which we are willing to accept are the beautiful ones. It stands to argue that the concepts of mathematics, which invite the exercise of so much wit, have the quality of beauty. However, Einstein's observation can at best explain properties of theories which we are willing to believe and has no reference to the intrinsic accuracy of the theory. We shall, therefore, turn to this latter question.

A possible explanation of the physicist's use of mathematics to formulate his laws of nature is that he is a somewhat irresponsible person. As a result, when he finds a connection between two quantities which resembles a connection well-known from mathematics, he will jump at the conclusion that the connection *is* that discussed in mathematics simply because he does not know of any other similar connection. It is not the intention of the present discussion to refute the charge that the physicist is a somewhat irresponsible person. Perhaps he is. However, it is important to point out that the mathematical formulation of the physicist's often crude experience leads in an uncanny number of cases to an amazingly accurate description of a large class of phenomena. This shows that the mathematical language has more to commend it than being the only language which we can speak; it shows that it is, in a very real sense, the correct language. Let us consider a few examples.

The first example is the oft-quoted one of planetary motion. The laws of falling bodies became rather well established as a result of experiments carried out principally in Italy. These experiments could not be very accurate in the sense in which we understand accuracy today partly because of the effect of air resistance and partly because of the impossibility, at that time, to measure short time intervals. Nevertheless, it is not surprising that, as a result of their studies, the Italian natural scientists acquired a familiarity with the ways in which objects travel through the atmosphere. It was Newton who then brought the law of freely falling objects into relation with the motion of the moon, noted that the parabola of the thrown rock's path on the earth and the circle of the moon's path in the sky are particular cases of the same mathematical object of an ellipse, and postulated the universal law of gravitation on the basis of a single, and at that time very approximate, numerical coincidence. Philosophically, the law of gravitation as formulated by Newton was repugnant to his time and to himself. Empirically, it was based on very scanty observations. The mathematical language in which it was formulated contained the concept of a second derivative and those of us who have tried to draw an osculating circle to a curve know that the second derivative is not a very immediate concept. The law of gravity which Newton reluctantly established and which he could verify with an accuracy of about 4 per cent has proved to be accurate to less than a ten thousandth of a per cent and became so closely associated with the idea of absolute accuracy that only recently did physicists become again bold enough to inquire into the limitations of its accuracy. Certainly, the example of Newton's law, quoted over and over again, must be mentioned first as a monumental example of a law, formulated in terms which appear simple to the mathematician, which has proved accurate beyond all reasonable expectations. Let us just recapitulate our thesis on this example: first, the law, particularly since a second derivative appears in it, is simple only to the mathematician, not to common sense or to non-mathematically-minded freshmen; second, it is a conditional law of very limited scope. It explains nothing about the earth which attracts Galileo's rocks, or about the circular form of the moon's orbit, or about the planets of the sun. The explanation of these initial conditions is left to the geologist and the astronomer, and they have a hard time with them. . . .

A much more difficult and confusing situation would arise if we could, some day, establish a theory of the phenomena of consciousness, or of biology, which would be as coherent and convincing as our present theories of the inanimate world. Mendel's laws of inheritance and the subsequent work on genes may well form the beginning of such a theory as far as biology is concerned. Furthermore, it is quite possible that an abstract argument can be found which shows that there is a conflict between such a theory and the accepted principles of physics. The argument could be of such abstract nature that it might not be possible to resolve the conflict, in favor of one or of the other theory, by an experiment. Such a situation would put a heavy strain on our faith in our theories and on our belief in the reality of the concepts which we form. It would give us a deep sense of frustration in our search for what I called 'the ultimate truth'. The reason that such a situation is conceivable is that, fundamentally, we do not know why our theories work so well. Hence, their accuracy may not prove their truth and consistency. Indeed, it is this writer's belief that something rather akin to the situation which was described above exists if the present laws of heredity and of physics are confronted.

Let me end on a more cheerful note. The miracle of the appropriateness of the language of mathematics for the formulation of the laws of physics is a wonderful gift which we neither understand nor deserve. We should be grateful for it and hope that it will remain valid in future research and that it will extend, for better or for worse, to our pleasure, even though perhaps also to our bafflement, to wide branches of learning.

Notes

1. Schrödinger, E. (1932) *Uber Indeterminismus in der Physik*, Leipzig, J. A. Barth; also Dubislav, W. (1933) *Naturphilosophie*, Berlin, Junker & Dunnhaupt, ch. 4.

2. Wigner, E. P. (1949) 'Invariance in physical theory', *Proceedings of the American Philosophical Society*, 93, 521–6.
3. See, in this connection, the graphic essay of Deutsch, M. (1958) *Daedalus*, 87, 86. A. Shimony has called my attention to a similar passage in Peirce, C. S. (1957) *Essays in the Philosophy of Science*, New York, Liberal Arts, p. 237.
4. Schrödinger, in his *What Is Life?*, Cambridge, Cambridge University Press, 1945, p. 31, says that this second miracle may well be beyond human understanding.
5. It is attributed to Galileo. [See the quotation given in the introduction to reading 1.4 (ed.).]
6. Von Neumann, J. (1932) *Mathematische Grundlagen der Quantenmechanik*, Berlin, Springer. (English translation: *Mathematical Foundations of Quantum Mechanics*, Princeton, N.J., Princeton University Press, 1955.)
7. Dirac, P. A. M. (1947) *Quantum Mechanics*, 3rd ed., Oxford, Clarendon.

Part Two
Conceptions of Science

3 Method and discovery

Accounts of scientific method have traditionally formed an integral part of theories about the nature of science. Classics of this genre include Bacon's *Novum Organum*, Descartes' *Discourse on Method*, and Newton's 'Rules of reasoning in philosophy'; and Mill's *System of Logic* (1843) has remained, at least until relatively recently, a classic textbook of scientific method.[1] We include here an extract from this work in which Mill expounds his two main methods of experimental inquiry.

In recent years the assumption that to understand the nature of science is to understand its methods of proof and discovery has been widely challenged. One of the keenest critics of this assumption has been Karl Popper. An extract is included here from *The Logic of Scientific Discovery*,[2] in which Popper argues, firstly, that there cannot be proof of general scientific claims about the world and, secondly, that the process of scientific discovery is a matter of psychology rather than logic.

The question whether there are *methods* of scientific discovery or not may at least partially be resolved by considerations drawn from the history of science. For a study of historical examples may enable a distinction to be drawn between the kind of case where it was predictable that a discovery would soon be made by somebody or other and the kind of case where, but for a particular individual, the discovery might have been delayed for a long time. If scientific advances are predictable it may be partly because established methods of inquiry are being used. In the third extract, the physicist Paul Dirac claims that if Einstein had not existed then the state of physics would have been very different for a considerable time. At one level, Dirac's account supports Popper as against Mill, but only in so far as Popper's account fits great theoretical discoveries better than Mill's does. The case of Einstein is, on Dirac's account, at least very unusual. It may be, therefore, that Mill was right to believe that there are methodologies of discovery, employed at a more mundane level of scientific research, even if they are not summed up in the methods described in his *System of Logic*.

Notes

1. Bacon, Francis (1627) *Novum Organum, or True Suggestions for the Interpretation of Nature*, Wood, William, trans., London, William Pickering, 1844; Descartes, René (1639) *A Discourse on Method*, Veitch, John, trans., London, Dent/New York, Dutton, 1912; Newton, Isaac (1687) 'Rules of reasoning in philosophy' in book 3 of *Sir Isaac Newton's Mathematical Principles of Natural Philosophy . . .*, Motte, Andrew, trans., Berkeley, University of California Press, 1934 – best known simply as *Principia*; Mill, John Stuart (1843) *A System of Logic . . .*, 2 vols, London.
2. Popper, Karl R. (1935) *The Logic of Scientific Discovery*, London, Hutchinson, 1959.

3.1 THE METHODS OF AGREEMENT AND DIFFERENCE

JOHN STUART MILL (1806–1873), *from* A System of Logic, *book 3, ch. 8, 1–3: 'Of the four methods of experimental inquiry', London, Longmans, Green, 1843*

Experimental methods, for Mill, are *inductive*, i.e. they involve generalization from observed particulars. They are methods of 'discovery and proving laws of nature'. They are both, as Mill notes, methods of *elimination* but, of the two, the method of difference is the more 'efficacious'. The method of agreement serves to eliminate suspected causes but does not necessarily prove the actual cause of a phenomenon. Its advantage is that it is a method which is more practically applicable. The method of difference is less readily applicable but, where it can be applied, it offers positive proof of the cause of a phenomenon.

The simplest and most obvious modes of singling out from among the circumstances which precede or follow a phenomenon those with which it is really connected by an invariable law are two in number. One is, by comparing together different instances in which the phenomenon occurs. The other is, by comparing instances in which the phenomenon does occur, with instances in other respects similar in which it does not. These two methods may be respectively denominated the Method of Agreement and the Method of Difference.

In illustrating these methods, it will be necessary to bear in mind the twofold character of inquiries into the laws of phenomena, which may be either inquiries into the cause of a given effect, or into the effects or properties of a given cause. We shall consider the methods in their application to either order of investigation, and shall draw our examples equally from both.

We shall denote antecedents by the large letters of the alphabet, and the consequents corresponding to them by the small. Let A, then, be an agent of cause, and let the object of our inquiry be to ascertain what are the effects of this cause. If we can either find or produce the agent A in such varieties of circumstances that the different cases have no circumstance in common except A, then whatever effect we find to be produced in all our trials is indicated as the effect of A. Suppose, for example, that A is tried along with B and C, and that the effect is a b c; and suppose that A is next tried with D and E, but without B and C, and that the effect is a d e. Then we may reason thus: b and c are not effects of A, for they were not produced by it in the second experiment; nor are d and e, for they were not produced in the first. Whatever is really the effect of A must have been produced in both instances; now this condition is fulfilled by no circumstances except a. The phenomenon a cannot have been the effect of B or C, since it was produced where they were not; nor of D or E, since it was produced where they were not. Therefore it is the effect of A.

For example, let the antecedent A be the contact of an alkaline substance and an oil. This combination being tried under several varieties of circumstances, resembling each other in nothing else, the results agree in the production of a greasy and detersive or saponaceous substance: it is therefore concluded that the combination of an oil and an alkali causes the production of a soap. It is thus we inquire, by the Method of Agreement, into the effect of a given cause.

In a similar manner we may inquire into the cause of a given effect. Let a be the effect. Here we have only the resource of observation without experiment: we cannot take a phenomenon of which we know not the origin, and try to find its mode of production by producing it: if we succeeded in such a random trial it could only be by accident. But if we can observe a in two different combinations, $a\ b\ c$ and $a\ d\ e$; and if we know, or can discover, that the antecedent circumstances in these cases respectively were $A\ B\ C$ and $A\ D\ E$, we may conclude by a reasoning similar to that in the preceding example, that A is the antecedent connected with the consequent a by a law of causation. B and C, we may say, cannot be causes of a, since on its second occurrence they were not present; nor are D and E, for they were not present on its first occurrence. A, alone of the five circumstances, was found among the antecedents of a in both instances.

For example, let the effect a be crystallisation. We compare instances in which bodies are known to assume crystalline structure, but which have no other point of agreement; and we find them to have one, and, as far as we can observe, only one, antecedent in common: the deposition of a solid matter from a liquid state, either a state of fusion or of solution. We conclude, therefore, that the solidification of a substance from a liquid state is an invariable antecedent of its crystallisation. . . .

The mode of discovering and proving laws of nature, which we have now examined, proceeds on the following axiom. Whatever circumstance can be excluded, without prejudice to the phenomenon, or can be absent notwithstanding its presence, is not connected with it in the way of causation. The casual circumstance being thus eliminated, if only one remains, that one is the cause which we are in search of: if more than one, they either are, or contain among them, the cause; and so, *mutatis mutandis*, of the effect. As this method proceeds by comparing different instances to ascertain in what they agree, I have termed it the Method of Agreement; and we may adopt as its regulating principle the following canon.

First canon

If two or more instances of the phenomenon under investigation have only one circumstance in common, the circumstance in which alone all the instances agree is the cause (or effect) of the given phenomenon.

Quitting for the present the Method of Agreement, to which we shall almost immediately return, we proceed to a still more potent instrument of the investigation of nature, the Method of Difference.

In the Method of Agreement, we endeavoured to obtain instances which agreed in the given circumstance but differed in every other: in the present method we require, on the contrary, two instances resembling one another in every other respect, but differing in the presence or absence of the phenomenon we wish to study. If our object be to discover the effects of an agent A, we must procure A in some set of ascertained circumstances, as A B C, and having noted the effects produced, compare them with the effect of the remaining circumstances B C, when A is absent. If the effect of A B C is a b c, and the effect of B C, b c, it is evident that the effect of A is a. So again, if we begin at the other end, and desire to investigate the cause of an effect a, we must select an instance, as a b c, in which the effect occurs, and in which the antecedents were A B C, and we must look out for another instance in which the remaining circumstances, b c, occur without a. If the antecedents, in that instance, are B C, we know that the cause of a must be A: either A alone, or A in conjunction with some of the other circumstances present.

It is scarcely necessary to give examples of a logical process to which we owe almost all the inductive conclusions we draw in early life. When a man is shot through the heart, it is by this method we know that it was the gunshot which killed him: for he was in the fulness of life immediately before, all circumstances being the same, except the wound.

The axioms implied in this method are evidently the following. Whatever antecedent cannot be excluded without preventing the phenomenon, is the cause, or a condition of that phenomenon; whatever consequent can be excluded, with no other difference in the antecedents than the absence of a particular one, is the effect of that one. Instead of comparing different instances of a phenomenon, to discover in what they agree, this method compares an instance of its occurrence with an instance of its non-occurrence, to discover in what they differ. The canon which is the regulating principle of the Method of Difference may be expressed as follows.

Second canon

If an instance in which the phenomenon under investigation occurs, and an instance in which it does not occur, have every circumstance in common save one, that one occurring only in the former; the circumstance in which alone the two instances differ is the effect, or the cause, or an indispensable part of the cause, of the phenomenon.

The two methods which we have now stated have many features of resemblance, but there are also many distinctions between them. Both are methods of elimination. This term (employed in the theory of equations to denote the process by which one after another of the elements of a question is excluded, and the solution made to depend on the relation between the remaining elements only) is well suited to express the operation, analogous to this, which has been understood since the time of Bacon to be the foundation of experimental inquiry, namely, the successive exclusion of the various circumstances which are found to accompany a phenomenon in a given instance, in order to ascertain what are those among them which can be absent consistently with the existence of the phenomenon. The Method of Agreement stands on the ground that whatever can be eliminated is not connected with the phenomenon by any law. The Method of Difference has for its foundation, that whatever cannot be eliminated is connected with the phenomenon by a law. Of these methods, that of Difference is more particularly a method of artificial experiment; while that of Agreement is more especially the resource employed where experimentation is impossible. A few reflections will prove the fact, and point out the reason of it.

It is inherent in the peculiar character of the Method of Difference that the nature of the combinations which it requires is much more strictly defined than in the Method of Agreement. The two instances which are to be compared with one another must be exactly similar in all circumstances except the one which we are attempting to investigate: they must be in the relation of $A\ B\ C$ and $B\ C$, or of $a\ b\ c$ and $b\ c$. It is true that this similarity of circumstances need not extend to such as are already known to be immaterial to the result. And in the case of most phenomena we learn at once, from the commonest experience, that most of the co-existent phenomena of the universe may be either present or absent without affecting the given phenomenon; or, if present, are present indifferently when the phenomenon does not happen and when it does. Still, even limiting the identity which is required between the two instances, $A\ B\ C$ and $B\ C$, to such circumstances as are not already known to be indifferent; it is very seldom that nature affords two instances, of which we can be assured that they stand in this precise relation to one another. In the spontaneous operations of nature there is generally such complication and such obscurity, they are mostly either on so overwhelmingly large or on so inaccessibly minute a scale, we are so ignorant of a great part of the facts which really take place, and even those of which we are not ignorant are so multitudinous, and therefore so seldom exactly alike in any two cases, that a spontaneous experiment, of the kind required by the Method of Difference, is commonly not to be found. When, on the contrary, we obtain a phenomenon by an artificial experiment, a pair of instances such as the method requires is obtained almost as a matter of course, provided the process does not last a long time. A certain state of surrounding circumstances existed before we commenced the experiment; this is $B\ C$. We then introduce A; say, for instance, by merely bringing an object from another part of the room, before there has been time for any change in the other elements. It is, in short (as M. Gointe observes), the very nature of an experiment to introduce into the pre-existing state of circumstances a change perfectly definite. We choose a previous state of things with which we are well acquainted, so that no unforeseen alteration in that state is likely to pass unobserved: and into this we introduce, as rapidly as possible, the phenomenon which we wish to study; so that in general we are entitled to feel complete assurance that the pre-existing state, and the state which we have produced, differ in nothing except the presence or absence of that phenomenon. If a bird is taken from a cage, and instantly plunged into carbonic acid gas, the experimentalist may be fully assured (at all events after one or two repetitions) that no circumstances capable of causing suffocation had supervened in the interim, except the change from immersion in the atmosphere to immersion in carbonic acid gas. There is one doubt, indeed, which may remain in some cases of this description; the effect may have been produced not by the change, but by the means employed to produce the change. The possibility, however, of this last supposition generally admits of being conclusively tested by other experiments. It thus appears that in the study of the various kinds of phenomena which we can, by our voluntary agency, modify or control, we can in general satisfy the requisitions of the Method of Difference; but that by the spontaneous operations of nature those requisitions are seldom fulfilled.

The reverse of this is the case with the Method of Agreement. We do not here require instances of so special and determinate a kind. Any instances whatever, in which nature presents us with a phenomenon, may be examined for the purposes of this method; and if all such instances agree in anything, a conclusion of considerable value is already attained. We can seldom, indeed, be sure that the one point of agreement is the only one; but this ignorance does not, as in the Method of Difference, vitiate the conclusion; the certainty of the result, as far as it goes, is not affected. We have ascertained one invariable antecedent or consequent, however many other invariable antecedents or consequents may still remain unascertained. If $A\ B\ C$, $A\ D\ E$, $A\ F\ G$, are all equally followed by a, then a is an invariable consequent of A. If $a\ b\ c$, *a d e*, *a f g*, all number *A* among their antecedents, then *A* is connected as an antecedent, by some invariable law, with *a*. But to determine whether this invariable antecedent is a cause, or this invariable consequent an effect, we must be able, in addition, to produce the one by means of the other; or, at least, to obtain that which alone constitutes our assurance of having produced anything, namely, an instance in which the effect, *a*, has come into existence, with no other change in the pre-existing circumstances than the addition of *A*. And this, if we can do it, is an application of the Method of Difference, not of the Method of Agreement.

It thus appears to be by the Method of Difference alone that we can ever, in the way of direct experience, arrive with certainty at causes. The Method of Agreement leads only to laws of phenomena (as some writers call them, but improperly, since laws of causation are also laws of phenomena), that is, to uniformities, which either are not laws of causation, or in which the question of causation must for the present remain undecided. The Method of Agreement is chiefly to be resorted to as a means of suggesting applications of the Method of Difference (as in the last example the comparison of *A B C*, *A D E*, *A F G*, suggested that *A* was the antecedent on which to try the experiment whether it could produce *a*), or as an inferior resource in case the Method of Difference is impracticable; which, as we before showed, generally arises from the impossibility of artificially producing the phenomena. And hence it is that the Method of Agreement, though applicable in principle to either case, is more emphatically the method of investigation on those subjects where artificial experimentation is impossible; because on those it is generally our only resource of a directly inductive nature; while, in the phenomena which we can produce at pleasure, the Method of Difference generally affords a more efficacious process, which will ascertain causes as well as mere laws.

3.2 AGAINST METHODS OF DISCOVERY

KARL R. POPPER (1902–   ), *from* The Logic of Scientific Discovery, *revised English edition, London, Routledge & Kegan Paul, 1968 (first edition Hutchinson, 1959)*

Popper argues that there is no solution to the problem of induction and hence that there cannot be an inductive logic. His opinion is that it is a mistake to suppose that there is a logical method for arriving at hypotheses. What matters, according to Popper, is not how hypotheses are discovered but how they are tested. Processes of discovery are not rational and are a matter for psychological investigation. The method of science is a method for testing theories critically (see also reading 4.3).

A scientist, whether theorist or experimenter, puts forward statements, or systems of statements, and tests them step by step. In the field of the empirical sciences, more particularly, he constructs hypotheses, or systems of theories, and tests them against experience by observation and experiment.

I suggest that it is the task of the logic of scientific discovery, or the logic of knowledge, to give a logical analysis of this procedure; that is, to analyse the method of the empirical sciences.

But what are these 'methods of the empirical sciences'? And what do we call 'empirical science'?

1. The problem of induction

According to a widely accepted view − to be opposed in this book − the empirical sciences can be characterized by the fact that they use '*inductive methods*', as they are called. According to this view, the logic of scientific discovery would be identical with inductive logic, i.e. with the logical analysis of these inductive methods.

It is usual to call an inference 'inductive' if it passes from *singular statements* (sometimes also called 'particular' statements), such as accounts of the results of observations or experiments, to *universal statements*, such as hypotheses or theories.

Now it is far from obvious, from a logical point of view, that we are justified in inferring universal statements from singular ones, no matter how numerous; for any conclusion drawn in this way may always turn out to be false: no matter how many instances of white swans we may have observed, this does not justify the conclusion that *all* swans are white.

The question whether inductive inferences are justified, or under what conditions, is known as *the problem of induction*.

The problem of induction may also be formulated as the question of how to establish the truth of universal statements which are based on experience, such as the hypotheses and theoretical systems of the empirical sciences. For many people believe that the truth of these universal statements is '*known by experience*'; yet it is clear that an account of an experience − of an observation or the result of an experiment − can in the first place be only a singular statement and not a universal one. Accordingly, people who say of a universal statement that we know its truth from experience usually mean that the truth of this universal statement can somehow be reduced to the truth of singular ones, and that these singular ones are known by experience to be true; which amounts to saying that the universal statement is based on inductive inference. Thus to ask whether there are natural laws known to be true appears to be only another way of asking whether inductive inferences are logically justified.

Yet if we want to find a way of justifying inductive inferences, we must first of all try to establish a *principle of induction*. A principle of induction would be a statement with the help of which we could put inductive inferences into a logically acceptable form. In the eyes of the upholders of inductive logic, a principle of induction is of supreme importance for scientific method: '. . . this principle,' says Reichenbach, 'determines the truth of scientific theories. To eliminate it from science would mean nothing less than to deprive science of the power to decide the truth or falsity of its theories. Without it, clearly, science would no longer have the right to distinguish its theories from the fanciful and arbitrary creations of the poet's mind.'[1]

Now this principle of induction cannot be a purely logical truth like a tautology or an analytic statement. Indeed, if there were such a thing as a purely logical principle of induction, there would be no problem of induction; for in this case, all inductive inferences would have to be regarded as purely logical or tautological transformations, just like inferences in deductive logic. Thus the principle of induction must be a synthetic statement; that is, a statement whose negation is not self-contradictory but logically possible. So the question arises why such a principle should be accepted at all, and how we can justify its acceptance on rational grounds.

Some who believe in inductive logic are anxious to point out, with Reichenbach, that 'the principle of induction is unreservedly accepted by the whole of science and that no man can seriously doubt this principle in everyday life either'.[2] Yet even supposing this were the case − for after all, 'the whole of science' might err − I should still contend that a principle of induction is superfluous, and that it must lead to logical inconsistencies.

That inconsistencies may easily arise in connection with the principle of induction should have been clear from the work of Hume; also, that they can be avoided, if at all, only with difficulty. For the principle of induction must be a universal statement in its turn. Thus if we try to regard its truth as known from experience, then the very same problems which occasioned its introduction will arise all over again. To justify it, we should have to employ inductive inferences; and to justify these we should have to assume an inductive principle of a higher order; and so on. Thus the attempt to base the principle of induction on experience breaks down, since it must lead to an infinite regress. . . .

My own view is that the various difficulties of inductive logic here sketched are insurmountable. So also, I fear, are those inherent in the doctrine, so widely current today, that inductive inference, although not 'strictly valid', *can attain some degree of 'reliability' or of 'probability'*. According to this doctrine, inductive inferences are 'probable inferences'. 'We have described,' says Reichenbach, 'the principle of induction as the means whereby science decides upon truth. To be more exact, we should say that it serves to decide upon probability. For it is not given to science to reach either truth or falsity . . . but scientific statements can only attain continuous degrees of probability whose unattainable upper and lower limits are truth and falsity. . . .'[3]

The theory to be developed in the following pages stands directly opposed to all attempts to operate with the ideas of inductive logic. It might be described as the theory of *the deductive method of testing*, or as the view that a hypothesis can only be empirically *tested* − and only *after* it has been advanced.

Before I can elaborate this view (which might be called 'deductivism', in contrast to 'inductivism') I must first make clear the distinction between the *psychology of knowledge* which deals with empirical facts, and the *logic of knowledge* which is concerned only with logical relations. For the belief in inductive logic is largely due to a confusion of psychological problems with epistemological ones. It may be worth noticing, by the way, that this confusion spells trouble not only for the logic of knowledge but for its psychology as well.

2. Elimination of psychologism

I said above that the work of the scientist consists in putting forward and testing theories.

The initial stage, the act of conceiving or inventing a theory, seems to me neither to call for logical analysis nor to be susceptible of it. The question how it happens that a new idea occurs to a man − whether it is a musical theme, a dramatic conflict, or a scientific theory − may be of great interest to empirical psychology; but it is irrelevant to the logical analysis of scientific knowledge. This latter is concerned not with *questions of fact* (Kant's *quid facti?*), but only with questions of *justification or validity* (Kant's *quid juris?*). Its questions are of the following kind. Can a statement be justified? And if so, how? Is it testable? Is it logically dependent on certain other statements? Or does it perhaps contradict them? In order that a statement may be logically examined in this way, it must already have been presented to us. Someone must have formulated it, and submitted it to logical examination.

Accordingly I shall distinguish sharply between the process of conceiving a new idea, and the methods and results of examining it logically. As to the task of the logic of knowledge — in contradistinction to the psychology of knowledge — I shall proceed on the assumption that it consists solely in investigating the methods employed in those systematic tests to which every new idea must be subjected if it is to be seriously entertained.

Some might object that it would be more to the purpose to regard it as the business of epistemology to produce what has been called a '*rational reconstruction*' of the steps that have led the scientist to a discovery — to the finding of some new truth. But the question is: what, precisely, do we want to reconstruct? If it is the processes involved in the stimulation and release of an inspiration which are to be reconstructed, then I should refuse to take it as the task of the logic of knowledge. Such processes are the concern of empirical psychology but hardly of logic. It is another matter if we want to reconstruct rationally the *subsequent tests* whereby the inspiration may be discovered to be a discovery, or become known to be knowledge. In so far as the scientist critically judges, alters, or rejects his own inspiration we may, if we like, regard the methodological analysis undertaken here as a kind of 'rational reconstruction' of the corresponding thought-processes. But this reconstruction would not describe these processes as they actually happen: it can give only a logical skeleton of the procedure of testing. Still, this is perhaps all that is meant by those who speak of a 'rational reconstruction' of the ways in which we gain knowledge.

It so happens that my arguments in this book are quite independent of this problem. However, my view of the matter, for what it is worth, is that there is no such thing as a logical method of having new ideas, or a logical reconstruction of this process. My view may be expressed by saying that every discovery contains 'an irrational element', or 'a creative intuition', in Bergson's sense. In a similar way Einstein speaks of the 'search for those highly universal laws . . . from which a picture of the world can be obtained by pure deduction. There is no logical path,' he says, 'leading to these . . . laws. They can only be reached by intuition, based upon something like an intellectual love (*"Einfüh-lung"*) of the objects of experience.'[4]

3. Deductive testing of theories

According to the view that will be put forward here, the method of critically testing theories, and selecting them according to the results of tests, always proceeds on the following lines. From a new idea, put up tentatively, and not yet justified in any way — an anticipation, a hypothesis, a theoretical system, or what you will — conclusions are drawn by means of logical deduction. These conclusions are then compared with one another and with other relevant statements, so as to find what logical relations (such as equivalence, derivability, compatibility, or incompatibility) exist between them.

We may if we like distinguish four different lines along which the testing of a theory could be carried out. First there is the logical comparison of the conclusions among themselves, by which the internal consistency of the system is tested. Secondly, there is the investigation of the logical form of the theory, with the object of determining whether it has the character of an empirical or scientific theory, or whether it is, for example, tautological. Thirdly, there is the comparison with other theories, chiefly with the aim of determining whether the theory would constitute a scientific advance should it survive our various tests. And finally, there is the testing of the theory by way of empirical applications of the conclusions which can be derived from it.

The purpose of this last kind of test is to find out how far the new consequences of the theory — whatever may be new in what it asserts — stand up to the demands of practice, whether raised by purely scientific experiments, or by practical technological applications. Here too the procedure of testing turns out to be deductive. With the help of other statements, previously accepted, certain singular statements — which we may call 'predictions' — are deduced from the theory; especially predictions that are easily testable or applicable. From among these statements, those are selected which are not derivable from the current theory, and more especially those which the current theory contradicts. Next we seek a decision as regards these (and other) derived statements by comparing them with the results of practical applications and experiments. If this decision is positive, that is, if the singular conclusions turn out to be acceptable, or *verified*, then the theory has, for the time being, passed its test: we have found no reason to discard it. But if the decision is negative, or in other words, if the conclusions have been *falsified*, then their falsification also falsifies the theory from which they were logically deduced.

It should be noticed that a positive decision can only temporarily support the theory, for subsequent negative decisions may always overthrow it. So long as a theory withstands detailed and severe tests and is not superseded by another theory in the course of scientific progress, we may say that it has 'proved its mettle' or that it is '*corroborated*' by past experience.

Nothing resembling inductive logic appears in the procedure here outlined. I never assume that we can argue from the truth of singular statements to the truth of theories. I never assume that by force of 'verified' conclusions, theories can be established as 'true', or even as merely 'probable'.

Notes

1. Reichenbach, Hans (1930) Article in *Erkenntnis*, 1, 186.
2. ibid., p. 67.
3. ibid., p. 186.
4. Einstein, Albert (1935) *The World as I See It*, Harris, Alan, trans., London, John Lane, p. 168. (Originally published 1934 as *Mein Weitbild*, Amsterdam.)

3.3   THE TEST OF EINSTEIN

PAUL DIRAC (1902–   ), *from a lecture given at a UNESCO symposium on the impact of modern scientific ideas on society in 1978, published as 'The test of time' in the* Unesco Courier, *75, June 1979, pp. 17–23*

Dirac here describes the impact of Einstein's theory of gravitation, discussed elsewhere in this volume (4.3, 5.1), and considers how Einstein might have reacted if there had been a discrepancy between his theory and well-confirmed observations. He suggests that Einstein's procedure would not have been to abandon the fundamentals of his theory but to look for some secondary feature which could be modified to take care of the discrepancy. Dirac's view bears not only on the dispute between Popper and those who believe in a methodology of discovery but also that aired in the next chapter between Popper and those, like Kuhn, who hold that it is a mistake to think that fundamental scientific theories can be disproved. In this second dispute Dirac's position bears interesting comparison with that of Lakatos in reading 4.5.

The big discoveries in science are made in two ways. Sometimes the time is ripe for a certain discovery and there are many people hot on the trail. It becomes a race between them and whoever wins the race gets the credit.

If you look through the list of Nobel prize winners you will see that very often the prizes are awarded to two or three people who have worked on the same subject and the credit is divided between those who win the race. This kind of discovery is such that if one particular man had never existed the discovery would soon have been made by somebody else.

Now there is another kind of scientific discovery where one man works all alone, follows new lines of thought entirely by himself with no rivals and no competitors. He goes into new domains of thought which no one has previously entered. The work of Einstein is mostly of this kind.

If Einstein had not existed these discoveries would not have been made by anybody else for many years or for many decades. Einstein alone entirely changed the course of scientific history.

Einstein's theory of relativity remained unknown, except to a few specialists, until the end of 1918, when the First World War came to an end. It then came in with a terrific impact. It presented the world with a new style of thinking, a new philosophy.

It came at a time when everyone was sick of the war, those who had won as well as those who had lost. People wanted something new. Relativity provided just what was wanted and was seized upon by the general public and became the central topic of conversation. It allowed people to forget for a time the horrors of the war they had come through.

Innumerable articles about relativity were written in newspapers and magazines. Never before or since has a specific idea aroused so much and such widespread interest. Most of what was said and written referred to general philosophical ideas and did not have the precision required for serious scientific discussion. Very little precise information was available. But still people were happy just to expound their views.

I was an engineering student at Bristol University in England at the time, and of course the students took up this subject and discussed it extensively among themselves. But neither the students nor the professors had precise information about it or knew anything about the underlying mathematics. We could only talk about the philosophical implications and accept the universal belief that it was a good theory.

In England, one man, Arthur Eddington, really understood relativity and became the leader and the authority on the subject. He was very much concerned with the astronomical consequences of the theory and the possibility of checking it by astronomical observations.

Three possible tests of the theory were proposed.

The first of these concerned the motion of the planet Mercury. The perihelion of Mercury (the point in the planet's trajectory nearest to the sun) was observed to be advancing about forty-three seconds of arc more than it should be according to the Newtonian theory, a fact that had been bothering astronomers for a long time. Einstein's new theory predicted just this effect and Eddington's tests confirmed this prediction.

This was really a wonderful success for Einstein's theory, but it is said that Einstein himself was not very excited when he heard of Eddington's confirmation because he felt that his theory had to be right in any case.

The second test concerned the deflection of light passing close by the sun. Einstein's theory of gravitation requires that light passing close by the sun shall be deflected. The Newtonian theory also requires a deflection, but only half the amount of the Einstein theory. So, by observing stars on the far side of the sun, whose light has passed close to the sun to reach us, we can test Einstein's theory.

Now we can only observe the stars close to the sun at a time of total eclipse, when the sun's light is blotted out by the moon. There was a suitable total eclipse in 1919 and Eddington prepared two expeditions to observe this eclipse, leading one of them in person.

Both expeditions obtained results which confirmed Einstein's theory. However, the accuracy of this confirmation was not very great because of the difficulties in making these observations. So people were not altogether satisfied with it. At many total eclipses of the sun that have occurred since then, people have again checked for this effect and they have always got results agreeing with Einstein's theory with a greater or lesser accuracy.

More recently it has become possible to check this effect with radio waves instead of light waves. Radio stars have been discovered and when a radio star is behind the sun we can observe whether the radio waves passing close by the sun are deflected. This can be done without waiting for a total eclipse because the sun is only a very weak emitter of radio waves. Using radio waves instead of light waves there is an added complication because radio waves are deflected by the sun's corona. But this deflection is different for waves of different lengths, so by making the observations for two different wavelengths, we can separate the effect arising from the corona from the Einstein effect. The result is that Einstein's theory is confirmed with an accuracy much greater than can be attained with light waves.

The third test concerned the prediction of the general relativity theory that light waves which have been emitted from a source in a gravitational field will be deflected towards longer wavelengths, i.e. towards the red end of the spectrum, an effect known as the red shift. The obvious place to look for this effect is with a light that has come from the surface of the sun. But it is difficult to observe the Einstein effect there because of another phenomenon (the Doppler effect) arising from the motion of the matter in the sun's atmosphere which is quite large and which is not very well understood. Nevertheless, we can make estimates of the effects of this motion and obtain a rough agreement of the requirements of Einstein's theory.

The discovery of the white dwarf star provides a better way of testing for this effect. With the white dwarf stars we have matter in a very highly condensed state. The gravitational potential at the surface of a white dwarf is very much greater than it is at the surface of the sun and the Einstein effect is correspondingly greater. If we have enough information about the white dwarf to be able to infer what its mass is and its size, we can get a very good check of Einstein's theory. This effect can now also be checked by laboratory observations with greater accuracy than we can get with astronomical observations.

Recently a fourth test has been added to the three classical ones. This is concerned with the time taken by light to pass close by the sun. The Einstein theory requires a delay. This can be observed if we project radar waves to a planet on the far side of the sun, and then observe the time taken for the reflected waves to get back to earth. With the use of radar waves the retardation is affected by the sun's corona and again we have to use two different wavelengths to disentangle the corona effect from the Einstein effect.

The observations have been carried out by Irwin Shapiro and again there is good confirmation of the Einstein theory.

This enumeration of the successes of Einstein's theory is impressive. In every case Einstein's theory is confirmed, with greater or less accuracy depending on the precision with which the observations can be made and the uncertainties that they involve.

Let us now face the question, that a discrepancy has appeared, well confirmed and substantiated, between the theory and the observations. How should one react to it? How would Einstein himself have reacted to it? Should one then consider the theory to be basically wrong?

I would say that the answer to the last question is emphatically No. Anyone who appreciates the fundamental harmony connecting the way nature runs and general mathematical principles must feel that a theory with the beauty and elegance of Einstein's theory *has* to be substantially correct. If a discrepancy should appear in some application of the theory, it must be caused by some secondary feature relating to this application which has not been adequately taken into account, and not by a failure of the general principles of the theory.

Relativity of time. *Two widely separated light-houses flash a warning beacon at the same instant. A man on the ground, exactly half-way between the two towers, sees the two flashes simultaneously. But to an observer in the air-ship, moving towards the beacon at the left, the two flashes would not be simultaneous. Relative to him, the flash from the tower nearest to him would appear a fraction of a second ahead of the other, as it has less distance to cover.*

When Einstein was working on building up his theory of gravitation he was not trying to account for some results of observations. Far from it. His entire procedure was to search for a beautiful theory, a theory of a type that nature would choose.

He was guided only by the requirement that his theory should have the beauty and the elegance which one would expect to be provided by any fundamental description of nature. He was working entirely from these ideas of what nature ought to be like and not from the requirement to account for certain experimental results.

Of course it needs real genius to be able to imagine what nature should be like; just from abstract thinking about it. Einstein was able to do it.

Somehow he got the idea of connecting gravitation with the curvature of space. He was able to develop a mathematical scheme incorporating this idea. He was guided only by consideration of the beauty of the equations.

The result of such a procedure is a theory of great simplicity and elegance in its basic ideas. One has an overpowering belief that its foundations must be correct quite independent of its agreement with observation.

I had the privilege of meeting Einstein on various occasions. The first time was at the Solvay Conference in Brussels in 1927 at which the leading scientists of the world discussed recent developments.[1]

By that time Einstein's theory was firmly established and generally accepted and it was not a subject of discussion at that conference. The major topic was the new quantum theory of Heisenberg, Schrödinger and others. Of course, we all wanted to have Einstein's impressions of the new ideas.

Einstein was a little hostile to these ideas because he had obtained such a marvellous success with his own ideas of introducing geometry into physics and he thought that further development would also be on the lines of introducing more exotic kinds of geometry. He had spent many years of his life working on those lines without any very substantial success. Probably these ideas of Einstein are basically correct but they have not yet led to a satisfactory solution.

I also met Einstein at a later Solvay Conference; then he came to Cambridge, where I was working, and later went to Princeton and became a permanent member of the Institute for Advanced Study. I was also a temporary member of the Institute from time to time.

I attended lectures which Einstein gave and sometimes he invited me to his house which was a great privilege. I got to know him personally on those occasions. I was able to see how scientific ideas dominated pretty well all his thoughts; even when you were given a cup of tea and you stirred it, the motion of the tea-leaves was something which Einstein figured out how to explain.

During the course of Einstein's discussions with physicists, he made one remark which has become very famous and is now carved into the stonework over the fireplace in the common-room of the Mathematics Institute at Princeton University. To appreciate this remark you really have to be a research physicist and understand that God has set certain problems which the research physicist is trying to solve. Furthermore, you must try to appreciate the mentality of God in setting these problems. Einstein summed up his view of this situation with these words: 'Raffiniert ist Gott, aber bosartig ist Er nicht', 'God is clever, but not dishonest.'

Note

1. The first Solvay Conference (so named after the Belgian industrialist Ernest Solvay who sponsored it) was held in Brussels in 1911 to discuss the consequences of Max Planck's law of black body radiation, formulated in 1901, which laid the foundation of the quantum theory. This group of scientists, perhaps the most prestigious ever gathered together, was responsible for advances in knowledge that form the basis of modern physics.

4   Science and pseudo-science

Major advances in science have sometimes been accompanied or followed by reappraisals of the nature of science. Both Isaac Newton and Albert Einstein broke in some measure with the ways of engaging in science established in their times. Since, nonetheless, their theories were accepted as outstanding contributions, they called for new conceptions of how science proper should be distinguished from activities which might be mistaken for it. Newton himself was aware that, in introducing the idea of universal gravitational attraction, he would be exposed to criticism from those who subscribed to the then orthodox view of science. To many of Newton's critics it seemed that Newton was invoking an 'occult quality' and returning to the kind of obscurantism they thought science had left behind. Newton, in the passage below, defends his failure to provide a clear account of the cause of gravitation by insisting that it was a matter of 'hypothesis' and that the evidence provided him with no basis for any conclusions about the cause of gravitational properties. Moreover, Newton goes on, such hypotheses have no place in science proper or what he calls 'experimental philosophy'. In other contexts Newton proved himself less of an enemy to hypotheses than this passage would lead one to expect. But for some time his remark 'Hypotheses non fingo' ['I frame no hypotheses'] was a watchcry for the ideologues of the 'experimental philosophy', among them John Stuart Mill. In the second extract, Mill invokes the authority of Newton in attempting to distinguish reputable from disreputable hypotheses.

The conception of scientific inquiry espoused, amongst others, by Mill, began to look too remote from the practice of established science once Einstein's theories had received acknowledgement. Popper, in proposing a different way of distinguishing science proper from pseudo-science, appeals to the testing of Einstein's theories as an example of the critical process he takes to be definitive of genuine science. There has been much debate about the demarcation criterion proposed by Popper and of which he provides an autobiographical resumé in the third extract. The last two extracts are contributions to a debate initiated by Popper. Thomas Kuhn, whose views (see 5.2, 5.3 and 9.3) are in some respects very different from Popper's, expresses doubt as to whether falsifiability can bear the emphasis Popper puts on it. On this point Imre Lakatos agrees with Kuhn. He rejects the 'instant rationality' which Popper's account, at least on a simple interpretation, appears to require. His position is, none the less, much closer to that of Popper in so far as he believes, like Popper, that the development of science is a thoroughly rational process. The debate about the distinction between science and pseudo-science has thus become inseparable from a debate about the nature of progress in science, a small part of which is included in the next chapter.

4.1 HYPOTHESES AND 'EXPERIMENTAL PHILOSOPHY'

ISAAC NEWTON (1642–1727), *from the general scholium to his* Philosophiae Naturalis Principia Mathematica [*Mathematical Principles of Natural Philosophy*] (*1687*), *Motte, Andrew, trans., Berkeley, University of California Press, 1934*

As indicated in the introductory remarks to this chapter, this short passage has had an unusual importance conferred on it by subsequent writers on the nature of scientific inquiry. It is included here for

that reason and not because it suffices as a summary
of Newton's attitude towards 'hypotheses'.

Hitherto we have explained the phaenomena of the heavens and of our
sea by the power of gravity, but have not yet assigned the cause of this
power. This is certain, that it must proceed from a cause that penetrates
to the very centres of the sun and planets, without suffering the least
diminution of its force; that operates not according to the quantity of
the surfaces of the particles upon which it acts (as mechanical causes use
to do), but according to the quantity of the solid matter which they
contain, and propagates its virtue on all sides to immense distances,
decreasing always in the duplicate proportion of the distances.
Gravitation towards the sun is made up out of the gravitations towards
the several particles of which the body of the sun is composed; and in
receding from the sun decreases accurately in the duplicate proportion
of the distances as far as the orb of Saturn, as evidently appears from the
quiescence of the aphelions of the planets; nay, and even to the remotest
aphelions of the comets, if those aphelions are also quiescent. But
hitherto I have not been able to discover the cause of those properties of
gravity from phaenomena, and I frame no hypotheses; for whatever is
not deduced from the phaenomena is to be called an hypothesis; and
hypotheses, whether metaphysical or physical, whether of occult
qualities or mechanical, have no place in experimental philosophy.
In this philosophy particular propositions are inferred from the
phaenomena, and afterwards rendered general by induction. Thus it
was that the impenetrability, the mobility, and the impulsive force of
bodies, and the laws of motion and of gravitation, were discovered. And
to us it is enough that gravity does really exist, and act according to the
laws which we have explained, and abundantly serves to account for all
the motions of the celestial bodies, and of our sea.

4.2   HYPOTHESES AND VERIFICATION

JOHN STUART MILL (1806–1873), *from* A System of
Logic, *book 3, ch. 14, pp. 554–6, London, Longmans, Green,
1843*

Mill, in book 3 of his *System of Logic*, put forward
four methods of experimental inquiry which he
proposed both as methods of discovery and as
methods of proof. These methods are the cornerstone

of Mill's inductive logic. Mill did not, however, consider that these methods provided an exhaustive description of the processes which mattered in science. On the contrary, he thought that hypotheses could be valuable, provided they put us on the road to proving scientific laws. The word *hypothesis* had become, in the eighteenth century, a way of labelling a speculation as unscientific. Mill, though remaining faithful to the idea that the object of science was to arrive at proofs, distinguishes between legitimate and illegitimate hypotheses.

An hypothesis is any supposition which we make (either without actual evidence, or on evidence avowedly insufficient) in order to endeavour to deduce from it conclusions in accordance with facts which are known to be real; under the idea that if the conclusions to which the hypothesis leads are known truths, the hypothesis itself either must be, or at least is likely to be, true. If the hypothesis relates to the cause or mode of production of a phenomenon, it will serve, if admitted, to explain such facts as are found capable of being deduced from it. And this explanation is the purpose of many, if not most, hypotheses. Since explaining, in the scientific sense, means resolving an uniformity which is not a law of causation into the laws of causation from which it results, or a complex law of causation into simpler and more general ones from which it is capable of being deductively inferred; if there do not exist any known laws which fulfil this requirement, we may feign or imagine some which would fulfil it; and this is making an hypothesis. . . .

It appears . . . to be a condition of the most genuinely scientific hypothesis, that it be not destined always to remain an hypothesis, but be of such a nature as to be either proved or disproved by comparison with observed facts. This condition is fulfilled when the effect is already known to depend on the very cause supposed, and the hypothesis relates only to the precise mode of dependence; the law of the variation of the effect according to the variations in the quantity or in the relations of the cause. With these may be classed the hypotheses which do not make any supposition with regard to causation, but only with regard to the law of correspondence between facts which accompany each other in their variations, though there may be no relation of cause and effect between them. Such were the different false hypotheses which Kepler made respecting the law of the refraction of light. It was known that the direction of the line of refraction varied with every variation in the direction of the line of incidence, but it was not known how; that is, what changes of the one corresponded to the different changes of the other. In this case any law, different from the true one, must have led to false results. And, lastly, we must add to these all hypothetical modes of merely representing, or describing, phenomena; such as the hypothesis of the ancient astronomers that the heavenly bodies moved in circles; the various hypotheses of excentrics, deferents, and epicycles, which were added to that original hypothesis; the nineteen false hypotheses which Kepler made and abandoned respecting the form of the planetary orbits; and even the doctrine in which he finally rested, that those orbits are ellipses, which was but an hypothesis like the rest until verified by facts.

In all these cases, verification is proof; if the supposition accords with the phenomena, there need be no other evidence of it. But in order that this may be the case, I conceive it to be necessary, when the hypothesis relates to causation, that the supposed cause should not only be a real phenomenon, something actually existing in nature, but should be already known to exercise, or at least to be capable of exercising, an influence of some sort over the effect. In any other case, it is not sufficient evidence of the truth of the hypothesis that we are able to deduce the real phenomena from it.

Is it, then, never allowable, in a scientific hypothesis, to assume a cause; but only to ascribe an assumed law to a known cause? I do not assert this. I only say, that in the latter case alone can the hypothesis be received as true merely because it explains the phenomena. In the former case it may be very useful by suggesting a line of investigation which may possibly terminate in obtaining real proof. But, for this purpose, as is justly remarked by M. Comte, it is indispensable that the cause suggested by the hypothesis should be in its own nature susceptible of being proved by other evidence. This seems to be the philosophical import of Newton's maxim (so often cited with approbation by subsequent writers), that the cause assigned for any phenomenon must not only be such as, if admitted, would explain the phenomenon, but must also be a *vera causa*. What he meant by a *vera causa* Newton did not indeed very explicitly define. . . . It is certainly not necessary that the cause assigned should be a cause already known; otherwise we should sacrifice our best opportunities of becoming acquainted with new causes. But what is true in the maxim is, that the cause, though not known previously, should be capable of being known thereafter; that its existence should be capable of being detected, and its connection with the effect ascribed to it should be susceptible of being proved, by independent evidence. The hypothesis, by suggesting observations and experiments, puts us on the road to that independent evidence if it be really attainable; and till it be attained, the hypothesis ought only to count for a more or less plausible conjecture.

This function, however, of hypotheses, is one which must be reckoned absolutely indispensable in science. When Newton said, 'Hypotheses non fingo,' he did not mean that he deprived himself of the facilities of investigation afforded by assuming in the first instance what he hoped ultimately to be able to prove. Without such assumptions, science could never have attained its present state: they are necessary steps in the progress to something more certain; and nearly everything which is now theory was once hypothesis. . . .

It is perfectly consistent with the spirit of the method, to assume in this provisional manner not only an hypothesis respecting the law of what we already know to be the cause, but an hypothesis respecting the cause itself. It is allowable, useful, and often even necessary, to begin by asking ourselves what cause *may* have produced the effect, in order that we may know in what direction to look out for evidence to determine whether it actually *did*. The vortices of Descartes would have been a perfectly legitimate hypothesis, if it had been possible, by any mode of exploration which we could entertain the hope of ever possessing, to bring the reality of the vortices, as a fact in nature, conclusively to the test of observation. The vice of the hypothesis was that it could not lead to any course of investigation capable of converting it from an hypothesis into a proved fact. It might chance to be *dis*proved, either by some want of correspondence with the phenomena it purported to explain, or (as actually happened) by some extraneous fact. 'The free passage of comets through the spaces in which these vortices should have been, convinced men that these vortices did not exist.' But the hypothesis would have been false, though no such direct evidence of its falsity had been procurable. Direct evidence of its truth there could not be. . . .

Mr Darwin's remarkable speculation on the Origin of Species[1] is an unimpeachable example of a legitimate hypothesis. What he terms 'natural selection' is not only a *vera causa*, but one proved to be capable of producing effects of the same kind with those which the hypothesis ascribes to it: the question of possibility is entirely one of degree. It is unreasonable to accuse Mr Darwin (as has been done) of violating the rules of Induction. The rules of Induction are concerned with the conditions of Proof. Mr Darwin has never pretended that his doctrine was proved. He was not bound by the rules of Induction, but by those of Hypothesis. And these last have seldom been more completely fulfilled. He has opened a path of inquiry full of promise, the results of which none can foresee. And is it not a wonderful feat of scientific knowledge and ingenuity to have rendered so bold a suggestion, which the first impulse of every one was to reject at once, admissible and discussable, even as a conjecture?

Note

1. This note was added to the 1862 and subsequent editions. Mill possessed a copy of the 1861 edition of *The Origin of Species*.

4.3 CONJECTURES AND REFUTATIONS

KARL R. POPPER (1902–   ), *from a lecture given in 1953 and originally published under the title 'Philosophy of science: a personal report' in* British Philosophy in the Mid-Century, *Mace, C. A., ed., London, George Allen & Unwin, 1957; reprinted as ch. 1 of* Conjectures and Refutations, *London, Routledge & Kegan Paul, 1963, 1978, pp. 33ff.*

Karl Popper is one of the most distinguished contemporary philosophers of science. In *The Logic of Scientific Discovery*[1] he rejects the requirement that a scientific theory must be capable of verification and proposed instead that 'it must be possible for an empirical scientific system to be refuted by experience'. In the following extract he explains how he came to formulate his criterion of demarcation and why he preferred it to the criterion adopted by other philosophers such as Mill.

Note

1. Popper, Karl R. (1935) *The Logic of Scientific Discovery*, London, Hutchinson, 1959 (rev. English ed. 1968).

When I received the list of participants in this course and realized that I had been asked to speak to philosophical colleagues I thought, after some hesitation and consultation, that you would probably prefer me to speak about those problems which interest me most, and about those developments with which I am most intimately acquainted. I therefore decided to do what I have never done before: to give you a report on my own work in the philosophy of science, since the autumn of 1919 when I first began to grapple with the problem, *'When should a theory be ranked as scientific?'* or *'Is there a criterion for the scientific character or status of a theory?'*

The problem which troubled me at the time was neither, 'When is a theory true?' nor, 'When is a theory acceptable?' My problem was different. *I wished to distinguish between* science and pseudo-science; knowing very well that science often errs, and that pseudo-science may happen to stumble on the truth.

I knew, of course, the most widely accepted answer to my problem: that science is distinguished from pseudo-science — or from 'metaphysics' — by its *empirical method*, which is essentially *inductive*, proceeding from observation or experiment. But this did not satisfy me. On the contrary, I often formulated my problem as one of distinguishing between a genuinely empirical method and a non-empirical or even a pseudo-empirical method — that is to say, a method which, although it appeals to observation and experiment, nevertheless does not come up to scientific standards. The latter method may be exemplified by astrology, with its stupendous mass of empirical evidence based on observation — on horoscopes and on biographies.

But as it was not the example of astrology which led me to my problem I should perhaps briefly describe the atmosphere in which my problem arose and the examples by which it was stimulated. After the collapse of the Austrian Empire there had been a revolution in Austria: the air was full of revolutionary slogans and ideas, and new and often wild theories. Among the theories which interested me Einstein's theory of relativity was no doubt by far the most important. Three others were Marx's theory of history, Freud's psycho-analysis, and Alfred Adler's so-called 'individual psychology'.

There was a lot of popular nonsense talked about these theories, and especially about relativity (as still happens even today), but I was fortunate in those who introduced me to the study of this theory. We all — the small circle of students to which I belonged — were thrilled with the result of Eddington's eclipse observations which in 1919 brought the first important confirmation of Einstein's theory of gravitation. It was a great experience for us, and one which had a lasting influence on my intellectual development.

The three other theories I have mentioned were also widely discussed among students at that time. I myself happened to come into personal contact with Alfred Adler, and even to cooperate with him in his social work among the children and young people in the working-class districts of Vienna where he had established social guidance clinics.

It was during the summer of 1919 that I began to feel more and more dissatisfied with these three theories — the Marxist theory of history, psycho-analysis, and individual psychology; and I began to feel dubious about their claims to scientific status. My problem perhaps first took the simple form, 'What is wrong with Marxism, psycho-analysis, and individual psychology? Why are they so different from physical theories, from Newton's theory, and especially from the theory of relativity?'

To make this contrast clear I should explain that few of us at the time would have said that we believed in the *truth* of Einstein's theory of gravitation. This shows that it was not my doubting the *truth* of those other three theories which bothered me, but something else. Yet neither was it that I merely felt mathematical physics to be more *exact* than the sociological or psychological type of theory. Thus what worried me was neither the problem of truth, at that stage at least, nor the problem of exactness or measurability. It was rather that I felt that these other three theories, though posing as sciences, had in fact more in common with primitive myths than with science; that they resembled astrology rather than astronomy.

I found that those of my friends who were admirers of Marx, Freud, and Adler, were impressed by a number of points common to these theories, and especially by their apparent *explanatory power*. These theories appeared to be able to explain practically everything that happened within the fields to which they referred. The study of any of them seemed to have the effect of an intellectual conversion or revelation, opening your eyes to a new truth hidden from those not yet initiated. Once your eyes were thus opened you saw confirming instances everywhere: the world was full of *verifications* of the theory. Whatever happened always confirmed it. Thus its truth appeared manifest; and unbelievers were clearly people who did not want to see the manifest truth; who refused to see it, either because it was against their class interest, or because of their repressions which were still 'un-analysed' and crying aloud for treatment.

The most characteristic element in this situation seemed to me the incessant stream of confirmations, of observations which 'verified' the theories in question; and this point was constantly emphasized by their adherents. A Marxist could not open a newspaper without finding on every page confirming evidence for his interpretation of history; not only in the news, but also in its presentation — which revealed the class bias of the paper — and especially of course in what the paper did *not* say. The Freudian analysts emphasized that their theories were con-stantly verified by their 'clinical observations'. As for Adler, I was much impressed by a personal experience. Once, in 1919, I reported to him a case which to me did not seem particularly Adlerian, but which he found no difficulty in analysing in terms of his theory of inferiority feelings, although he had not even seen the child. Slightly shocked, I asked him how he could be so sure. 'Because of my thousandfold experience,' he replied; whereupon I could not help saying: 'And with this new case, I suppose, your experience has become thousand-and-one-fold.'

What I had in mind was that his previous observations may not have been much sounder than this new one; that each in its turn had been interpreted in the light of 'previous experience', and at the same time counted as additional confirmation. What, I asked myself, did it confirm? No more than that a case could be interpreted in the light of the theory. But this meant very little, I reflected, since every conceivable case could be interpreted in the light of Adler's theory, or equally of Freud's. I may illustrate this by two very different examples of human behaviour: that of a man who pushes a child into the water with the intention of drowning it; and that of a man who sacrifices his life in an attempt to save the child. Each of these two cases can be explained with equal ease in Freudian and in Adlerian terms. According to Freud the first man suffered from repression (say, of some component of his Oedipus complex), while the second man had achieved sublimation. According to Adler the first man suffered from feelings of inferiority (producing perhaps the need to prove to himself that he dared to commit some crime), and so did the second man (whose need was to prove to himself that he dared to rescue the child). I could not think of any human behaviour which could not be interpreted in terms of either theory. It was precisely this fact − that they always fitted, that they were always confirmed − which in the eyes of their admirers constituted the strongest argument in favour of these theories. It began to dawn on me that this apparent strength was in fact their weakness.

With Einstein's theory the situation was strikingly different. Take one typical instance − Einstein's prediction, just then confirmed by the findings of Eddington's expedition. Einstein's gravitational theory had led to the result that light must be attracted by heavy bodies (such as the sun), precisely as material bodies were attracted. As a consequence it could be calculated that light from a distant fixed star whose apparent position was close to the sun would reach the earth from such a direction that the star would seem to be slightly shifted away from the sun; or, in other words, that stars close to the sun would look as if they had moved a little away from the sun, and from one another. This is a thing which cannot normally be observed since such stars are rendered invisible in daytime by the sun's overwhelming brightness; but during an eclipse it is possible to take photographs of them. If the same constellation is photographed at night one can measure the distances on the two photographs, and check the predicted effect.

Now the impressive thing about this case is the *risk* involved in a prediction of this kind. If observation shows that the predicted effect is definitely absent, then the theory is simply refuted. The theory is *incompatible with certain possible results of observation* − in fact with results which everybody before Einstein would have expected.[1] This is quite different from the situation I have previously described, when it turned out that the theories in question were compatible with the most divergent human behaviour, so that it was practically impossible to describe any human behaviour that might not be claimed to be a verification of these theories.

These considerations led me in the winter of 1919−20 to conclusions which I may now reformulate as follows.

(1) It is easy to obtain confirmations, or verifications, for nearly every theory − if we look for confirmations.

(2) Confirmations should count only if they are the result of *risky predictions*; that is to say, if, unenlightened by the theory in question, we should have expected an event which was incompatible with the theory − an event which would have refuted the theory.

(3) Every 'good' scientific theory is a prohibition: it forbids certain things to happen. The more a theory forbids, the better it is.

(4) A theory which is not refutable by any conceivable event is non-scientific. Irrefutability is not a virtue of a theory (as people often think) but a vice.

(5) Every genuine *test* of a theory is an attempt to falsify it, or to refute it. Testability is falsifiability; but there are degrees of testability: some theories are more testable, more exposed to refutation, than others; they take, as it were, greater risks.

(6) Confirming evidence should not count *except when it is the result of a genuine test of the theory*; and this means that it can be presented as a serious but unsuccessful attempt to falsify the theory. (I now speak in such cases of 'corroborating evidence'.)

(7) Some genuinely testable theories, when found to be false, are still upheld by their admirers − for example by introducing *ad hoc* some auxiliary assumption, or by re-interpreting the theory *ad hoc* in such a way that it escapes refutation. Such a procedure is always possible, but it rescues the theory from refutation only at the price of destroying, or at least lowering, its scientific status. (I later

described such a rescuing operation as a *'conventionalist twist'* or a *'conventionalist stratagem'*.)

One can sum up all this by saying that *the criterion of the scientific status of a theory is its falsifiability, or refutability, or testability.*

I may perhaps exemplify this with the help of the various theories so far mentioned. Einstein's theory of gravitation clearly satisfied the criterion of falsifiability. Even if our measuring instruments at the time did not allow us to pronounce on the results of the tests with complete assurance, there was clearly a possibility of refuting the theory.

Astrology did not pass the test. Astrologers were greatly impressed, and misled, by what they believed to be confirming evidence – so much so that they were quite unimpressed by any unfavourable evidence. Moreover, by making their interpretations and prophecies sufficiently vague they were able to explain away anything that might have been a refutation of the theory had the theory and the prophecies been more precise. In order to escape falsification they destroyed the testability of their theory. It is a typical soothsayer's trick to predict things so vaguely that the predictions can hardly fail: that they become irrefutable.

The Marxist theory of history, in spite of the serious efforts of some of its founders and followers, ultimately adopted this soothsaying practice. In some of its earlier formulations (for example in Marx's analysis of the character of the 'coming social revolution') their predictions were testable, and in fact falsified.[2] Yet instead of accepting the refutations the followers of Marx re-interpreted both the theory and the evidence in order to make them agree. In this way they rescued the theory from refutation; but they did so at the price of adopting a device which made it irrefutable. They thus gave a 'conventionalist twist' to the theory; and by this stratagem they destroyed its much advertised claim to scientific status.

The two psycho-analytic theories were in a different class. They were simply non-testable, irrefutable. There was no conceivable human behaviour which could contradict them. This does not mean that Freud and Adler were not seeing certain things correctly: I personally do not doubt that much of what they say is of considerable importance, and may well play its part one day in a psychological science which is testable. But it does mean that those 'clinical observations' which analysts naïvely believe confirm their theory cannot do this any more than the daily confirmations which astrologers find in their practice. And as for Freud's epic of the Ego, the Super-ego, and the Id, no substantially stronger claim to scientific status can be made for it than for Homer's collected stories from Olympus. These theories describe some facts, but in the manner of myths. They contain most interesting psychological suggestions, but not in a testable form.

At the same time I realized that such myths may be developed, and become testable; that historically speaking all — or very nearly all — scientific theories originate from myths, and that a myth may contain important anticipations of scientific theories. Examples are Empedocles' theory of evolution by trial and error, or Parmenides' myth of the unchanging block universe in which nothing ever happens and which, if we add another dimension, becomes Einstein's block universe (in which, too, nothing ever happens, since everything is, four-dimensionally speaking, determined and laid down from the beginning). I thus felt that if a theory is found to be non-scientific, or 'metaphysical' (as we might say), it is not thereby found to be unimportant, or insignificant, or 'meaningless', or 'nonsensical'.[3] But it cannot claim to be backed by empirical evidence in the scientific sense — although it may easily be, in some genetic sense, the 'result of observation'.

(There were a great many other theories of this pre-scientific or pseudo-scientific character, some of them, unfortunately, as influential as the Marxist interpretation of history; for example, the racialist interpretation of history — another of those impressive and all-explanatory theories which act upon weak minds like revelations.)

Thus the problem which I tried to solve by proposing the criterion of falsifiability was neither a problem of meaningfulness or significance, nor a problem of truth or acceptability. It was the problem of drawing a line (as well as this can be done) between the statements, or systems of statements, of the empirical sciences, and all other statements — whether they are of a religious or of a metaphysical character, or simply pseudo-scientific. Years later — it must have been in 1928 — I called this first problem of mine the '*problem of demarcation*'. The criterion of falsifiability is a solution to this problem of demarcation, for it says that statements or systems of statements, in order to be ranked as scientific, must be capable of conflicting with possible, or conceivable, observations.

Notes

1. This is a slight oversimplification, for about half of the Einstein effect may be derived from the classical theory, provided we assume a ballistic theory of light.
2. See, for example, Popper, Karl R. (1945) *The Open Society and Its Enemies*, 2 vols, London, Routledge & Kegan Paul, ch. 15, section 3 and notes 13–14.
3. The case of astrology, nowadays a typical pseudo-science, may illustrate this point. It was attacked by Aristotelians and other rationalists, down to Newton's day, for the

wrong reason − for its now accepted assertion that the planets had an 'influence' upon terrestrial ('sublunar') events. In fact Newton's theory of gravity, and especially the lunar theory of the tides, was historically speaking an offspring of astrological lore. . . .

4.4   THE SCIENCES AS PUZZLE-SOLVING TRADITIONS

THOMAS S. KUHN (1922–   ), *from* The Philosophy of Karl Popper, *2 vols, Schilpp, P. A., ed., La Salle, Ill., Open Court, 1974*

Kuhn maintains, in this extract, that Popper mistakes certain extraordinary episodes in science for events characteristic of scientific activity. He claims that the distinguishing mark of science is to be found in its 'normal' and 'puzzle-solving' phases rather than by examination of revolutionary phases. (For some explanation of Kuhn's terminology see reading 5.2.) Pseudo-sciences, such as astrology, do not generate puzzle-solving traditions.

Among the most fundamental issues on which Sir Karl and I agree is our insistence that an analysis of the development of scientific knowledge must take account of the way science has actually been practiced. That being so, a few of his recurrent generalizations startle me. One of these provides the opening sentences of the first chapter of the *Logic of Scientific Discovery*: 'A scientist,' writes Sir Karl, 'whether theorist or experimenter, puts forward statements, or systems of statements, and tests them step by step. In the field of the empirical sciences, more particularly, he constructs hypotheses, or systems of theories, and tests them against experience by observation and experiment.'[1] The statement is virtually a cliché, yet in application it presents three problems. It is ambiguous in its failure to specify which of two sorts of 'statements' or 'theories' are being tested. That ambiguity can, it is true, be eliminated by reference to other passages in Sir Karl's writings, but the generalization that results is historically mistaken. Furthermore, the mistake proves important, for the unambiguous form of the description misses just that characteristic of scientific practice which most nearly distinguishes the sciences from other creative pursuits.

There is one sort of 'statement' or 'hypothesis' that scientists do repeatedly subject to systematic test. I have in mind statements of an individual's best guesses about the proper way to connect his own research problem with the corpus of accepted scientific knowledge. He may, for example, conjecture that a given chemical unknown contains the salt of a rare earth, that the obesity of his experimental rats is due to a specified component in their diet, or that a newly discovered spectral pattern is to be understood as an effect of nuclear spin. In each case, the next steps in his research are intended to try out or test the conjecture or hypothesis. If it passes enough or stringent enough tests, the scientist has made a discovery or has at least resolved the puzzle he had been set. If not, he must either abandon the puzzle entirely or attempt to solve it with the aid of some other hypothesis. Many research problems, though by no means all, take this form. Tests of this sort are a standard component of what I have elsewhere labelled 'normal science' or 'normal research', an enterprise which accounts for the overwhelming majority of the work done in basic science. In no usual sense, however, are such tests directed to current theory. On the contrary, when engaged with a normal research problem, the scientist must *premise* current theory as the rules of his game. His object is to solve a puzzle, preferably one at which others have failed, and current theory is required to define that puzzle and to guarantee that, given sufficient brilliance, it can be solved.[2] Of course the practitioner of such an enterprise must often test the conjectural puzzle solution that his ingenuity suggests. But only his personal conjecture is tested. If it fails the test, only his own ability not the corpus of current science is impugned. In short, though tests occur frequently in normal science, these tests are of a peculiar sort, for in the final analysis it is the individual scientist rather than current theory which is tested.

This is not, however, the sort of test Sir Karl has in mind. He is above all concerned with the procedures through which science grows, and he is convinced that 'growth' occurs not primarily by accretion but by the revolutionary overthrow of an accepted theory and its replacement by a better one. (The subsumption under 'growth' of 'repeated overthrow' is itself a linguistic oddity whose *raison d'être* may become more visible as we proceed.) Taking this view, the tests which Sir Karl emphasizes are those which were performed to explore the limitations of accepted theory or to subject a current theory to maximum strain. Among his favourite examples, all of them startling and destructive in their outcome, are Lavoisier's experiments on calcination, the eclipse expedition of 1919, and the recent experiments on parity conservation. All, of course, are classic tests, but in using them to characterize scientific activity Sir Karl misses something terribly important about them. Episodes like these are very rare in the development of science. When they occur, they are generally called forth either by a prior crisis in the relevant field (Lavoisier's experiments or Lee and Yang's[3]) or by the existence of a theory which competes with the existing canons of research (Einstein's general relativity). These are, however, aspects of or occasions for what I have elsewhere called 'extraordinary research', an enterprise in which scientists do display very many of the characteristics Sir Karl emphasizes, but one which, at least in the past, has arisen only intermittently and under quite special circumstances in any scientific speciality.[4]

I suggest then that Sir Karl has characterized the entire scientific enterprise in terms that apply only to its occasional revolutionary parts. His emphasis is natural and common: the exploits of a Copernicus or Einstein make better reading than those of a Brahe or Lorentz; Sir Karl would not be the first if he mistook what I call normal science for an intrinsically uninteresting enterprise. Nevertheless, neither science nor the development of knowledge is likely to be understood if research is viewed exclusively through the revolutions it occasionally produces. For example, though testing of basic commitments occurs only in extra-ordinary science, it is normal science that discloses both the points to test and the manner of testing. Or again, it is for the normal, not the extraordinary practice of science that professionals are trained; if they are nevertheless eminently successful in displacing and replacing the theories on which normal practice depends, that is an oddity which must be explained. Finally, and this is for now my main point, a careful look at the scientific enterprise suggests that it is normal science, in which Sir Karl's sort of testing does not occur, rather than extraordinary science which most nearly distinguishes science from other enterprises. If a demarcation criterion exists (we must not, I think, seek a sharp or decisive one), it may lie just in that part of science which Sir Karl ignores.

In one of his most evocative essays, Sir Karl traces the origin of 'the tradition of critical discussion [which] represents the only practicable way of expanding our knowledge' to the Greek philosophers between Thales and Plato, the men who, as he sees it, encouraged critical discussion both between schools and within individual schools. The accompanying description of Presocratic discourse is most apt, but what is described does not at all resemble science. Rather it is the tradition of claims, counter-claims, and debates over fundamentals which, except perhaps during the Middle Ages, have characterized philosophy and much of social science ever since. Already by the Hellenistic period mathematics, astronomy, statics and the geometric parts of optics had abandoned this mode of discourse in favour of puzzle solving. Other sciences, in increasing numbers, have undergone the same transition since. In a sense, to turn Sir Karl's view on its head, it is precisely the abandonment of critical discourse that marks the transition to a science. Once a field has made that transition, critical discourse recurs only at moments of crisis when the bases of the field are again in jeopardy. Only when they must choose between competing theories do scientists behave like philosophers. That, I think, is why Sir Karl's brilliant description of the reasons for the choice between metaphysical systems so closely resembles my description of the reasons for choosing between scientific theories. In neither choice, as I shall shortly try to show, can testing play a quite decisive role.

There is, however, good reason why testing has seemed to do so, and in exploring it Sir Karl's duck may at last become my rabbit. No puzzle-solving enterprise can exist unless its practitioners share criteria which, for that group and for that time, determine when a particular puzzle has been solved. The same criteria necessarily determine failure to achieve a solution, and anyone who chooses may view that failure as the failure of a theory to pass a test. Normally, as I have already insisted, it is not viewed that way. Only the practitioner is blamed, not his tools. But under the special circumstances which induce a crisis in the profession (e.g. gross failure, or repeated failure by the most brilliant professionals) the group's opinion may change. A failure that had previously been personal may then come to seem the failure of a theory under test. Thereafter, because the test arose from a puzzle and thus carried settled criteria of solution, it proves both more severe and harder to evade than the tests available within a tradition whose normal mode is critical discourse rather than puzzle solving.

In a sense, therefore, severity of test-criteria is simply one side of the coin whose other face is a puzzle-solving tradition. That is why Sir Karl's line of demarcation and my own so frequently coincide. That coincidence is, however, only in their *outcome*; the *process* of applying them is very different, and it isolates distinct aspects of the activity about which the decision − science or non-science − is to be made. Examining the vexing cases, for example, psychoanalysis or Marxist historiography, for which Sir Karl tells us his criterion was initially designed, I concur that they cannot now properly be labelled 'science'. But I reach that conclusion by a route far surer and more direct than his. One brief example may suggest that of the two criteria, testing and puzzle solving, the latter is at once the less equivocal and the more fundamental.

To avoid irrelevant contemporary controversies, I consider astrology rather than, say, psychoanalysis. Astrology is Sir Karl's most frequently cited example of a 'pseudo-science'. He says:

> By making their interpretations and prophecies sufficiently vague they [astrologers] were able to explain away anything that might have been a refutation of the theory had the theory and the prophecies been more precise. In order to escape falsification they destroyed the testability of their theory.[5]

Those generalizations catch something of the spirit of the astrological enterprise. But taken at all literally, as they must be if they are to provide a demarcation criterion, they are impossible to support. The history of astrology during the centuries when it was intellectually reputable records many predictions that categorically failed. Not even astrology's most convinced and vehement exponents doubted the recurrence of such failures. Astrology cannot be barred from the sciences because of the form in which its predictions were cast.

Nor can it be barred because of the way its practitioners explained failure. Astrologers pointed out, for example, that, unlike general predictions about, say, an individual's propensities or a natural calamity, the forecast of an individual's future was an immensely complex task, demanding the utmost skill, and extremely sensitive to minor errors in relevant data. The configuration of the stars and eight planets was constantly changing; the astronomical tables used to compute the configuration at an individual's birth were notoriously imperfect; few men knew the instant of their birth with the requisite precision. No wonder, then, that forecasts often failed. Only after astrology itself became implausible did these arguments come to seem question-begging. Similar arguments are regularly used today when explaining, for example, failures in medicine or meteorology. In times of trouble they are also deployed in the exact sciences, fields like physics, chemistry and astronomy. There was nothing unscientific about the astrologer's explanation of failure.

Nevertheless, astrology was not a science. Instead it was a craft, one of the practical arts, with close resemblances to engineering, meterology and medicine as these fields were practised until little more than a century ago. The parallels to an older medicine and to contemporary psychoanalysis are, I think, particularly close. In each of these fields shared theory was adequate only to establish the plausibility of the discipline and to provide a rationale for the various craft-rules which governed practice. These rules had proved their use in the past, but no practitioner supposed they were sufficient to prevent recurrent failure. A more articulated theory and more powerful rules were desired, but it would have been absurd to abandon a plausible and badly needed discipline with a tradition of limited success simply because these desiderata were not yet at hand. In their absence, however, neither the astrologer nor the doctor could do research. Though they had rules to apply, they had no puzzles to solve and therefore no science to practice.

Compare the situations of the astronomer and the astrologer. If an astronomer's prediction failed and his calculations checked, he could hope to set the situation right. Perhaps the data were at fault: old observations could be re-examined and new measurements made, tasks which posed a host of calculational and instrumental puzzles. Or perhaps theory needed adjustment, either by the manipulation of epicycles, eccentrics, equants, etc, or by more fundamental reforms of astronomical technique. For more than a millennium these were the theoretical and mathematical puzzles around which, together with their instrumental counterparts, the astronomical research tradition was constituted. The astrologer, by contrast, had no such puzzles. The occurrence of failures could be explained, but particular failures did not give rise to research puzzles, for no man, however skilled, could make use of them in a constructive attempt to revise the astrological tradition. There were too many possible sources of difficulty, most of them beyond the astrologer's knowledge, control or responsibility. Individual failures were correspondingly uninformative, and they did not reflect on the competence of the prognosticator in the eyes of his professional compeers.[6] Though astronomy and astrology were regularly practiced by the same people, including Ptolemy, Kepler, and Tycho Brahe, there was never an astrological equivalent of the puzzle-solving astronomical tradition. And without puzzles, able first to challenge and then to attest the ingenuity of the individual practitioner, astrology could not have become a science even if the stars had, in fact, controlled human destiny.

In short, though astrologers made testable predictions and recognized that these predictions sometimes failed, they did not and could not engage in the sorts of activities that normally characterize all recognized sciences. Sir Karl is right to exclude astrology from the sciences, but his over-concentration on science's occasional revolutions prevents his seeing the surest reason for doing so.

That fact, in turn, may explain another oddity of Sir Karl's historiography. Though he repeatedly underlines the role of tests in the replacement of scientific theories, he is also constrained to recognize that many theories, for example the Ptolemaic, were replaced before they had in fact been tested.[7] On some occasions, at least, tests are not requisite to the revolutions through which science advances. But that is not true of puzzles. Though the theories Sir Karl cites had not been put to the test before their displacement, none of these was replaced before it had ceased adequately to support a puzzle-solving tradition. The state of astronomy was a scandal in the early sixteenth century. Most astronomers nevertheless felt that normal adjustments of a basically Ptolemaic model would set the situation right. In this sense the theory had not failed a test. But a few astronomers, Copernicus among them, felt that the difficulties must lie in the Ptolemaic approach itself rather than in the particular versions of Ptolemaic theory so far developed, and the results of that conviction are already recorded. The situation is typical.[8] With or without tests, a puzzle-solving tradition can prepare the way for its own displacement. To rely on testing as the mark of a science is to miss what scientists mostly do and, with it, the most characteristic feature of their enterprise.

Notes

1. Op. cit., 1968 ed., p. 27. See reading 3.2.
2. For an extended discussion of normal science, the activity which practitioners are trained to carry on, see Kuhn, Thomas S. (1962) *The Structure of Scientific Revolutions*, Chicago, University of Chicago Press, pp. 23–42, 135–42. It is important to notice that when I describe the scientist as a puzzle solver and Sir Karl describes him as a problem solver (e.g. in *Conjectures and Refutations*, London, Routledge & Kegan Paul, 1963, pp. 67, 222), the similarity of our terms disguises a fundamental divergence. Sir Karl writes (the italics are his), 'Admittedly, our expectations, and thus our theories, may precede, historically, even our problems. *Yet science starts only with problems.* Problems crop up especially when we are disappointed in our expectations, or when our theories involve us in difficulties, in contradictions.' I use the term 'puzzle' in order to emphasize that the difficulties which *ordinarily* confront even the very best scientists are, like crossword puzzles or chess puzzles, challenges only to his ingenuity. *He* is in difficulty, not current theory. My point is almost the converse of Sir Karl's.
3. For the work on calcination see Guerlac, Henry (1961) *Lavoisier – The Crucial Year*, Ithaca, N.Y., Cornell University Press. For the background of the parity experiments see Hafner, and Presswood (1965) 'Strong interference and weak interactions', *Science*, 149, 503–10.
4. See Kuhn, op. cit., 2nd ed. (1970), pp. 52–97.
5. *Conjectures and Refutations*, p. 37. See reading 4.3.
6. This is not to suggest that astrologers did not criticize each other. On the contrary, like practitioners of philosophy and some social sciences, they belonged to a variety of different schools, and the inter-school strife was sometimes bitter. But these debates ordinarily revolved about the *implausibility* of the particular theory employed by one or another school. Failures of individual predictions played very little role. Compare Thorndike, Lynn (1923–58) *A History of Magic and Experimental Science*, vol. 5, New York, Columbia University Press, p. 233.
7. *Conjectures and Refutations*, p. 246.
8. See Kuhn, op. cit., 1st ed., pp. 77–87.

4.5 SCIENCE AND PSEUDO-SCIENCE

IMRE LAKATOS (19 –   ), *from* Philosophy in the
Open, *Vesey, Godfrey, ed., Milton Keynes, Open University
Press, 1974, pp. 96–102*

In an important paper,[1] Lakatos put forward his
view that the key to the demarcation between science
and pseudo-science lies in the distinction between
progressive research programmes and degenerating
ones. As against Popper he allows that any scientific
research programme has a 'hard core' which is
belted against falsification by auxiliary hypotheses.
According to Lakatos it is this protective belt which is
adjusted in the light of unfavourable results. These
adjustments will lead, in the case of a progressive
programme, to an increase in the content of the
theory whereas, in the case of a degenerating programme, the theory becomes increasingly trivial and
empty. Lakatos insists, contrary to Kuhn, that the
changeover from one programme to another is a
wholly rational process even though it lacks the
'instant rationality' of a Popperian refutation. The
following extract is a radio talk given by Lakatos for
an Open University course. It is an informal account
of his position and includes some exaggeration
natural to the spoken word.

Note

1. Lakatos, Imre (1970) 'Falsification and the methodology of
   scientific research programmes', in Lakatos, I. and Musgrave, A. E., eds, *Criticism and the Growth of Knowledge*,
   Cambridge, Cambridge University Press.

Man's respect for knowledge is one of his most peculiar characteristics.
Knowledge in Latin is *scientia*, and science came to be the name of the
most respectable kind of knowledge. But what distinguishes knowledge
from superstition, ideology or pseudoscience? The Catholic Church
excommunicated Copernicans, the Communist Party persecuted
Mendelians on the ground that their doctrines were pseudoscientific.
The demarcation between science and pseudoscience is not merely a

problem of armchair philosophy: it is of vital social and political relevance.

Many philosophers have tried to solve the problem of demarcation in the following terms: a statement constitutes knowledge if sufficiently many people believe it sufficiently strongly. But the history of thought shows us that many people were totally committed to absurd beliefs. If the strength of beliefs were a hallmark of knowledge, we should have to rank some tales about demons, angels, devils, and of heaven and hell as knowledge. Scientists, on the other hand, are very sceptical even of their best theories. Newton's is the most powerful theory science has yet produced, but Newton himself never believed that bodies attract each other at a distance. So no degree of commitment to beliefs makes them knowledge. Indeed, the hallmark of scientific behaviour is a certain scepticism even towards one's most cherished theories. Blind commitment to a theory is not an intellectual virtue: it is an intellectual crime.

Thus a statement may be pseudoscientific even if it is eminently 'plausible' and everybody believes in it, and it may be scientifically valuable even if it is unbelievable and nobody believes in it. A theory may even be of supreme scientific value even if no one understands it, let alone believes it.

The cognitive value of a theory has nothing to do with its psychological influence on people's minds. Belief, commitment, understanding are states of the human mind. But the objective, scientific value of a theory is independent of the human mind which creates it or understands it. Its scientific value depends only on what objective support these conjectures have in facts. As Hume said:

> If we take in our hand any volume; of divinity, or school metaphysics, for instance; let us ask, does it contain any abstract reasoning concerning quantity or number? No. Does it contain any experimental reasoning concerning matter of fact and existence? No. Commit it then to the flames. For it can contain nothing but sophistry and illusion.

But what is 'experimental' reasoning? If we look at the vast seventeenth-century literature on witchcraft, it is full of reports of careful observations and sworn evidence — even of experiments. Glanvill, the house philosopher of the early Royal Society, regarded witchcraft as the paradigm of experimental reasoning. We have to define experimental reasoning before we start Humean book burning.

In scientific reasoning, theories are confronted with facts; and one of the central conditions of scientific reasoning is that theories must be supported by facts. Now how exactly can facts support theory?

Several different answers have been proposed. Newton himself thought that he proved his laws from facts. He was proud of not uttering mere hypotheses: he only published theories proven from facts. In particular, he claimed that he deduced his laws from the 'phenomena' provided by Kepler. But his boast was nonsense, since according to Kepler, planets move in ellipses, but according to Newton's theory, planets would move in ellipses only if the planets did not disturb each other in their motion. But they do. This is why Newton had to devise a perturbation theory from which it follows that no planet moves in an ellipse.

One can today easily demonstrate that there can be no valid derivation of a law of nature from any finite number of facts; but we still keep reading about scientific theories being proved from facts. Why this stubborn resistance to elementary logic?

There is a very plausible explanation. Scientists want to make their theories respectable, deserving of the title 'science', that is, genuine knowledge. Now the most relevant knowledge in the seventeenth century, when science was born, concerned God, the Devil, Heaven and Hell. If one got one's conjectures about matters of divinity wrong, the consequence of one's mistake was eternal damnation. Theological knowledge cannot be fallible: it must be beyond doubt. Now the Enlightenment thought that we were fallible and ignorant about matters theological. There is no scientific theology and, therefore, no theological knowledge. Knowledge can only be about Nature, but this new type of knowledge had to be judged by the standards they took over straight from theology: it had to be proven beyond doubt. Science had to achieve the very certainty which had escaped theology. A scientist, worthy of the name, was not allowed to guess: he had to prove each sentence he uttered from facts. This was the criterion of scientific honesty. Theories unproven from facts were regarded as sinful pseudoscience, heresy in the scientific community.

It was only the downfall of Newtonian theory in this century which made scientists realize that their standards of honesty had been utopian. Before Einstein most scientists thought that Newton had deciphered God's ultimate laws by proving them from the facts. Ampère, in the early nineteenth century, felt he had to call his book on his speculations concerning electromagnetism: *Mathematical Theory of Electrodynamic Phenomena Unequivocally Deduced from Experiment*. But at the end of the volume he casually confesses that some of the experiments were never performed and even that the necessary instruments had not been constructed!

If all scientific theories are equally unprovable, what distinguishes scientific knowledge from ignorance, science from pseudoscience?

One answer to this question was provided in the twentieth century by 'inductive logicians'. Inductive logic set out to define the probabilities of different theories according to the available total evidence. If the mathematical probability of a theory is high, it qualifies as scientific; if it is low or even zero, it is not scientific. Thus the hallmark of scientific honesty would be never to say anything that is not at least highly probable. Probabilism has an attractive feature: instead of simply providing a black-and-white distinction between science and pseudo-science, it provides a continuous scale from poor theories with low probability to good theories with high probability. But, in 1934, Karl Popper, one of the most influential philosophers of our time, argued that the mathematical probability of all theories, scientific or pseudo-scientific, given *any* amount of evidence is zero. If Popper is right, scientific theories are not only equally unprovable but also equally improbable. A new demarcation criterion was needed and Popper proposed a rather stunning one. A theory may be scientific even if there is not a shred of evidence in its favour, and it may be pseudoscientific even if all the available evidence is in its favour. That is, the scientific or non-scientific character of a theory can be determined independently of the facts. A theory is 'scientific' if one is prepared to specify in advance a crucial experiment (or observation) which can falsify it, and it is pseudoscientific if one refuses to specify such a 'potential falsifier'. But if so, we do not demarcate scientific theories from pseudoscientific ones, but rather scientific method from non-scientific method. Marxism, for a Popperian, is scientific if the Marxists are prepared to specify facts which, if observed, make them give up Marxism. If they refuse to do so, Marxism becomes a pseudoscience. It is always interesting to ask a Marxist, what conceivable event would make him abandon his Marxism. If he is committed to Marxism, he is bound to find it immoral to specify a state of affairs which can falsify it. Thus a proposition may petrify into pseudoscientific dogma or become genuine knowledge, depending on whether we are prepared to state observable conditions which would refute it.

Is, then, Popper's falsifiability criterion the solution to the problem of demarcating science from pseudoscience? No. For Popper's criterion ignores the remarkable tenacity of scientific theories. Scientists have thick skins. They do not abandon a theory merely because facts contradict it. They normally either invent some rescue hypothesis to explain what they then call a mere anomaly or, if they cannot explain the anomaly, they ignore it, and direct their attention to other problems. Note that scientists talk about anomalies, recalcitrant instances, not refutations. History of science, of course, is full of accounts of how crucial experiments allegedly killed theories. But such accounts are fabricated long after the theory had been abandoned. Had Popper ever asked a Newtonian scientist under what experimental conditions he would abandon Newtonian theory, some Newtonian scientists would have been exactly as nonplussed as are some Marxists.

What, then, is the hallmark of science? Do we have to capitulate and agree that a scientific revolution is just an irrational change in commitment, that it is a religious conversion? Tom Kuhn, a distinguished American philosopher of science, arrived at this conclusion after discovering the naïvety of Popper's falsificationism. But if Kuhn is right, then there is no explicit demarcation between science and pseudoscience, no distinction between scientific progress and intellectual decay, there is no objective standard of honesty. But what criteria can he then offer to demarcate scientific progress from intellectual degeneration?

In the last few years I have been advocating a methodology of scientific research programmes, which solves some of the problems which both Popper and Kuhn failed to solve.

First, I claim that the typical descriptive unit of great scientific achievements is not an isolated hypothesis but rather a research programme. Science is not simply trial and error, a series of conjectures and refutations. 'All swans are white' may be falsified by the discovery of one black swan. But such trivial trial and error does not rank as science. Newtonian science, for instance, is not simply a set of four conjectures − the three laws of mechanics and the law of gravitation. These four laws constitute only the 'hard core' of the Newtonian programme. But this hard core is tenaciously protected from refutation by a vast 'protective belt' of auxiliary hypotheses. And, even more importantly, the research programme has also a 'heuristic', that is, a powerful problem-solving machinery, which, with the help of sophisticated mathematical techniques, digests anomalies and even turns them into positive evidence. For instance, if a planet does not move exactly as it should, the Newtonian scientist checks his conjectures concerning atmospheric refraction, concerning propagation of light in magnetic storms, and hundreds of other conjectures which are all part of the programme. He may even invent a hitherto unknown planet and calculate its position, mass and velocity in order to explain the anomaly.

Now, Newton's theory of gravitation, Einstein's relativity theory, quantum mechanics, Marxism, Freudism, are all research programmes, each with a characteristic hard core stubbornly defended, each with its more flexible protective belt and each with its elaborate problem-solving machinery. Each of them, at any stage of its development, has unsolved problems and undigested anomalies. All theories, in this sense, are born refuted and die refuted. But are they equally good? Until now I have been describing what research programmes are like. But how can one distinguish a scientific or progressive programme from a pseudoscientific or degenerating one?

Contrary to Popper, the difference cannot be that some are still unrefuted, while others are already refuted. When Newton published his *Principia*, it was common knowledge that it could not properly explain even the motion of the moon; in fact, lunar motion refuted Newton. Kaufmann, a distinguished physicist, refuted Einstein's relativity theory in the very year it was published. But all the research programmes I admire have one characteristic in common. They all predict novel facts, facts which had been either undreamt of, or have indeed been contradicted by previous or rival programmes. In 1686, when Newton published his theory of gravitation, there were, for instance, two current theories concerning comets. The more popular one regarded comets as a signal from an angry God warning that He will strike and bring disaster. A little known theory of Kepler's held that comets were celestial bodies moving along straight lines. Now according to Newtonian theory, some of them moved in hyperbolas or parabolas never to return; others moved in ordinary ellipses. Halley, working in Newton's programme, calculated on the basis of observing a brief stretch of a comet's path that it would return in seventy-two years' time; he calculated to the minute when it would be seen again at a well-defined point of the sky. This was incredible. But seventy-two years later, when both Newton and Halley were long dead, Halley's comet returned exactly as Halley predicted. Similarly, Newtonian scientists predicted the existence and exact motion of small planets which had never been observed before. Or let us take Einstein's programme. This programme made the stunning prediction that if one measures the distance between two stars in the night and if one measures the distance between them during the day (when they are visible during an eclipse of the sun), the two measurements will be different. Nobody had thought to make such an observation before Einstein's programme. Thus in a progressive research programme theory leads to the discovery of hitherto unknown novel facts. In degenerating programmes, however, theories are fabricated only in order to accommodate known facts. Has, for instance, Marxism ever predicted a stunning novel fact successfully? Never! It has some famous unsuccessful predictions. It predicted the absolute impoverishment of the working class. It predicted that the first socialist revolution would take place in the industrially most developed society. It predicted that socialist societies would be free of revolutions. It predicted that there will be no conflict of interests between socialist countries. Thus the early predictions of Marxism were bold and stunning but they failed. Marxists explained all their failures: they explained the rising living standards of the working class by devising a theory of imperialism; they even explained why the first socialist revolution occurred in industrially backward Russia. They 'explained' Berlin 1953, Budapest 1956, Prague 1968. They 'explained' the Russian–Chinese conflict. But their auxiliary hypotheses were all cooked up after the event to protect Marxian theory from the facts. The Newtonian programme led to novel facts; the Marxian lagged behind the facts and has been running fast to catch up with them.

To sum up. The hallmark of empirical progress is not trivial verifications: Popper is right that there are millions of them. It is no success for Newtonian theory that stones, when dropped, fall towards the earth, no matter how often this is repeated. But so-called 'refutations' are not the hallmark of empirical failure, as Popper has preached, since all programmes grow in a permanent ocean of anomalies. What really count are dramatic, unexpected, stunning predictions: a few of them are enough to tilt the balance; where theory lags behind the facts, we are dealing with miserable degenerating research programmes.

Now, how do scientific revolutions come about? If we have two rival research programmes, and one is progressing while the other is degenerating, scientists tend to join the progressive programme. This is the rationale of scientific revolutions. But while it is a matter of intellectual honesty to keep the record public, it is not dishonest to stick to a degenerating programme and try to turn it into a progressive one.

As opposed to Popper the methodology of scientific research programmes does not offer instant rationality. One must treat budding programmes leniently: programmes may take decades before they get off the ground and become empirically progressive. Criticism is not a Popperian quick kill, by refutation. Important criticism is always constructive: there is no refutation without a better theory. Kuhn is wrong in thinking that scientific revolutions are sudden, irrational changes in vision. The history of science refutes both Popper and Kuhn: on close inspection both Popperian crucial experiments and Kuhnian revolutions turn out to be myths: what normally happens is that progressive research programmes replace degenerating ones.

The problem of demarcation between science and pseudoscience has grave implications also for the institutionalization of criticism. Copernicus's theory was banned by the Catholic Church in 1616 because it was said to be pseudoscientific. It was taken off the index in 1820 because by that time the Church deemed that facts had proved it and therefore it became scientific. The Central Committee of the Soviet Communist Party in 1949 declared Mendelian genetics pseudoscientific and had its advocates, like Academician Vavilov, killed in concentration camps; after Vavilov's murder Mendelian genetics was rehabilitated; but the Party's right to decide what is science and publishable and what is pseudoscience and punishable was upheld. The new liberal Establishment of the West also exercises the right to deny freedom of speech to what it regards as pseudoscience, as we have seen in the case of the debate concerning race and intelligence. All these judgements were inevitably based on some sort of demarcation criterion. This is why the problem of demarcation between science and pseudoscience is not a pseudo-problem of armchair philosophers: it has grave ethical and political implications.

5 Progress and revolution in science

One hundred years ago it would never have been suggested that a conception of scientific progress would need to accommodate the fact that there can be large-scale changes affecting far-reaching and well-established theories. Progress for Mill, for example (see 4.2), was progress towards something more certain and he would have found the idea of revolutionary change in scientific theory quite alien. Mill never dreamed that progress in science might be towards the brink of uncertainty. Yet, after his death, that was the direction in which Newtonian mechanics developed.

In the first extract, Sir Hermann Bondi gives his view of the revolution in modern physics and an account of scientific progress which owes, as Bondi acknowledges, much to the writings of Karl Popper. Popper has the last word in the discussion as reflected here. But perhaps the most seminal work on the nature of large-scale theoretical changes in science is Thomas Kuhn's *The Structure of Scientific Revolutions*.[1] Two extracts from this book are included here. The first sketches Kuhn's account of a revolution as a hiatus in the conduct of 'normal science' and a shift in the accepted 'paradigm'. Kuhn maintains that such a shift is not entirely rational (see also 4.4 and 9.3). Here we include his explanation of how he thinks that scientific development can nonetheless be seen as progress.

Note

1 Kuhn, Thomas S. (1962) *The Structure of Scientific Revolutions*, Chicago, University of Chicago Press.

5.1 WHAT IS PROGRESS IN SCIENCE?

HERMANN BONDI (1919–   ), *from his 1973 Herbert
Spencer lecture, published in* Problems of Scientific Revolution,
Harré, Rom, ed., *Oxford, Oxford University Press, 1975*

Bondi is concerned with the implications of the
rejection of Newton's theory of gravitation in favour
of Einstein's for an account of scientific progress.
This example is considered elsewhere in this volume
by another physicist, Paul Dirac (3.3), and by the
philosopher Karl Popper (4.3).

Obstacles to progress may be within the science itself or outside. You
can look at the problem psychologically, politically, or sociologically. I,
myself, in choosing to talk about *progress*, have, I think, a slightly easier
task than those who will talk of its obstacles, because progress in science
is presumably something that can be defined in internal terms intrinsic
to science. My thesis will be that the concept of progress in science is not
a simple concept. You might well say that it does not need a long lecture
to explain that something is *not* simple. Nevertheless, I will try to dispel
any prejudices that it might be simple.

To start then, I think I should try and define what science is. This is a
subject in which I am a whole-hearted follower of Karl Popper and his
criterion of demarcation, which is why I feel so honoured to have been
asked to start a series which will be completed by Karl Popper himself,
for whom I have such admiration.

I want to describe what Popper's concept is, in a very compressed
form. In his view it is the task of the scientist to propose a theory, a
theory that must naturally encompass what is known at the time, but
that over and above this *must* make forecasts of what future experiments or observations will show. If such experiments are then performed and the outcome is in agreement with what the theory has said,
then we must *never* say that the theory has been proved. We can only say
that it has stood a test successfully and it is the task of the theory to go on
making further deductions, further statements that can be tested empirically. If, however, such a test goes against the theory, then the
theory has been disproved and then one has got to start with a new
theory which may be a very difficult matter. This primacy of disproof is
an essential part of the scheme, and it grows naturally from the logical
structure: a scientific theory is always a *general* statement that all things
of this kind behave in a certain way. To put in the most elementary way

of which I am capable, you *may presume* from observation that *any* apples, when released, will drop, but you cannot possibly *deduce* this rule from your observations, because the theory that any apple when released will drop applies to all apples, past, present, and future. You may have tried it out with ten, or with a hundred, or with a thousand apples, but you will certainly not have tried it out with *all* apples, and therefore you can never prove the theory. But find only *one* apple that, when released, rises, and you have disproved the theory. With a particular instance you can disprove the general statement, but you can never logically deduce a general statement from a particular, however large, sample of experiments. The fact that you cannot deduce your scientific theory by any logical method shows that the vital part of the subject is originality and imagination. Formulating a scientific theory always involves an imaginative leap. We cannot imagine a mechanical process for going from a set of experiments or observations to a theory. A theory will be scientific if and only if it can be empirically disproved. I think this is a very important point. I suffer more at some times in my life than others from getting large numbers of letters with brilliant scientific ideas. The largest proportion of them, of course, comes from cranks. But with clever cranks it is not always immediately obvious that the writer is a crank and not somebody who has got perhaps quite a good idea oddly expressed. But when I come to the line, to which one often comes, 'Well, if the experiments go this way, they will fit in with my theory, and if they go any other way they will also fit in with my theory, so you see how good a theory it is', then my ample waste-paper basket is the right destination.

It is immediately clear, then, that with disproof playing such a very important role, we cannot expect any description of the progress of science to be smooth and straight. Indeed, it must be something very far from it. Let me again give you an example, perhaps the most extreme example that we have got, of Popper's criteria in action. When Newton's theory of gravitation was proposed, over three hundred years ago, there followed enormous numbers of tests. The theory was used by astronomers to predict the position of planets and satellites and to forecast when eclipses would occur, then to go backwards in time and date historical events by them — they would refer historical events to eclipses by calculating exactly when an eclipse would occur. To say that that theory was tested a hundred thousand times and passed each test brilliantly is, I am sure, numerically an understatement. But the fact that it had been tested so very often did not help the theory all that much when the first discrepancies between theory and observation emerged towards the end of the last century, with more and more accurate observations of the motion of the planets and more and more accurate methods of calculating the mutual perturbation of the planets. Newcombe then discovered before the turn of the century that there was a discrepancy in the motion of the planet Mercury (he referred to this in his calculations as the 'empirical term'). With hindsight, we can say that to a large extent this was a disproof of Newton's theory of gravitation, although in fact the progress to Einstein's theory came from a rather different side, a change in the intellectual climate, but the disproof was really there with Newcombe. And so you have the result that a theory that had been tested exhaustively, and passed all those tests brilliantly, was still liable to be disproved.

This disproof had a tremendous effect on the intellectual climate. It had been thought that whatever in the world might be difficult, might be complex, might be hard to understand, at least Newton's theory of gravitation was good and solid, tested well over a hundred thousand times. And when such a theory falls victim to the increasing precision of observation and calculation, one certainly feels that one can never again rest assured. This is the stuff of progress. You cannot therefore speak of progress as progress in a particular direction, as a progress in which knowledge becomes more and more certain and more and more all-embracing. At times we make discoveries that sharply reduce the knowledge that we have, and it is discoveries of this kind that are indeed the seminal point in science. It is they that are the real roots of progress and lead to the jumps in understanding, but in the first instance they reduce what we regard as assured knowledge.

It is, of course, important to remember that when a theory has passed a very large number of tests, like Newton's theory, and is then disproved − and we can certainly speak of its disproof now − you would not say that everything that was tested before − all those forecasts − were wrong. They were right, and you know therefore that although the theory *qua* general theory is no longer tenable, yet it is something that described a significant volume of experience quite well. And indeed, although we have a newer and better theory of gravitation − Einstein's theory and one or two variants of it in addition − nevertheless, whenever we do not want to carry out calculations of the motions of planets and satellites with extreme precision − we use Newton's theory because it is simpler. The difference lies in our attitude to it. When you formulate a theory it has universalist totalitarian claims. When you have tested it, then you know that that theory describes certain ranges of phenomena, a certain *limited* range, with a certain limited measure of accuracy and precision. And that description will hold. It is your interpretation of the theory as something that is the Truth (with a capital T) (a term that to my thinking has nothing to do with science anyway), that will have been shattered. And you will naturally look for a description that is *better* in the sense that it embraces a wider range of phenomena to higher precision, but is also disprovable. If it is not disprovable it is not scientifically interesting. So, the nature of progress is that crucial points in it are the *shattering* of knowledge, rather than the gaining of knowledge. But I would be quite wrong to say that the gaining of knowledge was not also progress. It just is not a very straight path.

It is implicit in Popper's description that we can perform more searching experiments tomorrow than we can perform today, that you can test the theory more thoroughly tomorrow than you can test it today. Otherwise there wouldn't be all that much point in this vulnerability in forecasting. Our faith that tomorrow we can test more searchingly than today is based on our faith in the progress of technology. It is the technology that supplies the experimenter and the observer with their means. It is a progressive technology that allows us to measure new things, or to measure old things more precisely. And what is the basis of the progress of technology? Of course, it is the progress of science; and so the idea that science, all beautiful and shining, leads, and technology follows, is a total misconception. The relation between the two is the relation between the chicken and the egg and progress in the one is often due to progress in the other as Popper has so well stated. There are in science itself, nevertheless, criteria which make us regard certain things as progress: namely that we can deal with more searching experiments. We can cover a larger area although our method of covering may by no means be simple.

The search for simplicity is a powerful driving force, but it does not necessarily get us there. The search for simplicity belongs more properly to the subject of the psychology of science than the subject of what constitutes progress, and we know from many examples in history that we have arrived at greater simplicity only to go forward to greater complexity afterwards. Some subjects get into states where they are very hard to describe, let alone understand, because they are so highly complex, although not so many years before there was a phase where they were very simple. We know that in certain circumstances we can hardly expect to find simplicity. On our own scale we know there is a lot of complexity because we know *we* are very complex indeed, so one's hope for simplicity is either to go to the very large or to the very small. Sometimes one is rewarded for certain periods in having a simpler situation and you say, 'Isn't it a marvellous piece of progress to know that we now know *all* the particles that go into making up an atom': only a few years later your simplicity is shattered and you discover that there is a whole zoo of particles. No doubt the time will come when they are again ordered. A very pretty story of the kind of zig-zag that is characteristic of progress in science concerns the atomic weights. When they were first determined with low precision it was thought likely that they all bore integral ratios to each other, that they were all whole-number multiples of some particular unit. Then, when it became possible to measure atomic weights more precisely, one discovered that this was certainly not the case. Next the brilliant idea of isotopes came along, viz. that elements might be made up of atoms the same in all respects other than their masses, and that different masses always occurred with the same relative abundance. This could be tested with precision, and again you could say they were all whole numbers. Before long the precision of measurement had increased yet further and one found that even the individual isotopes bore no whole-number ratios to each other. This way one found the mass defects which express the binding energy of the nuclei. Before very long one appreciated again then that the whole-number property was a very important property but it referred to the number of protons and neutrons in the nucleus of each isotope and not to the mass of the nucleus. And so, by somewhat re-defining your terms, you have had a whole chain: whole-number, not whole-number, whole-number, not whole-number; and that is called progress. And undoubtedly in our understanding it was progress, but it is not rectilinear in any sense.

5.2   THE ROUTE TO 'NORMAL SCIENCE'

THOMAS S. KUHN (1922–   ), *from* The Structure of Scientific Revolutions, *Chicago, University of Chicago Press, 2nd ed., 1970, pp. 10–13*

In this extract, Kuhn introduces some of the key ideas which he uses to analyse the structure of scientific revolutions, in particular 'normal science' and 'paradigm' (a later explication of paradigms, in response to criticism from Popper, is included in reading 4.4). Kuhn illustrates his analysis by reference to the history of physical optics.

In this essay, 'normal science' means research firmly based upon one or more past scientific achievements, achievements that some particular scientific community acknowledges for a time as supplying the foundation for its further practice. Today such achievements are recounted, though seldom in their original form, by science textbooks, elementary and advanced. These textbooks expound the body of accepted theory, illustrate many or all of its successful applications, and compare these applications with exemplary observations and experiments. Before such books became popular early in the nineteenth century (and until even more recently in the newly matured sciences), many of the famous classics of science fulfilled a similar function. Aristotle's *Physica*, Ptolemy's *Almagest*, Newton's *Principia* and *Opticks*, Franklin's *Electricity*, Lavoisier's *Chemistry*, and Lyell's *Geology* — these and many other works served for a time implicitly to define the legitimate problems and methods of a research field for succeeding generations of practitioners. They were able to do so because they shared two essential characteristics. Their achievement was sufficiently unprecedented to attract an enduring group of adherents away from competing modes of scientific activity. Simultaneously, it was sufficiently open-ended to leave all sorts of problems for the redefined group of practitioners to resolve.

Achievements that share these two characteristics I shall henceforth refer to as 'paradigms', a term that relates closely to 'normal science'. By choosing it, I mean to suggest that some accepted examples of actual scientific practice — examples which include law, theory, application, and instrumentation together — provide models from which spring particular coherent traditions of scientific research. These are the traditions which the historian describes under such rubrics as 'Ptolemaic astronomy' (or 'Copernican'), 'Aristotelian dynamics' (or 'Newtonian'), 'corpuscular optics' (or 'wave optics'), and so on. The study of paradigms, including many that are far more specialized than those named illustratively above, is what mainly prepares the student for membership in the particular scientific community with which he will later practice. Because he there joins men who learned the bases of their field from the same concrete models, his subsequent practice will seldom evoke overt disagreement over fundamentals. Men whose research is based on shared paradigms are committed to the same rules and standards for scientific practice. That commitment and the apparent consensus it produces are prerequisites for normal science, i.e. for the genesis and continuation of a particular research tradition. . . .

If the historian traces the scientific knowledge of any selected group of related phenomena backward in time, he is likely to encounter some minor variant of a pattern here illustrated from the history of physical optics. Today's physics textbooks tell the student that light is photons, i.e. quantum-mechanical entities that exhibit some characteristics of waves and some of particles. Research proceeds accordingly, or rather according to the more elaborate and mathematical characterization from which this usual verbalization is derived. That characterization of light is, however, scarcely half a century old. Before it was developed by Planck, Einstein, and others early in this century, physics texts taught that light was transverse wave motion, a conception rooted in a paradigm that derived ultimately from the optical writings of Young and Fresnel in the early nineteenth century. Nor was the wave theory the first to be embraced by almost all practitioners of optical science. During the eighteenth century the paradigm for this field was provided by Newton's *Opticks*, which taught that light was material corpuscles. At that time physicists sought evidence, as the early wave theorists had not, of the pressure exerted by light particles impinging on solid bodies.[1]

These transformations of the paradigms of physical optics are scientific revolutions, and the successive transition from one paradigm to another via revolution is the usual developmental pattern of mature science. It is not, however, the pattern characteristic of the period before Newton's work, and that is the contrast that concerns us here. No period between remote antiquity and the end of the seventeenth century exhibited a single generally accepted view about the nature of light. Instead there were a number of competing schools and sub-schools, most of them espousing one variant or another of Epicurean, Aristotelian, or Platonic theory. One group took light to be particles emanating from material bodies; for another it was a modification of the medium that intervened between the body and the eye; still another explained light in terms of an interaction of the medium with an emanation from the eye; and there were other combinations and modifications besides. Each of the corresponding schools derived strength from its relation to some particular metaphysic, and each emphasized, as paradigmatic observations, the particular cluster of optical phenomena that its own theory could do most to explain. Other observations were dealt with by *ad hoc* elaborations, or they remained as outstanding problems for further research.

At various times all these schools made significant contributions to the body of concepts, phenomena, and techniques from which Newton drew the first nearly uniformly accepted paradigm for physical optics. Any definition of the scientist that excludes at least the more creative members of these various schools will exclude their modern successors as well. Those men were scientists. Yet anyone examining a survey of physical optics before Newton may well conclude that, though the field's practitioners were scientists, the net result of their activity was something less than science. Being able to take no common body of belief for granted, each writer on physical optics felt forced to build his field anew from its foundations. In doing so, his choice of supporting observation and experiment was relatively free, for there was no standard set of methods or of phenomena that every optical writer felt forced to employ and explain. Under these circumstances, the dialogue of the resulting books was often directed as much to the members of other schools as it was to nature. That pattern is not unfamiliar in a number of creative fields today, nor is it incompatible with significant discovery and invention. It is not, however, the pattern of development that physical optics acquired after Newton and that other natural sciences make familiar today.

Note

1. Priestley, Joseph (1772) *The History and Present State of Discoveries, Relating to Vision, Light and Colours*, 2 vols, London, pp. 385–90.

5.3   PROGRESS THROUGH REVOLUTIONS

THOMAS S. KUHN (1922–   ), *from* The Structure of Scientific Revolutions, *Chicago, University of Chicago Press*, 2nd ed., 1970, *pp. 162–70, 171–3*

Kuhn's analysis of scientific revolutions raises the question why major scientific changes should, on his account, be supposed to constitute 'progress'. For he denies that it is possible to compare a new paradigm with the one it has replaced in such a way as to say that it is more true. In this extract, Kuhn puts forward a controversial view about the nature of progress in science (he himself refers to the controversy in reading 9.3).

Ask now why an enterprise like normal science should progress, and begin by recalling a few of its most salient characteristics. Normally, the members of a mature scientific community work from a single paradigm or from a closely related set. Very rarely do different scientific communities investigate the same problems. In those exceptional cases the groups hold several major paradigms in common. Viewed from within any single community, however, whether of scientists or of non-scientists, the result of successful creative work *is* progress. How could it possibly be anything else? We have, for example, just noted that while artists aimed at representation as their goal, both critics and historians chronicled the progress of the apparently united group. Other creative fields display progress of the same sort. The theologian who articulates dogma or the philosopher who refines the Kantian imperatives contributes to progress, if only to that of the group that shares his premises. No creative school recognizes a category of work that is, on the one hand, a creative success, but is not, on the other, an addition to the collective achievement of the group. If we doubt, as many do, that non-scientific fields make progress, that cannot be because individual schools make none. Rather, it must be because there are always competing schools, each of which constantly questions the very foundations of the others. The man who argues that philosophy, for example, has made no progress emphasizes that there are still Aristotelians, not that Aristotelianism has failed to progress.

These doubts about progress arise, however, in the sciences too. Throughout the pre-paradigm period when there is a multiplicity of competing schools, evidence of progress, except within schools, is very hard to find. This is the period . . . during which individuals practice science, but in which the results of their enterprise do not add up to science as we know it. And again, during periods of revolution when the fundamental tenets of a field are once more at issue, doubts are repeatedly expressed about the very possibility of continued progress if one or another of the opposed paradigms is adopted. Those who rejected Newtonianism proclaimed that its reliance upon innate forces would return science to the Dark Ages. Those who opposed Lavoisier's chemistry held that the rejection of chemical 'principles' in favor of laboratory elements was the rejection of achieved chemical explanation by those who would take refuge in a mere name. A similar, though more moderately expressed, feeling seems to underlie the opposition of Einstein, Bohm, and others, to the dominant probabilistic interpretation of quantum mechanics. In short, it is only during periods of normal science that progress seems both obvious and assured. During those periods, however, the scientific community could view the fruits of its work in no other way.

With respect to normal science, then, part of the answer to the problem of progress lies simply in the eye of the beholder. Scientific progress is not different in kind from progress in other fields, but the absence at most times of competing schools that question each other's aims and standards makes the progress of a normal-scientific community far easier to see. That, however, is only part of the answer and by no means the most important part. We have, for example, already noted that once the reception of a common paradigm has freed the scientific community from the need constantly to re-examine its first principles, the members of that community can concentrate exclusively upon the subtlest and most esoteric of the phenomena that concern it. Inevitably, that does increase both the effectiveness and the efficiency with which the group as a whole solves new problems. Other aspects of professional life in the sciences enhance this very special efficiency still further.

Some of these are consequences of the unparalleled insulation of mature scientific communities from the demands of the laity and of everyday life. That insulation has never been complete − we are now discussing matters of degree. Nevertheless, there are no other professional communities in which individual creative work is so exclusively addressed to and evaluated by other members of the profession. The most esoteric of poets or the most abstract of theologians is far more concerned than the scientist with lay approbation of his creative work, though he may be even less concerned with approbation in general. That difference proves consequential. Just because he is working only for an audience of colleagues, an audience that shares his own values and beliefs, the scientist can take a single set of standards for granted. He need not worry about what some other group or school will think and can therefore dispose of one problem and get on to the next more quickly than those who work for a more heterodox group. Even more important, the insulation of the scientific community from society permits the individual scientist to concentrate his attention upon problems that he has good reason to believe he will be able to solve. Unlike the engineer, and many doctors, and most theologians, the scientist need not choose problems because they urgently need solution and without regard for the tools available to solve them. In this respect, also, the contrast between natural scientists and many social scientists proves instructive. The latter often tend, as the former almost never do, to defend their choice of a research problem − e.g. the effects of racial discrimination or the causes of the business cycle − chiefly in terms of the social importance of achieving a solution. Which group would one then expect to solve problems at a more rapid rate?

The effects of insulation from the larger society are greatly intensified by another characteristic of the professional scientific community, the nature of its educational initiation. In music, the graphic arts, and literature, the practitioner gains his education by exposure to the works of other artists, principally earlier artists. Textbooks, except compendia of or handbooks to original creations, have only a secondary role. In history, philosophy, and the social sciences, textbook literature has a greater significance. But even in these fields the elementary college course employs parallel readings in original sources, some of them the 'classics' of the field, others the contemporary research reports that practitioners write for each other. As a result, the student in any one of these disciplines is constantly made aware of the immense variety of problems that the members of his future group have, in the course of time, attempted to solve. Even more important, he has constantly before him a number of competing and incommensurable solutions to these problems, solutions that he must ultimately evaluate for himself.

Contrast this situation with that in at least the contemporary natural sciences. In these fields the student relies mainly on textbooks until, in his third or fourth year of graduate work, he begins his own research. Many science curricula do not ask even graduate students to read in works not written specially for students. The few that do assign supplementary reading in research papers and monographs restrict such assignments to the most advanced courses and to materials that take up more or less where the available texts leave off. Until the very last stages in the education of a scientist, textbooks are systematically substituted for the creative scientific literature that made them possible. Given the confidence in their paradigms, which makes this educational technique possible, few scientists would wish to change it. Why, after all, should the student of physics, for example, read the works of Newton, Faraday, Einstein, or Schrödinger, when everything he needs to know about these works is recapitulated in a far briefer, more precise, and more systematic form in a number of up-to-date textbooks?

Without wishing to defend the excessive lengths to which this type of education has occasionally been carried, one cannot help but notice that in general it has been immensely effective. Of course, it is a narrow and rigid education, probably more so than any other except perhaps in orthodox theology. But for normal-scientific work, for puzzle-solving within the tradition that the textbooks define, the scientist is almost perfectly equipped. Furthermore, he is well equipped for another task as well − the generation through normal science of significant crises. When they arise, the scientist is not, of course, equally well prepared. Even though prolonged crises are probably reflected in less rigid educational practice, scientific training is not well designed to produce the man who will easily discover a fresh approach. But so long as somebody appears with a new candidate for paradigm – usually a young man or one new to the field – the loss due to rigidity accrues only to the individual. Given a generation in which to effect the change, individual rigidity is compatible with a community that can switch from paradigm to paradigm when the occasion demands. Particularly, it is compatible when that very rigidity provides the community with a sensitive indicator that something has gone wrong.

In its normal state, then, a scientific community is an immensely efficient instrument for solving the problems or puzzles that its paradigms define. Furthermore, the result of solving those problems must inevitably be progress. There is no problem here. Seeing that much, however, only highlights the second main part of the problem of progress in the sciences. Let us therefore turn to it and ask about progress through extraordinary science. Why should progress also be the apparently universal concomitant of scientific revolutions? Once again, there is much to be learned by asking what else the result of a revolution could be. Revolutions close with a total victory for one of the two opposing camps. Will that group ever say that the result of its victory has been something less than progress? That would be rather like admitting that they had been wrong and their opponents right. To them, at least, the outcome of revolution must be progress, and they are in an excellent position to make certain that future members of their community will see past history in the same way. . . .

When it repudiates a past paradigm, a scientific community simultaneously renounces, as a fit subject for professional scrutiny, most of the books and articles in which that paradigm had been embodied. Scientific education makes use of no equivalent for the art museum or the library of classics, and the result is a sometimes drastic distortion in the scientist's perception of his discipline's past. More than the practitioners of other creative fields, he comes to see it as leading in a straight line to the discipline's present vantage. In short, he comes to see it as progress. No alternative is available to him while he remains in the field.

Inevitably those remarks will suggest that the member of a mature scientific community is, like the typical character of Orwell's *1984*, the victim of a history rewritten by the powers that be. Furthermore, that suggestion is not altogether inappropriate. There are losses as well as gains in scientific revolutions, and scientists tend to be peculiarly blind to the former.[1] On the other hand, no explanation of progress through revolutions may stop at this point. To do so would be to imply that in the sciences might makes right, a formulation which would again not be entirely wrong if it did not suppress the nature of the process and of the authority by which the choice between paradigms is made. If authority alone, and particularly if non-professional authority, were the arbiter of paradigm debates, the outcome of those debates might still be revolution, but it would not be *scientific* revolution. The very existence of science depends upon vesting the power to choose between paradigms in the members of a special kind of community. Just how special that community must be if science is to survive and grow may be indicated by the very tenuousness of humanity's hold on the scientific enterprise. Every civilization of which we have records has possessed a technology, an art, a religion, a political system, laws, and so on. In many cases those facets of civilization have been as developed as our own. But only the civilizations that descend from Hellenic Greece have possessed more than the most rudimentary science. The bulk of scientific knowledge is a product of Europe in the last four centuries. No other place and time has supported the very special communities from which scientific productivity comes.

What are the essential characteristics of these communities? Obviously, they need vastly more study. In this area only the most tentative generalizations are possible. Nevertheless, a number of requisites for membership in a professional scientific group must already be strikingly clear. The scientist must, for example, be concerned to solve problems about the behavior of nature. In addition, though his concern with nature may be global in its extent, the problems on which he works must be problems of detail. More important, the solutions that satisfy him may not be merely personal but must instead be accepted as solutions by many. The group that shares them may not, however, be drawn at random from society as a whole, but is rather the well-defined community of the scientist's professional compeers. One of the strongest, if still unwritten, rules of scientific life is the prohibition of appeals to heads of state or to the populace at large in matters scientific. Recognition of the existence of a uniquely competent professional group and acceptance of its role as the exclusive arbiter of professional achievement has further implications. The group's members, as individuals and by virtue of their shared training and experience, must be seen as the sole possessors of the rules of the game or of some equivalent basis for unequivocal judgments. To doubt that they shared some such basis for evaluations would be to admit the existence of incompatible standards of scientific achievement. That admission would inevitably raise the question whether truth in the sciences can be one.

This small list of characteristics common to scientific communities has been drawn entirely from the practice of normal science, and it should have been. That is the activity for which the scientist is ordinarily trained. Note, however, that despite its small size the list is already sufficient to set such communities apart from all other professional groups. And note, in addition, that despite its source in normal science the list accounts for many special features of the group's response during revolutions and particularly during paradigm debates. We have already observed that a group of this sort must see a paradigm change as progress. Now we may recognize that the perception is, in important respects, self-fulfilling. The scientific community is a supremely efficient instrument for maximizing the number and precision of the problems solved through paradigm change.

Because the unit of scientific achievement is the solved problem and because the group knows well which problems have already been solved, few scientists will easily be persuaded to adopt a viewpoint that again opens to question many problems that had previously been solved. Nature itself must first undermine professional security by making prior achievements seem problematic. Furthermore, even when that has occurred and a new candidate for paradigm has been evoked, scientists will be reluctant to embrace it unless convinced that two all-important conditions are being met. First, the new candidate must seem to resolve some outstanding and generally recognized problem that can be met in no other way. Second, the new paradigm must promise to preserve a relatively large part of the concrete problem-solving ability that has accrued to science through its predecessors. Novelty for its own sake is not a desideratum in the sciences as it is in so many other creative fields. As a result, though new paradigms seldom or never possess all the capabilities of their predecessors, they usually preserve a great deal of the most concrete parts of past achievement and they always permit additional concrete problem-solutions besides.

To say this much is not to suggest that the ability to solve problems is either the unique or an unequivocal basis for paradigm choice. We have already noted many reasons why there can be no criterion of that sort. But it does suggest that a community of scientific specialists will do all that it can to ensure the continuing growth of the assembled data that it can treat with precision and detail. In the process the community will sustain losses. Often some old problems must be banished. Frequently, in addition, revolution narrows the scope of the community's professional concerns, increases the extent of its specialization, and attenuates its communication with other groups, both scientific and lay. Though science surely grows in depth, it may not grow in breadth as well. If it does so, that breadth is manifest mainly in the proliferation of scientific specialties, not in the scope of any single specialty alone. Yet despite these and other losses to the individual communities, the nature of such communities provides a virtual guarantee that both the list of problems solved by science and the precision of individual problem-solutions will grow and grow. At least, the nature of the community provides such a guarantee if there is any way at all in which it can be provided. What better criterion than the decision of the scientific group could there be?

These last paragraphs point the directions in which I believe a more refined solution of the problem of progress in the sciences must be sought. Perhaps they indicate that scientific progress is not quite what we had taken it to be. But they simultaneously show that a sort of progress will inevitably characterize the scientific enterprise so long as such an enterprise survives. In the sciences there need not be progress of another sort. We may, to be more precise, have to relinquish the notion, explicit or implicit, that changes of paradigm carry scientists and those who learn from them closer and closer to the truth. . . .

I cannot yet specify in any detail the consequences of this alternate view of scientific advance. But it helps to recognize that the conceptual transposition here recommended is very close to one that the West undertook just a century ago. It is particularly helpful because in both cases the main obstacle to transposition is the same. When Darwin first published his theory of evolution by natural selection in 1859, what most bothered many professionals was neither the notion of species change nor the possible descent of man from apes. The evidence pointing to evolution, including the evolution of man, had been accumulating for decades, and the idea of evolution had been suggested and widely disseminated before. Though evolution, as such, did encounter resistance, particularly from some religious groups, it was by no means the greatest of the difficulties the Darwinians faced. That difficulty stemmed from an idea that was more nearly Darwin's own. All the well-known pre-Darwinian evolutionary theories – those of Lamarck, Chambers, Spencer, and the German *Naturphilosophen* – had taken evolution to be a goal-directed process. The 'idea' of man and of the contemporary flora and fauna was thought to have been present from the first creation of life, perhaps in the mind of God. That idea or plan had provided the direction and the guiding force to the entire evolutionary process. Each new stage of evolutionary development was a more perfect realization of a plan that had been present from the start.

For many men the abolition of that teleological kind of evolution was the most significant and least palatable of Darwin's suggestions. The *Origin of Species* recognized no goal set either by God or nature. Instead, natural selection, operating in the given environment and with the actual organisms presently at hand, was responsible for the gradual but steady emergence of more elaborate, further articulated, and vastly more specialized organisms. Even such marvelously adapted organs as the eye and hand of man − organs whose design had previously provided powerful arguments for the existence of a supreme artificer and an advance plan − were products of a process that moved steadily *from* primitive beginnings but *toward* no goal. The belief that natural selection, resulting from mere competition between organisms for survival, could have produced man together with the higher animals and plants was the most difficult and disturbing aspect of Darwin's theory. What could 'evolution', 'development', and 'progress' mean in the absence of a specified goal? To many people, such terms suddenly seemed self-contradictory . . . the resolution of revolutions is the selection by conflict within the scientific community of the fittest way to practice future science. The net result of a sequence of such revolutionary selections, separated by periods of normal research, is the wonderfully adapted set of instruments we call modern scientific knowledge. Successive stages in that developmental process are marked by an increase in articulation and specialization. And the entire process may have occurred, as we now suppose biological evolution did, without benefit of a set goal, a permanent fixed scientific truth, of which each stage in the development of scientific knowledge is a better exemplar.

Note

1. Historians of science often encounter this blindness in a particularly striking form. The group of students who come to them from the sciences is very often the most rewarding group they teach. But it is also usually the most frustrating at the start. Because science students 'know the right answers', it is particularly difficult to make them analyze an older science in its own terms.

5.4   THE RATIONALITY OF SCIENTIFIC REVOLUTIONS

KARL R. POPPER (1902−   ), *from his 1973 Herbert Spencer lecture, published in* Problems of Scientific Revolution, *Harré, Rom, ed., Oxford, Oxford University Press, 1975, pp. 82−4*

Popper holds that the distinctive mark of a scientific theory is that it admits, in principle, of being falsified (see 4.3). He also holds that there is a logic of theory choice and that logical considerations should be sharply distinguished from psychological ones (see

3.2). The same sharp distinction between logical and causal questions is reflected in the beginning of this extract.

So far I have considered progress in science mainly from a biological point of view; however, it seems to me that the following two logical points are crucial.

First, in order that a new theory should constitute a discovery or a step forward it should conflict with its predecessor; that is to say, it should lead to at least some conflicting results. But this means, from a logical point of view, that it should contradict its predecessor: it should overthrow it.

In this sense, progress in science — or at least striking progress — is always revolutionary.

My second point is that progress in science, although revolutionary rather than merely cumulative, is in a certain sense always conservative: a new theory, however revolutionary, must always be able to explain fully the success of its predecessor. In all those cases in which its predecessor was successful, it must yield results at least as good as those of its predecessor and, if possible, better results. Thus in these cases the predecessor theory must appear as a good approximation to the new theory; while there should be, preferably, other cases where the new theory yields different and better results than the old theory.

The important point about the two logical criteria which I have stated is that they allow us to decide of any new theory, even before it has been tested, whether it will be better than the old one, provided it stands up to tests. But this means that, in the field of science, we have something like a criterion for judging the quality of a theory as compared with its predecessor, and therefore a criterion of progress. And so it means that progress in science can be assessed rationally. This possibility explains why, in science, only progressive theories are regarded as interesting; and it thereby explains why, as a matter of historical fact, the history of science is, by and large, a history of progress. (Science seems to be the only field of human endeavour of which this can be said.)

As I have suggested before, scientific progress is revolutionary. Indeed, its motto could be that of Karl Marx: 'Revolution in permanence.' However, scientific revolutions are rational in the sense that, in principle, it is rationally decidable whether or not a new theory is better than its predecessor. Of course, this does not mean that we cannot blunder. There are many ways in which we can make mistakes.

An example of a most interesting mistake is reported by Dirac. Schrödinger found, but did not publish, a relativistic equation of the electron, later called the Klein–Gordon equation, before he found and published the famous non-relativistic equation which is now called by his name. He did not publish the relativistic equation because it did not seem to agree with the experimental results as interpreted by the preceding theory. However, the discrepancy was due to a faulty interpretation of empirical results, and not to a fault in the relativistic equation. Had Schrödinger published it, the problem of the equivalence between his wave mechanics and the matrix mechanics of Heisenberg and Born might not have arisen; and the history of modern physics might have been very different.[1]

It should be obvious that the objectivity and the rationality of progress in science is not due to the personal objectivity and rationality of the scientist. Great science and great scientists, like great poets, are often inspired by non-rational intuitions. So are great mathematicians. As Poincaré and Hadamard have pointed out,[2] a mathematical proof may be discovered by unconscious trials, guided by an inspiration of a decidedly aesthetic character, rather than by rational thought. This is true, and important. But obviously, it does not make the result, the mathematical proof, irrational. In any case, a proposed proof must be able to stand up to critical discussion: to its examination by competing mathematicians. And this may well induce the mathematical inventor to check, rationally, the results which he reached unconsciously or intuitively. Similarly, Kepler's beautiful Pythagorean dreams of the harmony of the world system did not invalidate the objectivity, the testability, the rationality of his three laws; nor the rationality of the problem which these laws posed for an explanatory theory.

Notes

1. Dirac, P. (1963) 'The evolution of the physicist's picture of nature', *Scientific American*, 208(5).
2. Hadamard, J. S. (1945) *An Essay on the Psychology of Invention in the Mathematical Field*, Princeton, N.J., Princeton University Press. See also reading 1.2.

Part Three
Conceptions of Social Inquiry

6 A science of human behaviour?

The question of whether inquiry in the social sciences is essentially of the same nature as that in the natural sciences may look at first sight a relatively straight-forward one — as perhaps do the positions taken up in the various extracts given here. On this level, Mill, Easton and Hempel all basically advocate 'the methodological unity of all empirical science', as Hempel puts it. Lessnoff on the other hand queries this unity on the grounds that the study of *people* and their actions is radically different from the study of mindless matter. These represent two long-standing positions on the central question: first the empiricist view that the study of social and of natural phenomena are in principle the same, even while accepting that in practice 'social science' may not yet be as developed as the natural sciences; and second the view that since the phenomena of nature and of human activity are fundamentally different, primarily because of the dimension of 'meaning' in human action, their study must correspondingly be different — a stand outlined by Lessnoff in this chapter and followed up further in chapter 7, particularly in reading 7.1.

The question is a complex one however, and though the various answers given can be grouped roughly into those 'for' and those 'against' regarding the social sciences as in principle methodologically the same as the natural sciences, to leave it at that could be misleading. For one thing *different* models of scientific methodology are often involved. Social scientists who hotly argue that particular methodo-logical models are appropriate, or otherwise, for social inquiry are sometimes attacking or defending models of inquiry which are far from unquestionably accepted within the natural sciences themselves. Hempel's 'deductive-nomological' type of explanation for example, following in the same tradition as the 'hypothetico-deductive' model elaborated in Popper's writings, may or may not seem applicable to the social sciences − but the same or similar doubts may be expressed about its overall applicability to the natural sciences too. When the central question so often invokes implicitly different models of 'natural science' inquiry − as exemplified earlier in this volume − answers too may need to be understood in differing senses.

The ways in which social inquiry is seen as basically the same as, or different from, that in the natural sciences also vary. The similarity or difference may be in the assumed overall *aims* of scientific inquiry − a stress on, say, prediction or control or building up a deductive structure of universally applicable laws; it may be in the form of *explanation* involved − the aspect stressed by Hempel; or again it may relate to the prior *identification* and *classification* of the subject of study, a point which Lessnoff particularly emphasizes. The disagreements are thus sometimes more limited and less wholesale than may at first appear.

There is also a certain measure of agreement. It seems to be shared ground between both sides that ultimately *empirical* inquiry is involved, and that in this sense social science, and history, go along with natural sciences in being distinct from, say, abstract speculation or prophecy or moral exhortation. Furthermore, while both positions, as in the earlier discussion of the demarcation between science and non-science, invoke some shared descriptive assumptions about which inquiries would be widely accepted as examples of 'social science' and of 'natural science', there is also a heavy emphasis on prescription. 'Social' inquiries, it is implied, *ought* to be of such and such a kind even if there is a reluctance in some quarters to accept this.

6.1 THAT THERE IS, OR MAY BE, A SCIENCE OF HUMAN NATURE

JOHN STUART MILL (1806–1873), *from* A System of Logic, *book 6, ch. 3, London, Longmans, Green, 1843*

Mill's account is a clear statement of the classical empiricist view: human nature is as much a subject for science as any other natural phenomenon. The study of human nature, it is true, cannot form one of the *exact* sciences, such as astronomy, for unerring predictions are impossible and the laws involved are approximate rather than universal. But this is also so, Mill urges, in certain accepted sciences too – the study of tides, for example – and, as in some other sciences, the 'approximate generalizations' which can be reached about human nature can be connected deductively with the universal 'laws of nature from which they result'. The study of human nature is thus to be classed as one of the non-exact sciences, similar to the science of tides.

It is a common notion, or at least it is implied in many common modes of speech, that the thoughts, feelings, and actions of sentient beings are not a subject of science, in the same strict sense in which this is true of the objects of outward nature. This notion seems to involve some confusion of ideas, which it is necessary to begin by clearing up.

Any facts are fitted, in themselves, to be a subject of science, which follow one another according to constant laws; although those laws may not have been discovered, nor even be discoverable by our existing resources. Take, for instance, the most familiar class of meteorological phenomena, those of rain and sunshine. Scientific inquiry has not yet succeeded in ascertaining the order of antecedence and consequence among these phenomena, so as to be able, at least in our regions of the earth, to predict them with certainty or even with any high degree of probability. Yet no one doubts that the phenomena depend on laws, and that these must be derivative laws resulting from known ultimate laws, those of heat, electricity, vaporisation, and elastic fluids. Nor can it be doubted that if we were acquainted with all the antecedent circumstances, we could, even from those more general laws, predict (saving difficulties of calculation) the state of the weather at any future time.

Meteorology, therefore, not only has in itself every natural requisite for being, but actually is, a science; though, from the difficulty of observing the facts on which the phenomena depend (a difficulty inherent in the peculiar nature of those phenomena), the science is extremely imperfect; and were it perfect, might probably be of little avail in practice, since the data requisite for applying its principles to particular instances would rarely be procurable.

A case may be conceived of an intermediate character between the perfection of science and this its extreme imperfection. It may happen that the greater causes, those on which the principal part of the phenomena depends, are within the reach of observation and measurement; so that if no other causes intervened, a complete explanation could be given not only of the phenomenon in general, but of all the variations and modifications which it admits of. But inasmuch as other, perhaps many other causes, separately insignificant in their effects, cooperate or conflict in many or in all cases with those greater causes, the effect, accordingly, presents more or less of aberration from what would be produced by the greater causes alone. Now if these minor causes are not so constantly accessible, or not accessible at all to accurate observation, the principal mass of the effect may still, as before, be accounted for, and even predicted; but there will be variations and modifications which we shall not be competent to explain thoroughly, and our predictions will not be fulfilled accurately, but only approximately.

It is thus, for example, with the theory of the tides. No one doubts that Tidology (as Dr Whewell proposes to call it) is really a science. As much of the phenomena as depends on the attraction of the sun and moon is completely understood, and may in any, even unknown, part of the earth's surface be foretold with certainty; and the far greater part of the phenomena depends on those causes. But circumstances of a local or casual nature, such as the configuration of the bottom of the ocean, the degree of confinement from shores, the direction of the wind, etc., influence in many or in all places the height and time of the tide; and a portion of these circumstances being either not accurately knowable, not precisely measurable, or not capable of being certainly foreseen, the tide in known places commonly varies from the calculated result of general principles by some difference that we cannot explain, and in unknown ones may vary from it by a difference that we are not able to foresee or conjecture. Nevertheless, not only is it certain that these variations depend on causes, and follow their causes by laws of unerring uniformity; not only, therefore, is tidology a science, like meteorology, but it is what, hitherto at least, meteorology is not, a science largely available in practice. General laws may be laid down respecting the tides; predictions may be founded on those laws, and the result will in the main, though often not with complete accuracy, correspond to the predictions.

And this is what is or ought to be meant by those who speak of sciences which are not *exact* sciences. Astronomy was once a science, without being an exact science. It could not become exact until not only the general course of the planetary motions, but the perturbations also, were accounted for, and referred to their causes. It has become an exact science, because its phenomena have been brought under laws comprehending the whole of the causes by which the phenomena are influenced, whether in a great or only in a trifling degree, whether in all or only in some cases, and assigning to each of those causes the share of effect which really belongs to it. But in the theory of the tides, the only laws as yet accurately ascertained are those of the causes which affect the phenomenon in all cases, and in a considerable degree; while others which affect it in some cases only, or, if in all, only in a slight degree, have not been sufficiently ascertained and studied to enable us to lay down their laws, still less to deduce the completed law of the phenomenon, by compounding the effects of the greater with those of the minor causes. Tidology, therefore, is not yet an exact science; not from any inherent incapacity of being so, but from the difficulty of ascertaining with complete precision the real derivative uniformities. By combining, however, the exact laws of the greater causes, and of such of the minor ones as are sufficiently known, with such empirical laws or such approximate generalisations respecting the miscellaneous variations as can be obtained by specific observation, we can lay down general propositions which will be true in the main, and on which, with allowance for the degree of their probable inaccuracy, we may safely ground our expectations and our conduct.

The science of human nature is of this description. It falls far short of the standard of exactness now realised in Astronomy; but there is no reason that it should not be as much a science as Tidology is, or as Astronomy was when its calculations had only mastered the main phenomena, but not the perturbations.

The phenomena with which this science is conversant being the thoughts, feelings, and actions of human beings, it would have attained the ideal perfection of a science if it enabled us to foretell how an individual would think, feel, or act throughout life, with the same certainty with which astronomy enables us to predict the places and the occultations of the heavenly bodies. It needs scarcely be stated that nothing approaching to this can be done. The actions of individuals could not be predicted with scientific accuracy, were it only because we cannot foresee the whole of the circumstances in which those individuals will be placed. But further, even in any given combination of (present) circumstances, no assertion, which is both precise and universally true, can be made respecting the manner in which human beings will think, feel, or act. This is not, however, because every person's modes of thinking, feeling, and acting do not depend on causes; nor can we doubt that if, in the case of any individual, our data could be complete, we even now know enough of the ultimate laws by which mental phenomena are determined to enable us in many cases to predict, with tolerable certainty, what, in the greater number of supposable combinations of circumstances, his conduct or sentiments would be. But the impressions and actions of human beings are not solely the result of their present circumstances, but the joint result of those circumstances and of the characters of the individuals; and the agencies which determine human character are so numerous and diversified (nothing which has happened to the person throughout life being without its portion of influence), that in the aggregate they are never in any two cases exactly similar. Hence, even if our science of human nature were theoretically perfect, that is, if we could calculate any character as we can calculate the orbit of any planet, *from given data*; still, as the data are never all given, nor ever precisely alike in different cases, we could neither make positive predictions, nor lay down universal propositions.

Inasmuch, however, as many of those effects which it is of most importance to render amenable to human foresight and control are determined, like the tides, in an incomparably greater degree by general causes, than by all partial causes taken together; depending in the main on those circumstances and qualities which are common to all mankind, or at least to large bodies of them, and only on a small degree on the idiosyncrasies of organisation or the peculiar history of individuals; it is evidently possible, with regard to all such effects, to make predictions which will *almost* always be verified, and general propositions which are almost always true. And whenever it is sufficient to know how the great majority of the human race, or of some nation or class of persons, will think, feel, and act, these propositions are equivalent to universal ones. For the purposes of political and social science this *is* sufficient . . . an approximate generalisation is, in social inquiries, for most practical purposes equivalent to an exact one; that which is only probable when asserted of individual human beings indiscriminately selected, being certain when affirmed of the character and collective conduct of masses.

It is no disparagement, therefore, to the science of Human Nature that those of its general propositions which descend sufficiently into detail to serve as a foundation for predicting phenomena in the concrete are for the most part only approximately true. But in order to give a genuinely scientific character to the study, it is indispensable that these approximate generalisations, which in themselves would amount only to the lowest kind of empirical laws, should be connected deductively with the laws of nature from which they result − should be resolved into the properties of the causes on which the phenomena depend. In other words, the science of Human Nature may be said to exist in proportion as the approximate truths which compose a practical knowledge of mankind can be exhibited as corollaries from the universal laws of human nature on which they rest, whereby the proper limits of those approximate truths would be shown, and we should be enabled to deduce others for any new state of circumstances, in anticipation of specific experience.

6.2   THEORY AND BEHAVIOURAL RESEARCH

DAVID EASTON (1917−   ), *from ch. 1 of* A Framework for Political Analysis, *Englewood Cliffs, N.J., Prentice-Hall, 1965, pp. 6−7, 11−16, abridged*

Easton's account arises from the influential 'behavioralist' position which, originating in the United States, became a strong and self-conscious movement in social science research from the 1950s on, stirring up much consequent controversy. Easton states the position's main aims and assumptions at the outset, and goes on to develop the hope that a common unit of analysis can be found in social theory which could be used rather in the same way as molecules in the natural sciences − as the 'particles out of which all social behavior is formed'. Easton differs from Mill in certain of his emphases and in his references to more recent work in the social sciences, but over all he takes up the same basic empiricist position: 'a commitment to the assumptions and methods of empirical science'.

Most students of politics, even those unwilling to accept classification as behavioralists, would probably agree about the general nature of behavioral assumptions and objectives, although strong differences might arise concerning the precise emphasis to be given to any one of these.

What is the nature of these assumptions and objectives, the intellectual foundation stones on which this movement has been constructed? No single way of characterizing them is satisfactory to everyone, but the following itemized list provides a reasonably accurate and exhaustive account of them.

1. *Regularities.* There are discoverable uniformities in political behavior. These can be expressed in generalizations or theories with explanatory and predictive value.
2. *Verification.* The validity of such generalizations must be testable, in principle, by reference to relevant behavior.
3. *Techniques.* Means for acquiring and interpreting data cannot be taken for granted. They are problematic and need to be examined self-consciously, refined, and validated so that rigorous means can be found for observing, recording, and analyzing behavior.
4. *Quantification.* Precision in the recording of data and the statement of findings requires measurement and quantification, not for their own sake, but only where possible, relevant, and meaningful in the light of other objectives.
5. *Values.* Ethical evaluation and empirical explanation involve two different kinds of propositions that, for the sake of clarity, should be kept analytically distinct. However, a student of political behavior is not prohibited from asserting propositions of either kind separately or in combination as long as he does not mistake one for the other.
6. *Systematization.* Research ought to be systematic, that is, theory and research are to be seen as closely intertwined parts of a coherent and orderly body of knowledge. Research untutored by theory may prove trivial, and theory unsupportable by data, futile.
7. *Pure science.* The application of knowledge is as much a part of the scientific enterprise as theoretical understanding. But the understanding and explanation of political behavior logically precede and provide the basis for efforts to utilize political knowledge in the solution of urgent practical problems of society.
8. *Integration.* Because the social sciences deal with the whole human situation, political research can ignore the findings of other disciplines only at the peril of weakening the validity and undermining the generality of its own results. Recognition of this interrelationship will help to bring political science back to its status

of earlier centuries and return it to the main fold of the social sciences. . . .

To appreciate how far the emergence of a behavioral approach goes beyond a methodological or merely technical reorientation, we have to put recent trends in political research into the context of the whole historical movement of the social sciences. The quickest way of doing this, without becoming enmeshed in the intricacies of their history, is to trace the evolution in names used to identify what we are coming to call the behavioral sciences. These names mirror the essence of the historical transformations relevant to our immediate purposes.

Historically, all social knowledge was originally one and indivisible; the intellectual specialization of labor appears late upon the scholarly scene in the Western world. For almost two thousand years, from the early classical Greek period to sometime in the eighteenth century, men basically saw each other not as specialists but as general seekers after wisdom and knowledge, as philosophers in the original sense of the word. It is true, as early as the Middle Ages, that law, theology, and medicine stood as separate and coordinate fields of learning and teaching in the universities; but philosophy still embraced the bulk of human knowledge about man in society.

With the increasing weight and differential rate and direction of the development of knowledge in the modern historical periods, however, this general corpus gradually began to break up into specialized segments. By the eighteenth century, for example, we can already distinguish what came to be called natural philosophy from moral philosophy, and, as knowledge in both these fields increased remarkably during that century, their names underwent a further subtle modification. Under the heightening prestige of chemistry, physics, and biology, they acquired the names natural and moral sciences. With further elaboration during the nineteenth century, especially under the impetus of Saint-Simon and Auguste Comte, with their sharp focus on human relationships in society, the moral sciences finally became known by the contemporary phrase, social sciences. Of course, ethical inquiry and philosophy persisted throughout all of what is a very complicated evolution of social knowledge. But, from a repository for almost all knowledge, philosophy has been left as a residual category which until today has continued to shrink in scope and, of necessity, to redefine its tasks periodically.

If this light survey of names associated with social knowledge at its various stages does nothing else, it alerts us to the fact that the emergence of a new name today is not unique. It occurs at a particular point in a history that has been under way for thousands of years and will undoubtedly continue. Each transition, from philosophy to natural and moral philosophy, to natural and moral sciences, then to the social sciences, and now to behavioral sciences, signals a stage in a truly linear movement in the nature and assumptions about our understanding of man in society. . . .

The new terminology reflects the fact that two new ingredients have been added to contemporary social research that will help to set it apart from all past eras. In the first place, never before has there been so great a demand for self-conscious attention to empirical theory at all levels of generality – middle range as well as general – that, in principle, can be reduced to testable propositions. In the second place, as part of this, the social sciences have been compelled to face up to the theoretical problem of locating stable units of analysis which might possibly play the role in social research that the particles of matter do in the physical sciences.

In part, this turn toward empirical theory has been related to a hope that has never been completely lost from sight in the whole history of increasing specialization of knowledge and which appeared again in particularly strong form in the 1930s and 1940s. This was the idea that the understanding of man in society would be immeasurably enriched if some way could be found to draw the social sciences together into a basic unity. For a time integration of the social sciences became something of an academic will-o'-the-wisp, and, although it has lost its initial momentum, it has left a vital residue behind.

It turned out that scholars could conceive of integration of the disciplines as occurring at several different levels. At the applied level one could bring the data of the social sciences together for the solution of whole social problems. Unification was to take place on the job, as it were. Housing, employment, peace and the like were not to be seen as sociological, or economic, or political matters exclusively; adequate consideration of these would include the use of knowledge from a whole range of disciplines. Teams of specialists working together for practical purposes might thereby provide one kind of disciplinary integration.

A second kind might emerge through programs of research training. Students would be expected to address themselves not to a discipline but to social problems in the hope that they would learn to bring to bear on them the modes of analysis and data from any area of knowledge and research that seemed relevant and appropriate. The student was supposed to ignore the walls between the disciplines and to consider himself simply a social scientist. In such programs reference to the formal name of a discipline might be strictly taboo.

Related to but nonetheless different from this approach was a third kind in which it was felt that thorough training of a person in two or three disciplines might bring about a limited integration in the mind of a single individual. It would at least encourage such a fusion within the limits of the capacity of a single person to absorb and independently to synthesize a number of social fields. Here training was to be disciplinary in its orientation, but in the outcome two or more disciplines would be integrally joined.

Each of these three levels had something to commend it, each has left its mark on curricula for the training of social scientists, and each has helped to create a new self-image of the social sciences, at least with respect to their intrinsic interconnections. But none of these paths led toward any integral unification of the disciplines; at most, what was proposed was some kind of cross-fertilization or exchange of knowledge. They left the way open to search for a means of genuinely synthesizing the disciplines, and this has come to form a possible fourth level of integration.

The key idea behind this approach has been the conviction that there are certain fundamental units of analysis relating to human behavior out of which generalizations can be formed and that these generalizations may provide a common base on which the specialized sciences of man in society could be built. In place of some mechanical combination of the social sciences, this substituted an underlying basic science of behavior. Although, in reductionist vein, some have argued for psychology as the already existing basic science and others have put in a plea for sociology or anthropology or even political science, the main effort has gone toward the search for an entirely new foundation.

The expectation and hope that it will be possible to develop a common underlying social theory impels research in certain inescapable directions. The most significant of these for our purposes is that it has led to the search for a common unit of analysis that could easily feed into the special subject matters of each of the disciplines. Ideally, the units would be repetitious, ubiquitous and uniform, molecular rather than molar. In this way they would constitute the particles out of which all social behavior is formed and which manifest themselves through different institutions, structures and processes. . . .

Most recently, *systems* have made their appearance as a possible focus, beginning with the smallest cell in the human body as a system and working up through ever more inclusive systems such as the human being as an organism, the human personality, small groups, broader institutions, societies, and collections of societies, such as the international system. The assumption is that behavior in these systems may be governed by analogous if not homologous processes. General systems analysis is perhaps an even more ambitious effort than action theory to draw disciplines into a common framework, for it spreads its net over all of the sciences, physical and biological as well as social, and views them all as behaving systems.

Let us disregard for the moment the particular answers designed to form the bridgework of a general theory. In its broadest sweep adoption of the label 'behavioral sciences' symbolizes the hope that, ultimately, some common variables may be discovered, variables of a kind that will stand at the core of a theory useful for the better understanding of human behavior in all fields. In some vague way there has been added to this the feeling that psychology, sociology, and anthropology are the core sciences out of which such a theory may well arise.

This approach, it is clear, reaffirms a commitment to the assumptions and methods of empirical science, especially for those disciplines such as political science that have hitherto been reluctant to adopt them.

6.3   EXPLANATION IN SCIENCE AND IN HISTORY

CARL G. HEMPEL (1905–   ), *ch. 1 of* Frontiers of Science and Philosophy, *Colodny, Robert G., ed., London, George Allen & Unwin, 1964, pp. 9–33*

Hempel's essay is concerned primarily with the logic of modes of *explanation* in inquiry and compares those in natural science and in history (one form of social inquiry). His interest lies in the two basic kinds of laws which he considers are developed in science: first those based primarily on deduction in which the thing to be explained is subsumed under a general law, often with a causal connection, and second the 'probabilistic-statistical' laws which refer to what *often* happens rather than what *always* happens – a similar point to that made by Mill. These, for Hempel, are the two basic modes of 'nomological explanation' (explanation through laws) in scientific inquiry. At first sight, explanations in historical inquiry may seem different, but, Hempel argues,

they turn out ultimately to fall under one or the other
of the two basic modes of scientific nomological
explanation already discussed — the deductive and
the probabilistic. In this sense 'explanation . . . is
basically the same in all areas of scientific inquiry'.

1. Introduction

Among the divers factors that have encouraged and sustained scientific
inquiry through its long history are two pervasive human concerns
which provide, I think, the basic motivation for all scientific research.
One of these is man's persistent desire to improve his strategic position in
the world by means of dependable methods for predicting and,
whenever possible, controlling the events that occur in it. The extent to
which science has been able to satisfy this urge is reflected impressively
in the vast and steadily widening range of its technological applications.
But besides this practical concern, there is a second basic motivation
for the scientific quest, namely, man's insatiable intellectual curiosity,
his deep concern to *know* the world he lives in, and to *explain*, and
thus to *understand*, the unending flow of phenomena it presents to
him.

In times past questions as to the *what* and the *why* of the empirical
world were often answered by myths; and to some extent, this is so even
in our time. But gradually, the myths are displaced by the concepts,
hypotheses and theories developed in the various branches of empirical
science, including the natural sciences, psychology, and sociological as
well as historical inquiry. What is the general character of the understanding attainable by these means, and what is its potential scope? In
this paper I will try to shed some light on these questions by examining
what seem to me the two basic types of explanation offered by the
natural sciences, and then comparing them with some modes of
explanation and understanding that are found in historical studies.

First, then, a look at explanation in the natural sciences.

2. Two basic types of scientific explanation

2.1 *Deductive-nomological explanation.* In his book, *How We Think,*[1]
John Dewey describes an observation he made one day when, washing
dishes, he took some glass tumblers out of the hot soap suds and put
them upside down on a plate: he noticed that soap bubbles emerged
from under the tumblers' rims, grew for a while, came to a standstill,

and finally receded inside the tumblers. Why did this happen? The explanation Dewey outlines comes to this: in transferring a tumbler to the plate, cool air is caught in it; this air is gradually warmed by the glass, which initially has the temperature of the hot suds. The warming of the air is accompanied by an increase in its pressure, which in turn produces an expansion of the soap film between the plate and the rim. Gradually, the glass cools off, and so does the air inside, with the result that the soap bubbles recede.

This explanatory account may be regarded as an argument to the effect that the event to be explained (let me call it the explanandum-event) was to be expected by reason of certain explanatory facts. These may be divided into two groups: (i) particular facts and (ii) uniformities expressed by general laws. The first group includes facts such as these: the tumblers had been immersed, for some time, in soap suds of a temperature considerably higher than that of the surrounding air; they were put, upside down, on a plate on which a puddle of soapy water had formed, providing a connecting soap film, etc. The second group of items presupposed in the argument includes the gas laws and various other laws that have not been explicitly suggested concerning the exchange of heat between bodies of different temperature, the elastic behavior of soap bubbles, etc. If we imagine these various presuppositions explicitly spelled out, the idea suggests itself of construing the explanation as a deductive argument of this form:

$$(D) \qquad\qquad \begin{array}{c} C_1, C_2, \ldots, C_k \\ L_1, L_2, \ldots, L_r \\ \hline E \end{array}$$

Here, $C_1, C_2, \ldots, C_k$ are statements describing the particular facts invoked; $L_1, L_2, \ldots, L_r$ are general laws: jointly, these statements will be said to form the explanans. The conclusion E is a statement describing the explanandum-event; let me call it the explanandum-statement, and let me use the word 'explanandum' to refer to either E or to the event described by it.

The kind of explanation thus characterized I will call *deductive-nomological explanation*; for it amounts to a deductive subsumption of the explanandum under principles which have the character of general laws: it answers the question '*Why* did the explanandum event occur?' by showing that the event resulted from the particular circumstances specified in $C_1, C_2, \ldots, C_k$ in accordance with the laws $L_1, L_2, \ldots, L_r$. This conception of explanation, as exhibited in schema (D), has therefore been referred to as the covering law model, or as the deductive model, of explanation.[2]

A good many scientific explanations can be regarded as deductive-nomological in character. Consider, for example, the explanation of mirror-images, of rainbows, or of the appearance that a spoon handle is bent at the point where it emerges from a glass of water: in all these cases, the explanandum is deductively subsumed under the laws of reflection and refraction. Similarly, certain aspects of free fall and of planetary motion can be accounted for by deductive subsumption under Galileo's or Kepler's laws.

In the illustrations given so far the explanatory laws had, by and large, the character of empirical generalizations connecting different observable aspects of the phenomena under scrutiny: angle of incidence with angle of reflection or refraction, distance covered with falling time, etc. But science raises the question 'why?' also with respect to the uniformities expressed by such laws, and often answers it in basically the same manner, namely, by subsuming the uniformities under more inclusive laws, and eventually under comprehensive theories. For example, the question, 'Why do Galileo's and Kepler's laws hold?' is answered by showing that these laws are but special consequences of the Newtonian laws of motion and of gravitation; and these, in turn, may be explained by subsumption under the more comprehensive general theory of relativity. Such subsumption under broader laws or theories usually increases both the breadth and the depth of our scientific under-standing. There is an increase in breadth, or scope, because the new explanatory principles cover a broader range of phenomena; for example, Newton's principles govern free fall on the earth and on other celestial bodies, as well as the motions of planets, comets and artificial satellites, the movements of pendulums, tidal changes and various other phenomena. And the increase thus effected in the depth of our understanding is strikingly reflected in the fact that, in the light of more advanced explanatory principles, the original empirical laws are usually seen to hold only approximately, or within certain limits. For example, Newton's theory implies that the factor g in Galileo's law, $s = \frac{1}{2}gt^2$, is not strictly a constant for free fall near the surface of the earth; and that, since every planet undergoes gravitational attraction not only from the sun, but also from the other planets, the planetary orbits are not strictly ellipses, as stated in Kepler's laws.

One further point deserves brief mention here. An explanation of a particular event is often conceived as specifying its *cause*, or causes. Thus, the account outlined in our first illustration might be held to explain the growth and the recession of the soap bubbles by showing that the phenomenon was *caused* by a rise and a subsequent drop of the temperature of the air trapped in the tumblers. Clearly, however, these temperature changes provide the requisite explanation only in conjunction with certain other conditions, such as the presence of a soap film, practically constant pressure of the air surrounding the glasses, etc. Accordingly, in the context of explanation, a cause must be allowed to consist in a more or less complex set of particular circumstances; these might be described by a set of sentences: $C_1, C_2, \ldots, C_k$. And, as suggested by the principle 'Same cause, same effect,' the assertion that those circumstances jointly caused a given event − described, let us say, by a sentence E − implies that whenever and wherever circumstances of the kind in question occur, an event of the kind to be explained comes about. Hence, the given causal explanation implicitly claims that there are general laws − such as $L_1, L_2, \ldots, L_r$ in schema (D) − by virtue of which the occurrence of the causal antecedents mentioned in $C_1, C_2, \ldots, C_k$ is a sufficient condition for the occurrence of the event to be explained. Thus, the relation between causal factors and effect is reflected in schema (D): causal explanation is deductive-nomological in character. (However, the customary formulations of causal and other explanations often do not explicitly specify all the relevant laws and particular facts: to this point, we will return later.)

The converse does not hold: there are deductive-nomological explanations which would not normally be counted as causal. For one thing, the subsumption of laws, such as Galileo's or Kepler's laws, under more comprehensive principles is clearly not causal in character: we speak of causes only in reference to *particular* facts or events, and not in reference to *universal facts* as expressed by general laws. But not even all deductive-nomological explanations of particular facts or events will qualify as causal; for in a causal explanation some of the explanatory circumstances will temporarily precede the effect to be explained: and there are explanations of type (D) which lack this characteristic. For example, the pressure which a gas of specified mass possesses at a given time might be explained by reference to its temperature and its volume at the same time, in conjunction with the gas law which connects simultaneous values of the three parameters.[3]

In conclusion, let me stress once more the important role of laws in deductive-nomological explanation: the laws connect the explanandum event with the particular conditions cited in the explanans, and this is what confers upon the latter the status of explanatory (and, in some cases, causal) factors in regard to the phenomenon to be explained.

2.2 *Probabilistic explanation.* In deductive-nomological explanation as schematized in (D), the laws and theoretical principles involved are of *strictly universal form*: they assert that in *all* cases in which certain specified conditions are realized an occurrence of such and such a kind will result; the law that any metal, when heated under constant pressure, will increase in volume, is a typical example; Galileo's, Kepler's, Newton's, Boyle's and Snell's laws, and many others, are of the same character.

Now let me turn next to a second basic type of scientific explanation. This kind of explanation, too, is nomological, i.e. it accounts for a given phenomenon by reference to general laws or theoretical principles; but some or all of these are of *probabilistic-statistical form*, i.e. they are, generally speaking, assertions to the effect that if certain specified conditions are realized, then an occurrence of such and such a kind will come about with such and such a statistical probability.

For example, the subsiding of a violent attack of hay fever in a given case might well be attributed to, and thus explained by reference to, the administration of 8 milligrams of chlor-trimeton. But if we wish to connect this antecedent event with the explanandum, and thus to establish its explanatory significance for the latter, we cannot invoke a universal law to the effect that the administration of 8 milligrams of that antihistamine will invariably terminate a hay fever attack: this simply is not so. What can be asserted is only a generalization to the effect that administration of the drug will be followed by a relief with high statistical probability, i.e. roughly speaking, with a high relative frequency in the long run. The resulting explanans will thus be of the following type:

> John Doe had a hay fever attack and took 8 milligrams of chlor-trimeton.
> The probability for subsidence of a hay fever attack upon administration of 8 milligrams of chlor-trimeton is high.

Clearly, this explanans does not deductively imply the explanandum, 'John Doe's hay fever attack subsided'; the truth of the explanans makes the truth of the explanandum not certain (as it does in a deductive-nomological explanation) but only more or less likely or, perhaps 'practically' certain.

Reduced to its simplest essentials, a probabilistic explanation thus takes the following form:

$$(P) \quad \left. \frac{Fi \qquad\qquad}{Oi} \; p(O, F) \text{ is very high} \; \right\} \text{ makes very likely}$$

The explanandum, expressed by the statement 'Oi', consists in the fact that in the particular instance under consideration, here called i (e.g. John Doe's allergic attack), an outcome of kind O (subsidence) occurred. This is explained by means of two explanans-statements. The first of these, 'Fi', corresponds to $C_1, C_2, \ldots, C_k$ in (D); it states that in case i, the factors F (which may be more or less complex) were realized. The second expresses a law of probabilistic form, to the effect that the statistical probability for outcome O to occur in cases where F is realized is very high (close to 1). The double line separating explanandum from explanans is to indicate that, in contrast to the case of deductive-nomological explanation, the explanans does not logically imply the explanandum, but only confers a high likelihood upon it. The concept of likelihood here referred to must be clearly distinguished from that of statistical probability, symbolized by 'p' in our schema. A statistical probability is, roughly speaking, the long-run relative frequency with which an occurrence of a given kind (say, F) is accompanied by an 'outcome' of a specified kind (say, O). Our likelihood, on the other hand, is a relation (capable of gradations) not between kinds of occurrences, but between statements. The likelihood referred to in (P) may be characterized as the strength of the inductive support, or the degree of rational credibility, which the explanans confers upon the explanandum; or, in Carnap's terminology, as the *logical*, or *inductive* (in contrast to statistical) *probability* which the explanandum possesses relative to the explanans.

Thus, probabilistic explanation, just like explanation in the manner of schema (D), is nomological in that it presupposes general laws; but because these laws are of statistical rather than of strictly universal form, the resulting explanatory arguments are inductive rather than deductive in character. An inductive argument of this kind *explains* a given phenomenon by showing that, in view of certain particular events and certain statistical laws, its occurrence was to be expected with high logical, or inductive, probability.

By reason of its inductive character, probabilistic explanation differs from its deductive-nomological counterpart in several other important respects; for example, its explanans may confer upon the explanandum a more or less high degree of inductive support; in this sense, probabilistic explanation admits of degrees, whereas deductive-nomological explanation appears as an either-or affair: a given set of universal laws and particular statements either does or does not imply a given explanandum statement. A fuller examination of these differences, however, would lead us far afield and is not required for the purposes of this paper.[4]

One final point: the distinction here suggested between deductive-nomological and probabilistic explanation might be questioned on the ground that, after all, the universal laws invoked in a deductive explanation can have been established only on the basis of a finite body of evidence, which surely affords no exhaustive verification, but only more or less strong probability for it; and that, therefore, all scientific laws have to be regarded as probabilistic. This argument, however, confounds a logical issue with an epistemological one: it fails to distinguish properly between the *claim* made by a given law-statement and the *degree of confirmation*, or *probability*, which it possesses on the available evidence. It is quite true that statements expressing laws of either kind can be only incompletely confirmed by any given finite set – however large – of data about particular facts; but law-statements of the two different types make claims of different kind, which are reflected in their logical forms: roughly, a universal law-statement of the simplest kind asserts that *all* elements of an indefinitely large reference class (e.g. copper objects) have a certain characteristic (e.g. that of being good conductors of electricity); while statistical law-statements assert that in the long run, a specified proportion of the members of the reference class have some specified property. And our distinction of two types of law and, concomitantly, of two types of scientific explanation, is based on this difference in claim as reflected in the difference of form.

The great scientific importance of probabilistic explanation is eloquently attested to by the extensive and highly successful explanatory use that has been made of fundamental laws of statistical form in genetics, statistical mechanics, and quantum theory.

3. Elliptic and partial explanations: explanation sketches

As I mentioned earlier, the conception of deductive-nomological explanation reflected in our schema (D) is often referred to as the covering law model, or the deductive model, of explanation: similarly, the conception underlying schema (P) might be called the probabilistic or the inductive-statistical, model of explanation. The term 'model' can serve as a useful reminder that the two types of explanation as characterized above constitute ideal types or theoretical idealizations and are not intended to reflect the manner in which working scientists actually formulate their explanatory accounts. Rather, they are meant to provide explications, or rational reconstructions, or theoretical models, of certain modes of scientific explanation.

In this respect our models might be compared to the concept of mathematical proof (within a given theory) as construed in meta-mathematics. This concept, too, may be regarded as a theoretical model: it is not intended to provide a descriptive account of how proofs are formulated in the writings of mathematicians: most of these actual formulations fall short of rigorous and, as it were, ideal, meta-mathematical standards. But the theoretical model has certain other functions: it exhibits the rationale of mathematical proofs by revealing the logical connections underlying the successive steps; it provides standards for a critical appraisal of any proposed proof constructed within the mathematical system to which the model refers; and it affords a basis for a precise and far-reaching theory of proof, provability, decidability, and related concepts. I think the two models of explanation can fulfil the same functions, if only on a much more modest scale. For example, the arguments presented in constructing the models give an indication of the sense in which the models exhibit the rationale and the logical structure of the explanations they are intended to represent.

I now want to add a few words concerning the second of the functions just mentioned; but I will have to forgo a discussion of the third.

When a mathematician proves a theorem, he will often omit mention of certain propositions which he presupposes in his argument and which he is in fact entitled to presuppose because, for example, they follow readily from the postulates of his system or from previously established theorems or perhaps from the hypothesis of his theorem, if the latter is in hypothetical form; he then simply assumes that his readers or listeners will be able to supply the missing items if they so desire. If judged by ideal standards, the given formulation of the proof is elliptic or incomplete; but the departure from the ideal is harmless: the gaps can readily be filled in. Similarly, explanations put forward in every-day discourse and also in scientific contexts are often *elliptically formulated*. When we explain, for example, that a lump of butter melted because it was put into a hot frying pan, or that a small rainbow appeared in the spray of the lawn sprinkler because the sunlight was reflected and refracted by the water droplets, we may be said to offer elliptic formulations of deductive-nomological explanations; an account of this kind omits mention of certain laws or particular facts which it tacitly takes for granted, and whose explicit citation would yield a complete deductive-nomological argument.

In addition to elliptic formulation, there is another, quite important, respect in which many explanatory arguments deviate from the theoretical model. It often happens that the statement actually in-cluded in the explanans, together with those which may reasonably be assumed to have been taken for granted in the context at hand, explain the given explanandum only *partially*, in a sense which I will try to indicate by an example. In his *Psychopathology of Everyday Life*, Freud offers the following explanation of a slip of the pen that occurred to him:

> On a sheet of paper containing principally short daily notes of business interest, I found, to my surprise, the incorrect date, 'Thursday, October 20th,' bracketed under the correct date of the month of September. It was not difficult to explain this anticipation as the expression of a wish. A few days before I had returned fresh from my vacation and felt ready for any amount of professional work, but as yet there were few patients. On my arrival I had found a letter from a patient announcing her arrival on the 20th of October. As I wrote the same date in September I may certainly have thought '*X*. ought to be here already; what a pity about that whole month!', and with this thought I pushed the current date a month ahead.[5]

Clearly, the formulation of the intended explanation is *at least incomplete* in the sense considered a moment ago. In particular, it fails to mention any laws or theoretical principles in virtue of which the subconscious wish, and the other antecedent circumstances referred to, could be held to explain Freud's slip of the pen. However, the general theoretical considerations Freud presents here and elsewhere in his writings suggests strongly that his explanatory account relies on a hypothesis to the effect that when a person has a strong, though perhaps unconscious, desire, then if he commits a slip of pen, tongue, memory, or the like, the slip will take a form in which it expresses, and perhaps symbolically fulfils, the given desire.

Even this rather vague hypothesis is probably more definite than what Freud would have been willing to assert. But for the sake of the argument let us accept it and include it in the explanans, together with the particular statements that Freud did have the subconscious wish he mentions, and that he was going to commit a slip of the pen. Even then, the resulting explanans permits us to deduce only that the slip made by Freud would, *in some way or other*, express and perhaps symbolically fulfil Freud's subconscious wish. But clearly, such expression and fulfilment might have been achieved by many other kinds of slip of the pen than the one actually committed.

In other words, the explanans does not imply, and thus fully explain, that the particular slip, say *s*, which Freud committed on this occasion, would fall within the narrow class, say *W*, of acts which consist in writing the words 'Thursday, October 20th'; rather, the explanans implies only that s would fall into a wider class, say F, which includes W as a proper subclass, and which consists of all acts which would express and symbolically fulfil Freud's subconscious wish *in some way or other*.

The argument under consideration might be called a *partial explanation*: it provides complete, or conclusive, grounds for expecting s to be a member of F, and since W is a subclass of F, it thus shows that the explanandum, i.e. s falling within W, accords with, or bears out, what is to be expected in consideration of the explanans. By contrast, a deductive-nomological explanation of the form (D) might then be called *complete* since the explanans here does imply the explanandum.

Clearly, the question whether a given explanatory argument is complete or partial can be significantly raised only if the explanandum sentence is fully specified; only then can we ask whether the explanandum does or does not follow from the explanans. Completeness of explanation, in this sense, is relative to our explanandum sentence. Now, it might seem much more important and interesting to consider instead the notion of a complete explanation of some *concrete event*, such as the destruction of Pompeii, or the death of Adolf Hitler, or the launching of the first artificial satellite: we might want to regard a particular event as completely explained only if an explanatory account of deductive or of inductive form had been provided for all of its aspects. This notion, however, is self-defeating; for any particular event may be regarded as having infinitely many different aspects or characteristics, which cannot all be accounted for by a finite set, however large, of explanatory statements.

In some cases, what is intended as an explanatory account will depart even further from the standards reflected in the model schemata (D) and (P) above. An explanatory account, for example, which is not explicit and specific enough to be reasonably qualified as an elliptically formulated explanation or as a partial one, can often be viewed as an *explanation sketch*: it may suggest, perhaps quite vividly and persuasively, the general outlines of what, it is hoped, can eventually be supplemented so as to yield a more closely reasoned argument based on explanatory hypotheses which are indicated more fully, and which more readily permit of critical appraisal by reference to empirical evidence.

The decision whether a proposed explanatory account is to be qualified as an elliptically formulated deductive or probabilistic explanation, as a partial explanation, as an explanation sketch, or perhaps as none of these is a matter of judicious interpretation; it calls for an appraisal of the intent of the given argument and of the background assumptions that may be assumed to have been tacitly taken for granted, or at least to be available, in the given context. Unequivocal decision rules cannot be set down for this purpose any more than for determining whether a given informally stated inference which is not deductively valid by reasonably strict standards is to count nevertheless as valid but enthymematically formulated, or as fallacious, or as an instance of sound inductive reasoning, or perhaps, for lack of clarity, as none of these.

4. Nomological explanation in history

So far, we have examined nomological explanation, both deductive and inductive, as found in the natural sciences; and we have considered certain characteristic ways in which actual explanatory accounts often depart from the ideal standards of our two basic models. Now it is time to ask what light the preceding inquiries can shed on the explanatory procedures used in historical research.

In examining this question, we will consider a number of specific explanatory arguments offered by a variety of writers. It should be understood from the beginning that we are here concerned, not to appraise the factual adequacy of these explanations, but only to attempt an explication of the claims they make and of the assumptions they presuppose.

Let us note first, then, that some historical explanations are surely nomological in character: they aim to show that the explanandum phenomenon resulted from certain antecedent, and perhaps, con-comitant, conditions; and in arguing these, they rely more or less explicitly on relevant generalizations. These may concern, for example, psychological or sociological tendencies and may best be conceived as broadly probabilistic in character. This point is illustrated by the following argument, which might be called an attempt to explain Parkinson's Law by subsumption under broader psychological principles:

> As the activities of the government are enlarged, more people develop a vested interest in the continuation and expansion of governmental functions. People who have jobs do not like to lose them; those who are habituated to certain skills do not welcome change; those who have become accustomed to the exercise of a certain kind of power do not like to relinquish their control − if anything, they want to develop greater power and correspondingly greater prestige. . . . Thus, government offices and bureaus, once created, in turn institute drives, not only to fortify themselves against assault, but to enlarge the scope of their operations.[6]

The psychological generalizations here explicitly adduced will reasonably have to be understood as expressing, not strict uniformities, but strong *tendencies*, which might be formulated by means of rough probability statements; so that the explanation here suggested is probabilistic in character.

As a rule, however, the generalizations underlying a proposed historical explanation are largely left unspecified; and most concrete explanatory accounts have to be qualified as partial explanations or as explanation sketches. Consider, for example, F. J. Turner's essay 'The significance of the frontier in American history',[7] which amplifies and defends the view that

> Up to our own day American history has been in a large degree the history of the colonization of the Great West. The existence of an area of free land, its continuous recession, and the advance of American settlement westward explain American development. . . . The peculiarity of American institutions is the fact that they have been compelled to adapt themselves . . . to the changes involved in crossing a continent, in winning a wilderness, and in developing at each area of this progress, out of the primitive economic and political conditions of the frontier, the complexity of city life.[8]

One of the phenomena Turner considers in developing his thesis is the rapid westward advance of what he calls the Indian trader's frontier. 'Why was it', Turner asks, 'that the Indian trader passed so rapidly across the continent?'; and he answers,

> The explanation of the rapidity of this advance is bound up with the effects of the trader on the Indian. The trading post left the unarmed tribes at the mercy of those that had purchased firearms − a truth which the Iroquois Indians wrote in blood, and so the remote and unvisited tribes gave eager welcome to the trader. . . . This accounts for the trader's power and the rapidity of his advance.[9]

There is no explicit mention here of any laws, but it is clear that this sketch of an explanation presupposes, first of all, various particular facts, such as that the remote and unvisited tribes had heard of the efficacy and availability of firearms, and that there were no culture patterns or institutions precluding their use by those tribes; but in addition, the account clearly rests also on certain assumptions as to how human beings will tend to behave in situations presenting the kinds of danger and of opportunity that Turner refers to.

Similar comments apply to Turner's account of the westward advance of what he calls the farmer's frontier:

Omitting those of the pioneer farmers who move from the love of adventure, the advance of the more steady farmer is easy to understand. Obviously the immigrant was attracted by the cheap lands of the frontier, and even the native farmer felt their influence strongly. Year by year the farmers who lived on soil, whose returns were diminished by unrotated crops, were offered the virgin soil of the frontier at nominal prices. Their growing families demanded more lands, and these were dear. The competition of the unexhausted, cheap, and easily tilled prairie lands compelled the farmer either to go West . . . or to adopt intensive culture.[10]

This passage is clearly intended to do more than describe a sequence of particular events: it is meant to afford an understanding of the farmers' westward advance by pointing to their interests and needs and by calling attention to the facts and the opportunities facing them. Again, this explanation takes it for granted that under such conditions normal human beings will tend to seize new opportunities in the manner in which the pioneer farmers did.

Examining the various consequences of this moving-frontier history, Turner states that 'the most important effect of the frontier has been in the promotion of democracy here and in Europe',[11] and he begins his elaboration of this theme with the remark that 'the frontier is productive of individualism. . . . The tendency is anti-social. It produces antipathy to control, and particularly to any direct control':[12] and this is, of course, a sociological generalization in a nut-shell.

Similarly, any explanation that accounts for a historical phenomenon by reference to economic factors or by means of general principles of social or cultural change are nomological in import, even if not in explicit formulation.

But if this be granted there still remains another question, to which we must now turn, namely, whether, in addition to explanations of a broadly nomological character, the historian also employs certain other distinctly historical ways of explaining and understanding whose import cannot be adequately characterized by means of our two models. The question has often been answered in the affirmative, and several kinds of historical explanation have been adduced in support of this affirmation. I will now consider what seem to me two especially interesting candidates for the role of specifically historical explanation; namely first, genetic explanation, and secondly, explanation of an action in terms of its underlying rationale.

5. Genetic explanation in history

In order to make the occurrence of a historical phenomenon intelligible, a historian will frequently offer a 'genetic explanation' aimed at exhibiting the principal stages in a sequence of events which led up to the given phenomenon.

Consider, for example, the practice of selling indulgences as it existed in Luther's time. H. Boehmer, in his work, *Luther and the Reformation*, points out that until about the end of the 19th century, 'the indulgence was in fact still a great unknown quantity, at sight of which the scholar would ask himself with a sigh: "Where did it come from?"'[13] An answer was provided by Adolf Gottlob,[14] who tackled the problem by asking himself what led the Popes and Bishops to offer indulgences. As a result,

> origin and development of the unknown quantity appeared clearly in the light, and doubts as to its original meaning came to an end. It revealed itself as a true descendant of the time of the great struggle between Christianity and Islam, and at the same time a highly characteristic product of Germanic Christianity.[15]

In brief outline,[16] the origins of the indulgence appear to go back to the 9th century, when the Popes were strongly concerned with the fight against Islam. The Mohammedan fighter was assured by the teachings of his religion that if he were to be killed in battle his soul would immediately go to heaven; but the defender of the Christian faith had to fear that he might still be lost if he had not done the regular penance for his sins. To allay these doubts, John VII, in 877, promised absolution for their sins to crusaders who should be killed in battle.

> Once the crusade was so highly thought of, it was an easy transition to regard participation in a crusade as equivalent to the performance of atonement . . . and to promise remission of these penances in return for expeditions against the Church's enemies.[17]

Thus, there was introduced the indulgence of the Cross, which granted complete remission of the penitential punishment to all those who participated in a religious war. 'If it is remembered what inconveniences, what ecclesiastical and civil disadvantages the ecclesiastical penances entailed, it is easy to understand that the penitents flocked to obtain this indulgence.'[18] A further strong incentive came from the belief that whoever obtained an indulgence secured liberation not only from the ecclesiastical penances, but also from the corresponding suffering in purgatory after death. The benefits of these indulgences were next extended to those who, being physically unfit to participate in a religious war, contributed the funds required to send a soldier on a crusade: in 1199, Pope Innocent III recognized the payment of money as adequate qualification for the benefits of a crusading indulgence.

When the crusades were on the decline, new ways were explored of raising funds through indulgences. Thus, there was instituted a 'jubilee indulgence', to be celebrated every hundred years, for the benefit of pilgrims coming to Rome on that occasion. The first of these indulgences, in 1300, brought in huge sums of money; and the time interval between successive jubilee indulgences was therefore reduced to 50, 33 and even 25 years. And from 1393 on the jubilee indulgence was made available, not only in Rome, for the benefit of pilgrims, but everywhere in Europe, through special agents who were empowered to absolve the penitent of their sins upon payment of an appropriate amount. The development went even further: in 1477, a dogmatic declaration by Sixtus IV attributed to the indulgence the power of delivering even the dead from purgatory.

Undeniably, a genetic account of this kind can enhance our understanding of a historical phenomenon. But its explanatory role, far from being *sui generis*, seems to me basically nomological in character. For the successive stages singled out for consideration surely must be qualified for their function by more than the fact that they form a temporal sequence and that they all precede the final stage, which is to be explained: the mere enumeration in a yearbook of 'the year's important events' in the order of their occurrence clearly is not a genetic explanation of the final event or of anything else. In a genetic explanation each stage must be shown to 'lead to' the next, and thus to be linked to its successor by virtue of some general principle which makes the occurrence of the latter at least reasonably probable, given the former. But in this sense, even successive stages in a physical phenomenon such as the free fall of a stone may be regarded as forming a genetic sequence whose different stages — characterized, let us say, by the position and the velocity of the stone at different times — are interconnected by strictly universal laws; and the successive stages in the movement of a steel ball bouncing its zigzaggy way down a Galton pegboard may be regarded as forming a genetic sequence with probabilistic connections.

The genetic accounts given by historians are not, of course, of the purely nomological kind suggested by these examples from physics. Rather, they combine a certain measure of nomological interconnecting with more or less large amounts of straight description. For consider an intermediate stage mentioned in a genetic account: some aspects of it will be presented as having evolved from the preceding stages (in virtue of connecting laws, which often will be no more than hinted at); while other aspects, which are not accounted for by information about the preceding development, will be descriptively added because they are relevant to an understanding of subsequent stages in the genetic sequence. Thus, schematically speaking, a genetic explanation will begin with a pure description of an initial stage; thence, it will proceed to an account of a second stage, part of which is nomologically linked to, and explained by, the characteristic features of the initial stage; while the balance is simply described as relevant for a nomological account of some aspects of the third stage; and so forth.[19]

In our illustration the connecting laws are hinted at in the mention made of motivating factors: the explanatory claims made for the interest of the popes in securing a fighting force and in amassing ever larger funds clearly presuppose suitable psychological generalizations as to the manner in which an intelligent individual will act, in the light of his factual beliefs, when he seeks to attain a certain objective. Similarly, general assumptions underly the reference to the fear of purgatory in explaining the eagerness with which indulgences were bought. And when, referring to the huge financial returns of the first jubilee indulgence, Schwiebert says 'This success only whetted the insatiable appetite of the popes. The intervening period of time was variously reduced from 100 to 50, to 33, to 25 years . . .',[20] the explanatory force here implied might be said to rest on some principle of reinforcement by rewards. As need hardly be added, even if such a principle were explicitly introduced, the resulting account would provide at most a partial explanation; it could not be expected to show, for example, why the intervening intervals should have the particular lengths here mentioned.

In the genetic account of the indulgences, those factors which are simply described (or tacitly presupposed) rather than explained include, for example, the doctrines, the organization, and the power of the Church; the occurrence of the crusades and their eventual decline; and innumerable other factors which are not even explicitly mentioned, but which have to be understood as background conditions if the genetic survey is to serve its explanatory purpose.

The general conception here outlined of the logic of genetic explanation could also be illustrated by reference to Turner's studies of the American frontier; this will be clear even from the brief remarks made earlier on Turner's ideas.

Some analysts of historical development put special emphasis on the importance of the laws underlying a historical explanation; thus, e.g., A. Gerschenkron maintains,

Historical research consists essentially in application to empirical material of various sets of empirically derived hypothetical generalizations and in testing the closeness of the resulting fit, in the hope that in this way certain uniformities, certain typical situations, and certain typical relationships among individual factors in these situations can be ascertained,[21]

and his subsequent substantive observations include a brief genetic survey of patterns of industrial development in 19th century Europe, in which some of the presumably relevant uniformities are made reasonably explicit.

6. Explanation by motivating reasons

Let us now turn to another kind of historical explanation that is often considered as *sui generis*, namely, the explanation of an action in terms of the underlying *rationale*, which will include, in particular, the ends the agent sought to attain, and the alternative courses of action he believed to be open to him. The following passage explaining the transition from the indulgence of the Cross to the institution of the jubilee indulgence illustrates this procedure:

> in the course of the thirteenth century the idea of a crusade more and more lost its power over men's spirits. If the Popes would keep open the important source of income which the indulgence represented, they must invent new motives to attract people to the purchase of indulgences. It is the merit of Boniface VIII to have recognized this clearly. By creating the jubilee indulgence in 1300 he assured the species a further long development most welcome to the Papal finances.[22]

This passage clearly seeks to explain the establishment of the first jubilee indulgence by suggesting the reasons for which Boniface VIII took this step. If properly spelled out, these reasons would include not only Boniface's objective of ensuring a continuation of the income so far derived from the indulgence of the Cross, but also his estimate of the relevant empirical circumstances, including the different courses of action open to him, and their probable efficacy as well as potential difficulties in pursuing them and adverse consequences to which they might lead.

The kind of explanation achieved by specifying the rationale underlying a given action is widely held to be fundamentally different from nomological explanation as found in the natural sciences. Various reasons have been adduced in support of this view; but I will limit my discussion largely to the stimulating ideas on the subjects that have been set forth by Dray.[23] According to Dray, there is an important type of historical explanation whose features 'make the covering law model peculiarly inept'; he calls it 'rational explanation', i.e. 'explanation which displays the *rationale* of what was done', or, more fully, 'a reconstruction of the agent's *calculation* of means to be adopted toward his chosen end in the light of the circumstances in which he found himself'. The object of rational explanation is not to subsume the explanandum under general laws, but 'to show that what was done was the thing to have done for the reasons given, rather than merely the thing that is done on such occasions, perhaps in accordance with certain laws'. Hence, a rational explanation has 'an element of *appraisal*' in it: it 'must exhibit what was done as appropriate or justified'. Accordingly, Dray conceives a rational explanation as being based on a standard of appropriateness or of rationality of a special kind which he calls a '*principle of action*', i.e. ' a judgment of the form "When in a situation of type $C_1, C_2, \ldots C_n$ the thing to do is X" '.

Dray does not give a full account of the kind of 'situation' here referred to; but to do justice to his intentions, these situations must evidently be taken to include, at least, items of the following three types: (i) the end the agent was seeking to attain; (ii) the empirical circumstances, as seen by the agent, in which he had to act; (iii) the moral standards or principles of conduct to which the agent was committed. For while this brief list requires considerable further scrutiny and elaboration, it seems clear that only if at least these items are specified does it make sense to raise the question of the appropriateness of what the agent did in the given 'situation'.

It seems fair to say, then, that according to Dray's conception a rational explanation answers a question of the form 'Why did agent A do X?' by offering an explanans of the following type (our formulation replaces the notation '$C_1, C_2, \ldots C_n$' by the simpler 'C', without, of course, precluding that the kind of situation thus referred to may be extremely complex):

(R) A was in a situation of type C
        In a situation of type C, the appropriate thing to do is X

But can an explanans of this type possibly serve to explain A's having in fact done X? It seems to me beyond dispute that in any adequate explanation of an empirical phenomenon the explanans must provide good grounds for believing or asserting that the explanandum phenomenon did in fact occur. Yet this requirement, which is necessary though not sufficient [24] for an adequate explanation, is not met by a rational explanation as conceived by Dray. For the two statements included in the contemplated explanans (R) provide good reasons for believing that the appropriate thing for A to do was X, but not for believing that A did in fact do X. Thus, a rational explanation in the sense in which Dray appears to understand it does not explain what it is meant to explain. Indeed, the expression 'the thing to do' in the standard formulation of a principle of action, 'functions as a value term', as Dray himself points out: but then, it is unclear, on purely logical grounds, how the valuational principle expressed by the second sentence in (R), in conjunction with the plainly empirical, non-valuational first sentence, should permit any inferences concerning empirical matters such as A's action, which could not be drawn from the first sentence alone.

To explain, in the general vein here under discussion, why A did in fact do X, we have to refer to the underlying rationale not by means of a normative principle of action, but by descriptive statements to the effect that, at the time in question A was a rational agent, or had the disposition to act rationally; and that a rational agent, when in circumstances of kind C, will always (or: with high probability) do X. Thus construed, the explanans takes on the following form:

(R')   (a) A was in a situation of type C
       (b) A was disposed to act rationally
       (c) Any person who is disposed to act rationally will, when in a situation of type C, invariably (with high probability) do X

But by this explanans A's having done X is accounted for in the manner of a deductive or of a probabilistic nomological explanation. Thus, in so far as reference to the rationale of an agent does explain his action, the explanation conforms to one of our nomological models.

An analogous diagnosis applies, incidentally, also to explanations which attribute an agent's behavior in a given situation not to rationality and more or less explicit deliberation on his part, but to other dispositional features, such as his character and emotional make-up. The following comment on Luther illustrates this point:

Even stranger to him than the sense of anxiety was the allied sense of fear. In 1527 and 1535, when the plague broke out in Wittenberg, he was the only professor besides Bugenhagen who remained calmly at his post to comfort and care for the sick and dying. . . . He had, indeed, so little sense as to take victims of the plague into his house and touch them with his own hand. Death, martyrdom, dishonor, contempt . . . he feared just as little as infectious disease.[25]

It may well be said that these observations give more than a description: that they shed some explanatory light on the particular occurrences mentioned. But in so far as they explain, they do so by presenting Luther's actions as manifestations of certain personality traits, such as fearlessness; thus, the particular acts are again subsumed under generalizations as to how a fearless person is likely to behave under certain circumstances.

It might seem that both in this case and in rational explanation as construed in (R'), the statements which we took to express general laws − namely, (c) in (R'), and the statement about the probable behavior of a fearless person in our last illustration − do not have the character of empirical laws at all, but rather that of analytic statements which simply express part of what is *meant* by a rational agent, a fearless person, or the like. Thus, in contrast to nomological explanations, these accounts in terms of certain dispositional characteristics of the agent appear to presuppose no general laws at all. Now, the idea of analyticity gives rise to considerable philosophical difficulties; but let us disregard these here and take the division of statements into analytic and synthetic to be reasonably clear. Even then, the objection just outlined cannot be upheld. For dispositional concepts of the kind invoked in our explanations have to be regarded as governed by entire clusters of general statements − we might call them symptom statements − which connect the given disposition with various specific manifestations, or symptoms, of its presence (each symptom will be a particular mode of 'responding', or acting, under specified 'stimulus' conditions); and the whole cluster of these symptom statements for a given disposition will have implications which are plainly not analytic (in the intuitive sense here assumed). Under these circumstances it would be arbitrary to attribute to some of the symptom statements the analytic character of partial definitions.

The logic of this situation has a precise representation in Carnap's theory of reduction sentences.[26] Here, the connections between a given disposition and its various manifest symptoms are assumed to be expressed by a set of so-called reduction sentences (these are characterized by their logical form). Some of these state, in terms of manifest characteristics, sufficient conditions for the presence of the given disposition; others similarly state necessary conditions. The reduction sentences for a given dispositional concept cannot, as a rule, all be qualified as analytic; for jointly they imply certain non-analytic consequences which have the status of general laws connecting exclusively the manifest characteristics; the strongest of the laws so implied is the so-called representative sentence, which 'represents, so to speak, the factual content of the set' of all the reduction sentences for the given disposition concept. This representative sentence asserts, in effect, that whenever at least one of the sufficient conditions specified by the given reduction sentences is satisfied, then so are all the necessary conditions laid down by the reduction sentences. And when A is one of the manifest criteria sufficient for the presence of a given disposition, and B is a necessary one, then the statement that whenever A is present so is B will normally turn out to be synthetic.

So far then, I have argued that Dray's construal of explanation by motivating reasons is untenable; that the normative principles of action envisaged by him have to be replaced by statements of a dispositional kind; and that, when this is done, explanations in terms of a motivating rationale, as well as those referring to other psychological factors, are seen to be basically nomological.

Let me add a few further remarks on the idea of rational explanation. First: in many cases of so-called purposive action, there is no conscious deliberation, no rational calculation that leads the agent to his decision. Dray is quite aware of this; but he holds that a rational explanation in his sense is still possible; for

> in so far as we say an action is purposive at all, no matter at what level of conscious deliberation, there is a calculation which could be constructed for it: the one the agent would have gone through if he had had time, if he had not seen what to do in a flash, if he had been called upon to account for what he did after the event, etc. And it is by eliciting some such calculation that we explain the action.[27]

But the explanatory significance of reasons or 'calculations' which are 'reconstructed' in this manner is certainly puzzling. If, to take Dray's example, an agent arrives at his decision 'in a flash' rather than by deliberation, then it would seem to be simply false to say that the decision can be accounted for by some argument which the agent might have gone through under more propitious circumstances, or which he might produce later if called upon to account for his action; for, by hypothesis, no such argument was in fact gone through by the agent at the crucial time; considerations of appropriateness or rationality played no part in shaping his decision; the rationale that Dray assumes to be adduced and appraised in the corresponding rational explanation is simply fictitious.

But, in fairness to Dray, these remarks call for a qualifying observation: in at least some of the cases Dray has in mind it might not be fictitious to ascribe the action under study to a disposition which the agent acquired through a learning process whose initial stages did involve conscious ratiocination. Consider, for example, the various complex maneuvers of accelerating, braking, signalling, dodging jaywalkers and animals, swerving into and out of traffic lanes, estimating the changes of traffic lights, etc., which are involved in driving a car through city traffic. A beginning driver will often perform these only upon some sort of conscious deliberation or even calculation; but gradually, he learns to do the appropriate thing automatically, 'in a flash', without giving them any conscious thought. The habit pattern he has thus acquired may be viewed as consisting in a set of dispositions to react in certain appropriate ways in various situations; and a particular performance of such an appropriate action would then be explained, not by a 'constructed' calculation which actually the agent did not perform but by reference to the disposition just mentioned and thus, again, in a nomological fashion.

The method of explaining a given action by 'constructing', in Dray's sense, the agent's calculation of means faces yet another, though less fundamental, difficulty: it will frequently yield a rationalization rather than an explanation, especially when the reconstruction relies on the reasons the agent might produce when called upon to account for his action. As G. Watson remarks,

> Motivation, as presented in the perspective of history, is often too simple and straightforward, reflecting the psychology of the Age of Reason. . . . Psychology has come . . . to recognize the enormous weight of irrational and intimately personal impulses in conduct. In history, biography, and in autobiography, especially of public characters, the tendency is strong to present 'good' reasons instead of 'real' reasons.[28]

Accordingly, as Watson goes on to point out, it is important, in examining the motivation of historical figures, to take into account the significance of such psychological mechanisms as reaction formation, 'the dialectic dynamic by which stinginess cloaks itself in generosity, or rabid pacifism arises from the attempt to repress strong aggressive impulses'.[29]

These remarks have a bearing also on an idea set forth by P. Gardiner in his illuminating book on historical explanation.[30] Commenting on the notion of the 'real reason' for a man's action, Gardiner says: 'In general, it appears safe to say that by a man's "real reasons" we mean those reasons he would be prepared to give under circumstances where his confession would not entail adverse consequences to himself.' And he adds 'An exception to this is the psychoanalyst's usage of the expression where different criteria are adopted.'[31] This observation might be taken to imply that the explanation of human actions in terms of underlying motives is properly aimed at exhibiting the agent's 'real reasons' in the ordinary sense of the phrase, as just described; and that, by implication, reasons in the psychoanalyst's sense require less or no consideration. But such a construal of explanation would give undue importance to considerations of ordinary language. Gardiner is entirely right when he reminds us that the 'language in which history is written is for the most part the language of ordinary speech'[32]; but the historian in search of reasons that will correctly explain human actions will obviously have to give up his reliance on the everyday conception of 'real reasons' if psychological or other investigations show that real reasons, thus understood, do not yield as adequate an account of human actions as an analysis in terms of less familiar conceptions such as, perhaps, the idea of motivating factors which are kept out of the agent's normal awareness by processes of repression and reaction formation.

I would say, then, first of all, that historical explanation cannot be bound by conceptions that might be implicit in the way in which ordinary language deals with motivating reasons. But secondly, I would doubt that Gardiner's expressly tentative characterization does justice even to what we ordinarily mean when we speak of a man's 'real reasons'. For considerations of the kind that support the idea of sub-conscious motives are quite familiar in our time, and we are therefore prepared to say in ordinary, non-technical discourse that the reasons given by an agent may not be the 'real reasons' behind his action, even if his statement was subjectively honest, and he had no grounds to expect that it would lead to any adverse consequences for him. For no matter whether an explanation of human actions is attempted in the language of ordinary speech or in the technical terms of some theory, the over-riding criterion for what-if-anything should count as a 'real', and thus explanatory, reason for a given action is surely not to be found by examining the way in which the term 'real reason' has thus far been used, but by investigating what conception of real reason would yield the most satisfactory explanation of human conduct; and ordinary usage gradually changes accordingly.

7. Concluding remarks

We have surveyed some of the most prominent candidates for the role of characteristically historical mode of explanation; and we have found that they conform essentially to one or the other of our two basic types of scientific explanation.

This result and the arguments that led to it do not in any way imply a mechanistic view of man, of society, and of historical processes; nor, of course, do they deny the importance of ideas and ideals for human decision and action. What the preceding considerations do suggest is, rather, that the nature of understanding, in the sense in which explanation is meant to give us an understanding of empirical phenomena, is basically the same in all areas of scientific inquiry; and that the deductive and the probabilistic model of nomological explanation accommodate vastly more than just the explanatory arguments of, say, classical mechanics: in particular, they accord well also with the character of explanations that deal with the influence of rational deliberation, of conscious and subconscious motives, and of ideas and ideals on the shaping of historical events. In so doing, our schemata exhibit, I think, one important aspect of the methodological unity of all empirical science.

Notes

1. See Dewey, John (1910) *How We Think*, Boston, ch. 6.
2. For a fuller presentation of the model and for further references, see, for example, Hempel, C. G. and Oppenheim, P. (1948) 'Studies in the logic of explanation', *Philosophy of Science*, 15, 135–75; sections 1–7 of this article, which contain all the fundamentals of the presentation, are reprinted in Feigl, H. and Brodbeck, M. eds (1953) *Readings in the Philosophy of Science*, New York, 1953. The suggestive term 'covering law model' is W. Dray's; cf. Dray, W. (1957) *Laws and Explanation in History*, Oxford, ch. 1. Dray characterizes this type of explanation as 'subsuming what is to be explained under a general law' (op. cit., p. 1), and then rightly urges, in the name of methodological realism, that 'the requirement of a *single* law be dropped' (op. cit., p. 24; original italics): it should be noted, however, that, as in schema (*D*) above, several earlier publications on the subject (among them Hempel and Oppenheim, op. cit.) make explicit provision for the inclusion of more laws than one in the explanans.
3. The relevance of the covering law model to causal explanation is examined more fully in section 4 of Hempel, C. G. (1962) 'Deductive-nomological *vs.* statistical explanation', in Feigl, H., et al., eds, *Minnesota Studies in the Philosophy of Science*, vol. 3, Minneapolis.
4. The concept of probabilistic explanation, and some of the peculiar logical and methodological problems engendered by it, are examined in some detail in Hempel, op. cit., part 2.
5. Freud, S. (1951) *Psychopathology of Everyday Life*, Brill, A. A., trans., New York, p. 64.
6. McConnell, D. W., et al. (1939) *Economic Behavior*, New York, pp. 894–5.
7. First published in 1893, and reprinted in several publications, among them: Edwards, Everett E., ed. (1938) *The Early Writings of Frederick Jackson Turner*, Madison, Wisconsin.
8. In Edwards, op. cit., pp. 185–6.
9. ibid., pp. 200–1.
10. ibid., p. 210.
11. ibid., p. 219.

12. ibid., p. 220.
13. Boehmer, H. (1930) *Luther and the Reformation*, Potter, E. S. G., trans., London, p. 91.
14. Gottlob's study, *Kreuzablass und Almosenablass*, was published in 1906; cf. the references to the work of Gottlob and other investigators in Schwiebert, E. G. (1950) *Luther and His Times*, St Louis, notes to ch. 10.
15. Boehmer, op. cit., p. 91.
16. This outline follows the accounts given by Boehmer, op. cit., ch. 3 and by Schwiebert, op. cit., ch. 10.
17. Boehmer, op. cit., p. 92.
18. ibid., p. 93.
19. The logic of genetic explanations in history is examined in some detail in Nagel, E. (1961) *The Structure of Science*, New York, pp. 564–8. The conception outlined in the present paper, though arrived at without any knowledge of Nagel's work on this subject, accords well with the latter's results.
20. Schwiebert, op. cit., p. 304.
21. Gerschenkron, A. (1952) 'Economic backwardness in historical perspective', in Hoselitz, B. F., ed., *The Progress of Underdeveloped Areas*, Chicago, pp. 3–29.
22. Boehmer, op. cit., pp. 93–4.
23. op. cit., ch. 5, original emphasis throughout.
24. Empirical evidence supporting a given hypothesis may afford strong grounds for believing the latter without providing an explanation for it.
25. Boehmer, op. cit., p. 234.
26. See especially the classical essay: Carnap, R. (1936–7) 'Testability and meaning', *Philosophy of Science*, 3, 419–71 and 4, 1–40; reprinted, with some omissions, in Feigl and Brodbeck, op. cit. On the point here under discussion, see sec. 9 and particularly sec. 10 of the original essay or sec. 7 of the reprinted version.
27. Dray, op. cit., p. 123.
28. Watson, G. (1940) 'Clio and Psyche: some interrelations of psychology and history', in Ware, C. F., ed., *The Cultural Approach to History*, New York, pp. 34–47, p. 36.
29. ibid.
30. Gardiner, P. (1952) *The Nature of Historical Explanation*, Oxford.
31. ibid., p. 136.
32. ibid., p. 63.

6.4 MINDS AND SOCIAL SCIENCE

MICHAEL LESSNOFF (1940–   ), *from* The Structure of Social Science, *London, George Allen & Unwin, 1974, ch. 2, pp. 32–41, 43–4, 47, abridged*

Lessnoff takes issue with the broadly empiricist assumptions of the previous analyses. In this extract he in a sense begins further back by concentrating not on modes of explanation or the nature of scientific inquiry as such, but on the *subject matter* of social

science and of how to identify and classify this in
embarking on a social inquiry. He points to the
mental phenomena in any social inquiry – thinking,
purposive action, meaning – and argues that this
provides an essential difference from the non-
conscious phenomena concentrated on in the natural
sciences (especially physics). In taking up this view
Lessnoff allies himself with one strongly established
tradition in the social sciences, with those who, like
Max Weber, emphasize the *subjective meaning* of
human action as central to social inquiry. His
terminology – and that of others who take up this
basic position – not surprisingly tends to differ from
that in the empiricist tradition: he writes not about
human 'nature' or 'behaviour', with their implications respectively of permanence and of externally
measurable and observable manifestations, nor
about laws and deductive systems, but of social
'action', with its connotation of purposive and
meaningful human activity.

The success of the physical sciences, especially physics itself, gives rise to
dispute over whether they provide a good model for social science to
follow. There seem to be reasons to think so. All sciences, it can
plausibly be held, have, almost by definition, basically the same task –
to describe and explain phenomena as economically as the facts will
allow; hence the model of physics is the model for scientific success in
general. On the other hand, physics, unlike the social sciences, does not
deal with *people* as such. People of course do have a physical aspect,
and considered simply as bodies are as subject to physical laws as any
other; but people considered as people behave in ways that cannot (at
present, anyway) be derived from these laws. And because the
behaviour of people (considered as people) provides the subject-matter
of the social sciences, the model of physics is, I believe, inappropriate
for them, in several (not all) respects. For people have not only physical
bodies, but also (at least according to common belief) conscious *minds*.
Whether and in what sense this is true, and whether if true it affects the
applicability of the model of physics – differences over these issues are
at the root of many controversies in the philosophy of social science.

For social science to exist at all, the first prerequisite is to *identify* its
subject-matter, the social. Further basic tasks of social science are to

classify social phenomena into various kinds, and to *explain* why social phenomena are what they are. I shall argue that all three of these tasks require an approach different from that suggested by the model of physics. In this chapter I shall deal with the first two, leaving explanation till later.

The idea of the social has to do with the fact that human beings relate to one another. These relations manifest themselves in the interdependence of their actions; that a social phenomenon exists implies some pattern of interdependent actions. It follows, then, that identification of the social depends on a prior identification of human action. What does this imply?

Sociological empiricism

Many who would accept the above brief characterization of the social would hold that the identification and classification of social phenomena should proceed by the same methods of empirical observation that are appropriately used in the physical sciences to identify and classify physical things. Physical scientists take note of such observable features of things as shape, size, position, colour, pitch, loudness, etc. — characteristics perceptible to the senses; social scientists, on this view (which we can label 'sociological empiricism'), should do the same. But if social science is concerned with people, the empiricist view must somehow deal with the phenomena of the human mind — that is, with people's beliefs, desires, purposes, intentions, moral principles, values, etc. — for these appear to be closely connected with their actions (and interactions), but to lack the sorts of characteristics that empiricists consider the only ones science can take note of. Broadly there are two positions open to empiricists here (some seem to hold both, though they are incompatible). Either they may accept that mental phenomena are not empirically observable, and draw the conclusion that social science must completely ignore them, building up its own forms of description and classification on a genuinely scientific (i.e. empirical) basis; or else they may hold that an empiricist social science *can* study mental phenomena, because they *correspond* to overt phenomena (of behaviour) which are open to empirical observation. On the latter view, mental phenomena can be observed, to all intents and purposes, by observing the corresponding overt behaviour; but the typically mental terms normally used to describe them are in principle dispensable because replaceable by terms referring to the corresponding behaviour. Many adherents of both empiricist positions put great stress on the observation of overt behaviour, and can appropriately be called 'behaviourists'.

It is not hard to understand the popularity of such views. The notion of a mind which is not available for inspection by the empirical methods of the physical sciences seems to savour of the occult. If it cannot be so inspected, what can one say about it? Or rather, what can one *not* say about it? What objective check can there be on the validity of accounts of such minds? And if there can be none, how can such accounts be called scientific? It may be that valid knowledge of an empirically unobservable mind is in principle always available to one person − the person whose mind it is; that one knows directly what one's own desires, intentions, beliefs and principles are, even if others have no direct access to them. But this, even if true, would not solve the problem. Science deals with 'public knowledge'.[1] In science the authority of a single individual cannot be accepted; any assertion must be open to checking by all members of the relevant scientific community. In any case, testimony as to the contents of particular minds from the owners of these minds is often unavailable to social scientists.

Such considerations as these, reinforced by an emotional predilection for the unity of scientific method, have led to a strong current of empiricism among social scientists, especially those who have been self-consciously concerned with the scientific status of their discipline. Thus for Auguste Comte, the originator of the idea of a science of sociology, since science is based on observations of the external world, it can treat individual minds only as physiology or as overt behaviour.[2] The celebrated anthropologist Malinowski endorsed the behaviourist position: for him, 'thoughts', 'beliefs', 'ideas' and 'values' can be introduced into social science only if 'fully defined in terms of overt, observable, physically ascertainable behaviour'.[3] A third prominent exponent of sociological empiricism is Emile Durkheim, highly esteemed as a 'founding father' of modern sociology. Since Durkheim is still much studied, it is worth devoting some attention to the views he expressed in his *Rules of Sociological Method*.

Durkheim insisted on a radical dichotomy between collective 'ways of thinking', and ideas in individual minds; the former are data for the social scientist, the latter are not. His reason for this distinction is partly an empiricist one: collective ways of thinking, unlike the ideas of individuals, can manifest themselves to sensory observation by assuming stable, standardized forms such as written law codes, written creeds, etc. They thereby achieve the status of 'things', as distinct from mere ideas. . . .[4]

More recently, the empiricist standpoint has been defended with some vigour by the American sociologist, George Lundberg. Lundberg's polemic on the subject is perhaps more impressive as an extreme example of a particular frame of mind than as an argument, but he does raise some important issues, and expresses some representative opinions. Lundberg adheres to both of the incompatible empiricist positions mentioned above. Science, he points out, describes and classifies phenomena in ways which are inevitably different from those of common-sense and pre-scientific ways of thinking, and as it develops continually substitutes new descriptions for old. In this process, says Lundberg, there has been a constant expansion of the 'physical' at the expense of the 'mental'.[5] We could if we wished impute such mental attributes as will and motive to stones or the wind (indeed, it was once common), but it is simply unscientific to do so; similarly with human behaviour. Scientific descriptions must be 'objective', that it, such that different observers agree on the description of a given phenomenon; and mental descriptions are not objective. But in the social sciences the evolution of mental concepts into physical concepts is still incomplete. ' "Will", "feeling", "ends", "motives", "values" etc. . . . are the phlogiston of the social sciences.'[6] In other words, mental concepts belong to an immature stage of social science (as the concept 'phlogiston' belonged to an immature stage of chemistry), they are in no sense inherent in social data, and should be replaced by purely physical concepts as quickly as possible.

On the other hand, Lundberg elsewhere disclaims any wish to ignore 'the phenomena of "thought" or "consciousness" '.[7] He admits that 'organisms behave with reference to the anticipated results of behaviour'. However:

> Such 'ends' whenever they figure in a behaviour situation, exist in the form of symbols of some kind, and organisms respond to these symbols just as they respond to other stimuli. These symbols and whatever they stand for are from our point of view merely part of the data of the situation and have the same power of influencing conduct as any other phenomena that precipitate responses.[8]

In other words, people's intentions are expressed in *language* (symbols), which is to be studied by the methods of empirical science; for symbolic expressions of ideas and beliefs 'are as observable and objective data as . . . the seasonal flight of birds, or the jump of an electric spark'.[9] Here it is not a question of ridding ourselves of mental concepts, but of finding objective physical expressions of them in observable behaviour, often 'symbolic behaviour' (i.e. speech and writing).[10] Like Durkheim,

Lundberg seems to think that an empiricist description of the phenomena will reveal which of them are expressions of ideas.

For more rigorous argument in support of such views, we must turn to philosophers of empiricist leanings. According to one of the most distinguished of the latter, Rudolph Carnap, every term used to describe a mental state is reducible to terms that refer to observable physical things.[11] To ascribe a mental state (such as anger) to a person is equivalent to saying that in given circumstances he will behave in a particular way, and this behaviour, which can be described in *observable thing-terms* (as Carnap calls them), is thus a symptom of the mental state. Like Lundberg, Carnap attaches particular importance to linguistic behaviour, for every mental state has an observable linguistic symptom that can be elicited in appropriate circumstances, namely an utterance of the form 'I am (or was) in mental state Q', (for example 'I am angry') which is describable in physical thing-terms. If a person's being in a particular mental state were not equivalent to his behaving in a certain way in certain circumstances, Carnap holds, it would be impossible to ascribe mental states to other people.

Human action

The tendency of Durkheim, Lundberg and Carnap is to dispense with the mental in favour of the physical. Undoubtedly human beings could be scientifically studied on this basis – but not, I believe, *as* human beings, and certainly not as social beings. This follows from the fact, previously pointed out, that a study of the social relations of men depends on the ability to recognize human action.

How do we find out what people are doing or have done, and how do we describe and classify their actions? No one would deny that, in an obvious sense, actions can be observed, nor that they present empirically describable characteristics to the observer. When people perform actions their bodies can be seen to move relative to other objects, parts of the body change their spatial orientation and relations, sounds can be heard coming from them, and so on. But this description of the physical aspect of behaviour is clearly not a description of *actions*, of people doing things. Nor could it become one simply by increasing the detail of the physical descriptions – by, for example, giving a phonetic description of the sounds, or a description of the movements in terms of precise measurements. As A. I. Melden has pointed out in a well-known book,[12] an arm rising relative to a body is not the same thing as a man raising his arm, although the former always happens when the latter does. The difference is precisely that between the movement of an

object and a human action. Yet, in a sense, both are the very same event
– or rather, alternative descriptions of the same event. This is the crux
of the matter. In order to see an event as a human action, it is necessary
to interpret its empirically observable features in terms of mental
categories, to assume the applicability of these categories to what is
observed. Only if one assumes that the body whose arm rises is a *man*
with intentions, purposes and desires, and that the rising of his arm is in
fact an intentional act of his – only then does one see a man raising his
arm.

As several writers have pointed out, it is the purposive aspect of
behaviour, not its physical aspects, that constitutes the unity of an
action. Consider a rather complex action, such as building a house.
This is made up of a number of simpler actions, physically quite
disparate (perhaps clearing ground, shaping stones, sawing wood,
mixing cement, etc.) and possibly performed discontinuously and even
in different places. All of these can be understood as parts of a complex
action of house-building only in terms of the agent's purpose in
performing them. Equally, similar simple actions can belong to quite
different complex actions: in sawing wood one may be building a house
or preparing a fire, and it is the sawer's purpose, not his overt movements, that distinguishes the one from the other. . . .

Social action

Not all human actions fall within the purview of the social sciences.
According to Max Weber, another of the 'founding fathers', these
sciences attempt to understand and explain 'social action', which he
defines as follows:

> In 'action' is included all human behaviour when and insofar as the
> acting individual attaches a subjective meaning to it. . . . Action is
> social insofar as, by virtue of the subjective meaning attached to it by
> the acting individual (or individuals), it takes account of the
> behaviour of others.[13]

He goes on:

> The term 'social relationship' [denotes] the behaviour of a plurality of
> actors insofar as, in its meaningful content, the action of each takes
> account of that of others and is oriented in these terms.[14]

Weber's definition of action is very much in accord with the notion of
action developed above, for his concept of behaviour to which the agent
attaches a 'subjective meaning' is pretty much the same as that of

purposive behaviour. Social action, then, is, on Weber's definition, action conditioned by the agent's *subjective awareness* of other people's behaviour, and a social *relationship*, in turn, involves a reciprocal social awareness on the part of several people. It follows that, in order to identify social actions and social relationships, the observer must not only interpret the empirically describable features of behaviour in terms of a set of mental categories, he must attribute to the people involved a specific sort of mental orientation, namely an awareness of *others* as *people* having intentions, purposes, desires, etc. Not only must the social scientist be able to recognize human actions, he must suppose that those whose actions he studies can do so too.

Although on Weber's account the social sciences are concerned with only a particular category of actions, all human actions are to some extent a social product. Man is a social animal. A person's intentions and purposes, his very capacity to have intentions and purposes, depend on his experience of social relationships, especially those of early childhood. Peter Winch has drawn attention to a particular sense in which all human actions depend on the social, a sense which is highly relevant to the present context. It has to do with the way in which a person is able to attach what Weber calls a 'subjective meaning' to his behaviour. That behaviour is subjectively meaningful implies that the agent has a conception, under some particular description, of what the purpose or point of the behaviour is − he could (assuming he possesses the normal means of expression) describe its point, and thus the nature of the action as he conceives it. 'Building a house' would be one such description of the nature of an action, corresponding to the agent's conception of the point of the behaviour involved. That the agent has such a conception implies that he understands a *language* which includes some expression equivalent in meaning to 'building a house'. But language is, of course, a *social* institution: it is a set of conventions shared by a social group, by virtue of which meanings are attached to sounds and marks (words). Thus, a person's attaching a particular subjective meaning to his action depends on his belonging to a community whose language includes appropriate concepts.

Whether the social scientist, in classifying actions in which he is interested, must use the same description as the agent would use, is a vexed question consideration of which can be postponed. But it seems clear that a grasp of the agent's own understanding of his action is essential to a scientific understanding of it.

Language

It is by now evident (and is not in any case very controversial) that a social scientist's knowledge of what goes on in a community depends on an understanding of its language. Indeed, the amount of actual observation of action that social scientists perform is relatively small — they are to a large extent dependent on linguistic *accounts* of action, both written and oral. Political scientists, for example, do not observe Cabinet meetings — their knowledge of them is derived from linguistic descriptions by participants of what (purportedly) happened in them; nor do they observe how electors vote — they depend on linguistic information supplied by the electors. Again, criminologists rarely observe crimes being committed — what they know about the numbers and types of crimes rests largely on official enumerations, which in turn are based on linguistic reports. All sorts of social scientists depend on linguistic information given in reply to questionnaires. Perhaps the only social scientists who habitually *observe* their subject-matter are social anthropologists, and those who study small groups; and even they, obviously, must take account of their subjects' use of language. This means that they must either themselves understand their subjects' language, or rely on the translations of those who do. As has often been pointed out, the experience of anthropologists in unfamiliar communities gives the lie to any idea that the identification of actions is in principle a straightforward matter, simply requiring careful observation of the physical characteristics that social life presents to the observer. On the contrary, it takes a considerable time before these manifestations become comprehensible as particular sorts of actions; and they do so as the anthropologist acquires knowledge of the group's language, which is both an essential part of their social life and a means of questioning participants about that life. . . .

Knowledge of a community's language enables a social scientist to *question* its members. This is a privilege denied to physical scientists, but one which must, as is well known, be used with care, for it gives rise to the possibility of *misunderstanding*, perhaps especially where the investigator might be tempted to suppose that he and his subject-matter share exactly the same language. Social scientists who use questionnaires have frequently got into trouble through mistakenly supposing that, for example, manual workers understand relatively abstract terms like 'class' in the same way as they themselves do.[15] This of course reinforces the general lesson that the social scientist has to understand the subjective meaning of language to its user — not just observe its empirical characteristics. But usually it will not be enough for the social scientist just to understand his respondent's meaning: social scientists normally wish to use respondents' assertions that something is the case as *evidence* that it in fact is. Assuming that a respondent has the necessary knowledge to give correct information, this involves also a judgement about his state of *mind* − i.e. that he wishes to convey that information in his response. This, of course, need not be so − many respondents may have motives for misleading the questioner. The physical scientist, though he too may have difficulties in interpreting his observations, need not worry that his subject-matter may be trying to deceive him. . . .

Unobservables and explanation

I have argued that the model of physics is inapplicable in the social sciences because the existence of social facts always implies the existence of mental states − intentions, purposes, beliefs, expectations, aware-ness of rules − which are not observable by empirical methods. It is, however, possible to accept the premise without accepting the con-clusion. After all, physics too deals with unobservable phenomena, namely the theoretical entities . . . such as electrons, magnetic fields, etc. Do not our mental phenomena, perhaps, have a similar status to these? The theoretical entities of physics are to be considered as real entities capable of causing empirical phenomena. Thus, an observed phenomenon (such as a track in a cloud chamber) can be explained using a law (or laws) concerning the effects of interaction of un-observable entities of a particular sort (such as electrons) with other sorts of matter. If mental entities such as intentions and purposes were comparable to these theoretical physical entities, they would be capable of causing certain empirically observable phenomena, and would have lawful connections with them similar to those between electrons and tracks in cloud chambers.

But even if this were the case, it would not follow that mental states have a similar status in the social sciences to that of the theoretical entities in physical science. The empirical phenomena caused by mental states would be, presumably, bodily movements. There might, for example, be a causal connection between the intention to raise one's arm, and the rising of one's arm. Social science is not, however, interested in bodily movements like the rising of arms, nor in any possible causal connections between these movements and mental states. It is interested in the description and explanation of (social) *actions*, and these cannot (unlike the observable effects of theoretical entities) be described in purely physical terms. The significance of mental states for the social sciences is, in the first place, not to explain bodily movements, but to constitute a framework of concepts in terms of which these movements can be understood as actions.

Notes

1. To quote the title of a well-known book on the nature of science by John Ziman (1968) *Public Knowledge*, Cambridge, Cambridge University Press.
2. Comte's views are quoted and discussed in Hayek, F. A. (1964) *The Counter-Revolution of Science*, Glencoe, Ill., Free Press, p. 172.
3. Malinowski, B. (1960) *A Scientific Theory of Culture*, New York, Oxford University Press, p. 23.
4. Durkheim, Emile (1964) *The Rules of Sociological Method*, Glencoe, Ill., Free Press, pp. 2–4, 7, 29–30.
5. Lundberg, George A. (1963) 'The postulates of science and their implications for sociology', in Natanson, M., ed., *Philosophy of the Social Sciences*, New York, Random House, pp. 34n., 39–40, 43, 53–4.
6. ibid., p. 44.
7. ibid., p. 55.
8. ibid., p. 34n.
9. ibid., p. 53.
10. ibid., p. 55.
11. See Carnap, R. (1969) 'Logical foundations of the unity of science', reprinted in Krimerman, L. I., ed., *The Nature and Scope of Social Science*, New York, Appleton-Century-Crofts, pp. 362–73, esp. 369–71.
12. Melden, A. I. (1961) *Free Action*, London, Routledge & Kegan Paul, esp. chs 6 and 13.
13. Weber, Max (1964) *The Theory of Social and Economic Organization*, Glencoe, Ill., Free Press, p. 88.
14. ibid., p. 118.
15. Another example is given in Rickman, H. P. (1967) *Understanding and the Human Studies*, London, Heinemann, p. 68.

7 Understanding and explaining human action

The extracts in this chapter follow on from the idea raised in the previous chapter, particularly in Lessnoff's piece, that there may be something distinctive in the subject-matter of social inquiry itself. Since social science inquiries are about conscious or thinking people, this, it can be argued, means that social science inquiry must be conducted on a different basis from natural science.

But, if this argument is accepted, what *is* this basis? Once again this raises a continuing debate. It is a controversy which is perhaps most clearly expressed when facing the problems of how to study and analyse an unfamiliar society — and many of the examples cited here are thus from social anthropology — but it is one which extends throughout the other social sciences also.

The chapter is fittingly introduced by an extract from Peter Winch, whose book *The Idea of a Social Science*, first published in 1958, has had such an impact on the philosophy of the social sciences. He strongly challenges the often-accepted parallels between social and natural sciences, especially the view of Mill about the possibility of predicting and generalizing about human behaviour. Winch argues forcefully that since human action intrinsically involves meaning and deliberation, the analyst must understand this 'from the inside', as it were, if he is to understand it *as human* action: it is not just a matter of observing from the outside as in natural science. MacIntyre agrees with much of this assessment but takes issue with Winch over whether understanding the local views and ideas is enough: Should not (and does not) the social scientist do something *more* as well in order to reach a satisfactory analysis? Unlike MacIntyre, Beattie does not address himself directly to Winch's position, but his presentation, expressed primarily in terms of the methods and subject matter of social anthropology, shares some of the same assumptions. Like Winch and MacIntyre he takes it as incontestable that ideas and values form an essential part of social action and social institutions and must be understood as such. But at the same time he points out that in all inquiry, and perhaps in social inquiry above all, 'pure description' is never feasible. We never come with totally open minds to the data — thus even the prior understanding of local ideas and values will rest on certain implicit theoretical interpretations by the observer. He also holds that explanation in terms of functions which may not form a conscious part of the local system of beliefs is also acceptable in social science.

Despite their disagreements on certain aspects, it is noticeable that all these extracts share a tendency to speak of 'understanding', 'explanation', or 'meanings', rather than following the kind of terminology which emphasizes such concepts as 'general laws', 'measurement' or 'verification'. This difference in emphasis — and hence in overall theoretical outlook — from the stance of Mill, Easton and the so-called 'positivist' writers like Durkheim is also exemplified by their stress not on 'laws of human nature' nor on 'behaviour' but on meaningful 'human action'. They also share the conviction, though without in these extracts fully defining their terms, that there is a 'social' aspect of human affairs, distinct from the acts and nature of man as a purely *physical* being, which it is meaningful for the social scientist to inquire into and which is *different* from the subject matter of the natural scientists.

7.1   UNDERSTANDING SOCIAL INSTITUTIONS

PETER WINCH (1926–   ), *from* The Idea of a Social Science, *London, Routledge & Kegan Paul, 1958, extracts from chs 3 and 5, pp. 86–90, 131–2, 134–6*

This influential book was prefaced by a quotation from Lessing, which well sets out the main theme.

> It may indeed be true that moral actions are always the same in themselves, however different may be the times and however different the societies in which they occur; but still, the same actions do not always have the same names, and it is unjust to give any action a different name from that which it used to bear in its own times and amongst its own people.[1]

Winch is taking issue with the idea, put forward by Mill and others, that it is possible to construct generalizations about human behaviour, as if the units of measurement and analysis could be regarded as the same in all societies. On the contrary, he argues, one of the marks of human beings (*qua* human) is their possession of ideas and values, and it is only through understanding these, and the associated norms and rules which govern meaningful action in differing societies, that the inquirer can reach a proper understanding of social action. Because human action can only be thoroughly understood by taking account of the concepts of the actors, the social scientist is involved in a different kind of inquiry from that into physical processes.

Note

1. Lessing, Gotthold Ephraim, *Anti-Goeze*.

Mill's view is that understanding a social institution consists in observing regularities in the behaviour of its participants and expressing these regularities in the form of generalizations. Now if the position of the sociological investigator (in a broad sense) can be regarded as comparable, in its main logical outlines, with that of the natural scientist, the following must be the case. The concepts and criteria according to which the sociologist judges that, in two situations, the same thing has happened, or the same action performed, must be understood *in relation to the rules governing sociological investigation*. But here we run against a difficulty; for whereas in the case of the natural scientist we have to deal with only one set of rules, namely those governing the scientist's investigation itself, here *what the sociologist is studying*, as well as his study of it, is a human activity and is therefore carried on according to rules. And it is these rules, rather than those which govern the sociologist's investigation, which specify what is to count as 'doing the same kind of thing' in relation to that kind of activity.

An example may make this clearer. Consider the parable of the Pharisee and the Publican (*Luke* 18 : 9). Was the Pharisee who said 'God, I thank Thee that I am not as other men are' doing the same kind of thing as the Publican who prayed 'God be merciful unto me a sinner'? To answer this one would have to start by considering what is involved in the idea of prayer; and that is a *religious* question. In other words, the appropriate criteria for deciding whether the actions of these two men were of the same kind or not belong to religion itself. Thus the sociologist of religion will be confronted with an answer to the question: Do these two acts belong to the same kind of activity?; and this answer is given according to criteria which are not taken from sociology, but from religion itself.

But if the judgements of identity − and hence the generalizations − of the sociologist of religion rest on criteria taken from religion, then his relation to the performers of religious activity cannot be just that of observer to observed. It must rather be analogous to the participation of the natural scientist with his fellow-workers in the activities of scientific investigation. Putting the point generally, even if it is legitimate to speak of one's understanding of a mode of social activity as consisting in a knowledge of regularities, the nature of this knowledge must be very different from the nature of knowledge of physical regularities. So it is quite mistaken in principle to compare the activity of a student of a form of social behaviour with that of, say, an engineer studying the workings of a machine; and one does not advance matters by saying, with Mill, that the machine in question is of course immensely more complicated than any physical machine. If we are going to compare the social student to an engineer, we shall do better to compare him to an apprentice engineer who is studying what engineering − that is, the activity of engineering − is all about. His understanding of social phenomena is more like the engineer's understanding of his colleagues' activities than it is like the engineer's understanding of the mechanical systems which he studies.

This point is reflected in such common-sense considerations as the following: that a historian or sociologist of religion must himself have some religious feeling if he is to make sense of the religious movement he is studying and understand the considerations which govern the lives of its participants. A historian of art must have some aesthetic sense if he is to understand the problems confronting the artists of his period; and without this he will have left out of his account precisely what would have made it a history of *art*, as opposed to a rather puzzling external account of certain motions which certain people have been perceived to go through.

I do not wish to maintain that we must stop at the unreflective kind of understanding of which I gave as an instance the engineer's understanding of the activities of his colleagues. But I do want to say that any more reflective understanding must necessarily presuppose, if it is to count as genuine understanding at all, the participant's unreflective understanding. And this in itself makes it misleading to compare it with the natural scientist's understanding of his scientific data. Similarly, although the reflective student of society, or of a particular mode of social life, may find it necessary to use concepts which are not taken from the forms of activity which he is investigating, but which are taken rather from the context of his own investigation, still these technical concepts of his will imply a previous understanding of those other concepts which belong to the activities under investigation.

For example, liquidity preference is a technical concept of economies: it is not generally used by business men in the conduct of their affairs but by the economist who wishes to *explain* the nature and consequences of certain kinds of business behaviour. But it is logically tied to concepts which do enter into business activity, for its use by the economist presupposes his understanding of what it is to conduct a business, which in turn involves an understanding of such business concepts as money, profit, cost, risk, etc. It is only the relation between his account and these concepts which makes it an account of economic activity as opposed, say, to a piece of theology.

Again, a psychoanalyst may explain a patient's neurotic behaviour in terms of factors unknown to the patient and of concepts which would be unintelligible to him. Let us suppose that the psychoanalyst's explanation refers to events in the patient's early childhood. Well, the description of those events will presuppose an understanding of the concepts in terms of which family life, for example, is carried on in our society; for these will have entered, however rudimentarily, into the relations between the child and his family. A psychoanalyst who wished to give an account of the aetiology of neuroses amongst, say, the Trobriand Islanders, could not just apply without further reflection the concepts developed by Freud for situations arising in our own society. He would have first to investigate such things as the idea of fatherhood amongst the islanders and take into account any relevant aspects in which their idea differed from that current in his own society. And it is almost inevitable that such an investigation would lead to some modification in the psychological theory appropriate for explaining neurotic behaviour in this new situation. . . .

This view of the matter may make possible a new appreciation of Collingwood's conception of all human history as the history of thought. That is no doubt an exaggeration and the notion that the task of the historian is to re-think the thoughts of the historical participants is to some extent an intellectualistic distortion. But Collingwood is right if he is taken to mean that the way to understand events in human history, even those which cannot naturally be represented as conflicts between or developments of discursive ideas, is more closely analogous to the way in which we understand expressions of ideas than it is to the way we understand physical processes. . . .

The relation between sociological theories and historical narrative is less like the relation between scientific laws and the reports of experiments or observations than it is like that between theories of logic and arguments in particular languages. Consider for instance the explanation of a chemical reaction in terms of a theory about molecular structure and valency: here the theory *establishes* a connection between what happened at one moment when the two chemicals were brought together and what happened at a subsequent moment. It is only *in terms of the theory* that one can speak of the events being thus 'connected' (as opposed to a simple spatio-temporal connection); the only way to grasp the connection is to learn the theory. But the application of a logical theory to a particular piece of reasoning is not like that. One does not have to know the theory in order to appreciate the connection between the steps of the argument; on the contrary, it is only in so far as one can already grasp logical connections between particular statements in particular languages that one is even in a position to understand what the logical theory is all about. . . . Whereas in natural science it is your theoretical knowledge which enables you to explain occurrences you have not previously met, a knowledge of logical theory on the other hand will not enable you to understand a piece of reasoning in an unknown language; you will have to learn that language, and that in itself *may* suffice to enable you to grasp the connections between the various parts of arguments in that language.

Consider now an example from sociology. Georg Simmel writes:

The degeneration of a difference in convictions into hatred and fight occurs only when there were essential, original similarities between the parties. The (sociologically very significant) 'respect for the enemy' is usually absent where the hostility has arisen on the basis of previous solidarity. And where enough similarities continue to make confusions and blurred outlines possible, points of difference need an emphasis not justified by the issue but only by that danger of confusion. This was involved, for instance, in the case of Catholicism in Berne . . . Roman Catholicism does not have to fear any threat to its identity from external contact with a church so different as the Reformed Church, but quite from something as closely akin as Old Catholicism.[1]

Here I want to say that it is not *through* Simmel's generalization that one understands the relationship he is pointing to between Roman and Old Catholicism: one understands that only to the extent that one understands the two religious systems themselves and their historical relations. The 'sociological law' may be helpful in calling one's attention to features of historical situations which one might otherwise have overlooked and in suggesting useful analogies. Here for instance one may be led to compare Simmel's example with the relations between the Russian Communist Party and, on the one hand, the British Labour Party and, on the other, the British Conservatives. But no historical situation can be understood simply by 'applying' such laws, as one applies laws to particular occurrences in natural science. Indeed, it is only in so far as one has an *independent* historical grasp of situations like this one that one is able to understand what the law amounts to at all. That is not like having to know the kind of experiment on which a scientific theory is based before one can understand the theory, for there it makes no sense to speak of understanding the connections between the parts of the experiment except in terms of the scientific theory. But one could understand very well the nature of the relations between Roman Catholicism and Old Catholicism without ever having heard of Simmel's theory, or anything like it.

Note

1. Simmel, Georg (1955) *Conflict*, Glencoe, Ill., Free Press, ch. 1.

7.2   THE IDEA OF A SOCIAL SCIENCE

ALASDAIR MACINTYRE (1929–   ), *from 'The idea of a social science'*, Proceedings of the Aristotelian Society, *supp. vol. 41, 1967, pp. 95–114 also published in* Against the Self-Images of the Age, *London, Duckworth, 1971, pp. 211–29 and elsewhere; shortened, the major omission being section 3 of the original*

MacIntyre accepts Winch's criticisms of Mill and Durkheim for trying to characterize the institutions of other societies in the outside analyst's terms rather than that of people's own concepts, and agrees that a society's own self-description – i.e. the actors' concepts and values – is the essential starting point for the social inquirer. But, argues MacIntyre, this is *only* the starting point and not 'the whole task of the social scientist'. Unless social scientists also go beyond this in their analyses, effective comparison between societies is impossible, nor, even more important, is there any opening for comparing what people actually do with what they say and believe they do (or even think they ought to do). Without this additional step, there is no possibility of querying the local evaluation of events.

My aim in this essay is to express dissent from the position taken in Mr Peter Winch's book[1] whose title is also the title of this essay. Winch's book has been the subject of a good deal of misunderstanding, and he has been accused on the one hand of reviving familiar and long-refuted views[2] and on the other of holding views so eccentric in relation to social science as it actually is that they could not possibly have any practical effect on the conduct of that science.[3] In fact, however, Winch articulates a position which is at least partly implicit in a good deal of work already done, notably in anthropology, and he does so in an entirely original way. He writes in a genre recognizable to both sociologists and philosophers. Talcott Parsons and Alain Touraine have both found it necessary to preface their sociological work by discussions of norms and actions and have arrived at rather different conclusions from those of Winch; the importance of his work is therefore undeniable.

1

Wittgenstein says somewhere that when one gets into philosophical difficulties over the use of some of the concepts of our language, we are like savages confronted with something from an alien culture. I am simply indicating a corollary of this: that sociologists who misinterpret an alien culture are like philosophers getting into difficulty over the use of their own concepts.[4]

This passage epitomizes a central part of Winch's thesis with its splendid successive characterizations of the figure baffled by an alien culture; a savage at one moment, he has become a sociologist at the next. And this is surely no slip of the pen. According to Winch, the successful sociologist has simply learned all that the ideal native informant could tell him; sociological knowledge is the kind of knowledge possessed in implicit and partial form by the members of a society rendered explicit and complete.[5] It is not at first entirely clear just how far Winch is at odds in this contention with, for example, Malinowski, who insisted that the native Trobriander's account of Trobriand society must be inadequate, that the sociologists' account of institutions is a construction not available to the untutored awareness of the native informant.[6] For Winch of course is willing to allow into the sociologist's account concepts 'which are not taken from the forms of activity which he is investigating; but which are taken rather from the context of his own investigation', although he adds that 'these technical concepts will imply a prior understanding of those other concepts which belong to the activities under investigation'. Perhaps this might seem sufficient to remove the apparent disagreement of Winch and Malinowski, until we remember the conclusion of Malinowski's critique of the native informant's view. The sociologist who relies upon that view, he says,

> obtains at best that lifeless body of laws, regulations, morals, and conventionalities which *ought* to be obeyed, but in reality are often only evaded. For in actual life rules are never entirely conformed to, and it remains, as the most difficult but indispensable part of the ethnographer's work, to ascertain the extent and mechanism of the deviations.[7]

This makes two points clear.

First, Malinowski makes a distinction between the rules acknowledged in a given society and the actual behaviour of individuals in that society, whereas Winch proclaims the proper object of sociological study to be that behaviour precisely as rule-governed. The second is that in the study of behaviour Malinowski is willing to use notions such as that of mechanism which are clearly causal; whereas Winch warns us against comparing sociological understanding with understanding in terms of 'statistics and causal laws' and says of the notion of function, so important to Malinowski, that it 'is a quasi-causal notion, which it is perilous to apply to social institutions'.[8]

It does appear, therefore, that, although Winch and Malinowski agree in seeing the ideal native informant's account of his own social life as incomplete by comparison with the ideal sociologist's account, they do disagree about the nature of that incompleteness and about how it is to be remedied. My purpose in this essay will be to defend Malinowski's point of view on these matters against Winch's, but this purpose can only be understood if one reservation is immediately added. It is that in defending Malinowski's views on these points I must not be taken to be endorsing Malinowski's general theoretical position. I have in fact quoted Malinowski on these matters, but I might have quoted many other social scientists. For on these matters Malinowski speaks with the consensus.

2

A regularity or uniformity is the constant recurrence of the same kind of event on the same kind of occasion; hence statements of uniformities presuppose judgments of identity. But . . . criteria of identity are necessarily relative to some rule: with the corollary that two events which count as qualitatively similar from the point of view of one rule would count as different from the point of view of another. So to investigate the type of regularity studied in a given inquiry is to examine the nature of the rule according to which judgments of identity are made in that inquiry. Such judgments are intelligible only relatively to a given mode of human behavior, governed by its own rules.[9]

This passage is the starting-point for Winch's argument that J. S. Mill was mistaken in supposing that to understand a social institution is to formulate empirical generalizations about regularities in human behaviour, generalizations which are causal and explanatory in precisely the same sense that generalizations in the natural sciences are. For the natural scientist makes the relevant judgements of identity according to *his* rules (that is, the rules incorporated in the practice of his science); whereas the social scientist must make his judgements of identity in accordance with the rules governing the behaviour of those whom he studies. *Their* rules, not *his*, define the object of his study.

So it is quite mistaken in principle to compare the activity of a student of a form of social behavior with that of, say, an engineer studying the working of a machine. If we are going to compare the social student to an engineer, we shall do better to compare him to an apprentice engineer who is studying what engineering − that is, the activity of engineering − is all about.[10]

What the type of understanding which Winch is commending consists in is made clearer in two other passages. He says that, although prediction is possible in the social sciences, it 'is quite different from predictions in the natural sciences, where a falsified prediction always implies some sort of mistake on the part of the predictor: false or inadequate data, faulty calculation, or defective theory'.[11] This is because 'since understanding something involves understanding its contradictory, someone who, with understanding, performs X must be capable of envisaging the possibility of doing not-X'.[12] Where someone is following a rule, we cannot predict how he will interpret what is involved in following that rule in radically new circumstances; where decisions have to be made, the outcome 'cannot be *definitely* predicted', for otherwise 'we should not call them decisions'.

These points about prediction, if correct, reinforce Winch's argument about the difference between the natural sciences and the social sciences. . . .

From all this one can set out Winch's view of understanding and explanations in the social sciences in terms of a two-stage model. An action is *first* made intelligible as the outcome of motives, reasons, and decisions; and is then made *further* intelligible by those motives, reasons, and decisions being set in the context of the rules of a given form of social life. These rules logically determine the range of reasons and motives open to a given set of agents and hence also the range of decisions open to them. Thus Winch's contrast between explanation in terms of causal generalizations and explanations in terms of rules turns out to rest upon a version of the contrast between explanations in terms of causes and explanations in terms of reasons. This latter contrast must therefore be explored, and the most useful way of doing this will be to understand better what it is to act for a reason.

Many analyses of what it is to act for a reason have written into them an incompatibility between acting for a reason and behaving from a cause, just because they begin from the apparently simple and uncomplicated case where the action is actually performed, where the agent had one and only one reason for performing it, and where no doubt could arise for the agent as to why he had done what he had done. By concentrating attention upon this type of example, a basis is laid for making central to the analyses a contrast between the agent's knowledge of his own reasons for acting and his and others' knowledge of causes of his behaviour. For clearly in such a case the agent's claim that he did X for reason Y does not seem to stand in need of any warrant from a generalization founded upon observation; while equally clearly any claim that one particular event or state of affairs was the cause of another does stand in need of such a warrant. But this may be misleading. Consider two somewhat more complex cases than that outlined above. The first is that of a man who has several quite different reasons for performing a given action. He performs the action; how can he as agent know whether it was the conjoining of all the different reasons that was sufficient for him to perform the action or whether just one of the reasons was by itself alone sufficient or whether the action was overdetermined in the sense that there were two or more reasons, each of which would by itself alone have been sufficient? The problem arises partly because to know that one or other of these possibilities was indeed the case entails knowing the truth of certain unfulfilled conditionals.

A second case worth considering is that of two agents, each with the same reasons for performing a given action; one does not in fact perform it, the other does. Neither agent had what seemed to him a good reason or indeed had any reason for not performing the action in question. Here we can ask what made these reasons or some subset of them productive of action in the one case, but not in the other. In both these types of case we need to distinguish between the agent's having a reason for performing an action (not just in the sense of there being a reason for him to perform the action, but in the stronger sense of his being aware that he has such a reason) and the agent's being actually moved to action by his having such a reason. The importance of this point can be brought out by reconsidering a very familiar example, that of post-hypnotic suggestion.

Under the influence of post-hypnotic suggestion a subject will not only perform the action required by the hypnotist, but will offer apparently good reasons for performing it, while quite unaware of the true cause of the performance. So someone enjoined to walk out of the room might, on being asked why he was doing this, reply with all sincerity that he had felt in need of fresh air or decided to catch a train. In this type of case we would certainly not accept the agent's testimony as to the connection between reason and action, unless we are convinced of the untruth of the counter-factual. 'He would have walked out of the room, if no reason for doing so had occurred to him' and the truth of the counter-factual, 'he would not have walked out of the room, if he had not possessed some such reason for so doing'. The question of the truth or otherwise of the first of these is a matter of the experimentally established facts about post-hypnotic suggestion, and these facts are certainly expressed as causal generalizations. To establish the truth of the relevant generalization would entail establishing the untruth of the second counter-factual. But since to establish the truth of such causal generalizations entails consequences concerning the truth or untruth of generalizations about reasons, the question inevitably arises as to whether *the possession of a given reason* may not be the cause of an action in precisely the same sense in which hypnotic suggestion may be the cause of an action. The chief objection to this view has been that the relation of reason to action is internal and conceptual, not external and contingent, and cannot therefore be a causal relationship; but although nothing could count as a reason unless it stood in an internal relationship to an action, *the agent's possessing a reason* may be a state of affairs identifiable independently of the event which is *the agent's performance of the action*. Thus it does seem as if the possession of a reason by an agent is an item of a suitable type to figure as a cause, or an effect. But if this is so then to ask whether it was the agent's reason that roused him to act is to ask a causal question, the true answer to which depends upon what causal generalizations we have been able to establish. This puts in a different light the question of the agent's authority as to what roused him to act; for it follows from what has been said that this authority is at best prima facie. Far more of course needs to be said on this and related topics; but perhaps the argument so far entitles us to treat with scepticism Winch's claim that understanding in terms of rule-following and causal explanations have mutually exclusive subject-matters.

This has obvious implications for social science, and I wish to suggest some of these in order to provide direction for the rest of my argument. Clearly if the citing of reasons by an agent, with the concomitant appeal to rules, is not necessarily the citing of those reasons which are causally effective, a distinction may be made between those rules which agents in a given society sincerely profess to follow and to which their actions may in fact conform, but which do not in fact direct their actions, and those rules which, whether they profess to follow them or not, do in fact guide their acts by providing them with reasons and motives for acting in one way rather than another. The making of this distinction is essential to the notions of *ideology* and of *false consciousness*, notions which are extremely important to some non-Marxist as well as to Marxist social scientists.

But to allow that these notions could have application is to find oneself at odds with Winch's argument at yet another point. For it seems quite clear that the concept of ideology can find application in a society where the concept is not available to the members of the society, and furthermore that the application of this concept implies that criteria beyond those available in the society may be invoked to judge its rationality; and as such it would fall under Winch's ban as a concept unsuitable for social science. Hence there is a connection between

Winch's view that social science is not appropriately concerned with causal generalizations and his view that only the concepts possessed by the members of a given society (or concepts logically tied to those concepts in some way) are to be used in the study of that society. Furthermore, it is important to note that Winch's views on those matters necessarily make his account of rules and their place in social behaviour defective. . . .

4

. . . The positive value of Winch's book is partly as a corrective to the Durkheimian position which he rightly castigates. But it is more than a corrective because what Winch characterizes as the whole task of the social sciences is in fact their true starting-point. Unless we begin by a characterization of a society in its own terms, we shall be unable to identify the matter that requires explanation. Attention to intentions, motives and reasons must precede attention to causes; description in terms of the agent's concepts and beliefs must precede description in terms of our concepts and beliefs. The force of this contention can be brought out by considering and expanding what Winch says about Durkheim's *Suicide*.[13] Winch invites us to notice the connection between Durkheim's conclusion that the true explanation of suicide is in terms of factors outside the consciousness of the agents themselves such that the reasons of the agents themselves are effectively irrelevant and his initial decision to give the term 'suicide' a meaning quite other than that which it had for those agents. What is he inviting us to notice?

A number of points, I suspect, of which one is a central insight, the others in error. The insight is that Durkheim's particular procedure of giving to 'suicide' a meaning of his own *entails* the irrelevance of the agent's reasons in the explanation of suicide. Durkheim does in fact bring forward independent arguments designed to show that reasons are either irrelevant or inaccessible, and very bad arguments they are. But even if he had not believed himself to have grounds drawn from these arguments, he would have been unable to take reasons into account, given his decision about meaning. Durkheim arbitrarily equates the concept of *suicide* with that of *doing anything that the agent knows will bring about his own death* and thus classifies as suicide both the intended self-destruction of the Prussian or English officer who shoots himself to save the regiment the disgrace of a court martial and the death in battle of such an officer who has courageously headed a charge in such a way that he knows that he will not survive. (I choose these two examples because they both belong to the same category in

Durkheim's classification.) Thus he ignores the distinction between *doing X intending that Y shall result* and *doing X knowing that Y will result*. Now clearly if these two are to be assimilated, the roles of deliberation and the relevance of the agent's reasons will disappear from view. For clearly in the former case the character of *Y* must be central to the reasons the agent has for doing *X*, but in the latter case the agent may well be doing *X* either in spite of the character of *Y*, or not caring one way or the other about the character of *Y*, or again finding the character of *Y* desirable, but not desirable enough for him for it to constitute a reason or a motive for doing *X*. Thus the nature of the reasons *must* differ in the two cases, and if the two cases are to have the same explanation the agent's reasons can scarcely figure in that explanation. That is, Durkheim is forced by his initial semantic decision to the conclusion that the agent's reasons are in cases of what agents in the society which he studies would have called suicide (which are included as a subclass of what he calls suicide) *never* causally effective.

But there are two further conclusions which might be thought to, but do not in fact, follow. It does not follow that all such decisions to bring actions under descriptions other than those used by the agents themselves are bound to lead to the same *a priori* obliteration of the explanatory role of reasons; for this obliteration was in Durkheim's case, as I have just shown, a consequence of certain special features of his treatment of the concept of suicide, and not a consequence of any general feature of the procedure of inventing new descriptive terms in social sciences. Secondly, from the fact that explanation in terms of reason ought not to be excluded by any initial decision of the social scientist, it does not follow that such explanation is incompatible with causal explanation. Here my argument in the second section of this essay bears on what Winch says about Weber. Winch says that Weber was confused because he did not realize that 'a context of humanly followed rules . . . cannot be combined with a context of causal laws' without creating logical difficulties, and he is referring specifically to Weber's contention that the manipulation of machinery and the manipulation of his employees by a manufacturer may be understood in the same way, so far as the logic of the explanation is concerned. So Weber wrote, 'that in the one case "events of consciousness" do enter into the causal chain and in the other case do not, makes "logically" not the slightest difference'. I also have an objection to Weber's argument, but it is in effect that Weber's position is too close to Winch's. For Weber supposes that in order to introduce causal explanation he must abandon description of the social situation in terms of actions, roles, and the like. So he proposes speaking not of the workers being paid, but of their being handed pieces of metal. In so doing Weber concedes Winch's point that descriptions in terms of actions, reasons, and all that falls under his term 'events of consciousness' cannot figure in causal explanations without a conceptual mistake being committed. But in this surely he is wrong.

Compare two situations: first, one in which managers minimize shop-floor trade-union activity in a factory by concentrating opportunities of extra overtime and of earning bonuses in those parts of the factory where such activity shows signs of flourishing; and then one in which managers similarly minimize trade-union activity by a process of continual transfers between one part of the factory and another or between different factories. In both cases it may be possible to explain the low level of trade-union activity causally by reference to the managers' policies; but in the former case the reasons which the workers have for pursuing overtime and bonuses can find a place in the explanation without it losing its causal character and in both cases a necessary condition of the managers' actions being causally effective may well be that the workers in question remain ignorant of the policy behind the actions. The causal character of the explanations can be brought out by considering how generalizations might be formulated in which certain behaviour of the managers can supply either the neces-sary or the sufficient condition or both for the behaviour of the workers. But in such a formulation one important fact will emerge; namely, that true causal explanations cannot be formulated − where actions are concerned − unless intentions, motives and reasons are taken into account. That is, it is not only the case as I have argued in the second section of this essay that a true explanation in terms of reasons must entail some account of the causal background; it is also true that a causal account of action will require a corresponding account of the intentions, motives and reasons involved. It is this latter point that Durkheim misses and Winch stresses. In the light of this it is worth returning to one aspect of the explanation of suicide.

In modern cities more than one study has shown a correlation between the suicide rate for different parts of the city and the pro-portion of the population living an isolated, single-room apartment existence. What are the conditions which must be satisfied if such a correlation is to begin to play a part in explaining why suicide is committed? First it must be shown that at least a certain proportion of the individuals who commit suicide live in such isolated conditions; otherwise (unless, for example, it was the landlord of such apartments who committed suicide) we should find the correlation of explanatory assistance only in so far as it pointed us towards a common explanation of the two rates. But suppose that we do find that it is the individuals who live in such isolated conditions who are more likely to commit suicide. We still have to ask whether it is the pressure on the emotions of the isolation itself, or whether it is the insolubility of certain other problems in conditions of isolation which leads to suicide. Unless such questions about motives and reasons are answered, the causal generalization 'isolated living of a certain kind tends to lead to acts of suicide' is not so much an explanation in itself as an additional fact to be explained, even though it is a perfectly sound generalization and even though to learn its truth might be to learn how the suicide rate could be increased or decreased in large cities by changing our housing policies.

Now we cannot raise the questions about motives and reasons, the answers to which would explain why isolation has the effect which it has, unless we first of all understand the acts of suicide in terms of the intentions of the agents and therefore in terms of their own action descriptions. Thus Winch's starting-point proves to be the correct one, provided it is a starting-point. We could not even formulate our initial causal generalization about isolation and suicide, in such a way that the necessary question about motives and reasons could be raised later, unless the expression 'suicide' and kindred expressions which figured in our causal generalizations possessed the same meaning as they did for the agents who committed the acts. We can understand very clearly why Winch's starting-point must be substantially correct if we remember how he compares sociological understanding with understanding a language.[14] The crude notion that one can first learn a language and then secondly and separately go on to understand the social life of those who speak it can only flourish where the languages studied are those of peoples whose social life is so largely the same as our own that we do not notice the understanding of social life embodied in our grasp of the language; but attempts to learn the alien language of an alien culture soon dispose of it. Yet the understanding that we thus acquire, although a necessary preliminary, is only a preliminary. It would be equally harmful if Winch's attempt to make of this preliminary the substance of social science were to convince, or if a proper understanding of the need to go further were not to allow for the truth in his arguments.

5

These dangers are likely to be especially inhibiting in the present state of parts of social science. Two important essays by anthropologists, Leach's *Rethinking Anthropology* and Goldschmidt's *Comparative Functionalism*[15] . . . , focus upon problems to which adherence to

Winch's conclusions would preclude any solution. At the outset I contrasted Winch with Malinowski, but this was in respects in which most contemporary social scientists would take the standpoint quoted from Malinowski for granted. We owe also to Malinowski, however, the tradition of what Goldschmidt calls 'the detailed internal analysis of individual cultures' with the further comparison of institutional arrangements in different societies resting on such analyses. This tradition has been criticized by both Leach and Goldschmidt; the latter believes that because institutions are defined by each culture in its own terms, it is not at the level of institutions that cross-cultural analyses will be fruitful. The former has recommended us to search for recurrent topological patterns in, for example, kinship arrangements, with the same aim of breaking free from institutional ethnocentrism. I think that both Leach and Goldschmidt are going to prove to be seminal writers on this point and it is clear that their arguments are incompatible with Winch's. It would therefore be an important lacuna in this essay if I did not open up directly the question of the bearing of Winch's arguments on this topic.

Winch argues, consistently with his rejection of any place for causal laws in social science, that comparison between different cases is not dependent on any grasp of theoretical generalizations,[16] and he sets limits to any possible comparison by his insistence that each set of activities must be understood solely in its own terms. In so doing he must necessarily reject for example all those various theories which insist that religions of quite different kinds express unacknowledged needs of the same kind. (No such theory needs to be committed to the view that religions are and do no more than this.) Indeed in his discussion of Pareto[17] he appears to make such a rejection explicit by the generality of the grounds on which he rejects Pareto's comparison of Christian baptism with pagan rites. I hold no brief for the theory of residues and derivations. But when Winch insists that each religious rite must be understood in its own terms to the exclusion of any generalization about religion or that each social system must be so understood to the exclusion of any generalization about status and prestige, he must be pressed to make his grounds precise. In his later discussion of Evans-Pritchard, one aspect of Winch's views becomes clear; namely, the implication of his remark that 'criteria of logic are not a direct gift of God, but arise out of, and are only intelligible in the context of, ways of living or modes of social life'.[18] Winch's one substantial point of difference with Evans-Pritchard in his treatment of witchcraft among the Azande is that he thinks it impossible to ask whether the Zande beliefs about witches are true.[19] We can ask from within the Zande system of beliefs if there are witches and will receive the answer 'Yes'. We can ask from within the system of beliefs of modern science if there are witches and will receive the answer 'No'. But we cannot ask which system of beliefs is the superior in respect of rationality and truth; for this would be to invoke criteria which can be understood independently of any particular way of life, and in Winch's view there are no such criteria.

This represents a far more extreme view of the difficulties of cultural comparison than Goldschmidt, for example, advances. Both its extreme character and its error can be understood by considering two arguments against it. The first is to the effect that in Winch's view certain actual historical transitions are made unintelligible; I refer to those transitions from one system of beliefs to another which are necessarily characterized by raising questions of the kind that Winch rejects. In seventeenth-century Scotland, for example, the question could not but be raised, 'but are there witches?' If Winch asks, from within what way of social life, under what system of belief was this question asked, the only answer is that it was asked by men who confronted alternative systems and were able to draw out of what confronted them independent criteria of judgement. Many Africans today are in the same situation.

This type of argument is of course necessarily inconclusive; any historical counter-example to Winch's thesis will be open to questions of interpretation that will make it less than decisive. But there is another important argument. Consider the statement made by some Zande theorist or by King James VI and I, 'there are witches' and the statement made by some modern sceptic, 'there are no witches'. Unless one of these statements denies what the other asserts, the negation of the sentence expressing the former could not be a correct translation of the sentence expressing the latter. Thus if we could not deny from our own standpoint and in our own language what the Azande or King James assert in theirs, we should be unable to translate their expression into our language. Cultural idiosyncrasy would have entailed linguistic idiosyncrasy and cross-cultural comparison would have been rendered logically impossible. But of course translation is not impossible.

Yet if we treat seriously, not what I take to be Winch's mistaken thesis that we cannot go beyond a society's own self-description, but what I take to be his true thesis that we must not do this except and until we have grasped the criteria embodied in that self-description, then we shall have to conclude that the contingently different conceptual schemes and institutional arrangements of different societies make translation difficult to the point at which attempts at cross-cultural generalization too often become little more than a construction of lists.

Goldschmidt and Leach have both pointed out how the building up of typologies and classificatory schemes becomes empty and purposeless unless we have a theory which gives point and criteria to our classificatory activities. Both have also pointed out how, if we compare for example marital institutions in different cultures, our definition of 'marriage' will either be drawn from one culture in terms of whose concepts other cultures will be described or rather misdescribed, or else will be so neutral, bare and empty as to be valueless.[20] That is, the understanding of a people in terms of their own concepts and beliefs does in fact tend to preclude understanding them in any other term. To this extent Winch is vindicated. But an opposite moral to his can be drawn. We may conclude not that we ought not to generalize but that such generalization must move at another level. Goldschmidt argues for the recommendation: do not ask what an institution means for the agents themselves, ask what necessary needs and purposes it serves. He argues for this not because he looks for functionalist explanations of a Malinowskian kind, but because he believes that different institutions, embodying different conceptual schemes, may be illuminatingly seen as serving the same social necessities. To carry the argument further would be to raise questions that are not and cannot be raised within the framework of Winch's book. It is because I believe writers such as Goldschmidt are correct in saying that one must transcend such a framework that I believe also that Winch's book deserves close critical attention.

Notes

1. Winch, Peter (1958) *The Idea of a Social Science*, London, Routledge & Kegan Paul.
2. See, e.g. Rudner, Richard (1967) *The Philosophy of Social Science*, Englewood Cliffs, N.J., Prentice-Hall, pp. 81–3.
3. See the review by Louch, A. R. (1963) in *Inquiry*, 6, 273.
4. Winch, op. cit., p. 114.
5. ibid., p. 88.
6. Malinowski, Bronislaw (1932) *The Sexual Life of Savages in North-Western Melanesia*, New York/London, Harcourt, Brace & Jovanovich/Routledge & Kegan Paul, pp. 425–9.
7. ibid., pp. 428–9.
8. Winch, op. cit., p. 116.
9. ibid., pp. 83–4.
10. ibid., p. 88.
11. ibid., pp. 91–2.
12. ibid., p. 91.
13. ibid., p. 110. Durkheim, Emile (1897) *Le Suicide*, Paris. (Translated 1952 by Spaulding, John A. and Simpson, George, London, Routledge & Kegan Paul.)
14. ibid., p. 115.

15. Leach, E. R. (1966) *Rethinking Anthropology*, London, Athlone; Goldschmidt, Walter (1966) *Comparative Functionalism*, Berkeley, University of California Press.
16. Winch, op. cit., pp. 134—6.
17. ibid., pp. 104—11.
18. ibid., p. 100.
19. *American Philosophical Quarterly* (1964), 1(4), 309; Evans-Pritchard, E. E. (1937) *Witchcraft, Oracles and Magic among the Azande*, Oxford.
20. See Gough, Kathleen (1964) 'The Nayars and the definition of marriage', in Hammond, P. B., ed. *Cultural and Social Anthropology*, New York, Macmillan; Leach, op. cit., 'Polyandry, inheritance and the definition of marriage with particular reference to Sinhalese customary law'; and Goldschmidt, op. cit., pp. 17—26.

7.3   INQUIRY IN SOCIAL ANTHROPOLOGY

JOHN BEATTIE (1915–   ), *from* Other cultures: aims, methods and achievements in social anthropology, *London, Cohen & West, 1964, extracts from chs 3, 4, and 5, pp. 41–4, 49–55, 74–7, abridged*

In these extracts from a much-cited book on the methods and approach of social anthropology, Beattie argues that even the most descriptive account of the 'facts' about a foreign society — whether about their ideas or their activities — is essentially theory-laden. Even in presenting the local view of events, the analyst is to some extent inevitably bringing in something of his own interpretation.

Beattie shares Winch's insistence on the need for understanding a foreign society 'from the inside' as far as possible, without imposing outside categories on the material. But, like MacIntyre, he suggests that understanding ideas and beliefs in their own terms is not the only kind of explanation open to the social inquirer: there is also classification of foreign ideas and customs under general headings (a type of explanation); and the relating of social action either to its historical antecedents or, more common in social anthropology, to its functional interconnections, something which may be 'implicit rather than explicit in the minds of the people they are studying, if indeed they are aware of them at all'.

1. The need for theory

It may be said that the anthropologist's first task is descriptive: in any empirical enquiry we must know what the facts are before we can analyse them. But it is plain . . . that although the distinction between description and analysis is indispensable it can be misleading, especially in the social sciences. The difference is not simply between studies which imply abstraction and those which do not, for even the most common-sense descriptions are shot through with abstractions, generally unanalysed and implicit ones. This must be so, for a description of anything must be in general terms, and general terms are the names of classes, that is of abstractions, and not the names of things. So description always does more than just describe; to some degree at least it also explains. Theories are involved in even the simplest descriptions; not only do they determine the kinds of facts which are selected for attention, but also they dictate the ways in which these facts shall be ordered and put together. So the important question is not whether an account of a social institution (or of anything else) implies generalization and abstraction, for it is bound to do this. The critical questions are, rather, what is the level of abstraction, and what are the kinds of theories involved? It is especially necessary to be explicit about these matters in social anthropology, for the social situations it deals with are often unfamiliar ones. This means that our common-sense notions about them, implicitly derived from our own culture, are likely to be quite inappropriate and may be gravely misleading. This is why there is a special need for explicit theory in social anthropology, that is, for a systematic consideration of the kinds of questions which are to be asked. For it is not at all obvious *prima facie* what kinds of questions are appropriate to what kinds of data. Owing to deficient theory, anthropologists have often framed their questions in such terms that they are unanswerable.

These considerations also explain why amateurs' accounts of simpler and unfamiliar cultures are rarely as satisfactory by present-day standards as those of professional anthropologists. It is not that they are less careful or conscientious observers; it is simply that the kinds of questions modern social anthropologists ask, and the kinds of interconnections they look for, derive from a body of theoretical ideas which have grown up over the past half-century or so, and which have to be learnt. As in other sciences, though more recently than in most, the amateur's day is over. No scientist can approach his material with, literally, an open mind; he is bound to have some theoretical preconceptions. Since this is so, it is desirable first that these should be as explicit as possible and second, that they should both be appropriate to the kind of material being investigated and be conceived in terms of current theory.

Of course no sensible social anthropologist approaches his study with a set of cast-iron, currently fashionable categories, and then forces his material into them, regardless of its uniqueness and individuality. At the start of a field investigation the appropriateness of any particular body of theory, explanatory framework, or set of questions (all these phrases mean very much the same thing), is bound to be a hit-or-miss affair, subject to continuing revision, modification and reformulation. The difference between the professional and the amateur is not that one has theories about what he is doing and the other has not: nobody in his senses tries to do something without the least idea of what he is trying to do, and his statement of what he is trying to do and how he proposes to do it (if he takes the trouble to make such a statement) is his theory. The difference between them lies rather in the explicitness and appropriateness of their theories, of the questions they are trying to answer. It will become clearer in later chapters that questions which are appropriate in regard to one of the three aspects of social relationships which I distinguished earlier (that is, their aspects as systems of action, systems of beliefs, or systems of values) may be quite inappropriate in regard to another.

Social anthropologists, then, seek to understand the data they study, and what they mostly study are social relationships. Now there are two important ways in which an unfamiliar social relationship can be understood. First, we can learn enough about the culture in which it is found to see the situation as the parties to it see it, and secondly, we can place it in a causal context as both effect and cause. These two kinds of understanding correspond to the two major aspects of human social relationships which I distinguished earlier, their aspect as systems of ideas and beliefs, and their aspect as systems of action. Though analytically distinguishable, these are almost always combined in the actual explanations which social scientists give. But it is worth noting that the first of them, understanding by, as it were, imaginatively putting oneself in the place of the parties to the relationship being examined, is peculiar to the social sciences. It is no part of the chemist's or the physicist's job to identify himself imaginatively with the entities he is studying; to do so would hinder rather than help his researches. But it is an essential part of the social anthropologist's task. . . .

A word must be said on the general notion of explanation in the social sciences, and especially in social anthropology. There are many different ways of explaining things, some appropriate to some kinds of data, others to other kinds, and they are often confused. But what is common to all kinds of explanation is that they relate what is to be explained to something else, or to some order of things or events, so that it no longer appears to hang in the air, as it were detached and isolated. As the social anthropologist Nadel has put it, explanation 'adds meaning to "just so" existence'. What is not fully intelligible when considered in and by itself becomes so as soon as it is seen as a part of a wider whole or process, or as an exemplification of some principle or pattern already understood. So explaining something means putting it in an appropriate context.

Now there are various ways in which things can be related to other things, and so explained: I consider some of them in the next chapter. Here I note only that there is a very broad sense in which it may be said that all explanation, deductively considered, is merely a process of bringing what is to be explained under some general rule or principle. But this is too general for our purpose. Certainly all explanation does involve the assimilation of what is to be explained to some body of existing knowledge, but essentially this process is only classificatory; what we are doing here is referring what is to be explained to some category or class with which we are already familiar. Where we already know something about the class to which our explicandum is referred, then the process of subsuming the particular under the general certainly adds to our understanding of it, and so far it is explanatory. Thus, for example, our understanding of such apparently diverse institutions as the *kula* (in which the natives of some Melanesian islands ceremonially exchange certain ornaments), the *potlatch* (in which members of some North American Indian tribes conspicuously destroy useful goods), and of bridewealth (common in Africa and elsewhere and involving a payment by the groom to the bride's relatives on marriage), is greatly advanced when all these institutions are shown to be special types of the general class of presentations or gift-exchanges. What we are really doing here is bringing what we are attempting to explain within the range of an already existing explanation. So it is not simply the process of generalization that is explanatory − though some have written as though it were − in the last resort what is being invoked is some explanatory synthesis, as yet unspecified, of another kind. . . .

2. Explanation in social anthropology: social function

. . . Explanation is putting things in contexts. Now there are different kinds of contexts into which social scientists may put their findings; I have already discussed one of them, subsuming things under rules, or classifying them. Thus we may explain certain features of the institution of bridewealth by pointing out that it is a case of the wider class of gift-exchanges, and that as such it must have certain characteristics, such as a reciprocating element. But what we really want to know is why this should be so, and no amount of generalizing can tell us this. If we are to add to our understanding, and not just to summarize or apply what we know already, we need some new synthesis, some hitherto unthought-of way of looking at things.

But what kind of synthesis? I stressed earlier that the notion of a social institution involves, on the one hand, a framework of action, and on the other, a framework of ideas, beliefs and values. Corresponding to this distinction, there are two broad types of explanatory synthesis used by social anthropologists. The first has reference to causes; the second to meanings. The two levels interact, and indeed explanation on either level requires some reference to the other. But they imply two quite different kinds of interests in the social institutions being studied.

Until very recently most social anthropologists, especially in Britain, have stressed the analysis of social systems as systems of action, that is, in causal terms. The most celebrated contributions of the past half-century deriving through Radcliffe-Brown and Malinowski from Durkheim and his predecessors, have been made at this level. This is not surprising. . . . The key which opened the door to the systematic understanding of the simpler, 'primitive' societies was the organic analogy, which derived from French sociology. And the functioning of organisms, like the working of machines, makes sense without any reference to the states of mind (if any) of their constituent parts. Scholars on the Continent and in America, and a few social anthropologists in this country, have throughout sustained an interest in people's thoughts and ideas, both on their own account and as causally effective elements in systems of action. But the theoretical models most characteristic of modern social anthropology have been those which take societies as systems of action, and which either explicitly or implicitly invoke the organic analogy. It is only in the last few years that the study of social and cultural institutions as systems of meanings has again become a primary concern. Here I discuss explanatory theory at the 'action' level, where causal connections rather than 'meanings' are paramount. In the next chapter [below, p. 220] I consider advances in the anthropological study of other peoples' ideas and values.

On the 'action' level, two different though associated kinds of questions can be asked about social institutions, both concerned with causes. The first relates to the problem of how things came to be as they are, and so is essentially historical. A certain existing state of affairs is better understood if it can be shown to have followed from some pre-existing state of affairs in accordance with principles of causation already familiar from other contexts. So if it can be shown (as of course it very often cannot) that a certain social institution is as it is because of certain historical happenings, social anthropologists take (or should take) note of these happenings, provided that there is sufficient evidence for them. And these happenings need not themselves be physical events on the 'action' plane of social reality; we know that ideas and values may play an important part in history. History is important for sociology not only as a chain of causes and effects running back into the past; from a different point of view it is also important as a body of contemporary beliefs about these events. Such ideas may be potent forces in current social attitudes and relations, and as such they are plainly the social anthropologist's concern.

But causal, temporal processes may be regarded not only as making up unique chains of antecedents and consequents culminating in the present; they may also be seen as current, habitual and repetitive. This provides the second and major dimension of the social anthropologist's interest in causes. For it is one thing to ask how a society, or a social institution, came to be as it is; it is quite another thing to ask how it works or 'functions'. This is the central difference between the historical approach and what has come to be called the 'functional' approach in social anthropology. Both are concerned with causes, but the questions which one asks are aetiological or historical, while the questions which the other asks are operational or functional. An example of a historical question is 'did the kingship of the Baganda originate in conquest by an outside power?': an example of a functional or sociological question is 'what are the causal implications of the Ganda kingship for other institutions in the society, such as the economic system or the system of social control?' Both kinds of questions are concerned with causes, but in the second case, unlike the first, the causes and effects are thought of as repetitive or continuous in time and not as constituting a unique series. Also they are currently observable, or at least inferable, by the investigator.

These functional causal connections are not always obvious; they have to be looked for. So a characteristic of the functional approach is its concern to discover connections between things which at first sight seem to be quite separate. This is why functionalism as a technique of investigation had to await the development of intensive fieldwork. For to perceive causal connections between different social institutions in real-life situations it is first of all necessary to understand these institutions thoroughly; to know both how they work and what those who participate in them think about them (since their ideas may be causally effective). And this kind of understanding, at least in exotic and unfamiliar contexts, was impossible until intensive field studies of working communities began to be made. The chief importance of functional anthropology for modern fieldworkers is that it provides them with hypotheses about possible interconnections between institutions, and if and when these are established they afford reasonably adequate and satisfying explanations at the 'action' level. For example, witchcraft beliefs in a particular society may be shown to be closely connected with social control, since men may fear to invite either attack by witches or suspicion of witchcraft by socially disapproved behaviour. If this is shown to be the case, our understanding both of the social significance of witchcraft and of the maintenance of social order is much enhanced. . . .

Durkheim's explanation of suicide statistics by demonstrating causal links with such other social factors as marital status and church membership is a classic example [of such functional interconnections]. Another instance is the type of explanations anthropologists give of the widespread institution of marriage-payment or bridewealth by showing how it is linked with other co-existing social institutions. Thus it may provide a means of legitimizing the status of children, or maintain certain kinds of relationships between groups of people. The pointing out of such necessary but not always obvious interdependences is the fieldworker's most important task. Indeed, *qua* sociologist, it is difficult to see what else he could do, and as a fieldwork method there is not much more to functionalism than this. It has even been argued that there is no such thing as a specifically functional method, distinct from other kinds of sociological enquiry. The field sociologist's job, it may be said, is neither more nor less than to try to determine the nature of the social institutions he is studying, and the manner of their inter-connections.

But there is a little more to functionalism than this. Causal connections between things can only be detected if the investigator has in mind hypotheses about the kinds of interconnections which he expects to find. And he is looking for consequences as well as causes. In this sense functionalism is forward-looking; and usually functional explanation involves either explicit or implicit reference to some end or purpose, which is seen − or presumed − to be served by the causal interdependences which have been discovered. Functional theory looms so large in modern social anthropology that I must say something here about these presumed ends or purposes.

Because it looks forward to some kind of end, and not backwards to a beginning, functionalism is evidently (in some sense) teleological. But the notion of teleology contains a fundamental ambiguity, and this has led to much confusion. In the first place, teleological explanation consists in showing that it is a quality of what is being explained to have certain consequences. But not just any consequences. To say, for example, that it is a quality of fire to burn things is not to offer a teleological explanation of fire, even though it certainly adds to our understanding of what fire is. For an explanation to be teleological it is necessary that the consequence should be for some sort of meaningful complex or system, which the investigator already has in his mind, whether it is precisely formulated there or not. This means that when the causal implications for that complex of what is being explained have become plain to him, he may say: 'so that is the point of it!' or, more naïvely, 'so that is what it's for!' In precisely this manner the functioning of the lungs is teleologically explained by pointing out that it provides for the reoxygenization of the blood and so for the maintenance of the life of the whole organism.

Thus teleological explanation is not just reference from a cause to an effect, the simple reverse of historical explanation or explanation by efficient causation, which refers an effect to an antecedent cause. Essential to it is the notion that what is explained has causal implications for some previously comprehended complex or system. And this complex or system possesses some kind of pre-existent interest, and so some kind of value, for the investigator. What is being explained is teleologically understood when it is shown how it contributes to the working or maintenance of that system. This is the strict meaning of teleological explanation; Herbert Spencer called it 'legitimate teleology'.[1] It can be seen that it does not necessarily imply either that what is brought about is somehow foreseen by somebody or something (other than the investigator himself), or that the causally effective agent is as it is because it has the consequences it does have. It involves no reference to goals or purposes as dynamic, causally effective agents.

But just as in explanation by reference to antecedent events the mind finds it hard to rest content with mere correlation in space and time but demands efficient causation, so in the case of teleological explanation efficient causation may be as it were reversed, and the factor to be explained understood to be as it is *because* it has the consequences it does have. This provides the second meaning of teleology; Spencer's 'illegitimate' teleology. The end brought about is thought of as somehow foreseen (by somebody or something), and the thing to be explained is understood when it is seen to be designed (by somebody or something) to bring about this end. That is 'why' it is there.

This second kind of teleological explanation is evidently appropriate to much human behaviour, for people do act teleologically, in that they try to bring about certain ends, at least some of the time. But it is very much less helpful in dealing with social institutions. Here is an example. It makes very good sense to say that a man is slaughtering a goat for the purpose of making a feast. It makes very much less sense, and in fact may be quite false, to say (for instance) that the purpose of sacrifice is to bring the members of a certain community together in mutual harmony – even though this may be a consequence of the institution. 'Whose purpose?' we may legitimately ask: the institution itself obviously cannot have an intention, as an individual can. It may be that the members of a community know that one consequence of their sacrificial institutions is to increase group harmony, and they may even sustain these institutions for this reason; but it is altogether more likely that they are quite unaware of it. By far the larger number of functional correlations identified by anthropological and sociological fieldworkers are implicit rather than explicit in the minds of the people they are studying, if indeed they are aware of them at all.

Recognition of this has led to the formulation of the important distinction between those kinds of social consequences of which the members of the society are themselves aware, and those of which they are unaware, and which are identified only by the sociologist. Professor Merton has phrased this distinction as that between manifest and latent function. Of course there are difficulties about the notion of awareness in this context (for example what degree of explicitness constitutes awareness?), but the distinction is valid and important. It expresses an aspect of the distinction already referred to between the 'folk system', the social system as seen by its members, and the analytical system which the observer builds up in the light of his theoretical interests . . . there is an important difference between saying that a certain institution has significant implications for other institutions, and saying that this is *why* it has the character it has.

So we have here a 'how' question and a 'why' question. First, we may ask what happens; does such-and-such an event contribute to the working of a particular system of which we have already formed an idea, and if so, how does it do so? And secondly, we may ask the quite different question why it does so; how does it come about that things are as they are? Now this second question is really not a teleological one at all, for it expects an answer referring to some antecedent event, for example to someone's previous act of intelligence or will. An example of the first kind of question is: how are we to understand the form of a particular marriage institution? And a strictly teleological answer would be: by observing that it tends to produce or maintain a certain system of social relations, such as the integration of separate social groups. Once this is seen, the particular form which has puzzled us is, so far, explained. An example of the second kind of question is: why does that particular institution have the form it has − in other words, how has it come about that it is so conveniently adapted to the consequences by reference to which we explain it? This is really a historical question, for instead of looking forward to an end, it looks backward to a beginning.

Now in social anthropology, as in the other social sciences, the teleological approach which looks for the social functions served by institutions has proved to be most useful, but the attempt to provide genetic explanations of existing institutions in terms of somebody's purposes or intentions is much more rarely so. This is partly because social anthropologists have concentrated on the analysis of social institutions rather than on the study of the human individuals who have these institutions. And it is the individuals, not the institutions, that are motivated by ends, aims and purposes. Thus questions about intentions may, and indeed must be asked about the behaviour of human individuals; but they have little relevance to institutional analysis. And equally, questions which may usefully be asked about social institutions are often quite inappropriate in regard to individual people. It is entirely sensible to ask what are the social functions of an institution like marriage: it is very much less so to ask what are the social functions of particular husbands or wives. The frames of reference are quite different, but it is very easy to confuse them.

The existence of a certain institution and the fact that it contributes to certain socially significant ends may be due historically to any of a number of causes. It may be due to the conscious intention of past or present members of the society; it may be an unintended consequence of behaviour directed to quite different ends; it may be due to diffusion from elsewhere, or to some kind of social 'natural selection'. Or it may be, and most likely is, due to a combination of some or all of these factors. Where the answers to these historical questions are ascertainable they are of considerable interest to social anthropologists, especially if they are studying processes of social change. But usually in the case of simple, preliterate societies, we cannot know how social institutions came to be as they are, and then understanding in a different (if more restricted) dimension may be afforded by teleological explanation in its narrower and more exact sense. We can see the point of a marriage regulation or an economic institution when we have understood its causal implications for other aspects of the social system, even when we do not know how it came to be as it is.

So functional explanation in social anthropology does more than merely demonstrate that different, apparently independent, modes of social behaviour are causally connected in certain systematic ways. It looks also for their implications for institutional systems. This is the teleological content of functionalism. The accent is not only on the discovery of causal links, important though this is; it is also, and especially, on the part which one mode of institutionalized behaviour plays in a systematic and already conceptually prefigured complex of interlocking institutions. We are dealing with what may be regarded *analytically* as part-whole relationships. For example, the institution of vassalage is explained functionally (and teleologically) when it is shown that it contributes to the maintenance of the complex of social institutions which is usually called feudalism. And the institution of avoidance between certain relatives-in-law, found in some societies, is understood functionally when it is shown that by tending to obviate social conflict it makes possible harmonious relations in a broad range of contacts between the two groups concerned. . . .

3. Beliefs and values

It is quite impossible to assess the relevance of particular values or systems of values to particular social relationships or systems of relationships until the values have been understood in themselves. A conscientious field anthropologist is bound to concern himself with the values of the people he is studying, without prejudging their sociological significance. Belief and action, values and social institutions, are inextricably bound up with one another, and I remarked earlier that social anthropologists have always given some account of the values and beliefs of the peoples they have studied. Where these have had clear relevance to social institutions the links have usually been pointed out. In his study of Zande witchcraft Evans-Pritchard[2] shows how beliefs in witchcraft and oracles may have important implications for a system of political authority, and in his account of ancestral cult and social structure among the Lugbara of Uganda[3] Middleton shows that the status of clan elders depends on how effectively (in the Lugbara view) they can invoke the ancestral ghosts. But we do not abandon interest where such precise links cannot be established; human cosmologies and religious systems are of interest to social anthropologists in their own right as well as in their relationships, if any, to systems of action. The social anthropologist's method of working in and through the culture he is studying peculiarly qualifies him for this kind of study, at least in preliterate or only recently literate communities. Indeed it might be claimed that social anthropology's contribution to the understanding of other cultures has been at least as important in the study of beliefs and values, as it has been in the functional analysis of social systems.

Let us take this a step further. People's ways of thought may differ not only in the kinds of symbolism they use, and in the kinds of things they think important, but even in the very ways in which they represent to themselves the physical, social, and moral universe they live in. It is an epistemological commonplace that people see what they expect to see, and the categories of their perception are largely if not wholly determined by their social and cultural background. The pastoral Nuer can distinguish, by reference to colour and shape of horn, between several hundred kinds of cattle, and they have names for all of them; to the agriculturalist a cow is just a cow. Distinctions are made in some cultures which are not made, or are made differently, in others. Here is a very simple example from kinship. A western European regards the brothers of both of his parents as relatives of the same kind, and he calls them all 'uncle'. But in many other cultures a man regards paternal and maternal uncles as entirely different kinds of relatives, and he calls them by completely different terms . . . this usage is wholly consistent with a certain way of thinking about kin, in the context of which the European practice would seem absurd. Here is another quite different example. Western law makes a clear distinction between accidental death, and death caused by homicide or suicide − intentional killings. But in many cultures no such distinction is recognized; all deaths are thought to be intentional, whether the intention is thought to be that of a living person practising sorcery or witchcraft, or that of a ghost or spirit. Evidently such a way of regarding death must have important social implications.

So members of different cultures may see the world they live in very differently. And it is not just a matter of reaching different conclusions about the world from the 'same' evidence; the very evidence which is given to them as members of different cultures may be different. If in one sense all men everywhere inhabit the same world, in another and important sense they inhabit very different ones. And where these differences are culturally determined social anthropologists are centrally interested in them.

We can be more explicit. It has been argued that even such fundamental categories as 'time' and 'substance' may be very differently conceived by members of different cultures. From a study of the language of the Hopi people of the American South-West, and of the way they use it, the American linguist-anthropologist Whorf argued that Hopi do not imagine time, as we do, as a kind of continuum analogous with

space, in which different events occupy different positions in an unending sequence of before and after.[4] Rather they think in terms of
immediately experienced duration − 'earlier', 'later', 'now' − and they
distinguish events by reference to their immediacy, their certainty, or
their expectedness, not by reference to an objectified time-scale,
embodied in a tense structure. Similarly, Whorf claims, Hopi modes of
describing spatial relations do not postulate a sort of pre-existent 'space'
which things are 'in' as eggs are in a basket; they imply only things and
their positional interrelations.

So, according to Whorf, the linguistic forms of Hopi thought
dispense with many unnecessary and non-existent 'entities' with which
our particular language structure saddles us. Here is a further example.
Where we say 'it's raining', thereby raising the quite unreal question:
'what is?', Hopi simply say 'raining!', or 'rain is happening'. In this way
they eliminate a whole world of unknowable entities, and replace them
by happenings or events. Whorf argued with a good deal of plausibility
that a language of this kind and the ways of thinking about the world
that it implies might well be more appropriate to the kind of thinking
involved in modern physics than the Aristotelian substance-accident
mode in which most Western philosophy and science have been cast.

But however this may be (and not all social anthropologists would go
all the way with Whorf), his point that the ways of thought or 'collective
representations' of members of other cultures may differ in quite fundamental and unexpected ways from our own, is crucially important.
Innumerable difficulties and confusions, both theoretical and practical, have arisen because members of one culture have found it almost
impossible to see things as they are seen by members of another culture.
It is not just a matter of 'seeing the other fellow's point of view', essential
though that is. The problem is the very much more difficult one of comprehending the unacknowledged and unanalysed standpoints from
which his views are taken. Of course this can never be wholly achieved.
We can enter in some degree into other people's ways of thought, and
we can attain some understanding of their beliefs and values, but we
can never see things *exactly* as they see them. If we did we should have
ceased to be members of our own culture and gone over to theirs. But we
can go a long way towards achieving this kind of comprehension, while
still retaining a foothold in our own world. Perhaps social anthropology's chief claim to respect is that it has achieved some success in
doing this.

Notes

1. Spencer, Herbert (1890) *The Data of Ethics*, London.

2. Evans-Pritchard, E. E. (1937) *Witchcraft, Oracles and Magic amongst the Azande*, Oxford, Clarendon Press.
3. Middleton, John (1960) *Lugbara Religion: Ritual and Authority among an East African People*, London, Oxford University Press.
4. Whorf, Benjamin L. (1950) 'Time, space and language', in Thompson, Laura M., *Culture in Crisis: A Study of the Hopi Indians*, New York, Harper & Bros.

Part Four
Conceptions of Inquiry

8 Forms of inquiry

The extracts in this chapter reflect different traditions of thinking about the division of knowledge rather than a debate within a particular tradition. Each has a rather different epistemology. For Hume the division into forms of inquiry is a hierarchical one. On Hume's account the distinction between history, which is concerned with particular facts, and politics, which is concerned with general facts, is a more basic distinction than the distinction between history and astronomy. Hume's account admits morals, criticism and theology as sub-branches of inquiry, but only as special areas of experimental reasoning. Paul H. Hirst is far removed from the empiricist assumptions of Hume and owes, in his account of the forms of knowledge, a considerable intellectual debt to Kant and Wittgenstein. A form of knowledge is to be acknowledged as such only if it is 'autonomous', i.e. cannot be reduced to another form of knowledge. On his account, morals and religion emerge as distinct forms of knowledge and this status is also given to the distinction between the natural sciences and the human. Hirst's procedure and assumptions differ considerably from Hume's and his map of human knowledge may be said to be a pluralist one. Hirst cites as support for recognizing religious knowledge as a distinct form the failure of programmes designed to reduce it to other forms of knowledge.

Hume and Hirst appeal to broadly logical considerations which they see as independent of historical facts about how individual disciplines have developed. Foucault, by contrast, takes a thoroughly historical view of forms of knowledge or what he calls 'discourses'. His list (science, literature, philosophy, religion, history, fiction, etc.) bears some resemblance to that of Hirst. But Foucault holds that these distinctions are specified by the 'archive' of a society.

8.1 THE OBJECTS OF HUMAN INQUIRY

DAVID HUME (1711–1776), *from the 1749 work*, An Enquiry Concerning Human Understanding, *sections 4 and 12, in Selby-Bigge, L. A., ed.*, Hume's Enquiries, *Oxford, Clarendon, 1894, pp. 25ff. and 164ff.*

In the first of these two short extracts, Hume makes his most fundamental distinction, between propositions which are about the world but are only contingently true or false and propositions which are necessarily true or false but tell us only about the 'Relations of Ideas'. All reasoning from experience is of the former kind and, in the second extract, Hume is concerned with forms of 'experimental reasoning', i.e. reasoning from experience. Hume concludes with strictures against metaphysics in particular, which pretends to *a priori* knowledge of matters of fact in breach of his basic dichotomy, and against moral and theological writing of a metaphysical character.

All the objects of human reason or enquiry may naturally be divided into two kinds, to wit, Relations of Ideas, and Matters of Fact. Of the first kind are the sciences of Geometry, Algebra, and Arithmetic; and in short, every affirmation which is either intuitively or demonstratively certain. That the square of the hypothenuse is equal to the square of the two sides, is a proposition which expresses a relation between these figures. That three times five is equal to the half of thirty, expresses a relation between these numbers. Propositions of this kind are discoverable by the mere operation of thought, without dependence on what is anywhere existent in the universe. Though there never were a circle or triangle in nature, the truths demonstrated by Euclid would for ever retain their certainty and evidence.

Matters of fact, which are the second objects of human reason, are not ascertained in the same manner; nor is our evidence of their truth, however great, of a like nature with the foregoing. The contrary of every matter of fact is still possible; because it can never imply a contradiction, and is conceived by the mind with the same facility and distinctness, as if ever so conformable to reality. That the sun will not rise tomorrow is no less intelligible a proposition, and implies no more contradiction than the affirmation, that it will rise. We should in vain, therefore, attempt to demonstrate its falsehood. Were it demonstratively false, it would imply a contradiction, and could never be distinctly conceived by the mind. . . .

It is only experience, which teaches us the nature and bounds of cause and effect, and enables us to infer the existence of one object from that of another. Such is the foundation of moral reasoning, which forms the greater of human knowledge, and is the source of all human action and behaviour.

Moral reasonings are either concerning particular or general facts. All deliberations in life regard the former; as also all disquisitions in history, chronology, geography, and astronomy.

The sciences, which treat of general facts, are politics, natural philosophy, physic, chemistry, etc. where the qualities, causes and effects of a whole species of objects are enquired into.

Divinity or Theology, as it proves the existence of a Deity, and the immortality of souls, is composed partly of reasonings concerning particular, partly concerning general facts. It has a foundation in reason, so far as it is supported by experience. But its best and most solid foundation is faith and divine revelation.

Morals and criticism are not so properly objects of the understanding as of taste and sentiment. Beauty, whether moral or natural, is felt, more properly than perceived. Or if we reason concerning it, and endeavour to fix its standard, we regard a new fact, to wit, the general tastes of mankind, or some such fact, which may be the object of reasoning and enquiry.

When we run over libraries, persuaded of these principles, what havoc must we make? If we take in our hand any volume; of divinity or school metaphysics, for instance; let us ask, Does it contain any abstract reasoning concerning quantity or number? No. Does it contain any experimental reasoning concerning matter of fact and existence? No. Commit it then to the flames: for it can contain nothing but sophistry and illusion.

8.2 FORMS OF KNOWLEDGE

PAUL H. HIRST (1927–   ), *from 'Liberal education and
the nature of knowledge'*, Archambault, R. P., ed., Philosophical Analysis and Education, *London, Routledge & Kegan
Paul, 1963*

In the following extract, Hirst states what he means
by 'a form of knowledge' and makes some suggestions
as to what should be accepted as such forms, particularly that moral knowledge should be so
accepted. He also stresses that there are other
important classifications of knowledge.

By a form of knowledge is meant a distinct way in which our experience
becomes structured round the use of accepted public symbols. The symbols
thus having public meaning, their use is in some way testable against
experience and there is the progressive development of series of tested
symbolic expressions. In this way experience has been probed further and
further by extending and elaborating the use of the symbols and by means
of these it has become possible for the personal experience of individuals to
become more fully structured, more fully understood. The various forms of
knowledge can be seen in low level developments within the common area
of our knowledge of the everyday world. From this there branch out the
developed forms which, taking certain elements in our common knowledge
as a basis, have grown in distinctive ways. In the developed forms of
knowledge the following related distinguishing features can be seen:

(1) They each involve certain central concepts that are peculiar in
    character to the form. For example, those of gravity, acceleration,
    hydrogen, and photo-synthesis characteristic of the sciences;
    number, integral and matrix in mathematics; God, sin and pre-
    destination in religion; ought, good and wrong in moral knowledge.
(2) In a given form of knowledge these and other concepts that denote,
    if perhaps in a very complex way, certain aspects of experience,
    form a network of possible relationships in which experience can be
    understood. As a result the form has a distinctive logical structure.
    For example, the terms and statements of mechanics can be
    meaningfully related in certain strictly limited ways only, and the
    same is true of historical explanation.
(3) The form, by virtue of its particular terms and logic, has expressions
    or statements (possibly answering a distinctive type of question) that
    in some way or other, however indirect it may be, are testable
    against experience. This is the case in scientific knowledge, moral

knowledge, and in the arts, though in the arts no questions are explicit and the criteria for the tests are only partially expressible in words. Each form, then, has distinctive expressions that are testable against experience in accordance with particular criteria that are peculiar to the form.

(4) The forms have developed particular techniques and skills for exploring experience and testing their distinctive expressions, for instance the techniques of the sciences and those of the various literary arts. The result has been the amassing of all the symbolically expressed knowledge that we now have in the arts and the sciences.

Though the various forms of knowledge are distinguishable in these ways it must not be assumed that all there is to them can be made clear and explicit by these means. All knowledge involves the use of symbols and the making of judgments in ways that cannot be expressed in words and can only be learnt in a tradition. The art of scientific investigation and the development of appropriate experimental tests, the forming of an historical explanation and the assessment of its truth, the appreciation of a poem: all of these activities are high arts that are not in themselves communicable simply by words. Acquiring knowledge of any form is therefore to a greater or lesser extent something that cannot be done simply by solitary study of the symbolic expressions of knowledge, it must be learnt from a master on the job. No doubt it is because the forms require particular training of this kind in distinct worlds of discourse, because they necessitate the development of high critical standards according to complex criteria, because they involve our coming to look at experience in particular ways, that we refer to them as disciplines. They are indeed disciplines that form the mind.

Yet the dividing lines that can be drawn between different disciplines by means of the four suggested distinguishing marks are neither clear enough nor sufficient for demarcating the whole world of modern knowledge as we know it. The central feature to which they point is that the major forms of knowledge, or disciplines, can each be distinguished by their dependence on some particular kind of test against experience for their distinctive expressions. On this ground alone however certain broad divisions are apparent. The sciences depend crucially on empirical experimental and observational tests, mathematics depends on deductive demonstrations from certain sets of axioms. Similarly moral knowledge and the arts involve distinct forms of critical tests though in these cases both what the tests are and the ways in which they are applied are only partially statable. (Some would in fact dispute the status of the arts as a form of knowledge for this very reason.) Because of their particular logical features it seems to me necessary to distinguish also as separate disciplines both historical and religious knowledge, and there is perhaps an equally good case, because of the nature of their central concepts, for regarding the human sciences separately from the physical sciences. But within these areas further distinctions must be made. These are usually the result of the groupings of knowledge round a number of related concepts, or round particular skills or techniques. The various sciences and the various arts can be demarcated within the larger units of which they are in varying degrees representative in their structure, by these means.

But three other important classifications of knowledge must in addition be recognised. First there are those organisations which are not themselves disciplines or subdivisions of any discipline. They are formed by building together round specific objects, or phenomena, or practical pursuits, knowledge that is characteristically rooted elsewhere in more than one discipline. It is not just that these organisations make use of several forms of knowledge, for after all the sciences use mathematics, the arts use historical knowledge and so on. Many of the disciplines borrow from each other. But these organisations are not concerned, as the disciplines are, to validate any one logically distinct form of expression. They are not concerned with developing a particular structuring of experience. They are held together simply by their subject matter, drawing on all forms of knowledge that can contribute to them. Geography, as the study of man in relation to his environment, is an example of a theoretical study of this kind, engineering an example of a practical nature. I see no reason why such organisations of knowledge, which I shall refer to as 'fields', should not be endlessly constructed according to particular theoretical or practical interests. Second, whilst moral knowledge is a distinct form, concerned with answering questions as to what ought to be done in practical affairs, no specialised subdivisions of this have been developed. In practical affairs, moral questions, because of their character, naturally arise alongside questions of fact and technique, so that there have been formed 'fields' of practical knowledge that include distinct moral elements within them, rather than the subdivisions of a particular discipline. Political, legal and educational theory are perhaps the clearest examples of fields where moral knowledge of a developed kind is to be found. Thirdly, there are certain second order forms of knowledge which are dependent for their existence on the other primary areas. On the one hand there are the essentially scientific studies of language and symbolism as in grammar and philology. On the other hand there are the logical and philosophical studies of meaning and justification. These would seem to constitute a distinct discipline by virtue of their particular concepts and criteria of judgment.

In summary, then, it is suggested that the forms of knowledge as we have them can be classified as follows:

I. Distinct disciplines or forms of knowledge (subdivisible): mathematics, physical sciences, human sciences, history, religion, literature and the fine arts, philosophy.
II. Fields of knowledge: theoretical, practical (these may or may not include elements of moral knowledge).

It is the distinct disciplines that basically constitute the range of unique ways we have of understanding experience if to these is added the category of moral knowledge.

8.3   THE FORMS OF KNOWLEDGE REVISITED

PAUL H. HIRST (1927–   ), *from* Knowledge and the Curriculum, *London, Routledge & Kegan Paul, 1974, pp. 84–100*

Hirst offers further reflections on his thesis in the previous extract in the light of various criticisms, for instance that literature and the fine arts do not constitute a distinctive form of knowledge, nor does religion. He argues that each form of knowledge has its own forms of objective judgement. He defends his thesis against the charge that it leads to social relativism.

In . . . 'Liberal education and the nature of knowledge'[1] . . . I tried to outline a coherent concept of liberal education concerned simply with the development of the pupil's knowledge and understanding, the diversity of its content being determined by the diversity of the forms that human knowledge and understanding in fact take. An essential part of that argument was the suggestion that within the domain of knowledge a number of forms can be distinguished which are different in their logical character. The account given of those forms was necessarily very brief and its inadequacies have provoked a certain amount of critical comment.[2] Precisely what I was trying to do has been the subject of some debate, as well as the satisfactoriness of some of the arguments I deployed. Since then I have returned to this subject in a number of places, in particular in *The Logic of Education*,[3] written in collaboration with Professor R. S. Peters. Over the years, the thesis originally advanced has undergone a number of minor modifications which mark either certain developments in my own thoughts on the subject, or applications of the central ideas to somewhat different educational problems. It is the object [here] . . . to outline my present reflections on the original 'forms of knowledge' thesis. . . .

<h1 style="text-align:center">I</h1>

The central element in the original thesis was that the domain of human knowledge can be seen to be differentiated into a number of logically distinct 'forms', none of which is ultimately reducible in character to any of the others, either simply or in combination. For this property of mutual irreducibility I have from time to time used the terms logically 'distinct', 'autonomous', 'independent', 'unique', 'fundamental', and have talked of 'categorial divisions' within knowledge. All these terms carry connotations that make them far from ideal. Some are, no doubt, more misleading than others. But whatever terms are best, the claim I have been concerned with rests on a specific view of the nature of knowledge and the necessary features of knowledge. The domain of knowledge I take to be centrally the domain of true propositions or statements, and the question of their being logically distinct forms of knowledge to be the question of their being logically distinct types of true propositions or statements. Certainly we speak not only of knowing truths but also of knowing people and places and knowing how to do things. Detailed analysis suggests, however, that there are in fact only two distinct types of knowledge here, that in which the objects of knowledge are true propositions and that in which the objects are practical performances of some kind, knowledge of people and places being reducible to complexes of knowledge of these two types based on certain specific forms of experience. Taking this to be so, and not in this context being concerned with practical knowledge, the question of distinguishing autonomous areas of knowledge does reduce to distinguishing types of true propositions.

But what does this involve? Types of propositions can of course be distinguished in many different ways and how are we then to judge which of these, if any, shows the domain of knowledge to consist of a number of fundamentally distinct and irreducible categories? We shall get at the logically fundamental characteristics of true propositions only by looking at those features which are necessary to all such propositions and the question is whether or not within them there exist mutually irreducible categories. On these grounds, the three elements in which the differences are to be found are the concepts and the logical structure propositions employ, and the criteria for truth in terms of which they are assessed.

I do not wish to be interpreted as saying that these three elements within which the distinctions are drawn are logically independent of each other, when manifestly they are not. Nor should it be thought that anything in this approach prejudges the question as to whether in fact the domain of knowledge is logically monolithic or differentiable into a number of distinct forms. That question can be answered only by a detailed analysis of the character of true propositions in the light of these terms and any answer must therefore rest on the results of an extensive range of philosophical work. My original suggestion, that there are at present some seven areas which must be regarded as at least having serious claims to being logically distinct forms of knowledge, rests on my own reading of philosophical work concerned with differences in concepts and logical structures and truth criteria. What I have written therefore must be regarded as disputable at a level where philosophers are indeed not all agreed and subject to revision in the light of new philosophical clarification.

In addition to the three features I have mentioned, I originally suggested a fourth feature in which to distinguish differences between forms of knowledge, that of the methodology employed for amassing true propositions. Forms of knowledge are I think distinguishable in this way, but only in a secondary sense, and in later accounts I have not emphasised this feature. Differences in the methods used to establish true propositions not surprisingly will follow differences in the character of those propositions. These differences in methodology certainly mark out important differences in the pursuit of knowledge in the distinguishable forms, and are therefore most important in education and research. But they do not themselves add anything to the strictly logical distinctions which mark out possible forms of knowledge and I have therefore not referred to them in later writing which has concentrated solely on the logical distinctions.

Over the years, I have modified the terms used to label the forms I consider distinguishable in the light of the three fundamental features, but because of one area of uncertainty only. It has been suggested that I have wavered as to whether moral knowledge constitutes a distinct form. This is however not so. The question that for some while worried me considerably was the character of history and the social sciences, as my original reading of work in philosophy of history and philosophy of the social sciences left me unclear as to their status. It now seems to me that both history and the social sciences as pursued in universities and schools are, like most curriculum areas, logically complex in character. In part they are concerned with truths that are matters of empirical observation and experiment, truths that logically differ not at all from the kind with which the physical or natural sciences are concerned. Large tracts of sociology and psychology, and indeed parts of history, are therefore of the strictly physical science variety. That some of these truths are about the past, or are singular rather than general in character, is irrelevant for the purposes of the fundamental distinctions being made. After all, many of the statements made by biologists, physicists and chemists have these features. On the other hand, history and some of the social sciences are in large measure not concerned simply with an understanding of observable phenomena in terms of physical causation, but with explanations of human behaviour in terms of intentions, will, hopes, beliefs, etc. The concepts, logical structure and truth criteria of propositions of this latter kind are, I would now argue, different from, and not reducible to, those of the former kind. For this reason it now seems to me correct to speak of one form of knowledge as being concerned with the truths of the physical world and another as concerned with truths of a mental or personal kind. Knowledge of one's own states of mind and those of others, sometimes referred to as inter-personal knowledge, is of course here regarded as, in principle at any rate, fully propositionalisable. In these terms, I now think it best not to refer to history or the social sciences in any statement of the forms of knowledge as such. These pursuits like so many other so-called 'subjects' may well be concerned with truths of several different logical kinds and only detailed examination can show to what extent any one example of such a subject is or is not logically complex and in what ways. The labels that I have used for distinct forms of knowledge are to be understood as being strictly labels for different classes of true propositions. In so far as these terms are used for parts of the curricula of universities and schools, they may therefore cover very much more than an interest in one particular type of proposition. Even a term like mathematics, which may appropriately label a great deal of one form of knowledge because of the distinctive features of mathematical propositions, is frequently used in educational institutions to cover a concern not only for propositions of this kind, but also a concern for truths about the physical world and occasionally the history and philosophy of mathematics. I have no desire to legislate on the use of terms. I only wish it to be clear that what I mean by a form of knowledge may have little in common with what elsewhere falls under the same label.

II

The suggestion that in literature and the fine arts and also in religion we have distinct forms of knowledge has not surprisingly provoked opposition. Let me therefore make it clear that they can to my mind only be regarded as such in so far as they involve expressions that have the features of true propositions. We certainly do talk of the arts and religion as being cognitive, as providing distinctive types of knowledge. Whether this is justifiable and there is a form of knowledge in the arts, depends on whether or not artistic works themselves have features parallel to those of propositions with related objective tests.

It is my concern to take seriously the possibility that we can legitimately refer to knowledge in the arts as well as in mathematics, the sciences and other areas, that has led me to state less clearly than perhaps I should have, the third of my criteria for a form of knowledge: that necessitating unique truth criteria. Wittgenstein's work on meaning and language-games suggests that works of art can well be seen as symbolic expressions having meaning, simply because they have properties logically equivalent to those of propositions. Recent reconsideration of the concept of truth, and the correspondence theory in particular, suggests that the notion of truth is centrally a demand for objective judgment, and there is nothing to be gained by restricting it to one particular form of such judgment. In that case, works of art might well be seen as judgeable in a manner logically equivalent to that appropriate to propositions. It might of course be insisted that terms like 'concept', 'logical structure' and 'truth' are not appropriate in these circumstances, but I fail to see the real force of this objection. Lacking other suitable general terms to draw attention to the features I am interested in, I have therefore used these terms, and that of 'knowledge', as possibly applicable with very good reason to the arts. Whether in fact they are, is a matter of disagreement amongst philosophers. It is however my desire to keep open this possibility that has led me to talk sometimes of 'truth criteria', sometimes of 'validity', sometimes of 'objective tests' and sometimes of 'testable against experience'. Nothing in my purpose turns on using any one of these phrases rather than another. I am in each case simply referring to tests that have the logical function that truth tests have for propositions.

In looking at the arts as possibly propositional, I have not denied for one moment that art may have many other functions that other areas of knowledge may or may not have, say in relation to the expression of emotion or the creation of delight. In considering religion it is also to be recognised that it likewise has concerns beyond the mere pursuit of knowledge. My interest here is simply whether or not it can lay claim, amongst other things, to being a logically unique form of knowledge. On the answer to that question few would dare to pronounce categorically. My own view, as in the case of the arts, is that in the present state of affairs we must at least take the claim to knowledge seriously. Against this, it has been suggested that religious claims may constitute an area of belief or of non-cognitive discourse which does not justify the label 'form of knowledge' in my terms. Certainly, some have sought to give an account of religious meaning which has seen its cognitive core to be totally reducible to knowledge belonging to other forms (usually moral, historical, or esthetic) and the rest to be emotive in character. If such a reduction can be legitimately carried through, then there can here be no distinct form of religious knowledge. But can it? That I doubt. Equally, it seems to me unclear that one can coherently claim that there is a logically unique domain of religious *beliefs* such that none of them can be known to be true, all being matters of faith. The reason for this is just that the meaning of religious propositions, as any others, rests on a grasp of the truth criteria for such propositions. If these propositions belong to a logically unique form, then their truth criteria must be unique. Religious propositions are then only intelligible to those who know these unique truth criteria. But can such unique truth conditions be known without our actually being able to judge any propositions of this kind true or false? Can there be unique truth criteria that are never satisfied? If meaning is tied to knowing a unique set of truth criteria, is not meaning tied to our actually satisfying these in judging some propositions true or false? In so far then as religion is cognitive at all, it seems to me its claims must be understood as being totally reducible to one or more of the other forms of knowledge or as being at least in part a unique form of knowledge itself. The claim to an irreducible, unique form of propositional meaning, thus seems to necessitate that at last some proposition of this kind be known to be true. If so, there can only be a unique form of meaning if there is a unique form of knowledge, and the claim that religion involves a unique form of belief only, is incoherent.

III

If my original thesis has appeared to many too strong in claiming the existence of knowledge in all the seven different forms, it being doubted whether there are truth criteria in some of these areas, it has also been considered too strong in claiming unique concepts and logical structure for each form. Are there not many concepts that are shared by at least several forms? What about the concepts of 'space' and 'time' which manifestly pervade not only our knowledge of the physical world, but also our knowledge of persons, moral knowledge, artistic knowledge? What about the notion of 'truth' which the thesis itself suggests is a necessary feature of all the forms? And are there not certain fundamental logical laws which all forms of knowledge respect, for example those of identity and non-contradiction?

That there may be such common, even universal elements, I am perfectly willing to accept. What I do not see is how, if they exist, they undermine the thesis of the logical uniqueness, mutual irreducibility, call it what you will, of the forms that I have sought to defend. It was no part of the thesis even in its earliest formulation that the forms of knowledge are totally independent of each other, sharing no concepts or logical rules. That the forms are interrelated has been stressed from the start. Manifestly the concepts of 'space' and 'time' figure in several forms and are presupposed by concepts in other areas. Propositions of a moral kind employ concepts for features of the physical world. Moral argument uses the same deductive rules as does scientific argument. Religious claims presuppose truths about the world and about persons. The conceptual and logical elements shared between forms and the interrelations they indicate are considerable. Yet it remains the case that every proposition can be distinguished by the different kinds of truth criteria it involves, and is tied to the kind of concept applied in the proposition. Put another way every concept has criteria for its application which are the truth criteria for any proposition in which that concept is applied. In this way all concepts can be given a character. There are those that directly or indirectly distinguish features of the physical world. Others distinguish states of mind. Yet others, the moral characters of actions. No concept in one of these areas, even if it presupposes concepts from other areas, is entirely analysable into those presupposed concepts. Moral concepts are not reducible to concepts for objects in the physical world, nor vice versa, even though moral concepts presuppose concepts of objects in the physical world. In that sense, every form of knowledge, for all the concepts it may share with other forms, or presuppose from other forms, involves concepts which are distinctive, are unique, to it.

If this is so, it would seem to follow that there is a network of relations between concepts in each case which will in certain respects be distinctive. Moral concepts involve complex relations with each other and with other kinds of concepts that produce a unique structure. If there are different kinds of criteria for truth in the areas concerned, then, for instance, moral argument, being concerned with the application of moral concepts, and not the application of physical world concepts, must have a different logical structure from that of arguments in science. The idea that the relations between concepts and propositions in all forms of knowledge must conform to those of mathematical or scientific knowledge is a matter of pure dogmatism. We must examine these relations for their own structure in each case. Looser forms of relations are not necessarily suspect as these may be of the nature of these concepts. Nevertheless, certain elements within a moral argument may be identical in form with those in a scientific argument. If it can be shown that certain concepts or logical laws are common to all areas of knowledge, that would simply mean no more than that certain elements of knowledge of a specific form are presupposed by elements in all the other forms. This is no way denies any specific determinate character to those concepts or logical laws. In particular I see no reason to think that it implies the existence of an area of common sense knowledge quite distinct from the particular forms of knowledge which is in some sense presupposed by them. In so far as concepts have application, it seems to me they have a specific character, and that goes for all those within common sense as well as for those in more advanced areas of knowledge. Common sense knowledge is to my mind simply that collection of elementary knowledge, or what is claimed to be such, from the different forms, which is largely taken for granted in a given society.

The logical interrelations between the different forms of knowledge are manifestly many and complex. How far a general map of these can be outlined, I am far from clear. It might be thought that the sharpness of the demarcation lines I have drawn only accentuates the problem of seeing the relations. Certainly the relations of concepts and propositions across the divisions of knowledge are legion. Yet the distinctions I have emphasised, if they are fundamental, must be recognised for what they are, and the interrelations seen in terms of these. It has been suggested that there might be an overall hierarchical pattern in which logical and mathematical knowledge is seen as presupposed by knowledge in the physical sciences which in its turn is presupposed by a knowledge of persons. The sequence might be continued to give an order of say moral, religious, artistic and philosophical knowledge. With such a strictly logical hierarchy, not to be seen in any way as a hierarchy of value or metaphysical hierarchy, I have much sympathy. It is, however, a suggestion that would seem to oversimplify the very complex relations there are between elements of the forms, seeing them in too linear a way, particularly where those occurring later in the sequence are concerned. The present state of our detailed conceptual mapping of these areas is, however, such that one can at present do little more than make conjectures about an overall pattern. The thesis for which I have argued is tied to no particular position on this matter.

IV

It will be apparent from various points I have already made that although I was originally concerned simply with distinguishing various fundamentally different forms of knowledge, the approach by means of a classification of true propositions has thereby also provided a classification of the concepts applied in those propositions. From this it follows that if one holds, as I hold, that all forms of experience are intelligible only by virtue of the concepts under which we have them, a classification of forms of knowledge provides also a classification of forms of experience. What is more, the distinctions between the forms that I have been concerned with are what I understand by categorial distinctions, being matters of the types of concepts, logical structures and truth criteria which are irreducible to each other. I did not use the terminology of categories in the first instance, not wishing to be involved in expressing in detail the fundamental categorial concepts in each case. The examples of concepts applied in propositions within the different forms of knowledge that I have repeatedly given have therefore not been chosen for their categorial status within each domain. The isolation of the categorial concepts is a technical matter of great difficulty and I am not aware that anything turns on being able to isolate amongst the concepts of a form of knowledge or experience those which have this ultimate status in relation to the rest. Categories can be distinguished within our concepts even when we are uncertain which are the categorial concepts themselves, that fundamentally characterise the different domains uniquely. Indeed I see no reason to assume that we have in fact explicitly isolated all the categorial concepts in our forms of knowledge, some may well occur only implicitly within the more familiar complex concepts we employ. The concepts of 'space', 'time', and 'causality' would seem to be categorial where knowledge of the physical world is concerned and these are closely tied to the kind of truth criteria distinctive of scientific knowledge. Examples of concepts widely regarded as categorial in other domains can readily be given: ought, God, intention. Yet giving these raises a new important question, for one becomes only too readily aware of the shifts these concepts have undergone in the history of human thought. If this is so, what precisely is the status of the distinctions between the forms of knowledge and experience that I have sought to emphasise? How ultimate are they? Are they to be regarded as absolute divisions or expressions of a purely contemporary situation?

V

Although one of the fundamental purposes of . . . 'Liberal education and the nature of knowledge'[4] was an endeavour to characterise liberal education while rejecting the doctrines of metaphysical and epistemological realism with which it has been historically associated, I have not infrequently been taken to be asserting the existence of a series of absolute domains, having at least the status of Kantian *a priori* categories, if not that of categories of Platonic 'forms'. My use of the terms 'category' and 'form' may give some superficial support to such a view, but superficial it is, and the terms in which I suggest the forms are to be distinguished carry no such implications. The conceptual and logical analysis which indicates the divisions I have stressed is a matter of the logical relations and truth criteria to be found at present in our conceptual schemes. Notions of what is and what is not intelligible are employed, but these are questions of coherent thought and communication in public discourse. As distinct from a Kantian approach, it is not my view that in elucidating the fundamental categories of our understanding we reach an unchanging structure that is implicit, indeed *a priori*, in all rational thought in all times and places. That there exist any elements in thought that can be known to be immune to change, making transcendental demands on us, I do not accept. I see no grounds for accepting that being rational in any sphere is a matter of adherence to a set of principles that are of their character invariant, nor do I see why formal systems of relations of a mathematical kind should be regarded as providing any necessary ideal of rationality against which all other forms must be assessed. Being rational I see rather as a matter of developing conceptual schemes by means of public language in which words are related to our form of life, so that we make objective judgments in relation to some aspect of that form of life. The precise character of those schemes is a matter of investigation, not something that can be laid down in advance, in terms of some ideal, no matter how successful or attractive one particular scheme may be. How far such schemes do as a matter of fact have an invariant structure, is a question for research. Intelligibility in public language and objectivity of judgment would seem to be the demands of reason. What varied forms these at present take is the question I have been implicitly concerned with.

Looked at this way, reason is a human creation that depends on a whole range of factors all of which we are now prepared to see as variable. The capacity of man for linguistic development, like his sensory apparatus, is an evolutionary product. The environment in which he lives, physical as well as social, is similarly the outcome of change. All of this continues in flux, though the time scale of change for different elements varies hugely. Even the notions of reason, intelligibility and objectivity are within this situation. Nothing can any more be supposed fixed eternally. Yet none of this means that we cannot discern certain necessary features of intelligibility and reason as we have them. Although the nature of man may be changing and we are within a great context of total change, nevertheless we can pick out those concepts and principles which are necessary and fundamental to anything we could at present call understanding, as well as to the understanding we actually have. The ultimacy of these elements is there and they mark out the limits of anything we can intelligibly conceive. What is more, all intelligibility that we can have is tied to the creation of concepts within a setting that being given, we cannot escape, and which is in large measure not of our creating. We are the beings we are with our given capacities and contexts. Even if these are in the process of change, they have now the character they have and not another. Intelligibility is itself a development in this context, and one that is of its nature hedged in and limited by it. To assume that this framework is in any sense necessarily fixed now seems absurd. But to imagine it is not setting limits to what is right now intelligible is equally absurd. Those limits may change, but right now intelligibility is what it is. To ignore 'the bounds of sense' is to produce not a higher sense, but nonsense.

And built into the whole nature of intelligibility and sense, is the notion of objectivity. Whatever conceptual schemes we may in our languages devise for judging what is the case in the physical world, what is indeed the case when we use those concepts, is not of our deciding. Even in our situation of total flux, there is a distinction which is part of our making sense of our experience at all and without which that particular enterprise would itself seem unintelligible, that is the distinction between thoughts, concepts and propositions on the one hand and that to which they are applied on the other. Nor is this distinction applicable only in science. It is there in all our understanding. The first setting up of words in relation to what is a given in experience is necessary to intelligibility. It is only because we can so establish a relation, because we can agree in the judgments of application it involves, that there is meaning. This is the anchor of reason and sense. Where the principles laid down in the development of such a form of discourse are violated, reason and sense are lost. Not that these principles are simple or all of a piece in any form of discourse. Sense can be retained in part by sticking to some of the principles, or to the principles in general whilst misapplying them in a particular case.

Forms of discourse and types of objectivity may also vary radically in kind because the relationship between words and some element of what is 'given' may vary. Indeed that is again just what the distinction between 'forms of knowledge' is all about.

In terms of this approach, the possibility of objectivity and sense, even if not resting on absolute principles, would seem to rest on a fair degree of stability of judgment and agreement between men. This therefore raises once more the question as to how far as a matter of fact there are universal forms of thought. The concepts of mathematics and those of space, time and causality that Kant considered *a priori*, manifestly have enormous stability. Yet these are historical products, and we now recognise that they do not have the unlimited application in our experience that Kant thought. It is hard to believe that any other concepts that might be proposed in their place could come off any better. Yet the generality of certain conceptual schemes and their relatively timeless status are surely worthy of note. They are no doubt a measure of the stability and near universality of very significant features in human nature and the human situation. Social diversity may overlay these features so that more fundamental conceptual similarities are not very apparent. Yet man's universal empirical and social concerns, his own characteristics and those of his context are so alike, no other form of explanation seems necessary for the prevalence of certain categories. What is further, these common features would seem to cast serious doubt on the view that major forms of thought of different communities are mutually incomprehensible. There may be considerable difficulty in understanding the conceptual schemes of another society without comprehensive immersion in its culture. Yet in so far as its purposes and context are shared with one's own, the fundamental basis for understanding would seem to be there. The idea of total lack of communication in many areas of life would seem unlikely. The values and judgments made in one society may not be translatable into the conceptual schemes used by another, but that is of itself no denial of intelligibility. Nor is the fact that the values and judgments of two societies are incompatible.

What is more, the idea that notions of reason are entirely socially relative is also suspect. Reason is expressed in forms of language and thought developing in these circumstances of considerable stability in which many non-social elements are involved. It might then in general be expected to take similar structures in different societies. But, further, if the notion of reason is tied necessarily to that of objectivity, this is for it to be explicitly tied to the 'given', much of which is not a social construction and is common to societies. It is true that what is given can only be judged by means of socially constructed concepts, but what is so judged is not itself a merely conceptual creation. Objectivity may figure in different conceptual schemes in different societies, but in so far as societies share the concern for objectivity in similar human activities, their achievements can here be related and assessed. I see no reason to assume that objectivity is the concern of only a limited number of societies.

In distinguishing forms of knowledge, it is the forms of objective judgment that we now have which I have been seeking to separate. If the thesis is correct, there are some seven types of discourse in which objectivity is at present seriously claimed. In some of these that objectivity might be well articulated, and the agreement in judgments very precise and clear. In others, it might be much less precise and not well characterised. If the ways in which words can be related to experience expressing such judgments can be various and complex, and no one formula can be asserted as the only valid case, there is nothing surprising in that. We can only explore the claims that are made. The seven areas I have suggested are now distinct, have certainly not been so recognised in the past, though their presence in some sense may be discerned by hindsight. Maybe new forms are at present being slowly differentiated out. We can do little but wait and see. What other forms objectivity might come to take in due course is not being prejudged in any sense. Nor is the question of change in the notion of objectivity itself. The thesis is simply about the present state of affairs but that state of affairs is not to be regarded as either a transient articulation of a merely socially relative concept of knowledge, or the latest expression of an absolute and invariant framework implicit in knowledge.[5]

Notes

1. op. cit.
2. See particularly Gribble, J. H. (1970) 'The forms of knowledge', *Educational Philosophy and Theory*, 2(1); Phillips, D. C. (1971) 'The distinguishing features of forms of knowledge', *Educational Philosophy and Theory*, 3(2); Hindess, E. (1972) 'Forms of knowledge', *Proceedings of the Philosophy of Education Society of Great Britain*, 6(2); and Wilson, J. (1969) 'The curriculum: justification and taxonomy', *British Journal of Educational Studies*, 17(1).
3. Hirst, P. H. and Peters, R. S. (1970) *The Logic of Education*, London, Routledge & Kegan Paul. See also Hirst, P. H. (1966) 'Educational theory', in Tibble, J. W., ed., *The Study of Education*, London, Routledge & Kegan Paul.
4. op. cit.
5. The nature and significance of conceptual and categorial changes have been dealt with at some length in Körner, S. (1970) *Categorial Frameworks*, Oxford, Basil

Blackwell, and in Toulmin, S. (1972) *Human Understanding*, vol. 1, Oxford, Clarendon. The position outlined here, however, owes more to suggestions to be found in the writings of Professor D. W. Hamlyn, though I have no reason to suppose that he would agree with the particular use I have made of them. See especially Hamlyn, D. W. (1970) *The Theory of Knowledge*, London, Macmillan.

8.4 THE ARCHAEOLOGY OF KNOWLEDGE

M. FOUCAULT (1926–), *from* The Archaeology of Knowledge, *London, Tavistock, 1972, p. 22, pp. 43–5, 64 and 130ff.*

Foucault's context is different again from that of either Hume or Hirst. Whereas Hume is concerned to describe the form knowledge takes for an enlightened individual and Hirst the forms that should shape institutions of liberal education, Foucault's starting point has been the study of the growth and change in forms of knowledge themselves. After two studies of the growth of discipline,[1] Foucault responded to critics of his method with *The Archaeology of Knowledge*,[2] in which he tried to justify the philosophical presuppositions of what he had previously been doing. As part of this exercise, Foucault develops a theory of the forms of knowledge themselves.

The history of ideas has, Foucault argues, become more and more conscious of discontinuities, breaks in the lines tracing the influence of one group of thinkers on another or grouping thinkers together in schools or disciplines. The reason for this, he claims, is hidden doubt about the fundamental material of all history, documents. Because historians have come to regard their work as the exploration of documents, the reality that at one time they were supposed to bring to us, which united the disparate results in a combined history of England, of Europe, of the world, has been lost. History is no longer the memory of a society. The unity of history shattered, the archaeologist's skill of constructing an avowedly limited picture of ancient civilization *within* scattered fragments from the distant past reappears as a model. We need to discover how we can group together what we have to work on. But in order to decide on legitimate groupings, we need first to decide whether any of the given material has a right to priority. Notably, in the history of our own knowledge, we need to ask whether the different disciplines have to remain the same through different historical periods. And if, as Foucault claims, they do not, then what about the objects they describe, the rules for thinking accepted within them, their concepts or the aims of their researches? Foucault examines each of these and finds that they do not account for the character of each discipline. He therefore resorts to a notion of the 'archive' of a society, the practices that generate its knowledge, which is the proper study of the archaeology of knowledge.

Notes

1. Foucault, M. (1966) *Les Mots et les choses*, Paris, Gallimard (trans. 1970 as *The Order of Things*, London, Tavistock); (1961) *Histoire de la folie à l'âge classique*, Paris, Plon (trans. 1967 by Richard Howard, *Madness and Civilization: A History of Insanity in the Age of Reason*, London, Tavistock).
2. op. cit., originally (1969). Originally published as *L'Archéologie du Savoir*, Paris, Gallimard.

We must also question those divisions or groupings with which we have become so familiar. Can one accept, as such, the distinction between the major types of discourse, or that between such forms or genres as science, literature, philosophy, religion, history, fiction, etc., and which tend to create certain great historical individualities? We are not even sure of ourselves when we use these distinctions in our own world of discourse, let alone when we are analysing groups of statements which, when first formulated, were distributed, divided, and characterized in a quite different way: after all, 'literature' and 'politics' are recent categories, which can be applied to medieval culture, or even classical culture, only by a retrospective hypothesis, and by an interplay of formal analogies or semantic resemblances; but neither literature, nor politics, nor philosophy and the sciences articulated the field of discourse, in the seventeenth or eighteenth century, as they did in the nineteenth century. In any case, these divisions − whether our own, or those contemporary with the discourse under examination — are always themselves reflexive categories, principles of classification, normative rules, institutionalized types: they, in turn, are facts of discourse that deserve to be analysed beside others; of course, they also have complex relations with each other, but they are not intrinsic, autochthonous, and universally recognizable characteristics. . . .

In the sphere with which psychopathology dealt in the nineteenth century, one sees the very early appearance (as early as Esquirol) of a whole series of objects belonging to the category of delinquency: homicide (and suicide), *crimes passionels*, sexual offences, certain forms of theft, vagrancy — and then, through them, heredity, the neurogenic environment, aggressive or self-punishing behaviour, perversions, criminal impulses, suggestibility, etc. It would be inadequate to say that one was dealing here with the consequences of a discovery: of the sudden discovery by a psychiatrist of a resemblance between criminal and pathological behaviour, a discovery of the presence in certain delinquents of the classical signs of alienation, or mental derangement. Such facts lie beyond the grasp of contemporary research: indeed, the problem is how to decide what made them possible, and how these 'discoveries' could lead to others that took them up, rectified them, modified them, or even disproved them. Similarly, it would be irrelevant to attribute the appearance of these new objects to the norms of nineteenth-century bourgeois society, to a reinforced police and penal framework, to the establishment of a new code of criminal justice, to the introduction and use of extenuating circumstances, to the increase in crime. No doubt, all these processes were at work; but they could not of themselves form objects for psychiatric discourse; to pursue the description at this level one would fall short of what one was seeking.

If, in a particular period in the history of our society, the delinquent was psychologized and pathologized, if criminal behaviour could give rise to a whole series of objects of knowledge, this was because a group of particular relations was adopted for use in psychiatric discourse. The relation between planes of specification like penal categories and degrees of diminished responsibility, and planes of psychological characterization (faculties, aptitudes, degrees of development or involution, different ways of reacting to the environment, character types, whether acquired, innate, or hereditary). The relation between the authority of medical decision and the authority of judicial decision (a really complex relation since medical decision recognizes absolutely the authority of the judiciary to define crime, to determine the circumstances in which it is committed, and the punishment that it deserves; but reserves the right to analyse its origin and to determine the degree of responsibility involved). The relation between the filter formed by judicial interrogation, police information, investigation, and the whole machinery of judicial information, and the filter formed by the medical questionnaire, clinical examinations, the search for antecedents, and biographical accounts. The relation between the family, sexual and penal norms of the behaviour of individuals, and the table of pathological symptoms and diseases of which they are the signs. The relation between therapeutic confinement in hospital (with its own thresholds, its criteria of cure, its way of distinguishing the normal from the pathological) and punitive confinement in prison (with its system of punishment and pedagogy, its criteria of good conduct, improvement, and freedom). These are the relations that, operating in psychiatric discourse, have made possible the formation of a whole group of various objects.

Let us generalize: in the nineteenth century, psychiatric discourse is characterized not by privileged objects, but by the way in which it forms objects that are in fact highly dispersed. This formation is made possible by a group of relations established between authorities of emergence, delimitation and specification. One might say, then, that a discursive formation is defined (as far as its objects are concerned, at least) if one can establish such a group; if one can show how any particular object of discourse finds in it its place and law of emergence; if one can show that it may give birth simultaneously or successively to mutually exclusive objects, without having to modify itself. . . .

The conditions necessary for the appearance of an object of discourse, the historical conditions required if one is to 'say anything' about it, and if several people are to say different things about it, the conditions necessary if it is to exist in relation to other objects, if it is to establish with them relations of resemblance, proximity, distance, difference, transformation − as we can see, these conditions are many and imposing. Which means that one cannot speak of anything at any time; it is not easy to say something new; it is not enough for us to open our eyes, to pay attention, or to be aware, for new objects suddenly to light up and emerge out of the ground. . . .

Such discourses as economics, medicine, grammar, the science of living beings give rise to certain organizations of concepts, certain regroupings of objects, certain types of enunciation, which form, according to their degree of coherence, rigour and stability, themes or theories: the theme, in eighteenth-century grammar, of an original language (*langue*) from which all others derive, and of which all others carry within themselves a sometimes decipherable memory; a theory, in nineteenth-century philology, of a kinship between all the Indo-European languages, and of an archaic idiom that served as a common starting-point; a theme, in the eighteenth century, of an evolution of the species deploying in time the continuity of nature, and explaining the present gaps in the taxonomic table; a theory, propounded by the Physiocrats, of a circulation of wealth on the basis of agricultural production. Whatever their formal level may be, I shall call these themes and theories 'strategies'. The problem is to discover how they are distributed in history. Is it necessity that links them together, makes them invisible, calls them to their right places one after another, and makes of them successive solutions to one and the same problem? Or chance encounters between ideas of different origin, influences, discoveries, speculative climates, theoretical models that the patience or genius of individuals arranges into more or less well-constituted wholes? Or can one find a regularity between them and define the common system of their formation?

Between the *language* (*langue*) that defines the system of constructing possible sentences, and the *corpus* that passively collects the words that are spoken, the *archive* defines a particular level: that of a practice that causes a multiplicity of statements to emerge as so many regular events, as so many things to be dealt with and manipulated. It does not have the weight of tradition; and it does not constitute the library of all libraries, outside time and place; nor is it the welcoming oblivion that opens up to all new speech the operational field of its freedom; between tradition and oblivion, it reveals the rules of a practice that enables statements both to survive and to undergo regular modification. It is *the general system of the formation and transformation of statements.*

It is obvious that the archive of a society, a culture or a civilization cannot be described exhaustively; or even, no doubt, the archive of a whole period. On the other hand, it is not possible for us to describe our own archive, since it is from within these rules that we speak, since it is that which gives to what we can say — and to itself, the object of our discourse — its modes of appearance, its forms of existence and coexistence, its system of accumulation, historicity and disappearance. The archive cannot be described in its totality; and in its presence it is unavoidable. It emerges in fragments, regions and levels, more fully, no doubt, and with greater sharpness, the greater the time that separates us from it: at most, were it not for the rarity of the documents, the greater chronological distance would be necessary to analyse it. And yet could this description of the archive be justified, could it elucidate that which makes it possible, map out the place where it speaks, control its rights and duties, test and develop its concepts — at least at this stage of the search, when it can define its possibilities only in the moment of their realization — if it persisted in describing only the most distant horizons? Should it not approach as close as possible to the positivity that governs it and the archive system that makes it possible today to speak of the archive in general? Should it not illuminate, if only in an oblique way, that enunciative field of which it is itself a part? The analysis of the archive, then, involves a privileged region: at once close to us, and different from our present existence, it is the border of time that surrounds our presence, which overhangs it, and which indicates it in its otherness; it is that which, outside ourselves, delimits us. The description of the archive deploys its possibilities (and the mastery of its possibilities) on the basis of the very discourses that have just ceased to be ours; its threshold of existence is established by the discontinuity that separates us from what we can no longer say, and from that which falls outside our discursive practice; it begins with the outside of our own language (*langage*); its locus is the gap between our own discursive practices. In this sense, it is valid for our diagnosis. Not because it would enable us to draw up a table of our distinctive features, and to sketch out in advance the face that we will have in the future. But it deprives us of our continuities; it dissipates that temporal identity in which we are pleased to look at ourselves when we wish to exorcise the discontinuities of history; it breaks the thread of transcendental teleologies; and where anthropological thought once questioned man's being or subjectivity, it now bursts open the other, and the outside. In this sense, the diagnosis does not establish the fact of our identity by the play of distinctions. It establishes that we are difference, that our reason is the difference of discourses, our history the difference of times, our selves the difference of masks. That difference, far from being the forgotten and recovered origin, is this dispersion that we are and make.

The never completed, never wholly achieved uncovering of the archive forms the general horizon to which the description of discursive formations, the analysis of positivities, the mapping of the enunciative field belong. The right of words — which is not that of the philologists — authorizes, therefore, the use of the term *archaeology* to describe all these searches. This term does not imply the search for a beginning; it does not relate analysis to geological excavation. It designates the general theme of a description that questions the already-said at the level of its existence: of the enunciative function that operates within it, of the discursive formation, and the general archive system to which it belongs. Archaeology describes discourses as practices specified in the element of the archive.

9 Objectivity

Objectivity has been conceived as an ideal of all inquiry and a requirement of any inquiry which claims to be scientific. To deny that an inquiry is objective is to deny that it is to be taken seriously as an attempt to find out the truth. But, although 'objective' is a well-established term of praise and 'subjective' is often a term of disparagement, there is no single, agreed conception of objectivity.

Israel Scheffler has articulated what he regards as the 'standard' view of objectivity. The book from which this first extract is taken is a defence by Scheffler of this 'standard' view against various supposed attacks on the objectivity of science. Scheffler is concerned, in particular, to defend the independence of empirical facts from the theories to which they are relevant as evidence. The second extract includes Norwood Hanson's statement of the contrary view. The third extract is also from the work of a writer who is criticized by Scheffler, Thomas Kuhn. Here, however, we include a reply by Kuhn to those criticisms. Part of the original book of Kuhn's is included also in section 5.2.

The high value ascribed to objectivity in inquiry generally is partly due to the acknowledged success of the natural sciences by comparison with other inquiries. Discussions about objectivity often take the objectivity of the natural sciences for granted and raise the question whether inquiries in other areas, such as the humanities, come up to that standard. The paper by J. A. Passmore is a defence of the objectivity of history in relation to a number of criteria which, it has been claimed, the sciences satisfy but history does not.

9.1   THE 'STANDARD' VIEW OF OBJECTIVITY

ISRAEL SCHEFFLER (1923–   ), *from his* Science and Subjectivity, *Indianapolis, Bobbs-Merrill, 1967, pp. 1–4 and 8–10*

Scheffler holds that 'science is a systematic public enterprise, controlled by logic and empirical fact, whose purpose it is to formulate the truth about the natural world'. This 'standard' view is opposed to the idea that scientific disagreements may not be completely decideable by rational debate, either because observation is itself theory-laden or because theory choice is not wholly determined by logic and empirical fact.

A fundamental feature of science is its ideal of objectivity, an ideal that subjects all scientific statements to the test of independent and impartial criteria, recognizing no authority of persons in the realm of cognition. The claimant to scientific knowledge is responsible for what he says, acknowledging the relevance of considerations beyond his wish or advocacy to the judgment of his assertions. In assertion he is not simply expressing himself but making a claim; he is trying to meet independent standards, to satisfy factual requirements whose fulfilment cannot be guaranteed in advance.

To propound one's beliefs in a scientific spirit is to acknowledge that they may turn out wrong under continued examination, that they may fail to sustain themselves critically in an enlarged experience. It is, in effect, to conceive one's self of the here and now as linked through potential converse with a community of others, whose differences of location or opinion yet allow a common discourse and access to a shared world. It is accordingly to lay oneself open to criticism from any quarter and to acquire an impersonal regard for the judgments of others; for what matters is not who they are, but whether they properly voice the import of controlling standards. Assertions that purport to be scientific are, in sum, held subject to control by reference to independent checks.

Commitment to fair controls over assertion is the basis of the scientific attitude of impartiality and detachment; indeed, one might say that it constitutes this attitude. For impartiality and detachment are not to be thought of as substantive qualities of the scientist's personality or the style of his thought; scientists are as variegated in these respects as any other group of people. Scientific habits of mind are compatible with passionate advocacy, strong faith, intuitive conjecture and imaginative speculation. What is central is the acknowledgment of general controls to which one's dearest beliefs are ultimately subject. These controls, embodied in and transmitted by the institutions of science, represent the fundamental rules of its game. To devise fair controls for new ranges of assertion, and to guarantee the fairness of existing controls in the old, constitute the rationale of these rules. The cold and aloof scientist is, then, a myth.

It must be emphasized that the function of scientific controls is to channel critique and facilitate evaluation rather than to generate discoveries by routine. Control provides, in short, no mechanical substitute for ideas; there *are* no substitutes for ideas. The late Hans Reichenbach drew a sharp distinction in his philosophy of science between the 'context of discovery' and the 'context of justification', and he was right to do so. For the mechanical scientist is also a myth.[1]

Now, the ideal of objectivity, as thus far described, characterizes not only the scientist, but also the historian, the philosopher, the mathematician, the man of affairs — insofar as all make cognitive claims in a rational spirit. A parallel ideal is relevant for the moral person as well. The ideal of objectivity is, indeed, closely tied to the general notion of rationality, which is theoretically applicable to both the cognitive and the moral spheres. In both spheres, we honor demands for relevant reasons and acknowledge control by principle. In both, we suppose a commitment to general rules capable of running against one's own wishes in any particular case. In neither sphere is personal authority decisive; as S. I. Benn and R. S. Peters have put it,

> The procedural rules of science lay it down . . . that hypotheses must be decided on by looking at the evidence, not by appealing to a man. There are also, and can be, no rules to decide who will be the originators of scientific theories.
>
> In a similar way . . . a rule cannot be a moral one if it is to be accepted just because someone has laid it down or made a decision between competing alternatives. Reasons must be given for it, not originators or umpires produced. Of course, in both enterprises provisional authorities can be consulted. But there are usually good reasons for this choice and their pronouncements are never to be

regarded as final just because they have made them. In science and morality there are no appointed judges or policemen.[2]

There is thus no ground for restricting the applicability of the *ideal* of objectivity to *de facto* science, as contrasted, for example, with history, philosophy or human affairs.

Nevertheless, *de facto* science articulates, in a self-conscious and methodologically explicit manner, the demands of objectivity over a staggering range of issues of natural fact, subjecting these issues continuously to the joint tests of theoretical coherence and observational fidelity. 'It takes its starting points outside the mind in nature,' writes C. C. Gillispie, 'and winnows observations of events which it gathers under concepts, to be expressed mathematically if possible and tested experimentally by their success in predicting new events and suggesting new concepts.'[3] This it does in a logically deliberate and progressively more general manner, thereby providing us with a comprehensive model of the ideal of objectivity itself, stretching our earlier conceptions of its potentialities, and pointing the way to new and as yet undreamed of embodiments in a variety of realms.

What I am saying may be put summarily as follows: current science is continuous with other areas of life, and shares with them the distinctive features of the rational quest. However, in institutionalizing this quest so as to subject an ever wider domain of claims to refined and systematic test, science has given us a new appreciation of reason itself. Since reason is, moreover, a moral as well as an intellectual notion, we have thereby been given also a new and enlarged vision of the moral standpoint − of responsibility in belief, embodied not only in a firm commitment to impartial principles by which one's own assertions are to be measured, but in a further commitment to making those principles ever more comprehensive and rigorous. Thus, though science has certainly provided us with new and critically important knowledge of man's surroundings and capacities, such enlightenment far from exhausts its human significance. A major aspect of such significance has been the moral import of science: its dynamic articulation of the impulse to responsible belief, and its suggestion of the hope of an increased rationality and responsibility in all realms of conduct and thought. . . . How, if at all, is scientific objectivity possible?

In approaching this question, we shall begin by elaborating what has above been described as the 'standard view' of science. Fundamentally, as we have seen, this view affirms the objectivity of science; more specifically, it understands science to be a systematic public enterprise, controlled by logic and by empirical fact, whose purpose it is to formulate the truth about the natural world. The truth primarily sought is general, expressed in laws of nature, which tell us what is always and everywhere the case. Observation, however, supplies the particular empirical facts, the hard phenomenal data which our lawlike hypotheses strive to encompass, and for which it is the ultimate purpose of such hypotheses to account.

Laws or general hypotheses may be ordered in a hierarchy of increasing generality of scope, but a basic distinction is, in any event, to be drawn between observational or experimental laws on the one hand and theoretical laws on the other. Generalizing upon the data accessible to the senses, observational laws are couched in the language of observation and make reference to perceived things and processes. Theoretical laws, by contrast, are expressed in a more abstract idiom and typically postulate unobservable elements and functions; unlike observational laws, they cannot be subjected to the test of direct inspection or experiment. Their function is not to generalize observed phenomena, but rather to explain the laws which themselves generalize the phenomena. This they do by yielding such laws as deductive consequences of their own abstract postulations. They are, of course, indirectly testable by observation, for should one of their lawlike consequences break down on the level of experiment, such failure would count against them. However, they serve primarily to help relate diverse observational laws suitably within a comprehensive deductive scheme, and they are evaluated not only by their empirical yield but also by their simplicity, their intellectual familiarity, their accessibility to preferred models, and their manageability. They are, to be sure, also applied in the explanation of particular occurrences and in the solution of problems of prediction and control.

Any two theories of the same domain of phenomena may be compared to see if either is superior in accounting for the relevant empirical facts or, if equivalent on this score, if either surpasses the other in simplicity or convenience, etc. A hypothesis that does not itself clash with experience may yet be given up in favor of an alternative hypothesis that explains more facts or is simpler, or easier to handle. A given law may be absorbed into another, more general law by a process of reduction, through which it is shown to follow deductively from the more general law under plausible auxiliary assumptions.

When one hypothesis is superseded by another, the genuine facts it had purported to account for are not inevitably lost; they are typically passed on to its successor, which conserves them as it reaches out to embrace additional facts. Thus it is that science can be cumulative at the observational or experimental level, despite its lack of cumulativeness at the theoretical level; it strives always, and through varying theories, to save the phenomena while adding to them. And in the case of reduction, a reduced law is itself conserved, *in toto*, as a special consequence of its more general successor. Throughout the apparent flux of changing scientific beliefs, then, there is a solid growth of knowledge which represents progress in empirical understanding. Underlying historical changes of theory, there is, moreover, a constancy of logic and method, which unifies each scientific age with that which preceded it and with that which is yet to follow.

Such constancy comprises not merely the canons of formal deduction, but also those criteria by which hypotheses are confronted with the test of experience and subjected to comparative evaluation. We do not, surely, have explicit and general formulations of such criteria at the present time. But they are embodied clearly enough in scientific practice to enable communication and agreement in a wide variety of specific cases. Such communication and consensus indicate that there is a codifiable methodology underlying the conduct of the scientific enterprise. It is a methodology by which beliefs are objectively evaluated and exchanged, rather than an organon of discovery or theoretical invention. Yet it is this methodology which makes possible the cumulative growth of tested scientific knowledge as a public possession.

Now the public character of scientific procedure is not simply a matter of the free interchange of ideas. It is intimately related to the critical testing of beliefs, in the following way: If I put forward a hypothesis in scientific spirit, I suppose from the outset that I may be wrong, by independent tests to which I am prepared to submit my proposal. I suppose, in other words, that my present hypothesis is not to be prejudged as correct during the process of testing; I thus acknowledge that disagreement with respect to my proposal is no bar to further communication, nor indeed to agreement on the test itself. Indeed, from the latter sort of communication and agreement, consensus on my proposal may eventually grow. Further, insofar as testing involves an appeal to facts disclosed in common observation of things, I suppose that the same things can be observed from different perspectives, and consensus on observation reached without presupposing agreement on relevant theory. In sum, I acknowledge the possibility of common discourse with those who may differ with me in opinion, and assume shared access to an observed world with others who may be differently located or otherwise constituted than I. The methodological publicity of science involves the assumption that differing persons may yet talk intelligibly to one another, that they may observe together the phenomena bearing critically on issues which divide them, and that they may thus join in the testing of disputed conceptions in an effort to seek resolution.

Notes

1. Reichenbach, Hans (1938) *Experience and Prediction*, Chicago, University of Chicago Press, ch. 1, sec. 1.
2. Benn, S. I. and Peters, R. S. (1959) *Social Principles and the Democratic State*, London, George Allen & Unwin, p. 22.
3. Gillespie, C. C. (1960) *The Edge of Objectivity*, Princeton, N.J., Princeton University Press, p. 10.

9.2   OBSERVATION AS THEORY-LADEN

NORWOOD R. HANSON (1924–1967), *from his* Patterns of Discovery, *Cambridge, Cambridge University Press, 1958, pp. 129–46*

Hanson argues that there is a sense in which all seeing is theory-laden, i.e. what people say they see already presupposes something like a theory. In contrast with Scheffler (9.1), Hanson holds that an appeal to empirical fact can only succeed where the parties to a dispute share the same 'conceptual organization' of their experience.

Consider two microbiologists. They look at a prepared slide; when asked what they see, they may give different answers. One sees in the cell before him a cluster of foreign matter: it is an artefact, a coagulum resulting from inadequate staining techniques. This clot has no more to do with the cell, *in vivo*, than the scars left on it by the archaeologist's spade have to do with the original shape of some Grecian urn. The other biologist identifies the clot as a cell organ, a 'Golgi body'. As for techniques, he argues: 'The standard way of detecting a cell organ is by fixing and staining. Why single out this one technique as producing artefacts, while others disclose genuine organs?'

The controversy continues. It involves the whole theory of microscopical technique; nor is it an obviously experimental issue. Yet it affects what scientists say they see. Perhaps there is a sense in which two such observers do not see the same thing, do not begin from the same data, though their eyesight is normal and they are visually aware of the same object. . . .

Some philosophers have a formula ready for such situations: 'Of course they see the same thing. They make the same observation since they begin from the same visual data. But they interpret what they see differently. They construe the evidence in different ways.' The task is then to show how these data are moulded by different theories or inter-pretations or intellectual constructions.

Considerable philosophers have wrestled with this task. But in fact the formula they start from is too simple to allow a grasp of the nature of observation within physics. Perhaps the scientists cited above do not begin their inquiries from the same data, do not make the same observations, do not even see the same thing? Here many concepts run together. We must proceed carefully, for wherever it makes sense to say that two scientists looking at x do not see the same thing, there must always be a prior sense in which they do see the same thing. The issue is, then, 'Which of these senses is most illuminating for the understanding of observational physics?'

These biological examples are too complex. Let us consider Johannes Kepler: imagine him on a hill watching the dawn. With him is Tycho Brahe. Kepler regarded the sun as fixed: it was the earth that moved. But Tycho followed Ptolemy and Aristotle in this much at least: the earth was fixed and all other celestial bodies moved around it. *Do Kepler and Tycho see the same thing in the east at dawn?* . . .

The physical processes involved when Kepler and Tycho watch the dawn are worth noting. Identical photons are emitted from the sun; these traverse solar space, and our atmosphere. The two astronomers have normal vision; hence these photons pass through the cornea, aqueous humour, iris, lens and vitreous body of their eyes in the same way. Finally their retinas are affected. Similar electro-chemical changes occur in their selenium cells. The same configuration is etched on Kepler's retina as on Tycho's. So they see the same thing.

Seeing is an experience. A retinal reaction is only a physical state — a photochemical excitation. Physiologists have not always appreciated the differences between experiences and physical states. People, not their eyes, see. Cameras, and eyeballs, are blind. Attempts to locate within the organs of sight (or within the neurological reticulum behind the eyes) some nameable called 'seeing' may be dismissed. That Kepler and Tycho do, or do not, see the same thing cannot be supported by reference to the physical states of their retinas, optic nerves or visual cortices: there is more to seeing than meets the eyeball. . . .

Naturally, Tycho and Kepler see the same physical object. They are both visually aware of the sun. If they are put into a dark room and asked to report when they see something − anything at all − they may both report the same object at the same time. Suppose that the only object to be seen is a certain lead cylinder. Both men see the same thing: namely this object − whatever it is. It is just here, however, that the difficulty arises, for while Tycho sees a mere pipe, Kepler will see a telescope, the instrument about which Galileo has written to him.

Unless both are visually aware of the same object there can be nothing of philosophical interest in the question whether or not they see the same thing. Unless they both see the sun in this prior sense our question cannot even strike a spark.

Nonetheless, both Tycho and Kepler have a common visual experience of some sort. This experience perhaps constitutes their seeing the same thing. Indeed, this may be a seeing logically more basic than anything expressed in the pronouncement 'I see the sun' (where each means something different by 'sun'). If what they meant by the word 'sun' were the only clue, then Tycho and Kepler could not be seeing the same thing, even though they were gazing at the same object.

If, however, we ask, not 'Do they see the same thing?' but rather 'What is it that they both see?', an unambiguous answer may be forthcoming. Tycho and Kepler are both aware of a brilliant yellow − white disc in a blue expanse over a green one. Such a 'sense-datum' picture is single and uninverted. To be unaware of it is not to have it. Either it dominates one's visual attention completely or it does not exist.

If Tycho and Kepler are aware of anything visual, it must be of some pattern of colours. What else could it be? We do not touch or hear with our eyes, we only take in light. This private pattern is the same for both observers. Surely if asked to sketch the contents of their visual fields they would both draw a kind of semicircle on a horizon-line. They say they see the sun. But they do not see every side of the sun at once; so what they really see is discoid to begin with. It is but a visual aspect of the sun. In any single observation the sun is a brilliantly luminescent disc, a penny painted with radium.

So something about their visual experiences at dawn is the same for both: a brilliant yellow − white disc centred between green and blue colour patches. Sketches of what they both see could be identical − congruent. In this sense Tycho and Kepler see the same thing at dawn. The sun appears to them in the same way. The same view, or scene, is presented to them both.

In fact, we often speak in this way. Thus the account of a . . . solar eclipse:

Only a thin crescent remains; white light is now completely obscured; the sky appears a deep blue, almost purple, and the landscape is a monochromatic green . . . there are the flashes of light on the disc's circumference and now the brilliant crescent to the left. . . .[1]

Newton writes in a similar way in the *Opticks*:

These Arcs at their first appearance were of a violet and blue Colour, and between them were white Arcs of Circles, which . . . became a little tinged in their inward Limbs with red and yellow. . . .[2]

Every physicist employs the language of lines, colour patches, appearances, shadows. In so far as two normal observers use this language of the same event, they begin from the same data: they are making the same observation. Differences between them must arise in the interpretations they put on these data.

Thus, to summarize, saying that Kepler and Tycho see the same thing at dawn just because their eyes are similarly affected is an elementary mistake. There is a difference between a physical state and a visual experience. Suppose, however, that it is argued as above − that they see the same thing because they have the same sense-datum experience. Disparities in their accounts arise in *ex post facto* interpretations of what is seen, not in the fundamental visual data. If this is argued, further difficulties soon obtrude.

Normal retinas and cameras are impressed similarly by Figure 9.1. Our visual sense-data will be the same too. If asked to draw what we see, most of us will set out a configuration like Figure 9.1.

Do we all see the same thing? Some will see a perspex cube viewed from below. Others will see it from above. Still others will see it as a kind of polygonally-cut gem. Some people see only criss-crossed lines in a plane. It may be seen as a block of ice, an aquarium, a wire frame for a kite − or any of a number of other things.

Do we, then, all see the same thing? If we do, how can these differences be accounted for?

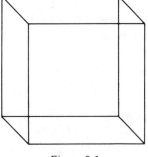

Figure 9.1

Here the 'formula' re-enters: 'These are different *interpretations* of what all observers see in common. Retinal reactions to Figure 9.1 are virtually identical; so too are our visual sense-data, since our drawings of what we see will have the same content. There is no place in the seeing for these differences, so they must lie in the interpretations put on what we see.'

This sounds as if I do two things, not one, when I see boxes and bicycles. Do I put different interpretations on Figure 9.1 when I see it now as a box from below, and now as a cube from above? I am aware of no such thing. I mean no such thing when I report that the box's perspective has snapped back into the page. If I do not mean this, then the concept of seeing which is natural in this connection does not designate two diaphanous components, one optical, the other inter-pretative. Figure 9.1 is simply seen now as a box from below, now as a cube from above; one does not first soak up an optical pattern and then clamp an interpretation on it. Kepler and Tycho just see the sun. That is all. That is the way the concept of seeing works in this connection.

'But,' you say, 'seeing Figure 9.1 first as a box from below, then as a cube from above, involves interpreting the lines differently in each case.' Then for you and me to have a different interpretation of Figure 9.1 just *is* for us to see something different. This does not mean we see the same thing and then interpret it differently. When I suddenly exclaim 'Eureka — a box from above', I do not refer simply to a dif-ferent interpretation. (Again, there is a logically prior sense in which seeing Figure 9.1 as from above and then as from below is seeing the same thing differently, i.e. being aware of the same diagram in dif-ferent ways. We can refer just to this, but we need not. In this case we do not.)

Besides, the word 'interpretation' is occasionally useful. We know where it applies and where it does not. Thucydides presented the facts objectively. Herodotus put an interpretation on them. The word does not apply to everything — it has a meaning. Can interpreting always be going on when we see? Sometimes, perhaps, as when the hazy outline of an agricultural machine looms up on a foggy morning and, with effort, we finally identify it. Is this the 'interpretation' which is active when bicycles and boxes are clearly seen? Is it active when the perspective of Figure 9.1 snaps into reverse? There was a time when Herodotus was half-through with his interpretation of the Graeco–Persian wars. Could there be a time when one is half-through interpreting Figure 9.1 as a box from above, or as anything else?

'But the interpretation takes very little time — it is instantaneous.' Instantaneous interpretation hails from the Limbo that produced unsensed sensibilia, unconscious inference, incorrigible statements, negative facts and *Objektive*. These are ideas which philosophers force on the world to preserve some pet epistemological or metaphysical theory.

Only in contrast to 'Eureka' situations (like perspective reversals, where one cannot interpret the data) is it clear what is meant by saying that though Thucydides could have put an interpretation on history, he did not. Moreover, whether or not an historian is advancing an interpretation is an empirical question: we know what would count as evidence one way or the other. But whether we are employing an interpretation when we see Figure 9.1 in a certain way is not empirical. What could count as evidence? In no ordinary sense of 'interpret' do I interpret Figure 9.1 differently when its perspective reverses for me. If there is some extraordinary sense of word it is not clear, either in ordinary language, or in extraordinary (philosophical) language. To insist that different reactions to Figure 9.1 *must* lie in the interpretations put on a common visual experience is just to reiterate (without reasons) that the seeing of x *must* be the same for all observers looking at x.

'But "I see the figure as a box" means: I am having a particular visual experience which I always have when I interpret the figure as a box, or when I look at a box. . . .' '. . . if I meant this, I ought to know it. I ought to be able to refer to the experience directly and not only indirectly. . . .'[3]

Ordinary accounts of the experiences appropriate to Figure 9.1 do not require visual grist going into an intellectual mill: theories and interpretations are 'there' in the seeing from the outset. How can interpretations 'be there' in the seeing? How is it possible to see an object according to an interpretation? 'The question represents it as a queer fact; as if something were being forced into a form it did not really fit. But no squeezing, no forcing took place here.' . . .[4] What has all this to do with suggesting that Tycho and Kepler may see different things in the east at dawn? Certainly the cases are different. But these reversible perspective figures are examples of different things being seen in the same configuration, where this difference is due neither to differing visual pictures, nor to any 'interpretation' superimposed on the sensation.

Some will see in Figure 9.2 an old Parisienne, others a young woman (à la Toulouse-Lautrec). All normal retinas 'take' the same picture; and our sense-datum pictures must be the same, for even if you see an old lady and I a young lady, the pictures we draw of what we see may turn out to be geometrically indistinguishable. (Some can see this *only* in one way, not both. This is like the difficulty we have after finding a face in a tree-puzzle; we cannot thereafter see the tree without the face.)

When what is observed is characterized so differently as 'young woman' or 'old woman', is it not natural to say that the observers see different things? Or must 'see different things' mean only 'see different objects'? This is a primary sense of the expression, to be sure. But is

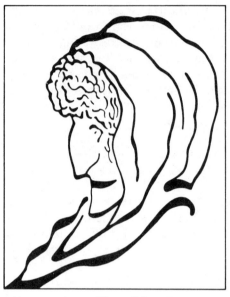

Figure 9.2

there not also a sense in which one who cannot see the young lady in Figure 9.2 sees something different from me, who sees the young lady? Of course there is. . . .

How does one describe the difference between the *jeune fille* and the *vieille femme* in Figure 9.2? Perhaps the difference is not describable: it may just show itself. That two observers have not seen the same things in Figure 9.2 could show itself in their behaviour. What is the difference between us when you see the zebra as black with white stripes and I see it as white with black stripes? Nothing optical. Yet there might be a context (for instance, in the genetics of animal pigmentation), where such a difference could be important.

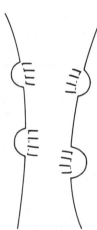

Figure 9.3

A third group of figures will stress further this organizational element of seeing and observing. They will hint at how much more is involved when Tycho and Kepler witness the dawn that 'the formula' suggests.

What is portrayed in Figure 9.3? Your retinas and visual cortices are affected much as mine are; our sense-datum pictures would not differ. Surely we could all produce an accurate sketch of Figure 9.3. Do we see the same thing?

I see a bear climbing up the other side of a tree. Did the elements 'pull together'/cohere/organize, when you learned this? You might even say with Wittgenstein 'it has not changed, and yet I see it differently. . . .'[5] Now, does it not have '. . . a quite particular "organization"'?

Organization is not itself seen as are the lines and colours of a drawing. It is not itself a line, shape, or a colour. It is not an element in the visual field, but rather the way in which elements are appreciated. Again, the plot is not another detail in the story. Nor is the tune just one more note. Yet without plots and tunes details and notes would not hang together. Similarly the organization of Figure 9.3 is nothing that registers on the retina along with other details. Yet it gives the lines and shapes a pattern. Were this lacking we would be left with nothing but an unintelligible configuration of lines.

How do visual experiences become organized? How is seeing possible? Consider Figure 9.4 in the context of Figure 9.5:

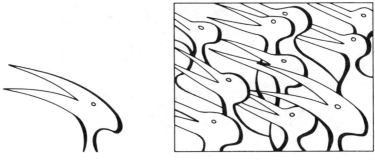

Figure 9.4   Figure 9.5

The context gives us the clue. Here, some people could not see the figure as an antelope. Could people who had never seen an antelope, but only birds, see an antelope in Figure 9.4?

In the context of Figure 9.6 the figure may indeed stand out as an antelope. It might even be urged that the figure seen in Figure 9.5 has no similarity to the one in Figure 9.6 although the two are congruent. Could anything be more opposed to a sense-datum account of seeing?

Figure 9.6

Of a figure similar to the Necker cube (Figure 9.1) Wittgenstein writes,

You could imagine [this] appearing in several places in a text-book. In the relevant text something different is in question every time: here a glass cube, there an inverted open box, there a wire frame of that shape, there three boards forming a solid angle. Each time the text supplies the interpretation of the illustration. But we can also see the illustration now as one thing, now as another. So we interpret it, and see it as we interpret it.[6]

Figure 9.7

Consider now the head-and-shoulders in Figure 9.7. The upper margin of the picture cuts the brow, thus the top of the head is not shown. The point of the jaw, clean shaven and brightly illuminated, is just above the geometric centre of the picture. A white mantle covers the right shoulder. The right upper sleeve is exposed as the rather black area at the lower left. The hair and beard are after the manner of a late mediaeval representation of Christ.

The appropriate aspect of the illustration is brought out by the verbal context in which it appears. It is not an illustration of anything determinate unless it appears in some such context. In the same way, I must talk and gesture around Figure 9.4 to get you to see the antelope when only the bird has revealed itself. I must provide a context. The context is part of the illustration itself.

Such a context, however, need not be set out explicitly. Often it is 'built into' thinking, imagining and picturing. We are set to appreciate the visual aspect of things in certain ways. Elements in our experience do not cluster at random.

A trained physicist could see one thing in Figure 9.8: an X-ray tube viewed from the cathode. Would Sir Lawrence Bragg and an Eskimo baby see the same thing when looking at an X-ray tube? Yes, and no. Yes – they are visually aware of the same object. No – the *ways* in which they are visually aware are profoundly different. Seeing is not only the having of a visual experience; it is also the way in which the visual experience is had.

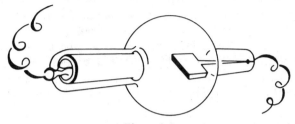

Figure 9.8

At school the physicist had gazed at this glass-and-metal instrument. Returning now, after years in University and research, his eye lights upon the same object once again. Does he see the same thing now as he did then? Now he sees the instrument in terms of electrical circuit theory, thermodynamic theory, the theories of metal and glass structure, thermionic emission, optical transmission, refraction, diffraction, atomic theory, quantum theory and special relativity.

Contrast the freshman's view of college with that of his ancient tutor. Compare a man's first glance at the motor of his car with a similar glance ten exasperating years later.

'Granted, one learns all these things,' it may be countered, 'but it all figures in the interpretation the physicist puts on what he sees. Though the layman sees exactly what the physicist sees, he cannot interpret it in the same way because he has not learned so much.'

Is the physicist doing more than just seeing? No; he does nothing over and above what the layman does when he sees an X-ray tube. What are you doing over and above reading these words? Are you interpreting marks on a page? When would this ever be a natural way of speaking? Would an infant see what you see here, when you see words and sentences and he sees but marks and lines? One does nothing beyond looking and seeing when one dodges bicycles, glances at a friend, or notices a cat in the garden.

'The physicist and the layman see the same thing,' it is objected, 'but they do not make the same thing of it.' The layman can make nothing of it. Nor is that just a figure of speech. I can make nothing of the Arab word for *cat*, though my purely visual impressions may be indistinguishable from those of the Arab who can. I must learn Arabic before I can see what he sees. The layman must learn physics before he can see what the physicist sees. . . .

The visitor must learn some physics before he can see what the physicist sees. Only then will the context throw into relief those features of the objects before him which the physicist sees as indicating resistance.

This obtains in all seeing. Attention is rarely directed to the space between the leaves of a tree, save when a Keats brings it to our notice. (Consider also what was involved in Crusoe's seeing a vacant space in the sand as a footprint.) Our attention most naturally rests on objects and events which dominate the visual field. What a blooming, buzzing, undifferentiated confusion visual life would be if we all arose tomorrow without attention capable of dwelling only on what had heretofore been overlooked.

The infant and the layman can see: they are not blind. But they cannot see what the physicist sees; they are blind to what he sees. We may not hear that the oboe is out of tune, though this will be painfully obvious to the trained musician. (Who, incidentally, will not hear the tones and *interpret* them as being out of tune, but will simply hear the oboe to be out of tune. We simply see what time it is; the surgeon simply sees a wound to be septic; the physicist sees the X-ray tube's anode overheating.) The elements of the visitor's visual field, though identical with those of the physicist, are not organized for him as for the physicist; the same lines, colours, shapes are apprehended by both, but not in the same way. There are indefinitely many ways in which a constellation of lines, shapes, patches, may be seen. *Why* a visual pattern is seen differently is a question for psychology, but *that* it may be seen differently is important in any examination of the concepts of seeing and observation. Here, as Wittgenstein might have said, the psychological is a symbol of the logical.

You see a bird, I see an antelope; the physicist sees an X-ray tube, the child a complicated lamp bulb; the microscopist sees coelenterate mesoglea, his new student sees only a gooey, formless stuff. Tycho and Simplicius see a mobile sun, Kepler and Galileo see a static sun.

It may be objected, 'Everyone, whatever his state of knowledge, will see Figure 9.1 as a box or cube, viewed as from above or as from below'. True; almost everyone, child, layman, physicist, will see the figure as box-like one way or another. But could such observations be made by people ignorant of the construction of box-like objects? No. This objection only shows that most of us − the blind, babies and dimwits excluded − have learned enough to be able to see this figure as a three-dimensional box. This reveals something about the sense in which Simplicius and Galileo do see the same thing (which I have never denied): they both see a brilliant heavenly body. The schoolboy and the physicist both see that the X-ray tube will smash if dropped. Examining how observers see different things in x marks something important about their seeing the same thing when looking at x. If seeing different things involves having different knowledge and theories about x, then perhaps the sense in which they see the same thing involves their sharing knowledge and theories about x. Bragg and the baby share no knowlege of X-ray tubes. They see the same thing only in that if they are looking at it they are both having some visual experience of it. Kepler and Tycho agree on more: they see the same thing in a stronger sense. Their visual fields are organized in much the same way. Neither sees the sun about to break out in a grin, or about to crack into ice cubes. (The baby is not 'set' even against these eventualities.) Most people today see the same thing at dawn in an even stronger sense: we share much knowledge of the sun. Hence Tycho and Kepler see different things, and yet they see the same thing. That these things can be said depends on their knowledge, experience, and theories.

Kepler and Tycho are to the sun as we are to Figure 9.4, when I see the bird and you see only the antelope. The elements of their experiences are identical; but their conceptual organization is vastly different. Can their visual fields have a different organization? Then they can see different things in the east at dawn.

It is the sense in which Tycho and Kepler do not observe the same thing which must be grasped if one is to understand disagreements within microphysics. Fundamental physics is primarily a search for intelligibility − it is philosophy of matter. Only secondarily is it a search for objects and facts (though the two endeavours are as hand and glove). Microphysicists seek new modes of conceptual organization. If that can be done the finding of new entities will follow. Gold is rarely discovered by one who has not got the lay of the land.

To say that Tycho and Kepler, Simplicius and Galileo, Hooke and Newton, Priestley and Lavoisier, Soddy and Einstein, De Broglie and Born, Heisenberg and Bohm all make the same observations but use them differently is too easy. It does not explain controversy in research science. Were there no sense in which they were different observations they could not be used differently. This may perplex some: that researchers sometimes do not appreciate data in the same way is a serious matter. It is important to realize, however, that sorting out differences about data, evidence, observation, may require more than simply gesturing at observable objects. It may require a comprehensive reappraisal of one's subject matter. This may be difficult, but it should not obscure the fact that nothing less than this may do.

There is a sense, then, in which seeing is a 'theory-laden' undertaking. Observation of x is shaped by prior knowledge of x. Another influence on observations rests in the language or notation used to express what we know, and without which there would be little we could recognize as knowledge.

Notes

1. BBC report, 30 June 1954.
2. Newton, Isaac (1704) *Opticks;* . . ., London, book 2, part 1.
3. Wittgenstein, L. (1953) *Philosophical Investigations*, Anscombe, G. E. M., trans., Oxford, Basil Blackwell, p. 194.
4. ibid., p. 200.
5. ibid., p. 193.
6. ibid.

9.3 VALUE JUDGEMENTS AND THEORY CHOICE

THOMAS S. KUHN (1922–   ), *from 'Objectivity, value judgment, and theory choice', in* The Essential Tension, *Chicago, University of Chicago Press, 1977*

Kuhn defends the claim of *The Structure of Scientific Revolutions*[1] that subjective factors enter into the choice of scientific theories. He denies that this is tantamount to asserting the irrationality of theory choice. He holds, rather, that scientists share certain values, such as consistency and simplicity, to which they may refer in arguing for the acceptance of one theory in preference to another. These shared values do not, however, completely determine the outcome of such a debate.

Note

1. Kuhn, Thomas, S. (1970) *The Structure of Scientific Revolutions*, Chicago, University of Chicago Press, 2nd edn.

In the penultimate chapter of a controversial book, *The Structure of Scientific Revolutions*,[1] I considered the ways scientists are brought to abandon one time-honored theory or paradigm in favor of another. Such decision problems, I wrote, 'cannot be resolved by proof'.[2] To discuss their mechanism is, therefore, to talk 'about techniques of persuasion, or about argument and counterargument in a situation in which there can be no proof'.[3] Under these circumstances, I continued, 'lifelong resistance [to a new theory] . . . is not a violation of scientific standards. . . . Though the historian can always find men − Priestley, for instance − who were unreasonable to resist for as long as they did, he will not find a point at which resistance becomes illogical or unscientific'.[4] Statements of that sort obviously raise the question of why, in the absence of binding criteria for scientific choice, both the number of solved scientific problems and the precision of individual problem solutions should increase so markedly with the passage of time. Confronting that issue, I sketched in my closing chapter a number of characteristics that scientists share by virtue of the training which licenses their membership in one or another community of specialists. In the absence of criteria able to dictate the choice of each individual, I argued, we do well to trust the collective judgment of scientists trained in this way. 'What better criterion could there be,' I asked rhetorically, 'than the decision of the scientific group?'[5]

A number of philosophers have greeted remarks like these in a way that continues to surprise me. My views, it is said, make of theory choice 'a matter for mob psychology'.[6] Kuhn believes, I am told, that 'the decision of a scientific group to adopt a new paradigm cannot be based on good reasons of any kind, factual or otherwise'.[7] The debates surrounding such choices must, my critics claim, be for me 'mere persuasive displays without deliberative substance'.[8] Reports of this sort manifest total misunderstanding, and I have occasionally said as much in papers directed primarily to other ends. But those passing protestations have had negligible effect, and the misunderstandings continue to be important. I conclude that it is past time for me to describe, at greater length and with greater precision, what has been on my mind when I have uttered statements like the ones with which I just began. If I have been reluctant to do so in the past, that is largely because I have preferred to devote attention to areas in which my views diverge more sharply from those currently received than they do with respect to theory choice.

What, I ask to begin with, are the characteristics of a good scientific theory? Among a number of quite usual answers I select five, not because they are exhaustive, but because they are individually important and collectively sufficiently varied to indicate what is at stake. First, a theory should be accurate: within its domain, that is, consequences deducible from a theory should be in demonstrated agreement with the results of existing experiments and observations. Second, a theory should be consistent, not only internally or with itself, but also with other currently accepted theories applicable to related aspects of nature. Third, it should have broad scope: in particular, a theory's consequences should extend far beyond the particular observations, laws, or subtheories it was initially designed to explain. Fourth, and closely related, it should be simple, bringing order to phenomena that in its absence would be individually isolated and, as a set, confused. Fifth — a somewhat less standard item, but one of special importance to actual scientific decisions — a theory should be fruitful of new research findings: it should, that is, disclose new phenomena or previously unnoted relationships among those already known.[9] These five characteristics — accuracy, consistency, scope, simplicity and fruitfulness — are all standard criteria for evaluating the adequacy of a theory. If they had not been, I would have devoted far more space to them in my book, for I agree entirely with the traditional view that they play a vital role when scientists must choose between an established theory and an upstart competitor. Together with others of much the same sort, they provide *the* shared basis for theory choice.

Nevertheless, two sorts of difficulties are regularly encountered by the men who must use these criteria in choosing, say, between Ptolemy's astronomical theory and Copernicus's, between the oxygen and phlogiston theories of combustion, or between Newtonian mechanics and the quantum theory. Individually the criteria are imprecise: individuals may legitimately differ about their application to concrete cases. In addition, when deployed together, they repeatedly prove to conflict with one another; accuracy may, for example, dictate the choice of one theory, scope the choice of its competitor. Since these difficulties, especially the first, are also relatively familiar, I shall devote little time to their elaboration. Though my argument does demand that I illustrate them briefly, my views will begin to depart from those long current only after I have done so.

Begin with accuracy, which for present purposes I take to include not only quantitative agreement but qualitative as well. Ultimately it proves the most nearly decisive of all the criteria, partly because it is less equivocal than the others but especially because predictive and explanatory powers, which depend on it, are characteristics that scientists are particularly unwilling to give up. Unfortunately, however, theories cannot always be discriminated in terms of accuracy. Copernicus's system, for example, was not more accurate than Ptolemy's until drastically revised by Kepler more than sixty years after Copernicus's death. If Kepler or someone else had not found other reasons to choose heliocentric astronomy, those improvements in accuracy would never have been made, and Copernicus's work might have been forgotten. More typically, of course, accuracy does permit discriminations, but not the sort that lead regularly to unequivocal choice. The oxygen theory, for example, was universally acknowledged to account for observed weight relations in chemical reactions, something the phlogiston theory had previously scarcely attempted to do. But the phlogiston theory, unlike its rival, could account for the metals' being much more alike than the ores from which they were formed. One theory thus matched experience better in one area, the other in another. To choose between them on the basis of accuracy, a scientist would need to decide the area in which accuracy was more significant. About that matter chemists could and did differ without violating any of the criteria outlined above, or any others yet to be suggested.

However important it may be, therefore, accuracy by itself is seldom or never a sufficient criterion for theory choice. Other criteria must function as well, but they do not eliminate problems. To illustrate I select just two – consistency and simplicity – asking how they functioned in the choice between the heliocentric and geocentric systems. As astronomical theories both Ptolemy's and Copernicus's were internally consistent, but their relation to related theories in other fields was very different. The stationary central earth was an essential ingredient of received physical theory, a tight-knit body of doctrine which explained, among other things, how stones fall, how water pumps function, and why the clouds move slowly across the skies. Heliocentric astronomy, which required the earth's motion, was inconsistent with the existing scientific explanation of these and other terrestrial phenomena. The consistency criterion, by itself, therefore, spoke unequivocally for the geocentric tradition.

Simplicity, however, favored Copernicus, but only when evaluated in a quite special way. If, on the one hand, the two systems were compared in terms of the actual computational labor required to predict the position of a planet at a particular time, then they proved substantially equivalent. Such computations were what astronomers did, and Copernicus's system offered them no labor-saving techniques; in that sense it was not simpler than Ptolemy's. If, on the other hand, one asked about the amount of mathematical apparatus required to explain, not the detailed quantitative motions of the planets, but merely their gross qualitative features – limited elongation, retrograde motion and the like – then, as every schoolchild knows, Copernicus required only one circle per planet, Ptolemy two. In that sense the Copernican theory was the simpler, a fact vitally important to the choices made by both Kepler and Galileo and thus essential to the ultimate triumph of Copernicanism. But that sense of simplicity was not the only one available, nor even the one most natural to professional astronomers, men whose task was the actual computation of planetary position.

Because time is short and I have multiplied examples elsewhere, I shall here simply assert that these difficulties in applying standard criteria of choice are typical and that they arise no less forcefully in twentieth-century situations than in the earlier and better-known examples I have just sketched. When scientists must choose between competing theories, two men fully committed to the same list of criteria for choice may nevertheless reach different conclusions. Perhaps they interpret simplicity differently or have different convictions about the range of fields within which the consistency criterion must be met. Or perhaps they agree about these matters but differ about the relative weights to be accorded to these or to other criteria when several are deployed together. With respect to divergences of this sort, no set of choice criteria yet proposed is of any use. One can explain, as the historian characteristically does, why particular men made particular choices at particular times. But for that purpose one must go beyond the list of shared criteria to characteristics of the individuals who make the choice. One must, that is, deal with characteristics which vary from one scientist to another without thereby in the least jeopardizing their adherence to the canons that make science scientific. Though such canons do exist and should be discoverable (doubtless the criteria of choice with which I began are among them), they are not by themselves sufficient to determine the decisions of individual scientists. For that purpose the shared canons must be fleshed out in ways that differ from one individual to another.

Some of the differences I have in mind result from the individual's previous experience as a scientist. In what part of the field was he at work when confronted by the need to choose? How long had he worked there; how successful had he been; and how much of his work depended on concepts and techniques challenged by the new theory? Other factors relevant to choice lie outside the sciences. Kepler's early election of Copernicanism was due in part to his immersion in the Neoplatonic and Hermetic movements of his day; German Romanticism predisposed those it affected toward both recognition and acceptance of energy conservation; nineteenth-century British social thought had a similar influence on the availability and acceptability of Darwin's concept of the struggle for existence. Still other significant differences are functions of personality. Some scientists place more premium than others on originality and are correspondingly more willing to take risks; some scientists prefer comprehensive, unified theories to precise and detailed problem solutions of apparently narrower scope. Differentiating factors like these are described by my critics as subjective and are contrasted with the shared or objective criteria from which I began.

Though I . . . question that use of terms, let me for the moment accept it. My point is, then, that every individual choice between competing theories depends on a mixture of objective and subjective factors, or of shared and individual criteria. Since the latter have not ordinarily figured in the philosophy of science, my emphasis upon them has made my belief in the former hard for my critics to see.

What I have said so far is primarily simply descriptive of what goes on in the sciences at times of theory choice. As description, furthermore, it has not been challenged by my critics, who reject instead my claim that these facts of scientific life have philosophic import. Taking up that issue, I shall begin to isolate some, though I think not vast, differences of opinion. Let me begin by asking how philosophers of science can for so long have neglected the subjective elements which, they freely grant, enter regularly into the actual theory choices made by individual scientists? Why have these elements seemed to them an index only of human weakness, not at all of the nature of scientific knowledge?

One answer to that question is, of course, that few philosophers, if any, have claimed to possess either a complete or an entirely well-articulated list of criteria. For some time, therefore, they could reasonably expect that further research would eliminate residual imperfections and produce an algorithm able to dictate rational, unanimous choice. Pending that achievement, scientists would have no alternative but to supply subjectively what the best current list of objective criteria still lacked. That some of them might still do so even with a perfected list at hand would then be an index only of the inevitable imperfection of human nature.

That sort of answer may still prove to be correct, but I think no philosopher still expects that it will. The search for algorithmic decision procedures has continued for some time and produced both powerful and illuminating results. But those results all presuppose that individual criteria of choice can be unambiguously stated and also that, if more than one proves relevant, an appropriate weight function is at hand for their joint application. Unfortunately, where the choice at issue is between scientific theories, little progress has been made toward the first of these desiderata and none toward the second. Most philosophers of science would, therefore, I think, now regard the sort of algorithm which has traditionally been sought as a not quite attainable ideal. I entirely agree and shall henceforth take that much for granted.

Even an ideal, however, if it is to remain credible, requires some demonstrated relevance to the situations in which it is supposed to apply. Claiming that such demonstration requires no recourse to subjective factors, my critics seem to appeal, implicitly or explicitly, to the well-known distinction between the contexts of discovery and of justification.[10] They concede, that is, that the subjective factors I invoke play a significant role in the discovery or invention of new theories, but they also insist that that inevitably intuitive process lies outside of the bounds of philosophy of science and is irrelevant to the question of scientific objectivity. Objectivity enters science, they continue, through the processes by which theories are tested, justified, or judged. Those processes do not, or at least need not, involve subjective factors at all. They can be governed by a set of (objective) criteria shared by the entire group competent to judge.

I have already argued that that position does not fit observations of scientific life and shall now assume that that much has been conceded. What is now at issue is a different point: whether or not this invocation of the distinction between contexts of discovery and of justification provides even a plausible and useful idealization. I think it does not and can best make my point by suggesting first a likely source of its apparent cogency. I suspect that my critics have been misled by science pedagogy or what I have elsewhere called textbook science. In science teaching, theories are presented together with exemplary applications, and those applications may be viewed as evidence. But that is not their primary pedagogic function (science students are distressingly willing to receive the word from professors and texts). Doubtless *some* of them were *part* of the evidence at the time actual decisions were being made, but they represent only a fraction of the considerations relevant to the decision process. The context of pedagogy differs almost as much from the context of justification as it does from that of discovery.

Full documentation of that point would require longer argument than is appropriate here, but two aspects of the way in which philosophers ordinarily demonstrate the relevance of choice criteria are worth noting. Like the science textbooks on which they are often modelled, books and articles on the philosophy of science refer again and again to the famous crucial experiments: Foucault's pendulum, which demonstrates the motion of the earth; Cavendish's demonstration of gravitational attraction; or Fizeau's measurement of the relative speed of sound in water and air. These experiments are paradigms of good reason for scientific choice; they illustrate the most effective of all the sorts of argument which could be available to a scientist uncertain which of two theories to follow; they are vehicles for the transmission of criteria of choice. But they also have another characteristic in common. By the time they were performed no scientist still needed to be convinced of the validity of the theory their outcome is now used to demonstrate. Those decisions had long since been made on the basis of significantly more equivocal evidence. The exemplary crucial experiments to which philosophers again and again refer would have been historically relevant to theory choice only if they had yielded unexpected results. Their use as illustrations provides needed economy to science pedagogy, but they scarcely illuminate the character of the choices that scientists are called upon to make.

Standard philosophical illustrations of scientific choice have another troublesome characteristic. The only arguments discussed are, as I have previously indicated, the ones favorable to the theory that, in fact, ultimately triumphed. Oxygen, we read, could explain weight relations, phlogiston could not; but nothing is said about the phlogiston theory's power or about the oxygen theory's limitations. Comparisons of Ptolemy's theory with Copernicus's proceed in the same way. Perhaps these examples should not be given since they contrast a developed theory with one still in its infancy. But philosophers regularly use them nonetheless. If the only result of their doing so were to simplify the decisions situation, one could not object. Even historians do not claim to deal with the full factual complexity of the situations they describe. But these simplifications emasculate by making choice totally unproblematic. They eliminate, that is, one essential element of the decision situations that scientists must resolve if their field is to move ahead. In those situations there are always at least some good reasons for each possible choice.

Notes

1. op. cit.
2. ibid., p. 148.
3. ibid., pp. 151f.
4. ibid., p. 159.
5. ibid., p. 170.
6. Lakatos, Imre (1970) 'Falsification and the methodology of scientific research programmes' in Lakatos, I. and Musgrave, A. E., eds, *Criticism and the Growth of Knowledge*, Cambridge, Cambridge University Press, p. 178.
7. Schapere, Dudley (1966) 'Meaning and scientific change', in Colodny, R. G., ed., *Mind and Cosmos: Essays in Contemporary Science and Philosophy*, Pittsburgh, p. 67.
8. Scheffler, op. cit., p. 81.
9. The last criterion, fruitfulness, deserves more emphasis than it has yet received. A scientist choosing between two theories ordinarily knows that his decision will have a bearing on his subsequent research career. Of course he is especially attracted by a theory that promises the concrete successes for which scientists are ordinarily rewarded.
10. The least equivocal example of this position is probably the one developed in Scheffler, op. cit., ch. 4.

9.4   THE OBJECTIVITY OF HISTORY

J. A. PASSMORE (1914–   ), 'The objectivity of history',
from Philosophy, 33(125), pp. 97–111, 1958

Passmore considers a number of different criteria of
objectivity and argues that in no case do these criteria
yield a sense in which science is objective and history
not so. He suggests that history differs from science in
not being concerned to discover general theories.
Historical inquiry is as much directed to finding out
'what really happens' as are the sciences.

'There's one thing certain,' said a historian of my acquaintance when he
heard the title of this paper, 'that's a problem which would never
perturb a working-historian.' He was wrong: a working-historian first
drew it to my attention; and in one form or another it raises its head
whenever historians discuss the nature of their own inquiries. Yet in a
way he was right. His mind had turned to the controversies of episte-
mologists, controversies about 'the possibility of knowledge'; historians,
he rightly felt, do not trouble their heads about such matters.

When, indeed, the historian asks whether history can be objective, he
is not suffering from a generalized, or epistemological, scepticism. That
some forms of inquiry − he would instance physics − can be objectively
conducted, he does not doubt; the only question, for him, is whether
this is true of history. One cannot allay his qualms, therefore . . . by an
appeal to 'the principle of non-vacuous contrast'.[1] This principle would
forbid us to deny that history is objective unless some forms of inquiry
are objective, but the distinction between objective and non-objective
need not be exhibited within history itself.

A striking feature of philosophical words, however, is that it is very
easy to fall into the trap of so defining them as to make them vacuous in
either of two directions: they may become vacuous through applying to
nothing at all, or through applying to everything, thereby losing their
usefulness as modes of distinguishing. Thus, for example, some philosophers have defined 'present' so rigidly that it would never be proper to
say of anything that it is 'present', others so loosely that the present
swallows up both the past and the future. Similar considerations apply
to 'objectivity'.

Consider the following arguments, the first constructed but by no
means, I think, implausible, the second a quotation from an article by

A. J. P. Taylor . . . intended to disprove the objectivity of history. *Argument One:* 'Of course history is objective: no one really doubts such facts as that Magna Charta was signed in 1215.' *Argument Two:* 'Historians seek to be detached, impassionate, impartial. In fact, however, no historian starts out with his mind a blank, to be gradually filled by the evidence.'[2]

Now if an inquiry is objectively conducted provided only that the inquirer sometimes asserts true propositions, then every inquiry is objective; the most arbitrary of partisans will tell the truth sometimes, if only by accident. On the other side, if only those inquiries are objective in which the inquirer begins with a blank mind, then no inquiry whatsoever is objective. By the time we begin to inquire we already, and inevitably, have beliefs, expectations, interests. What Hegel says of the historian − 'Even the average and mediocre historian who perhaps believes and pretends that he is merely receptive, merely surrendering to the data, is not passive in his thinking' − applies to all scientists. Not even the worst of them, the dreariest laboratory drudge, is objective − in Taylor's sense of the word. Thus on *Argument One* objectivity no longer discriminates; on *Argument Two* it no longer applies. Yet so treacherous is the ground on which we are now standing that neither of these arguments is wholly outrageous. Each has a certain contact with quite ordinary ways of using the word 'objective'.

Since it is my object to compare and contrast history with other forms of inquiry, I shall dismiss out of hand all proposed criteria of objectivity which would make it vacuous. But even then the range of possibilities is considerable; and we have no option but to canvass them in turn. 'Is history objective?' is a question to which one can only give the not very satisfactory answer 'it all depends on how high you set your standards'.

Criterion One (The Cartesian or mathematico-deductive): *An objective inquiry either (a) deduces its conclusions from self-evident axioms or (b) unfolds them from essences or definitions.*

It has sometimes been held, as by the Hegelians, that history consists in the gradual revelation of a plan, or an Idea; on this view, it might seem, the historian could satisfy the Cartesian criterion. But the conception of a plan, as Hegel explicitly says, emerges within a philosophy of history, in which history is made the starting-point for philosophical reflection. It cannot be so used as to obviate the need for historical investigation, enabling it to be replaced by logical analysis. 'History itself,' writes Hegel in his *Lectures on the Philosophy of History*, 'must be taken as it is; we have to proceed historically, empirically . . . only the study of world history can show that it has proceeded rationally.'[3] Hegel's most distinguished historical disciple, Ranke, sought his inspiration in the archives of Venice; if he was convinced that it was 'the hand of God' which he there sought to disclose, the fact remains that history disclosed God, not God history.

We can safely conclude, then, that if the 'objectivity' of a form of inquiry depends upon the possibility of deducing its content *a priori*, history must abandon all claims to objectivity. In this respect, however. it is in excellent company: company which includes at least all that scientific activity which Mr Toulmin describes, interestingly enough from our present point of view, as 'natural history'.[4]

Criterion Two (Mach's criterion): *An objective inquiry is one which begins from data which are literally such, i.e. which nakedly confront us.*

This ideal at once stirred the ambitions and disturbed the dreams of nineteenth-century historians. Events flow around us: why should we not, by restricting ourselves to their description, achieve a history which is barely, but truly, a record?

We might assail this ideal on purely epistemological grounds; we might argue that there are no 'pure data' in the Machian sense of that phrase. But we should not, by so doing, seriously perturb the positivistically-minded historian. The philosophical difficulty in nominating data which are strictly such has never interested the historian; he leaves anxiety on that point, we might say, to the physicist. For him it is enough if his 'data' are equal in status to the observations and experiments of the natural scientists; quite sensibly, he feels that if their work is not objective, the word ceases to have any methodological significance. His ideal-in-theory may be a science composed out of Machian data; his ideal-in-practice, the ideal to which he hopes to conform or despairs of realizing, transforms 'bare data' into observations, with no niggardliness, even then, in the use of the word 'observation'.

Thus he is not made uneasy by the objection that since the events which concern him are *past*, they cannot be data, but must always be inferences or reconstructions. For since the simplest of experiments and observations takes time, the restriction of 'data' to the 'immediately present' − presuming one can make some sense of that phrase − would carry with it the consequence that science knows nothing of data, either. And the historian's ideal, as we said, is natural science, not an epistemologist's Utopia.

For that reason, another objection has been taken more seriously. The natural scientist, it is argued, can always pass beyond the recorded facts to the facts themselves, and this direct reference to the facts is the essence of objectivity; the scientist confronts the world as it nakedly is, whereas the historian sees it, always, through the medium of someone else's testimony — a testimony he can never by the nature of the case penetrate beyond, because the events the testimony describes are gone forever. If a scientist doubts the testimony of some other scientist that when hydrochloric acid is poured on to zinc, hydrogen is produced, he can repeat the experiment for himself; if a historian doubts Ben Jonson's testimony about Shakespeare's character, he has no way of examining that character for himself — the most he can do is to set Jonson's testimony against somebody else's. Thus the historian cannot hope to achieve objectivity.

Criterion Three: An objective inquiry is a direct examination of the world which does not rely upon testimony.

One may note, in the first place, that there is implicit in this way of looking at the matter a curious kind of methodological solipsism. The contrast 'other people's testimony' — 'the facts' presumes that what *we* observe is a fact, whereas the best that other people can do is to 'express an opinion'. It is perhaps worth remembering that what *we* call 'our observations' are from the point of view of other people 'our testimony'.

Even historians are not exempt from a vulgar preference for what 'they can see with their own eyes'. Sir Henry Lambert, for example, suggests in his *The Nature of History* that the evidence that the Jameson raid took place is superior to the evidence that Napoleon was defeated at the Battle of Waterloo, because there are still people alive who took part in Jameson's raid.[5] This, it seems to me, is an obvious error: the historian is in a much better position to know that Napoleon was defeated at Waterloo than any participant in the battle could be. He can take a wider view of the situation than is accessible to any participant. Furthermore, if men are sometimes deceived by testimony, they are no less capable of deceiving themselves in the actual situation; indeed, this, rather than the risk of lying, is the principal reason for regarding their testimony with suspicion. There are some points of detail, of course, on which the evidence of a participant — who could be cross-examined — might happen to be useful, but these are of minor consequence. Historians do not in fact go in search of 'old soldiers'.

A second point is that what is called 'observation' is always to a considerable measure dependent upon testimony; we can never put ourselves in such a situation that we are relying on nothing except 'pure observation'. If we say that we have 'observed for ourselves' that hydrochloric acid acts on zinc to produce hydrogen, this observation, of course, depends on someone's testimony that what confront us in this case are hydrochloric acid, zinc and hydrogen; and if we wish to question any part of this testimony, we can do so only by depending upon some other testimony. So there can be nothing 'non-objective' about making use of testimony − unless 'objective' is vacuous − although this does not mean, of course, that any *particular* testimony is exempt from critical examination.

A third point is that considerable areas of physical science, in their reliance upon testimony, are in exactly the same position as history. Astronomy and seismology will serve as examples. One might, however, argue thus: the testimony on which the scientist has to rely is the careful recording of a fact by a trained observer; the historian, on the other hand, begins with chronicles, i.e. with testimonies composed by some-body who had an axe to grind. 'The so-called "sources" of history,' wrote Popper in *The Open Society*, 'only record such facts as appeared sufficiently interesting to record, so that sources will contain only facts that fit in with a preconceived theory.'[6]

Now, of course, the historian does occasionally find himself in a situation in which he has no 'sources' at his disposal except chronicles or, in the worst case, except *a* chronicle. But even then the historian is not quite at the mercy of the chronicler; he has his ways of testing chronicle accounts, and he can discover important facts from them which the chronicler had no intention whatever of recording. Mediaeval lives of saints, for example, are invaluable to the historian for the light they throw on the life of the Middle Ages, a life which the chronicler certainly would not have bothered deliberately to record. Furthermore, the greater part of the historian's sources, at least since Ranke's time, no chronicler compiled. They are, let us say, lists of tax-collections, drawn up by careful and certainly unimaginative bureaucrats for purposes quite temporary and official − not at all for the greater glory of the Emperor. Or the sources may be archaeological, rather than written documents − and rubbish-tips were not constructed to deceive the archaeologist. In short, the historian is not in the position of having to rely wholly on the propaganda of partisans.

It does not seem to me, then, that such a statement as 'Peter Pipkin paid twopence rent' need fear any comparison with 'this gas is oxygen'; or that it is possible to maintain, against history's objectivity, that it has no way of getting access to the facts. But one feature of the 'Peter Pipkin' state-ment deserves some little attention; it contains the phrase 'paid rent', and this is a phrase which refers to a set of rights and duties which are not precisely defined. Such 'open texture' is characteristic of the statements of historians, and is sometimes alleged against history's objectivity.

Thus E. M. Hulme in his *History and Its Neighbours* maintains that historical facts, in sharp distinction from scientific facts, are 'highly subjective'; taking as an example such an historical statement as that 'Lincoln is a great man' he argues that different historians have such different conceptions of 'a great man', that there is no objectivity in the fact the statement asserts.[7] On this showing, I suppose, a science proceeds objectively *only if its statements contain no expressions except those which 'mean the same' for all observers*. Let us call this *Criterion Four*. In its extreme form, we can, I think, dismiss it on the familiar ground that it makes objectivity vacuous. As has emerged very clearly from the chequered history of logical positivism, no language can be so constructed as to make misunderstanding impossible — to guarantee that everyone will have the same conception of the terms it employs. But it is characteristic of science that it uses expressions we can bring to 'the test', i.e. allowing that there is always the risk of misunderstanding, we can be given explanations which will enable us to see how to criticize the statements the scientist makes. History could certainly not be conducted objectively if its statements were not criticizable. And no doubt some historians make statements which are not in this sense 'objectively testable' — statements about 'the German spirit', for example. It will, I should say, be a sign of a good historian, that he avoids *ex parte* assertions like 'Lincoln was a great man', unless this is meant as a summary way of referring to a number of characteristics to which he has drawn attention; or that he makes it clear to us how, if at all, 'paying rent' differs from what we now understand by that same expression. So far as we can safely talk about degrees of open texture, I think we should have to admit that historical statements are 'more open' than chemical statements; but this does not entitle us to dismiss them as 'subjective'.

Suppose, however, it be admitted that there are historical facts; it might still be argued that history is incurably subjective because it is bound to *impose a pattern* on the facts. History consists not in the simple accumulation of facts but in telling some sort of connected story, and the choice of the pattern, so it is sometimes suggested, can only be a matter of arbitrary decision. We can take the implicit criterion in two different ways: as maintaining that the pattern is an arbitrary *construction*, or that it is an arbitrary *selection*.

Criterion Five: An inquiry is objective only if it keeps to atomic facts.

At this point, the argument is reminiscent of the British empiricist view that all relations are 'the work of the mind'. We can see this in the well-known text-book by Langlois and Seignobos, *Introduction to the Study of History*. 'Historical construction,' they write, 'has to be performed with an incoherent mass of minute facts, with detail-knowledge reduced as it were to a powder.'[8] If history really begins with an 'incoherent mass', then certainly it would be reasonable to conclude that a coherent history book is a merely personal construction: there would be no way whatever of checking the pattern it suggests. But Langlois and Seignobos break down this simple-minded empiricism when they go on to suggest that there are links and connections between these atomic facts. This is clearly so: indeed, as we have already suggested, to say that someone is 'paying rent' is already to have become conscious of a system of rights and duties. Relations and connections are ingredients within the simplest facts; they are not somehow imposed upon facts which are quite devoid of them. There is no *a priori* reason, then, for maintaining that order is imposed, as distinct from discovered. Let us turn then, rather, to:

Criterion Six: An inquiry is objective only if it does not select from within its material.

Here, for example, is L. B. Namier in *Avenues of History*:

> The function of the historian is akin to that of the painter and not of the photographic camera; to discover and set forth, to single out and stress that which is the nature of the thing and not to reproduce indiscriminately all that meets the eye. . . . History is therefore necessarily subjective and individual, conditioned by the interest and the vision of the historian.[9]

The historian regards certain facts as unimportant and others as important; in thus distinguishing them, so Namier is saying, he demonstrates that his inquiries are rooted in subjectivity. This complaint goes back to Descartes:

> Even the most accurate of histories, if they do not wholly misrepresent or exaggerate the value of things in order to render them more worthy of being read, at least omit in them all the circumstances which are basest and least notable; and from that fact it follows that what is retained is not portrayed as it really is.[10]

On the face of it, this is a queer criterion, because every form of inquiry is selective. Nothing is more irritating to the botanist or to the geologist than the presumption that every flower or every stone is of equal interest to him. A physicist is interested only in such physical operations as bear upon a problem he is investigating; a historian, similarly, will refer only to those facts which in some way bear upon the story he is telling.

The difficulty, however, lies in this conception of 'bearing upon'. We are accustomed, in discussing physical science, to talk in terms of problem, hypothesis, testing; if anybody asks us which facts are relevant, we shall say 'those which assist us to test the hypothesis'. Of course, we can overlook, or can unscrupulously ignore, relevant facts, but at least we have a relatively secure − and objective − test of relevance. Is there a comparable test of relevance in history?

Our discussion of this point is complicated by the tendency of a great many historians to speak as if description as such, description for its own sake, were their object − as if an ideal history would be one which described every social action which has ever taken place on the surface of the earth. Recognizing that it is not their object to discover general laws, and anxious, not unnaturally, to distinguish their work from that of the 'interpreters' or 'philosophers' of history, historians have concluded that their attention must be directed towards the *complete* description, in all its particularity, of a world which interests the sociologist, by comparison, only as exhibiting this or that social law. Then, since from this point of view one fact is as good as another, the historian lies open to the charge that the selectivity which is forced upon him is purely arbitrary; he has left himself with no way of distinguishing between what is important and what is unimportant, except in terms of arbitrary preference.

Historians write books, for example, with what seem to me to be preposterous titles − titles like *The History of England*. Then the critics complain: 'He says he is writing about the history of England, and yet he doesn't mention the Romantic Revival, or the institution of joint-stock companies, or the invention of the triple-expansion engine, or the publication of Newton's *Principia*.' And they allege these omissions as proof that the historian has a prejudice against literature, or against commerce, or science, or whatever else he fails to discuss. Since no historian can discuss everything, it is an easy step to the conclusion that history is irredeemably subjective.

The fact of the matter is that there is no such subject as *The History of England*: a book which purports to be a history of England is either a collection of fragments − like Trevelyan's *Social History* which, to borrow a metaphor from Butterfield, is a set of lantern-slides, not a moving picture − or else it tacitly confines itself to a more specific problem, say to the changes which have taken place in the distribution of sovereignty. Very often, the historian does not seem to know *what* he is doing; his instinct leads him to select a single problem for consideration, and yet he feels uneasily that since he is purporting to write about the 'History of England', he ought to say something about its literature, or its social life. So a good book is marred by perfunctory and irrelevant chapters; and the historian cannot defend himself against the charge of arbitrariness, since his selection is not determined by the structure of the work he has undertaken. History books, indeed, ought commonly to be more, not less, selective than they are; greater selectivity would be a step *towards* objectivity, not away from it. What the historian calls 'general history' is a fraud — resting for its plausibility upon the metaphysical notion that there is something called 'the whole community' which moves in the manner of a single man.

If this point be granted, the question still arises: how exactly is the historian to choose amongst his material? The determining factor, I have suggested, must be the nature of the problem from which he sets out, just as it is in the case of the physical scientist. There is, however, an important difference in the character of his problems; historical problems are more like a certain type of problem in applied science than they are like problems in pure science. This is a consequence of the fact that the historian is interested in what happens in a particular situation on a particular occasion; just as an engineer may have to ask himself: 'why did *that* aeroplane collapse?' so the historian asks: 'why did *that* monarchy collapse?' Furthermore, again like the engineer, he may, usually does, solve his problem by constructing a model. The engineer builds a scale model of the aeroplane, places it in what he takes to have been its environment on the fatal occasion, and shows it collapsing. What he shows can also be said, but only in a highly detailed form; 'aeroplanes with that sort of structure, with that length of span, etc., will not stand up to a wind of more than a certain force'. Similarly the historian constructs a narrative model of, say, the collapse of the monarchy in France — one which draws attention, he hopes, to the strains and stresses which were relevant to that collapse; then we see its collapse taking place. He may comment as well, bidding us pay special attention to this or that point in his narrative, as an engineer may comment on what is happening to his model aeroplane or (more irritatingly) a novelist on the development of his characters. Yet, at least in an important type of historical writing, the model, the narrative, is the central thing; and a 'relevant' fact is one which can be employed in the construction of a model. 'The last word of the historian,' as Butterfield writes in *The Whig Interpretation of History*, 'is not some firm general statement: it is a detailed piece of research.'[11]

The engineer, however, can test his model: if he puts the right stress on it, it collapses. What, if anything, corresponds, in history, to this testing process? Unless there is *some* test, it would seem, one model is as good as another; history, therefore, would fail to satisfy a familiar criterion for objectivity. Here, it might be said, is the crux of the matter: let it be granted that there are historical facts, let it be granted that these facts are 'important' or 'unimportant' in relation to a particular reconstruction, even then history fails to be objective because there are no grounds on which one historical reconstruction can rationally be preferred to another.

Criterion Seven: A branch of inquiry is objective only if it contains a method of deciding between conflicting hypotheses.

That history does not satisfy this criterion is persuasively argued by Popper in *The Open Society*.[12] Popper's criticism amounts to this: the hypotheses of history are *ad hoc* hypotheses, and we are free to choose as we like between *ad hoc* hypotheses. In contrast, the hypotheses of science are designed to apply to situations other than those which suggested them; in this way, the facts compel us to choose between them. We accept the hypothesis which leads us to expect, as other hypotheses do not, certain changes to take place which we then observe to occur. In history, however, all the relevant facts are already before us when we construct our hypothesis. Thus in choosing between hypotheses, the historian is not, as the physicist is, *constrained* by the facts, and in this difference the subjectivity of history resides.

In making this contrast, Popper is certainly exaggerating, I should say, the degree to which the physicist is constrained by his experiments. At the same time he is pointing to a real difficulty, even if it is perhaps not quite so serious as he imagines. I can illustrate the character of the difficulty most clearly by drawing on my own experience. Some little time ago, I wrote a book which purported to be an interpretation of Hume's philosophy.[13] One reviewer addressed me somewhat as follows: 'a possible interpretation, but other interpretations are equally possible'. How is one to reply? Obviously, this is a case where Popper's difficulty is at its most acute. I can produce as evidence nothing except passages in Hume's writings; I can do nothing which corresponds to predicting an as yet unobserved colour-shift in Mercury.

Yet at the same time my inquiry, as I conduct it, is not *ad hoc*. Why? Because what happens is something like this: an interpretation is suggested by certain passages in Hume; that interpretation is then confirmed by passages I had not previously so much as noticed, which the proposed interpretation serves to illuminate. Or I discover that passages which I previously could not understand now make good sense.

In the completed book, however, I lay all my cards on the table. All the passages are quoted as if they had equal confirmatory value. That explains why the interpretation has an *ad hoc* air. If a reader is convinced by my interpretation, this will be because he has himself been puzzled by passages in Hume, and my interpretation solves his puzzle for him. If, on the other hand, he approaches the book 'cold', with no problems of his own, it is bound to strike him as being at best ingenious, at worst wholly factitious.

The historian is very often in the position in which I found myself; it is not surprising, therefore, that to the outside observer his work has an *ad hoc* appearance, even if, as I have suggested, that appearance is distinctly misleading. Not infrequently, however, his position is a good deal more favourable. An hypothesis occurs to him, say, about the origins of the Peasants' Revolt; that hypothesis, were it true, would involve a revision of accepted views about population shifts after the Black Death; some ingenious inquirer discovers a quite new way of determining just what did happen to the population during those crucial years. He may, for example, light on the accounts of a mediaeval quarry whose stones were used exclusively for tombstones. Thus the historian's hypothesis is confirmed, at what seemed to be the weakest point, by evidence which was not at the disposal of its framer. The most that can be said against history, then, is that there is *sometimes* no known way of deciding between conflicting historical hypotheses; this difficulty is not peculiar to history and ought not to be alleged against its objectivity.

The question we have been considering, it should be observed, is substantially identical with one that has a more familiar ring about it: whether, as it is said, history employs a 'correspondence' or a 'coherence' theory of truth. For this amounts to asking whether there is any test of a historical hypothesis except that it 'makes sense', i.e. that the historian has constructed a plausible story. I have been suggesting that there often is such a test: we can look and see whether the hypothesis 'corresponds with the facts' — if we like to use that mode of expression — as they are dug up by the archaeologist or by the archive-ransacker. In ordinary life, if somebody gives us an account of what happened in a committee, we may believe him without further investigation — because the story has a familiar pattern — or else we may look for independent evidence. If we were asked whether we employed a coherence or a correspondence criterion of truth, we should look blank, as would the historian, quite rightly. Like the rest of us, he has various ways of testing his hypotheses, or his reconstructions, none of them committing him to a 'criterion of truth'.

So far, then, we have been arguing that the historian proceeds scientifically — in the sense that he puts forward hypotheses, or constructs narratives, which are subject to the constraint of facts. Yet, we may wonder, if this is so, how does it happen that historical works differ so notably one from another? The extent of this difference is perhaps the most popular of all grounds for denying the objectivity of history. Let us set out the implicit criterion thus:

Criterion Eight: In objective inquiries, conclusions are reached which are universally acceptable.

Compare, for example, Mr Walsh in his *Philosophy of History*:

> the main presuppositions of the thinking of physics are shared by all physicists and to think scientifically is to think in accordance with them. And this is at any rate one of the things that gives general validity to the conclusions of physicists; they do not depend to any important extent on the personal idiosyncrasies or private feelings of those who reach them, but are reached by a process in which complete abstraction is made from them.[14]

In this statement there is, I should say, more than a little exaggeration, a relic of the calculating-machine theory of science. The personal idio-syncrasies and private feelings of natural scientists are much more powerful agents both of discovery and of confusion than Mr Walsh allows. One does not doff an idiosyncrasy as easily as one dons a white coat. But we could put his point thus (this might be described as the ideal-in-practice of 'absolute impartiality'): physical scientists have developed regular ways of tackling scientific problems and of testing proposed solutions to them. Not to accept these methods is to be 'prejudiced', 'biassed', 'unscientific'.

One may well ask, however, whether the situation within history is so very different. There are generally accepted ways — involving a con-siderable level of expertness — of showing that a certain document (e.g. the *Donation of Constantine*) is a forgery, or that another (e.g. the *Kings of Rome*) is unreliable. If a man would not now be described as a 'physicist' who made assertions about physical operations without supporting them by experiment or calculation, so equally a man is 'no historian' who writes about past events without paying any attention to documentary evidence.

So much must be said; and yet the cases of history and natural science do not seem to be quite parallel. One distinguishes a Roman Catholic from a Protestant historian whereas one does not refer to the religion of a physicist; it seems sensible to talk about the Marxist interpretation of the French Revolution but not about the Marxist interpretation of the Doppler effect. Nor does this difficulty entirely vanish even after a dis-tinction is made between history and the interpretation of history; it is not just that the French Revolution is used by the Marxists to illustrate some particular sociological thesis and by other philosophers of history to illustrate a *different* thesis. The Marxist model of the events which took place will be incompatible at certain points with the model constructed by non-Marxists. Yet is not the same true, or could it not be true, of natural science? A footnote in Mr Walsh's book gives us pause: 'I am assuming,' he says, 'that "Soviet biology" and "bourgeois physics" are non-existent.' This we read with a smile of agreement, but should we? Imagine a situation in which there were Marxist universities in our midst, as there are Roman Catholic schools; the physics taught at these universities would certainly differ, in important respects, from the physics taught at non-Marxist universities. Would we then deny that physics is objective?

Furthermore, to make the contrast one between history and physics is certainly misleading; the identification of science and physics is a perpetual source of philosophical confusion. A peculiarity of physics — deriving not from its form as a branch of inquiry but from the nature of its subject-matter — is that the conclusions at which it arrives do not generally touch upon the non-theoretical interests of human beings. A physicist can come to recognize that Boyle's law is not universally applicable without concluding that he must abandon going to church, or voting conservative, or acting despotically as a father. The situation is quite different in psychology and sociology, and is somewhat different even in biology. Let us suppose that Freud's argument in *Totem and Taboo* were scientifically impregnable; could we contemplate a situation in which it was accepted by Roman Catholics?[15] There is an insignificant band of flat-earthers, a much larger group which refuses to accept the evolutionary theory of human origins — the difference is a matter of degree, only, if we pass on to psychology, to sociology, to history.

What ought to surprise and gratify us is the extent to which the spirit of objectivity has won its triumphs. Roman Catholic and Protestant accounts of the Reformation, considered as a story about social institutions, come more and more into conformity. If the test of objectivity is that there are regular ways of settling issues, by the use of which men of whatever party can be brought to see what actually happened, then I do not see how one can doubt the objectivity of history. But if we are satisfied with nothing less than the production of histories which all men the least rational will accept as final, then that would be a greater victory for the scientific spirit than we have any reason to expect. Such unanimity, however, is not to be found in any branch of human inquiry. Once again, if we press the criterion of objectivity too hard, it applies to no form of inquiry; slacken it slightly and history edges its way in with the rest.

One must emphasize, also, that very many of the differences which undoubtedly exist between, say, various histories of the French Revolution do not proceed from genuine differences of opinion, or oppositions in policy. The historian, I said, attempts to construct a narrative-model. Now for one thing there are models on different scales; the smaller the scale, the more we shall be told and the less we shall be shown. That is what makes school text-books so impossibly dull and so misleading, too, in their judgments. As Hegel puts this point: 'A history of this kind . . . must give up the individual presentation of reality, and abridge itself by means of abstraction. . . .' In so doing, we may argue, it quite falsifies the character of historical inquiry. Text-books in elementary science, however, are no less dull and no less misleading. Differences between history books derive in part from differences in the extent to which they simplify.

Secondly, although we talk happily enough about 'the French Revolution', or 'the English Civil War', obviously these descriptive phrases refer to extremely complex and diversified states of affairs. The 'French Revolution', for example, was at once the collapse of the monarchy and the collapse of the feudal economic system. The name 'French Revolution' is a convenient abbreviation for a complex of historical changes, any one of which can set for us a historical problem. Thus two history books, one of which emphasizes the importance, for any understanding of the French Revolution, of the separation between monarchy and people, and the other of which emphasizes the economic obstacles encountered by the rising bourgeoisie, need not really be in conflict with one another; each has as its subject a different aspect of the Revolution. Of course, if there were some single cause from which all the events of the French Revolution flowed, then certainly we should have to choose between the luxury of the court and the rise of the middle classes; we should have to say that one of these was the true cause and the other was not.

Professor Gallie has recently argued[16] . . . that the task of the historian is to draw attention to those *necessary* conditions which we might otherwise overlook, and that he quite misconceives the limits of his just ambitions if he tries to nominate *sufficient* conditions. This doctrine, for all its attractiveness, would be difficult to accept as it stands; for necessary conditions are endless − even necessary conditions we could easily overlook. It was a necessary condition of Gladstone's becoming Prime Minister that at the age of seven he took his mother's advice and changed his wet clothes; but scarcely a matter for the historian's consideration. What can, however, be said is that in the excitement of discovering a particular type of necessary condition, the historian is sometimes led into asserting that it is both necessary and sufficient − as happens also in a great many other cases, say in the germ theory of disease. Or again, a condition which is necessary and sufficient for the explanation of a certain phase, or a certain aspect, of a historical complex is wrongly supposed to be sufficient and necessary for other phases or other aspects, as if we could deduce from the economic origins of the French Revolution why the Goddess of Reason was worshipped. Once we recognize the complexity of historical changes, and the multitude of different problems they raise, we can hope to avoid the more gratuitous cases of this particular error.

One can understand, also, why each generation rewrites its history-books; a point sometimes urged in proof of history's incurable subjectivity. The explanation, often enough, is that men come to be interested in quite new aspects of past events; we look differently at the French Revolution now we have experienced the Russian Revolution, with a new interest in the way in which it passed into a dictatorship. In that sense, all history is contemporary history: our contemporary interests determine what we select for consideration from the past − as, for example, the working out of a propositional calculus, or of a modal logic, may cause us to examine from a new point of view the mediaeval doctrine of 'consequences'. But nothing of importance about the nature and status of historical inquiry follows from this fact.

What is our final conclusion about the 'placing' of history amongst forms of human activity? Well, one can see why there have been arguments about its relation both to literature and to science. If we mean by 'science' the attempt to find out what really happens, then history is a science. It demands the same kind of dedication, the same ruthlessness, the same passion for exactness, as physics. That is all I have been trying to show. If, however, we mean by science the search for general theories, then history is not science; indeed, in so far as it tries to show us something through a particularized pattern of action, it stands closer to the novel and the drama than it does to physics. It differs from literature, however, in two important respects: human society, not individual entanglements, provide it with its themes − and, more important for our present purposes, it is both sensible and necessary to ask whether its narrative 'really happened like that'. It is *history*, neither literature nor science, but sharing some of the properties of both. Its very existence, indeed, helps to bring home to us the connection and the distinction between these two forms of human endeavour.

Notes

1. Blake, Christopher (1955) 'Can history be objective?', *Mind*, January.

2. Taylor, A. J. P. (1956) *The Times Literary Supplement*, 6 January.
3. Hegel, G. W. F. (1852–98) *Lectures on the Philosophy of History*, Sibree, J. trans., London.
4. Toulmin, S. (1953) *The Philosophy of Science*, London, Hutchinson, pp. 44ff.
5. Lambert, Henry (1933) *The Nature of History*, London, Oxford University Press.
6. Popper, Karl R. (1945) *The Open Society and Its Enemies*, 2 vols, London, Routledge & Kegan Paul.
7. Hulme, E. M. (1942) *History and Its Neighbours*, London, Oxford University Press.
8. Langlois, C. V. and Seignobos, C. (1898) *Introduction to the Study of History*, Berry, G. G., trans., London. (Originally *Introduction aux études historiques*, Paris.)
9. Namier, L. B. (1952) *Avenues of History*, London, Hamish Hamilton.
10. Descartes, René (1639) *A Discourse on Method*, Veitch, John, trans., London, Dent/New York, Dutton, 1912, part 1.
11. Butterfield, Herbert (1931) *The Whig Interpretation of History*, London, G. Bell & Sons.
12. Op. cit.
13. Passmore, J. A. (1952) *Hume's Intentions*, Cambridge, Cambridge University Press. Of course, writing an interpretation is not the same thing as writing a history book. I do not wish at the moment to consider more precisely in what an interpretation consists. But the general point I am making, I trust, applies to history books and to interpretations alike.
14. Walsh, W. H. (1951) *An Introduction to Philosophy of History*, London, Hutchinson, p. 96.
15. Freud, Sigmund (1918) *Totem and Taboo*, Brill, A. A., trans., New York, Moffat, Yard.
16. Gallie, W. B. (1955) 'Explanations in history and the genetic sciences', *Mind*, April.

10 Values and inquiry

Like the discussion of 'objectivity' the subject of the
place of value judgements in inquiry has been much
debated. Do natural scientists separate their values
from their theories or their empirical observations?
In what sense if so? And if not, should they? And
what bearing do the differing answers to these questions have on social inquiry, the main focus in this
section? In so far as natural scientists can be shown to
separate their own values from their science, does
and can the same apply in the social sciences? Does
the different subject matter of social scientific
inquiry mean that it is harder, even impossible, to
keep the inquirer's values out of it? Or that when he
asserts his detachment and value-freedom this is no
more than a conscious or unconscious deceit?

There is general agreement that this set of
problems − or something like it − is a matter of
importance in social inquiry. Most social scientists
take up some position on it, implicit or explicit, not
infrequently building on certain assumptions about
the methods and criteria of the natural sciences.
There are few fully agreed answers, however, though
a certain grouping can be detected in the kinds of
approaches taken up; these are partly, though not
totally, linked with certain political alignments.

The extracts here represent three differing but in
some places overlapping views. First comes an extract
from Max Weber's influential writings on the
methodology of the social sciences in which he argues
that social scientists, *qua* social scientists, must confine themselves to empirically-based study: political and moral choices belong to the sphere of the

citizen, not the researcher in his role of professional
social scientist. This brings him ultimately within
the same frame of argument as the logical positivists
with their clear-cut logical distinction between fact
and value, and, together with the whole 'positivist'
tradition, his position has been much attacked by
recent writers, of which Gouldner's extract here is a
good example. Weber's argument however is a more
complex one than his opponents sometimes allow,
and includes awareness of the inevitable intrusion of
one's values into certain aspects of study, e.g. the
choice of topic, and of the moral and political responsibilities of the social scientist *qua* citizen.
Gouldner takes up the opposing view and, following
out an argument common to a number of Marxist
social scientists, urges that not only is it impossible to
keep values out of sociological inquiry, but that one
ought not to try to do so − value-free sociology is
both impossible and undesirable. Hesse accepts
certain assumptions in both the previous positions,
but arguing from the parallel with natural sciences
reaches yet a third view − that though there are
areas of social science inquiry where, as in the natural
sciences, values can and should be 'filtered out',
nevertheless the nature of theories in the social
sciences means that values there play a part parallel
to pragmatism in the natural sciences in supple-
menting the factual constraints which in themselves
cannot fully determine the choice of theories.

10.1 'OBJECTIVITY' IN SOCIAL SCIENCE

MAX WEBER (1864−1920), *from* The methodology of the
social sciences, Shils, E. A. and Finch, H. A., trans. and ed.,
New York, Free Press, 1949, extracts from pp. 52−9, abridged

The essay from which this extract is taken was written
by Max Weber when he took over the joint editorship
of the journal *Archiv für Sozialwissenschaft und
Sozialpolitik* and thus forms part of Weber's explanation about his (and the journal's) policy and aims. It
represents a statement of his views on a problem

which occupied him throughout his working life. Weber is clearly unprepared to exclude interest in values completely from social science, so he tries to elaborate a careful account of the sense in which they are relevant and allowable in social science inquiry. The point he is adamant on is his opposition to mixing up empirical knowledge and value judgements or presenting the latter under the guise of the former: and for a teacher it is 'an imperative requirement of intellectual honesty' to make 'relentlessly clear to his audience, and especially to himself, which of his statements are statements of logically deduced or empirically observed facts and which are statements of practical evaluations'.[1]

He was especially critical of teachers who used their professional position as a platform for their political views:

> Like everyone else, the professor has other facilities for the diffusion of his ideals. . . . But the professor should not demand the right as a professor to carry the marshal's baton of the statesman or reformer in his knapsack. This is just what he does when he uses the unassailability of the academic chair for the expression of political (or cultural—political) evaluations.[2]

Notes

1. op. cit., p. 2.
2. ibid., p. 5.

It can never be the task of an empirical science to provide binding norms and ideals from which directives for immediate practical activity can be derived.

What is the implication of this proposition? It is certainly not that value-judgments are to be withdrawn from scientific discussion in general simply because in the last analysis they rest on certain ideals and are therefore 'subjective' in origin. Practical action and the aims of our journal would always reject such a proposition. Criticism is not to be suspended in the presence of value-judgments. The problem is rather: what is the meaning and purpose of the scientific criticism of ideals and value-judgments? This requires a somewhat more detailed analysis.

All serious reflection about the ultimate elements of meaningful human conduct is oriented primarily in terms of the categories 'end' and 'means'. We desire something concretely either 'for its own sake' or as a means of achieving something else which is more highly desired. The question of the appropriateness of the means for achieving a given end is undoubtedly accessible to scientific analysis. Inasmuch as we are able to determine (within the present limits of our knowledge) which means for the achievement of a proposed end are appropriate or inappropriate, we can in this way estimate the chances of attaining a certain end by certain available means. In this way we can indirectly criticize the setting of the end itself as practically meaningful (on the basis of the existing historical situation) or as meaningless with reference to existing conditions. Furthermore, when the possibility of attaining a proposed end appears to exist, we can determine (naturally within the limits of our existing knowledge) the consequences which the application of the means to be used will produce in addition to the eventual attainment of the proposed end, as a result of the interdependence of all events. We can then provide the acting person with the ability to weigh and compare the undesirable as over against the desirable consequences of his action. Thus, we can answer the question: what will the attainment of a desired end 'cost' in terms of the predictable loss of other values! Since, in the vast majority of cases, every goal that is striven for does 'cost' or can 'cost' something in this sense, the weighing of the goal in terms of the incidental consequences of the action which realizes it cannot be omitted from the deliberation of persons who act with a sense of responsibility. One of the most important functions of the *technical criticism* which we have been discussing thus far is to make this sort of analysis possible. To apply the results of this analysis in the making of a decision, however, is not a task which science can undertake; it is rather the task of the acting, willing person: he weighs and chooses from among the values involved according to his own conscience and his personal view of the world. Science can make him realize that all action and naturally, according to the circumstances, inaction imply in their consequences the espousal of certain values — and herewith — what is today so willingly overlooked — the rejection of certain others. The act of choice itself is his own responsibility.

We can also offer the person, who makes a choice, insight into the significance of the desired object. We can teach him to think in terms of the context and the meaning of the ends he desires, and among which he chooses. We do this through making explicit and developing in a logically consistent manner the 'ideas' which actually do or which can underlie the concrete end. It is self-evident that one of the most important tasks of every science of cultural life is to arrive at a rational understanding of these 'ideas' for which men either really or allegedly struggle. This does not overstep the boundaries of a science which strives for an 'analytical ordering of empirical reality', although the methods which are used in this interpretation of cultural (*geistiger*) values are not 'inductions' in the usual sense. At any rate, this task falls at least partly beyond the limits of economics as defined according to the conventional division of labor. It belongs among the tasks of social philosophy. However, the historical influence of ideas in the development of social life has been and still is so great that our journal cannot renounce this task. It shall rather regard the investigation of this phenomenon as one of its most important obligations.

But the scientific treatment of value-judgments may not only understand and empathically analyze (*nacherleben*) the desired ends and the ideals which underlie them; it can also 'judge' them critically. This criticism can of course have only a dialectical character, i.e. it can be no more than a formal logical judgment of historically given value-judgments and ideas, a testing of the ideals according to the postulate of the internal *consistency* of the desired end. It can, insofar as it sets itself this goal, aid the acting, willing person in attaining self-clarification concerning the final axioms from which his desired ends are derived. It can assist him in becoming aware of the ultimate standards of value which he does not make explicit to himself, or which he must presuppose in order to be logical. The elevation of these ultimate standards, which are manifested in concrete value-judgments, to the level of explicitness is the utmost that the scientific treatment of value-judgments can do without entering into the realm of speculation. As to whether the person expressing these value-judgments *should* adhere to these ultimate standards is his personal affair; it involves will and conscience, not empirical knowledge.

An empirical science cannot tell anyone what he *should* do — but rather what he *can* do — and under certain circumstances — what he wishes to do. It is true that in our sciences, personal value-judgments have tended to influence scientific arguments without being explicitly admitted. They have brought about continual confusion and have caused various interpretations to be placed on scientific arguments even in the sphere of the determination of simple causal interconnections among facts according to whether the results increased or decreased the chances of realizing one's personal ideals, i.e. the possibility of desiring a certain thing. Even the editors and the collaborators of our journal will regard 'nothing human as alien' to them in this respect. But it is a long way from this acknowledgment of human frailty to the belief in an 'ethical' science of economics, which would derive ideals from its subject matter and produce concrete norms by applying general ethical imperatives. It is true that we regard as *objectively* valuable those innermost elements of the 'personality', those highest and most ultimate value-judgments which determine our conduct and give meaning and significance to our life. We can indeed espouse these values only when they appear to us as valid, as derived from our highest values and when they are developed in the struggle against the difficulties which life presents. Certainly, the dignity of the 'personality' lies in the fact that for it there exist values about which it organizes its life — even if these values are in certain cases concentrated exclusively within the sphere of the person's 'individuality', then 'self-realization' in *those* interests for which it claims *validity* as *values* is the idea with respect to which its whole existence is oriented. Only on the assumption of belief in the validity of values is the attempt to espouse value-judgments meaningful. However, to *judge* the *validity* of such values is a matter of *faith*. It may perhaps be a task for the speculative interpretation of life and the universe in quest of their meaning. But it certainly does not fall within the province of an empirical science in the sense in which it is to be practiced here. . . .

Nowhere are the interests of science more poorly served in the long run than in those situations where one refuses to see uncomfortable facts and the realities of life in all their starkness. The *Archiv* will struggle relentlessly against the severe self-deception which asserts that through the synthesis of several party points of view, or by following a line between them, practical norms of *scientific validity* can be arrived at. It is necessary to do this because, since this piece of self-deception tries to mask its own standards of value in relativistic terms, it is more dangerous to the freedom of research than the former naive faith of parties in the scientific 'demonstrability' of their dogmas. The capacity to distinguish between empirical knowledge and value-judgments, and the fulfillment of the scientific duty to see the factual truth as well as the practical duty to stand up for our own ideals constitute the program to which we wish to adhere with ever increasing firmness.

There is and always will be — and this is the reason that it concerns us — an unbridgeable distinction among (1) those arguments which appeal to our capacity to become enthusiastic about and our feeling for concrete practical aims or cultural forms and values, (2) those arguments in which, once it is a question of the validity of ethical norms, the appeal is directed to our conscience, and finally (3) those arguments which appeal to our capacity and need for *analytically ordering* empirical reality in a manner which lays claim to *validity* as empirical truth. This proposition remains correct, despite, as we shall see, the fact that those highest 'values' underlying the practical interest are and always will be decisively significant in determining the focus of attention of analytical activity (*ordnende Tätigkeit des Denkens*) in the sphere of the cultural sciences. It has been and remains true that a systematically correct scientific proof in the social sciences, if it is to achieve its purpose, must be acknowledged as correct even by a Chinese − or − more precisely stated − it must constantly *strive* to attain this goal, which perhaps may not be completely attainable due to faulty data. Furthermore, the successful *logical* analysis of the content of an ideal and its ultimate axioms and the discovery of the consequences which arise from pursuing it, logically and practically, must also be valid for the Chinese. At the same time, our Chinese can lack a 'sense' for our ethical imperative and he can and certainly often will deny the ideal itself and the concrete value-judgments derived from it. Neither of these two latter attitudes can affect the scientific value of the analysis in any way. . . .

There is one tenet to which we adhere most firmly in our work, namely, that a social science journal, in our sense, to the extent that it is *scientific* should be a place where those truths are sought, which − to remain with our illustration − can claim, even for a Chinese, the validity appropriate to an analysis of empirical reality.

10.2   ANTI-MINOTAUR: THE MYTH OF A VALUE-FREE SOCIOLOGY

ALVIN W. GOULDNER (1920−   ), '*Anti-minotaur: the myth of a value-free sociology*', *from* Social Problems *9(3), 1962; reprinted in Stein, M. and Vidich, A., eds*, Sociology on Trial, *Englewood Cliffs, N.J., Prentice-Hall, 1963, abridged*

This is a strong attack on Weber as the upholder of the ideal of a 'value-free' social science. Gouldner is sympathetic with some of Weber's points and also accepts the historical importance of the assertion of freedom from political and moral pressures in establishing sociology as an autonomous subject. But, he argues, sociologists have a responsibility not to retreat from involvement in social and political

questions, and a duty to speak out on the basis
of their professional knowledge. Furthermore an
apparent detachment in social scientific research can
in practice mask hidden values: by refraining from
critical analysis under the guise of 'neutrality' the
researcher is in fact committing himself to the
opposite political position, that of upholding the
status quo. In Gouldner's view the plea for 'value-
free' social science is often little more than a face-
saving device masking a 'tacit bargain' with the
authorities. Rather than going along with this
pretence of value-freedom, he argues, social scientists should declare (and teach) their values openly,
and not conceal their critical evaluations of the
present order. Social scientists have a particular
responsibility to use their professional insights to
combat 'moral indifference'. At root this is no
different from the physical scientists' duty to explore
their values and to take responsibility not only for
their students' technical competence but also for
their 'moral sense'.

This is an account of a myth created by and about a magnificent
minotaur named Max — Max Weber, to be exact; his myth was that
social science should and could be value-free. The lair of this minotaur,
although reached only by a labyrinthine logic and visited only by a few
who never return, is still regarded by many sociologists as a holy place.
In particular, as sociologists grow older they seem impelled to make a
pilgrimage to it and to pay their respects to the problem of the relations
between values and social science.

Considering the perils of the visit, their motives are somewhat
perplexing. Perhaps their quest is the first sign of professional senility;
perhaps it is the last sigh of youthful yearnings. And perhaps a concern
with the value problem is just a way of trying to take back something
that was, in youthful enthusiasm, given too hastily.

In any event, the myth of a value-free sociology has been a con-
quering one. Today, all the powers of sociology, from Parsons to
Lundberg, have entered into a tacit alliance to bind us to the dogma
that 'Thou shalt not commit a value judgment', especially as sociologists. Where is the introductory textbook, where the lecture course on
principles, that does not affirm or imply this rule?

In the end, of course, we cannot disprove the existence of minotaurs who, after all, are thought to be sacred precisely because, being half man and half bull, they are so unlikely. The thing to see is that a belief in them is not so much untrue as it is absurd. Like Berkeley's argument for solipsism, Weber's brief for a value-free sociology is a tight one and, some say, logically unassailable. Yet it is also absurd. For both arguments appeal to reason but ignore experience.

I do not here wish to enter into an examination of the *logical* arguments involved, not because I regard them as incontrovertible but because I find them less interesting to me as a sociologist. Instead what I will do is to view the belief in a value-free sociology in the same manner that sociologists examine any element in the ideology of any group. This means that we will look upon the sociologist just as we would any other occupation, be it the taxicab driver, the nurse, the coal miner or the physician. In short, I will look at the belief in a value-free sociology as part of the ideology of a working group and from the standpoint of the sociology of occupations.

The image of a value-free sociology is more than a neat intellectual theorem demanded as a sacrifice to reason; it is, also, a felt conception of a role and a set of (more or less) shared sentiments as to how sociologists should live. We may be sure that it became this not simply because it is true or logically elegant but, also, because it is somehow useful to those who believe in it. Applauding the dancer for her grace is often the audience's way of concealing its lust.

That we are in the presence of a group myth, rather than a carefully formulated and well-validated belief appropriate to scientists, may be discerned if we ask, just what is it that is believed by those holding sociology to be a value-free discipline? Does the belief in a value-free sociology mean that, in point of fact, sociology is a discipline actually free of values and that it successfully excludes all nonscientific assumptions in selecting, studying, and reporting on a problem? Or does it mean that sociology *should* do so? Clearly, the first is untrue and I know of no one who even holds it possible for sociologists to exclude completely their nonscientific beliefs from their scientific work; and if this is so, on what grounds can this impossible task be held to be morally incumbent on sociologists?

Does the belief in a value-free sociology mean that sociologists cannot, do not, or should not make value judgments concerning things outside their sphere of technical competence? But what has technical competence to do with the making of value judgments? If technical competence does provide a warrant for making value judgments then there is nothing to prohibit sociologists from making them within the area of their *expertise*. If, on the contrary, technical competence provides no warrant for making value judgments then, at least sociologists are as *free* to do so as anyone else; then their value judgments are at least as good as anyone else's, say, a twelve-year-old child's. And, by the way, if technical competence provides no warrant for making value judgments, then what does?

Does the belief in a value-free sociology mean that sociologists are or should be indifferent to the moral implications of their work? Does it mean that sociologists can and should make value judgments so long as they are careful to point out that these are different from 'merely' factual statements? Does it mean that sociologists cannot logically deduce values from facts? Does it mean that sociologists do not or should not have or express *feelings* for or against some of the things they study? Does it mean that sociologists may and should inform laymen about techniques useful in realizing their own ends, if they are asked to do so, but that if they are not asked to do so they are to say nothing? Does it mean that sociologists should never take the initiative in asserting that some beliefs that laymen hold, such as the belief in the inherent inferiority of certain races, are false even when known to be contradicted by the facts of their discipline? Does it mean that social scientists should never speak out, or speak out only when invited, about the probable outcomes of a public course of action concerning which they are professionally knowledgeable? Does it mean that social scientists should never express values in their roles as teachers or in their roles as researchers, or in both? Does the belief in a value-free sociology mean that sociologists, either as teachers or researchers, have a right to covertly and unwittingly express their values but have no right to do so overtly and deliberately?

I fear that there are many sociologists today who, in conceiving social science to be value-free, mean widely different things, that many hold these beliefs dogmatically without having examined seriously the grounds upon which they are credible, and that some few affirm a value-free sociology ritualistically without having any clear idea what it might mean. Weber's own views on the relation between values and social science, and some current today are scarcely identical. While Weber saw grave hazards in the sociologist's expression of value judgments, he also held that these might be voiced if caution was exercised to distinguish them from statements of fact. If Weber insisted on the need to maintain scientific objectivity, he also warned that this was altogether different from moral indifference.

Not only was the cautious expression of value judgments deemed permissible by Weber but, he emphasized, these were positively mandatory under certain circumstances. Although Weber inveighed against the professorial 'cult of personality', we might also remember that he was not against all value-imbued cults and that he himself worshipped at the shrine of individual responsibility. A familiarity with Weber's work on these points would only be embarrassing to many who today affirm a value-free sociology in his name. And should the disparity between Weber's own views and many now current come to be sensed, then the time is not far off when it will be asked, 'Who now reads Max Weber?'

What to Weber was an agonizing expression of a highly personal faith, intensely felt and painstakingly argued, has today become a hollow catechism, a password, and a good excuse for no longer thinking seriously. It has become increasingly the trivial token of professional respectability, the caste mark of the decorous; it has become the gentleman's promise that boats will not be rocked. Rather than showing Weber's work the respect that it deserves, by carefully re-evaluating it in the light of our own generation's experience, we reflexively reiterate it even as we distort it to our own purposes. Ignorance of the gods is no excuse but it can be convenient. For if the worshipper never visits the altar of his god, then he can never learn whether the fire still burns there or whether the priests, grown fat, are simply sifting the ashes.

The needs which the value-free conception of social science serves are both personal and institutional. Briefly, my contention will be that, among the main institutional forces facilitating the survival and spread of the value-free myth, was its usefulness in maintaining both the cohesion and the autonomy of the modern university, in general, and the newer social science disciplines, in particular. There is little difficulty, at any rate, in demonstrating that these were among the motives originally inducing Max Weber to formulate the conception of a value-free sociology. . . .

Without doubt the value-free principle did enhance the autonomy of sociology; it was one way in which our discipline pried itself loose − in some modest measure − from the clutch of its society, in Europe freer from political party influence, in the United States freer of ministerial influence. In both places, the value-free doctrine gave sociology a larger area of autonomy in which it could steadily pursue basic problems rather than journalistically react to passing events, and allowed it more freedom to pursue questions uninteresting either to the respectable or to the rebellious. It made sociology freer − as Comte had wanted it to be − to pursue all its own theoretical implications. In other words, the value-free principle did, I think, contribute to the intellectual growth and emancipation of our enterprise.

There was another kind of freedom which the value-free doctrine also allowed; it enhanced a freedom from moral compulsiveness; it permitted a partial escape from the parochial prescriptions of the sociologist's local or native culture. Above all, effective internalization of the value-free principle has always encouraged at least a temporary suspension of the moralizing reflexes built into the sociologist by his own society. From one perspective, this of course has its dangers — a disorienting normlessness and moral indifference. From another standpoint, however, the value-free principle might also have provided a *moral* as well as an intellectual *opportunity*. . . .

The value-free doctrine could have meant an opportunity for a more authentic morality. It could and sometimes did aid men in transcending the morality of their 'tribe', to open themselves to the diverse moralities of unfamiliar groups, and to see themselves and others from the standpoint of a wider range of significant cultures. But the value-free doctrine also had other, less fortunate, results as well.

Doubtless there were some who did use the opportunity thus presented; but there were, also, many who used the value-free postulate as an excuse for pursuing their private impulses to the neglect of their public responsibilities and who, far from becoming more morally sensitive, became morally jaded. Insofar as the value-free doctrine failed to realize its potentialities it did so because its deepest impulses were — as we shall note later — dualistic; it invited men to stress the separation and not the mutual connectedness of facts and values: it had the vice of its virtues. In short, the conception of a value-free sociology has had *diverse* consequences, not all of them useful or flattering to the social sciences.

On the negative side, it may be noted that the value-free doctrine is useful both to those who want to escape *from* the world and to those who want to escape *into* it. It is useful to those young, or not so young men, who live off sociology rather than for it, and who think of sociology as a way of getting ahead in the world by providing them with neutral techniques that may be sold on the open market to any buyer. The belief that it is not the business of a sociologist to make value judgments is taken, by some, to mean that the market on which they can vend their skills is unlimited. From such a standpoint, there is no reason why one cannot sell his knowledge to spread a disease just as freely as he can to fight it. Indeed, some sociologists have had no hesitation about doing market research designed to sell more cigarettes, although well aware of the implications of recent cancer research. In brief, the value-free doctrine of social science was sometimes used to justify the sale of one's talents to the highest bidder and is, far from new, a contemporary version of the most ancient sophistry.

In still other cases, the image of a value-free sociology is the armor of the alienated sociologist's self. Although C. Wright Mills may be right in saying this is the Age of Sociology, not a few sociologists, and Mills included, feel estranged and isolated from their society. They feel impotent to contribute usefully to the solution of its deepening problems and, even when they can, they fear that the terms of such an involvement require them to submit to a commercial debasement or a narrow partisanship, rather than contributing to a truly public interest. . . .

There is one way in which those who desert the world and those who sell out to it have something in common. Neither group can adopt an openly critical stance toward society. Those who sell out are accomplices; they may feel no critical impulses. Those who run out, while they do feel such impulses, are either lacking in any talent for aggression, or have often turned it inward into noisy but essentially safe university politics or into professional polemics. In adopting a conception of themselves as 'value-free' scientists, their critical impulses may no longer find a target in society. Since they no longer feel free to criticize society, which always requires a measure of courage, they now turn to the cannibalistic criticism of sociology itself and begin to eat themselves up with 'methodological' criticisms.

One latent meaning, then, of the image of a value-free sociology is this: 'Thou shalt not commit a critical or negative value judgment — especially of one's own society.' Like a neurotic symptom this aspect of the value-free image is rooted in a conflict; it grows out of an effort to compromise between conflicting drives: On the one side, it reflects a conflict between the desire to criticize social institutions, which since Socrates has been the legacy of intellectuals, and the fear of reprisals if one does criticize — which is also a very old and human concern. On the other side, this aspect of the value-free image reflects a conflict between the fear of being critical and the fear of being regarded as unmanly or lacking in integrity, if uncritical.

The doctrine of a value-free sociology resolves these conflicts by making it seem that those who refrain from social criticism are acting solely on behalf of a higher professional good rather than their private interests. In refraining from social criticism, both the timorous and the venal may now claim the protection of a high professional principle and, in so doing, can continue to hold themselves in decent regard. Persuade all that no one must bell the cat, then none of the mice need feel like a rat.

Should social scientists affirm or critically explore values they would of necessity come up against powerful institutions who deem the statement or protection of public values as part of their special business. Should social scientists seem to compete in this business, they can run afoul of powerful forces and can, realistically, anticipate efforts at external curbs and controls. In saying this, however, we have to be careful lest we needlessly exacerbate academic timorousness. Actually, my own firsthand impressions of many situations where sociologists serve as consultants indicate that, once their clients come to know them, they are often quite prepared to have sociologists suggest (not dictate) policy and to have them express their own values. Nor does this always derive from the expectation that sociologists will see things their way and share their values. Indeed, it is precisely the expected difference in perspectives that is occasionally desired in seeking consultation. I find it difficult not to sympathize with businessmen who jeer at sociologists when they suddenly become more devoted to business values than the businessmen themselves.

Clearly all this does not mean that people will tolerate disagreement on basic values with social scientists more equably than they will with anyone else. Surely there is no reason why the principles governing social interaction should be miraculously suspended just because one of the parties to a social relation is a social scientist. The dangers of public resentment are real but they are only normal. They are not inconsistent with the possibility that laymen may be perfectly ready to allow social scientists as much (or as little) freedom of value expression as they would anyone else. And what more could any social scientist want?

The value-free image of social science is not consciously held for expedience's sake; it is not contrived deliberately as a hedge against public displeasure. It could not function as a face-saving device if it were. What seems more likely is that it entails something in the nature of a tacit bargain: in return for a measure of autonomy and social support, many social scientists have surrendered their critical impulses. This was not usually a callous 'sell-out' but a slow process of mutual accommodation; both parties suddenly found themselves betrothed without a formal ceremony. . . .

The problem of a value-free sociology has its most poignant implications for the social scientist in his role as educator. If sociologists ought not express their personal values in the academic setting, how then are students to be safeguarded against the unwitting influence of these values which shape the sociologist's selection of problems, his preferences for certain hypotheses or conceptual schemes, and his neglect of others. For these are unavoidable and, in this sense, there is and can be no value-free sociology. The only choice is between an expression of one's values, as open and honest as it can be, this side of the psychoanalytical couch, and a vain ritual of moral neutrality which, because it invites men to ignore the vulnerability of reason to bias, leaves it at the mercy of irrationality.

If truth is the vital thing, as Weber is reputed to have said on his deathbed, then it must be all the truth we have to give, as best we know it, being painfully aware and making our students aware, that even as we offer it we may be engaged in unwitting concealment rather than revelation. If we would teach students how science is made, really made rather than as publicly reported, we cannot fail to expose them to the whole scientist by whom it is made, with all his gifts and blindnesses, with all his methods and his *values* as well. To do otherwise is to usher in an era of spiritless technicians who will be no less lacking in understanding than they are in passion, and who will be useful only because they can be used.

In the end, even these dull tools will through patient persistence and cumulation build a technology of social science strong enough to cripple us. Far as we are from a sociological atomic bomb, we already live in a world of the systematic brainwashing of prisoners of war and of housewives with their advertising-exacerbated compulsions; and the social science technology of tomorrow can hardly fail to be more powerful than today's.

It would seem that social science's affinity for modeling itself after physical science might lead to instruction in matters other than research alone. Before Hiroshima, physicists also talked of a value-free science; they, too, vowed to make no value judgments. Today many of them are not so sure. If we today concern ourselves exclusively with the technical proficiency of our students and reject all responsibility for their moral sense, or lack of it, then we may someday be compelled to accept responsibility for having trained a generation willing to serve in a future Auschwitz. Granted that science always has inherent in it both constructive and destructive potentialities. It does not follow from this that we should encourage our students to be oblivious to the difference. Nor does this in any degree detract from the indispensable norms of scientific objectivity; it merely insists that these differ radically from moral indifference.

I have suggested that, at its deepest roots, the myth of a value-free sociology was Weber's way of trying to adjudicate the tensions between two vital Western traditions: between reason and faith, between knowledge and feeling, between classicism and romanticism, between the head and the heart. Like Freud, Weber never really believed in an enduring peace or in a final resolution of this conflict. What he did was to seek a truce through the segregation of the contenders, by allowing each to dominate in different spheres of life. Although Weber's efforts at a personal synthesis brings him nearer to St Thomas, many of his would-be followers today tend to be nearer to the Latin Averroists with their doctrine of the twofold truth, with their conception of themselves as narrow technicians who reject responsibility for the cultural and moral consequences of their work. It is precisely because of the deeply dualistic implications of the current doctrine of a value-free sociology that I felt its most appropriate symbol to be the man-beast, the cleft creature, the Minotaur.

10.3   THEORY AND VALUE IN THE SOCIAL SCIENCES

MARY HESSE (1924–   ), from 'Theory and value in the social sciences', Hookway, C. and Pettit, P., eds, Action and Interpretation: Studies in the Philosophy of Social Interpretation, Cambridge, Cambridge University Press, 1978, pp. 1–16

Mary Hesse argues for one widely accepted view of science – that theories are, indeed, constrained by the facts, but they are not fully *determined* by them.[1] In the natural sciences, the additional criteria for the acceptance of a theory includes the *pragmatic* one, the test of how far a theory can lead to successful prediction and control. This however cannot easily be applied in some social science theories. In certain respects, therefore, the pragmatic criterion is in the social sciences replaced by value judgements as a means of selecting theories for attention. In this sense, she concludes, 'the proposal of a social theory is more like the arguing of a political case than like a natural science explanation'.

Note that Hesse is making a rather less sweeping case for the role of values than Gouldner. She is not arguing that *all* social science theories necessarily depend on value judgements (some *are* susceptible to the pragmatic criterion, she suggests, and in these value judgements can gradually be filtered out); nor does she wish to elevate the adoption of certain values as a binding part of the inquirer's political commitment. Rather she indicates that the search and respect for facts is a necessary condition for the acceptability of any scientific theory, but that since facts in themselves are not enough to decide between theories (nor, for some social science theories, are pragmatic criteria), value judgements in fact play some part in this selection, whether we realize this consciously or not. She urges the importance of becoming more aware of the value choices under-lying social science theories − values not just of the revolutionary left (on which attention is most often focused) but also those of the moderate centre and right.

Note

1. A view which rejects certain assumptions in Popper's account in favour of the kind of analysis put forward in Lakatos (see reading 4.5).

Many reasons have been given for supposing that the social sciences require different kinds of method and justification from the natural sciences, and conversely for supposing that these methods and justifi-cations are or ought to be the same. I don't want to rehearse all these arguments here, but rather to concentrate on two features of the *natural* sciences which already suggest that the conventional arguments about similarities and differences are inadequate. These features can be roughly summed up in the by now fairly uncontroversial proposition that all scientific theories are *underdetermined* by facts, and the much more problematic propositions that, this being the case, there are further criteria for scientific theories that have to be rationally dis-cussed, and that these may include considerations of value.

Whether the natural and the social sciences are seen as similar or different depends of course on the view we take of the natural sciences. The view I am going to presuppose, but not argue here, is that made familiar in recent post-deductivist discussions, with the addition of a crucial pragmatic dimension.[1] Let me summarise as follows:

(1) Theories are logically constrained by facts, but are underdeter-mined by them: i.e. while, to be acceptable, theories should be more or less plausibly coherent with facts, they can be neither con-clusively refuted nor uniquely derived from statements of fact alone, and hence no theory in a given domain is uniquely acceptable.

(2) Theories are subject to revolutionary change, and this involves even the language presupposed in 'statements of fact', which are irreducibly theory-laden: i.e. they presuppose concepts whose meaning is at least partly given by the context of theory.

(3) There are further determining criteria for theories which attain the status of rational postulates or conventions or heuristic devices at different historical periods − these include general metaphysical and material assumptions, e.g. about substance and causality, atoms or mechanisms, and formal judgments of simplicity, probability, analogy, etc.

(4) In the history of natural science, these further criteria have sometimes included what are appropriately called value judgments, but these have tended to be filtered out as theories developed.

(5) The 'filtering-out' mechanism has been powered by universal adoption of one overriding value for natural science, namely the criterion of increasingly successful prediction and control of the environment. In what follows I shall call this the *pragmatic criterion*.

Points 4 and 5 need further explanation.

Value judgments related to science may be broadly of two kinds. They may be evaluations of the *uses* to which scientific results are put, such as the value of cancer research, or the disvalue of the nuclear bomb. But they may also be evaluations that enter more intimately into theory-construction as *assertions* that it is desirable that the universe be of such and such a kind *and* that it is or is not broadly as it is desired to be. Examples of positive evaluations of what is the case are: belief in the perfection of spherical symmetry, and consequent belief that the heavens are spherically symmetrical; belief that men ought to be and therefore are at the physical centre of the universe, and that they are biologically superior and unique among organisms; belief that mind is devalued by regarding it as a natural mechanism, and therefore that mind is in fact irreducible to matter. An example of negative evaluation of what is the case is the Marxist belief that in this pre-revolutionary stage of the class struggle various elements of social life that look like valuable supports of social stability are to be unmasked as in fact being obstacles to the desirable revolution. In the light of such a belief, for example, the immiseration of the proletariat becomes a positive value, and tends to become the essential category in terms of which complex social facts are described.

It is the second type of evaluation in science that I shall be concerned with. All examples of this type issue in assertions rather than imperatives, and hence involve a transition from *ought* judgments to *is* judgments. Are they not therefore immediately condemned as illicit in any form of scientific argument? In reply to this objection two points can be made. First, there is no doubt that there are historical examples in which the genetic fallacy was not seen as a fallacy, so that in describing the thought processes involved in such examples the historian at least has to recognise forms of quasi-inference such as those just sketched. But the second and more important consideration depends on point 3 above, namely that since there is never *demonstrative* reasoning from evidence to theory, further determining criteria may well include factual judgments about the way the world is, and these are sometimes based persuasively on judgments of how it ought to be. There is no fallacy of logical inference, for logical inference is not appropriate here; there is rather the choice of some hypotheses for consideration among many other possible ones, in the hope that the world will be found to be good as the accepted value system describes the good.

In the case of the natural sciences, however, it may well be objected that the evaluative and teleological beliefs of past science either have been refuted, or have been eliminated by economy and simplicity criteria applied to theories. It would be a mistake to suppose that they could have been refuted by facts alone, because even if we do not accept the strong theory-ladenness thesis of point 2, it would generally be agreed that facts are susceptible of a multiplicity of theoretical interpretations, and that if such value judgments were regarded as of overriding importance (overriding, that is, all except logic), the facts could have been accommodated, though perhaps at a cost to economy. But the requirement of theoretical economy or simplicity is not an adequate general answer either, for at least two reasons. First, what have been held to be prima facie simple theories have often been abandoned for more complex ones. Examples are: field theories in place of action at a distance, atomic theories in place of phenomenal volume and weight relations in chemical reactions, and Copernicus's heliocentric universe, which in his theory required more parameters than the geocentric universe it replaced. In most such cases, what was of overriding importance was not facts plus prima facie simplicity, but facts plus interpretation in terms of some intelligible or desirable world-model. Secondly, no one has yet succeeded in presenting definitions of simplicity that are adequate for all the occasions on which appeal had been made to it. But it is at least clear that there is not one concept of simplicity but many, and the suspicion grows that simplicity is not in itself a final court of appeal but rather adapts itself to definition in terms of whatever other criteria of theory choice are taken to be overriding.

The most important of these other criteria in natural science is what I have called the *pragmatic criterion* of predictive success. In considering historical examples the question to be asked in philosophy of science is not so much what were the special local (social, biographical, psychological, etc.) factors at work in the immediate and short-term decisions of individuals, but rather whether there is any *general* criterion for the long-term acceptability of one theory rather than another, and for the replacement of old theories by new. This is to ask a question which presupposes that because all formal criteria such as verification, confirmation, and falsifiability seem to have broken down as criteria for theory choice in particular short-term scientific situations, therefore there are no general criteria of theory choice over the long term. But revolutionary accounts have not disposed of the objection that natural science, as well as being revolutionary in respect of *theories*, is also in some sense cumulative and progressive, and retains contact with the empirical world by means of long-term testing of theory complexes taken as wholes. If we press the question 'What is it that progresses?', the only possible long-term answer is the ability to use science to learn the environment, and to make predictions whose results we can rely on not to surprise us. It is this modification of the traditional empirical criteria of confirmation and falsifiability that I intend by the 'pragmatic criterion'.[2]

As successful prediction accumulates, the pragmatic criterion filters out both simplicity criteria and other value judgments. We can observe by hindsight that in the early stages of a science, value judgments (such as the centrality of man in the universe) provide some of the reasons for choice among competing underdetermined theories. As systematic theory and pragmatic success accumulate, however, such judgments may be overridden, and their proponents retire defeated from the scientific debate. Thus, the theological and metaphysical arguments against Copernicus, against Newton, and against Darwin became progressively more irrelevant to science. This is not to say, of course, that *our own* preferences in choices between underdetermined theories are not themselves influenced by our value judgments and by beliefs which we take for granted, or that these will not be visible to the hindsight of future historians of science.[3] This is very likely to be so, but it does not conflict with the notion of accumulation of pragmatic success in science past, present and future. There is also a sense in which value judgment enters into the very adoption of the pragmatic criterion itself — the judgment that the requirement of predictive success should override all other possible criteria of theory choice. This is the one value judgment that, of course, is *not* filtered out, but rather is presupposed in the pragmatic criterion. It is a judgment that has perhaps rarely been consciously adopted by any scientific society of the past, but it is one which, it is becoming increasingly apparent, may be consciously rejected in the future.

It is not my purpose here to discuss in detail the relation between what I have called the pragmatic criterion and more orthodox theories of objectivity and truth. But something more must be said to avoid misunderstanding. First, there is a difficulty about the notion of 'successful prediction'. If we were able to ignore the much-discussed difficulties referred to in point 2, and assume that there is a theory-neutral observation language for which there are clearly applicable truth criteria, we might be tempted to define 'increasingly successful prediction' in terms of an accumulating set of true observation statements deducible from the corpus of scientific theories. We cannot ignore these difficulties, however, or the consequent tendency to understand 'truth' not in a correspondence sense but as coherence within a given theory, and hence as theory-relative. Since theories of truth are themselves in considerable disarray, it is better to find some way of understanding 'successful prediction' independently of them. Here I suggest a pragmatic or ostensive appeal to the actual state of natural science since the seventeenth century, in which we can recognise an accumulation of successful prediction which overrides changing theories and is *independent* of particular conceptual schemes in which scientific successes are described in conflicting theories. The space-ship still goes, whether described in a basically Newtonian or relativistic framework. Pragmatic knowledge can be obtained without an absolutely theory-neutral descriptive language.

It may be illuminating to draw an analogy (only an analogy) between the method of natural science and the program of a computer designed to process environmental data and to learn to make successful predictions (for example, a character-recognition device). The criteria of success of such a device can be made independent of the actual 'language' system used in the computer to store and process data and to give the orders for testing theories on more data. Equal success in two or more computers is consistent with their having widely different internal language systems, although of course some language systems may be more convenient than others for given kinds of data, and indeed there may be feedback mechanisms in the program which permit change of language to a more convenient one when this is indicated by the success and failure rate.

A second possible misunderstanding of the pragmatic criterion arises from the fact that technological applications are the most striking examples of accumulating successful prediction. Philosophers of science should perhaps disengage themselves from the Popper-induced prejudice that pragmatic application has nothing to do with the logic of science. On the other hand, successful prediction does not necessarily issue in technical control. Many theories enlarge our pragmatic knowledge (for example, about fossils or quasars), without necessarily forming the basis of technology.

A third difficulty is that the relation between the pragmatic criterion and any theory of truth is obscure and needs much more examination than can be given to it here. But in the particular case of some kind of correspondence theory, to which philosophers of truth seem now to be increasingly drawn, there does not seem to be any prima facie conflict between such a theory and the pragmatic criterion. Current corres-pondence theories of truth tend to be expressed in terms of some rela-tion of 'satisfaction' which holds between the world and true statements, and are in themselves independent of the question how such satisfaction is identified in particular instances. There are notorious difficulties about such identifications − the same difficulties that underlie the notions of underdetermined theories and criticisms of the basic observation language. The pragmatic criterion trades these difficulties for others by bypassing the question of the reference of theoretical language, and resting on the non-linguistic concept of successful prediction.

In considering whether natural science as defined by points 1 to 5 is an adequate model for the social sciences, we can add two further points:

(6) There are not at present, and perhaps can never reasonably be expected to be, general theories in the social sciences that satisfy the pragmatic criterion of point 5 − namely, theories that provide increasingly successful prediction and control in the social domain.

(7) Moreover, since adoption of the pragmatic criterion itself implies a value judgment, it is possible to decide *against* it as an overriding goal for social science, and to adopt other value goals.

Point 7 does not presuppose the truth of point 6. I doubt if point 6 can be proved in any general way. On the actual present situation one can only observe what underlies complaints about the backwardness, theoretical triviality, and empirical rule-of-thumb character of most social science, in spite of limited success in establishing low-level laws in isolated areas. On the logical possibility, there have been attempts at general proof of the non-natural character of social science, attempts which derive from features of the social subject-matter such as complexity, instability, indeterminacy, irreducible experimental interference with data, self-reference of social theorising as part of its own subject-matter, etc. I do not believe such proofs can ever be conclusive, if only for the reason that most of these features are also found somewhere in the natural sciences. If we use as an analogy for the method of natural science the computer which learns to predict its environment, an immediate consequence is that there will be some environments and some types of data which do not permit learning by any computer of limited capacity, for any or all of the reasons just listed. The social environment *may*, wholly or partly, be such an environment. I doubt if anything stronger can be said, and I doubt whether any attempt to formalise the situation further at this general abstract level is worthwhile. Satisfaction of the pragmatic criterion by particular social-science theories needs to be argued case by case.

Point 7, however, remains. It is explicitly recognised in Marxist writings on the social sciences, and also in the older *Verstehen* tradition and in its more recent offshoot, hermeneutics (although the latter two traditions neglect the dimension of 'interest' that inevitably infects social theory according to Marxism). The rest of this paper will be devoted to exploring the consequences of point 7.

It is important to notice that point 7, together with points 1 to 5, imply a distinction between two sorts of 'value-ladenness' in social science. The first is analogous to theory-ladenness in natural science, and is the sense primarily in mind when empiricist philosphers have attempted to disentangle and exclude value judgments from scientific social theory. It is the sort of value judgment that I have mentioned in point 4, which becomes associated with theoretical interpretations by virtue either of the selective interest of the investigator (e.g. in preferring to investigate stable systems as norms), or of adoption of those hypotheses which assert the world actually to be in some respects as it is desired to be (e.g. acquired characteristics either are or are not inherited according to preferred ideology). I have suggested that the crucial point about the natural sciences is that though such judgments may function heuristically in hypotheses, operation of the pragmatic criterion frequently filters them out, and how the world 'ought to be' frequently fails in face of how the world is, or rather in face of the only plausible and coherent ways that can be found of interpreting facts and successful predictions. Where the pragmatic criterion works in social science we shall expect some value judgments to be filtered out in a similar way — for example, it seems not impossible that currently controversial questions about the relationship, if any, between intelligence quotient and racial origin might be sufficiently defined to be made rigorously testable, and laws might be derived which satisfy the criterion of successful prediction. (Whether it would be *desirable* to adopt and try to rigorously apply the pragmatic criterion here is entirely another question.)

But where the pragmatic criterion cannot be made to work in a convergent manner it is not possible to filter out value judgments in this way. A second type of value judgment may then be involved, which in varying degrees *takes the place of the pragmatic criterion* in selecting theories for attention. These judgments will be *value goals* for science that are alternatives to the pragmatic goal of predictive success. Such alternative goals have often been recognised in the literature, for example by Weber in his category of value-relevance, and by Myrdal in arguing for explicit adoption of a value standpoint, preferably one that corresponds to an actual power group in society.[4] But alternative value goals have usually been recognised in the negative sense of the 'unmasking' of so-called non-objective biases, rather than in the positive sense of being consciously adopted goals other than the pragmatic criterion. It is difficult to make such standpoints conscious and explicit while they are operative, but the literature is now full of studies in the critical sociology of sociology, where the standpoints of the past, and of other contemporary groups of sociologists, are 'unmasked'. It is a well-known Marxist ploy to uncover the non-intellectual interests even of self-styled positivists: those who argue most strongly for a value-free and objective social science are shown to be those whose social and economic interest is in the status quo, and in not having the boat rocked by encouragement to explicit criticism and value controversy. And such studies are not found only in Marxist writers. Robin Horton, for example, has given an interesting analysis of the styles in social anthropology during this century in terms of the changing attitudes of the West, in its imperialist and liberal phases, towards its former colonies as they become politically independent and aspire to cultural autonomy.[5]

Weber carefully distinguished value-relevance from the value-freedom of the social scientist with respect to political action. That is to say, he accepted that judgments of interest select the subject matter of the human sciences, but denied that the social scientist as such should use his theories to argue any particular political practice. Even with respect to value-relevance, he argued that theories must ultimately be shown to be causally adequate. Thus Weber's own value-interest in studying, for example, the interrelations of capitalism and the Protestant ethic was doubtless to refute Marx's contention that the ideological superstructure is unilaterally determined by the economic substructure. But Weber insists that his theory of such relationships must be shown to be a factual theory of cause and effect, confirmable by positive instances and refutable by negative. Without going into the detail of Weber's discussions of methodology, it can I think be fairly concluded that he sees the goal of knowledge and truth-assertion as essentially the same in the natural and social sciences, but that he has an over-simple view of the nature of causal laws in the natural sciences, which misleads him into extrapolating an almost naive Millean method into the social sciences. He does not doubt that judgments of value-relevance are separable from positive science, and can in this sense be 'filtered out' of cognitive conclusions. Thus he has not yet made the 'epistemological break' involved in recognising, questioning, and perhaps replacing the pragmatic criterion for social sciences, nor has he distinguished two sorts of judgments of value-relevance — those which can ultimately be eliminated by the pragmatic criterion and those which cannot because they depend on a view of causality that presupposes it.

There are others who have not understood the nature of this epistemological break. In a commentary on Myrdal's requirement of total explicitness of value standpoint and identification with some actual power-group, John Rex[6] finds an implied suggestion that objectivity inheres in the balance of power between such groups, and that this balance of power 'can be relatively objectively determined', as if what is determined by the standpoint of the most powerful group. However, while it may be true that the most powerful group can to a greater or lesser extent impose its will upon the development of the social system, it does not at all follow that the theory informed by its value standpoint gives the true dynamical laws of that system on a pragmatic criterion, or the best theory on any other criterion except that truth resides in the barrel of a gun. Whether the unions or the sheikhs eventually gain control in Britain is irrelevant to the theoretical acceptability of either of their implied economic doctrines. And Christ and Socrates may have the best theories after all.

Myrdal himself is more careful, but he too leaves largely unexamined the exact relation between objectivity as sought in the natural sciences and the value criteria which are inevitably adopted in social science. Of science in general he writes:

Our steadily increasing stock of observations and inferences is not merely subjected to continuous cross-checking and critical discussion but is deliberately scrutinized to discover and correct hidden preconceptions and biases. Full objectivity, however, is an ideal toward which we are constantly striving, but which we can never reach. The social scientist, too, is part of the culture in which he lives, and he never succeeds in freeing himself entirely from dependence on the dominant preconceptions and biases of his environment.[7]

If 'objectivity' in this sense is the ideal which is unattainable, then valuations are a necessary evil. Seen in such negative light, it is unlikely that the choice between valuations will be subjected to logical or philosophical scrutiny, and the vacuum is likely to be filled by power criteria or worse, in the manner of Rex. But if it is true that the ideal objectivity is unattainable and that valuations are necessary, the philosopher will surely be better advised to present this necessity in a positive light, and to critically examine the value choices that are then open. In points 4 to 7 I have attempted to articulate such a positive view by distinguishing value-laden theories, subject to the pragmatic criterion, from the value goals adopted for the total scientific enterprise.

Mannheim is another exponent of the sociology of sociology who has been misled by neglect of his distinction. As is well known, he adopts a relationism of total ideology according to which all knowledge (except logic, mathematics and natural science) is knowledge only in relation to some observer standpoint.[8] In our terms, this may be interpreted as a recognition of the value-ladenness of the social sciences, and the suggestion that some observer standpoint determines the criterion of evaluation. He then asks: Which standpoint is optimum for establishing truth? and goes on to reject the two classical Marxist answers − the proletariat, and the class-self-conscious Party subsection of the proletariat − and to put forward the intelligentsia, who, he claims, are powerless and interest-free, and understand the sociology of knowledge. Whatever be the merits of this particular choice, it is clear that Mannheim has now retreated from his fleeting glimpse of irreducible commitment to value goals and is asking for an ideal standpoint from which truth is seen in the same sense of truth as that appropriate to natural science. Apart from the falsity of the claim that the intelligentsia are disinterested, this leads Mannheim into the logical circle of sociology of knowledge that has often been discussed, namely: In relation to what observer standpoint is it *true* that the intelligentsia are disinterested? Whatever the answer, truth as thus defined is clearly still relational and not objective in the sense of the pragmatic or whatever other criterion is adopted for the natural sciences.

Of all writers on the sociology of knowledge, Alvin Gouldner perhaps comes closest to embracing point 7 explicitly. After a careful and devastating analysis of the sociological origins and determinants of American functional sociology, and a more brief analysis of Soviet sociology, he comes in his Epilogue ('The theorist pulls himself together, partially') to the crucial question: What then are the sociological origins and determinants of Gouldner's unmasking exercise in respect of the American sociologists? He goes on explicitly to reject the approach of those methodologists 'who stress the interaction of theory and research . . . the role of rational and cognitive forces',[9] that is, the orthodox philosophers of science who reject value commitments. Rather, the sociologist must be *reflexive* − self-aware of his own place in his own standpoint − and must accept his involvement in it in a manner that requires a new *praxis* − a new lifestyle in which there is no ultimate division of himself as sociologist from himself as man. But more significant than this note of introspective moralising is Gouldner's description of the sociologist's task in the following terms:

> Commonly, the social theorist is trying to reduce the tension between a social event or process that he takes to be real and some value which this has violated. Much of theory-work is initiated by a dissonance between an imputed reality and certain values, or by the indeterminate value of an imputed reality. Theory-making, then, is often an effort to cope with threat; it is an effort to cope with a threat to something in which the theorist himself is deeply and personally implicated and which he holds dear.[10]

Thus, 'the French Revolution, the rise of Socialism, the Great Depression of 1929, or a new world of advertising and salesmanship' are facts-as-personally-experienced, requiring not so much explanation in the sense of the natural sciences (which perhaps we can never have), as redescription (interpretation, understanding) in terms which make them cohere with a chosen order of values. One might compare with Weber's desire to rescue human ideals from dominance by substructures, whether economic or bureaucratic; Durkheim's sense of the need for social cohesion and stability in face of man's inordinate and irrational desires; the note of protest inseparably bound into Marx's 'scientific' concept of exploitation of man's labour power; and Gouldner's own quite unconcealed negative evaluation of the sociologies of Goffman and Garfinkel, whose origins he 'unmasks' and whose adequacy he judges not on grounds of a spurious 'objectivity' but on grounds of his own sense of the moral degradation of their pictures of the social world ('anything goes', 'espionage agents', 'demonic', 'camp', 'kicks', 'the cry of pain . . . is Garfinkel's triumphal moment', 'sadism').[11] In the light of Gouldner's rather clear-sighted adoption of criteria other than the pragmatic, we may accept the challenge implicit in his statement early in the book that 'whether social theories *unavoidably* require and must rest *logically* on some background concepts [valuations] is a question that simply does not concern me here . . . this is a problem for philosophers of science'.[12] Though he appears here to remain agnostic, if his own analysis is acceptable it provides strong grounds for the methodological adoption of point 7, that is for the recognition that where the pragmatic criterion is inoperative, other value goals for social science should be self-consciously adopted.[13]

By way of conclusion let me rebut some possible empiricist misunderstandings, draw a consequence for the sociology of knowledge, and suggest an analogy for the choice of value goals.

It may be objected that, in emphasising the need to make explicit choice of value goals for science as well as theoretical value assumptions, I have neglected the role that the pragmatic criterion (or indeed any realist criterion of truth that might be proposed) actually plays in the social sciences. To this objection I would reply that nothing I have said about the inapplicability of the pragmatic criterion or about the choice of value goals is intended to exclude the possibility that there are areas in the social sciences where the methods and criteria of the natural sciences are both workable and desirable. There are general laws of human behaviour (though I suspect only low-level laws rather closely circumscribed in domain), there are models and ideal types whose consequences can be explored deductively and tested, and there are limited predictions which are sometimes successful. Where these things are the case, we may speak of 'objectivity' in the social realm in whatever sense we wish to speak of it in the natural realm, and we *may* (not *must*) make the same choice of value goals for the social as for the natural sciences. What I am arguing is that it would be wilfully blind and neglectful of the responsibility of social science as a cognitive discipline to ignore the fact that much social science which is currently acceptable is not and probably never can be of this kind. I have been primarily concerned with the consequence that non-pragmatic value choices have to be made. There will of course be difficulties in demarcating one type of value choice from others, both where there are doubts about how far the pragmatic criterion can be taken and also about how far it should be taken, as in recent disputes, for example, about the racial inheritance of characteristics, or about whether Garfinkel should collect data that involve severe mental disorientation of people in their ordinary social relationships. No general rules can be given about such disputes, because they are themselves essentially value disputes about the goals of particular social researches. But all of this does not entail that there are no facts or laws in the social sciences, nor that where there are such, social theory should not be consistent with them. As in the natural sciences, social theories are *constrained* but not *determined* by facts. Whether we wish to extend the use of the concept of 'objectivity' beyond the domain of such facts to the recognition of value choice, as Myrdal does,[14] is partly a verbal matter.

A more fundamental empiricist objection, however, is the following.[15] It may be suggested, first, that there is great difficulty in actually articulating viable goals for social science which are alternatives to the pragmatic criterion, and second, that where such goals are apparently identified and described, their operation always in fact involves the pragmatic criterion. Traditionally various versions of the *Verstehen* thesis have been appealed to to provide alternative goals, but it seems that in any attempt to *understand* a person's behaviour, one is seeking to fulfil one's expectations about his future behaviour. Indeed, all human interaction depends on the success of some such predictions about mutual responsiveness, and this seems not unlike an application of the pragmatic criterion. This is surely correct, and it is not surprising to find successful fulfilment of expectations as a criterion in all reasoning about the world, including all lowest-level inductive generalisations, whether about objects or persons. But this argument must not be made to prove too much. It certainly does not show that the pragmatic criterion as described in point 5 is sufficient to determine uniquely the theoretical interpretation of people's behaviour, for in this context we lack the wide-ranging and systematic generality characteristic of natural science, and consequently we lack what I have called the filtering-out mechanism that eventually eliminates value judgments as criteria of theory choice.

Secondly, a remark about consequences for the programme of the sociology of knowledge. Whether or not we wish to use epistemologically loaded terms like 'cognition', 'knowledge', 'objectivity', and 'truth' for acceptable theories in social science, a consequence of my arguments is that criteria of acceptability are *pluralist* — as pluralist as our choices of value goals. And if we wish to talk of *choice* of values it also follows that we presuppose a certain area of freedom in the activity of theorising — we are not wholly constrained to adopt particular theories either by the facts, or by adoption of particular value goals, or by social and economic environment. Thus it would be inconsistent with the present thesis to hold a form of the sociology of knowledge according to which socio-economic substructure determines all forms of knowledge, including presumably adoption or non-adoption of the sociology of knowledge itself. As has often been pointed out, such a determinist view, while not actually self-contradictory, is somewhat self-defeating.[16]

But a weaker form of sociology of knowledge has been implicit in my presentation of the value basis of social science, because one of the grounds for holding that value choices are inseparable from social theories is precisely that other people's theories, and sometimes one's own, can be shown to be partially determined by social environment and interests. And yet if this 'can be shown' is taken in the sense of objective empirical knowledge, we are on the horns of the same dilemma: *either* here at least (and in the least likely place) we have got to accept a kind of sociology that is objectively empirical and interest-free, *or* it 'can be shown' only on the basis of yet another, and probably interest-influenced, value choice. The first horn of the dilemma is lethal, but the second is graspable just in virtue of the pluralist conception of value choice that has been generally adopted here. The question now becomes: Given that we are not *compelled* to adopt it, does the weaker sociology-of-knowledge thesis nevertheless commend itself to our value system as desirable — illuminative of dark areas in social interaction, and conducive to understanding of others and of ourselves? The question can only be answered by consideration of particular examples, and in terms of one's personal reaction to them. I would answer for myself that many examples in the work of Marx, Mannheim, Myrdal, Gouldner, and some current 'critical sociology'[17] do seem to be thus illuminating.

Finally, a convenient analogy. I suggest that the proposal of a social theory is more like the arguing of a political case than like a natural-science explanation. It should seek for and respect the facts when these are to be had, but it cannot await a possibly unattainable total explanation. It must appeal explicitly to value judgments and may properly use persuasive rhetoric. No doubt it should differ from most political argument in seeking and accounting for facts more conscientiously, and in constraining its rhetoric this side of gross special pleading and rabble-rousing propaganda. Here the inheritance of virtues from the natural sciences comes to the social scientist's aid, and I hope nothing I have said will be taken to undermine these virtues. The fact that the view of the social sciences presented here is more often associated with the particular choice of value goals of the revolutionary left[18] does not in the least invalidate the general argument, nor reduce — rather, it increases — the need for the moderate centre and right to look to its own value choices. Neither liberal denial that there are such value choices nor cynical right-wing suppression of them from consciousness will meet the case.

Hume attempted to divorce the question of truth from that of value, while certain scientific humanists have attempted to derive value from truth. A consequence of my argument on the other hand has been that, at least in the sciences of man, a sense of 'truth' that is not merely pragmatic may be derivable from prior commitment to values and goals.[19]

Notes

1. I have discussed these matters in Hesse, Mary (1974) *The Structure of Scientific Inference*, London, chs 1, 2, and 12; and (1976) 'Truth and the growth of scientific knowledge', in *PSA*, Suppe, F. and Asquith, P. D., eds, East Lansing, Michigan, Philosophy of Science Association. Since the notion of 'underdetermination' has been exploited particularly by Quine, I should say that I do not accept his distinction between 'normal scientific induction' and 'ontological indeterminism', according to which it seems to be implied that purely scientific theories can eventually be determined uniquely by inductive methods. Some of my reasons for this rejection will emerge below.

2. It was Duhem's holist account of theory-testing, in Duhem, P. M. M. (1954) *The Aim and Structure of Physical Theory*, Princeton, N.J., Princeton University Press (first published 1906 as *La théorie physique*, Paris), which foreshadowed the demise of later and narrower criteria of empirical test. The work of I. Lakatos has more recently familiarised philosophers of science with the problem of theoretical acceptability in long-term historical perspective, although his criteria for 'progressive research programmes' do not include the predictive aspects of the pragmatic criterion adopted here. See particularly Lakatos, Imre (1970) 'Falsification and the methodology of scientific research programmes', in Lakatos, I. and Musgrave, A., eds, *Criticism and the Growth of Knowledge*, Cambridge, Cambridge University Press.

3. Recent studies in the history and sociology of natural science indicate that there has been far more influence upon theories from evaluations and non-scientific standpoints than has generally been realised. See for example Forman, P. (1971) 'Weimar culture, causality, and quantum theory, 1918–1927: adaptation by German physicists and mathematicians to a hostile intellectual environment', in McCormmach, R., ed., *Historical Studies in the Physical Sciences*, vol. 3, Philadelphia; papers in Teich, M. and Young, R. M., eds (1973) *Changing Perspectives in the History of Science*, London, Heinemann; and many references in Barnes, Barry (1974) *Scientific Knowledge and Sociological Theory*, London, Routledge; and Bloor, David (1976) *Knowledge and Social Imagery*, London, Routledge.

4. Weber, M. (1949) *The Methodology of the Social Sciences*, New York, and (1947) *The Theory of Economic and Social Organization*, Oxford, ch. 1. The second part of *Methodology* and ch. 1 of *Theory* are reprinted in Brodbeck, M., ed. (1968) *Readings in the Philosophy of the Social Sciences*, New York. Myrdal, G. (1953) *The Political Element in the Development of Economic Theory*, London; (1958) *Value in Social Theory*, London; and (1970) *Objectivity in Social Research*, London, Heinemann.

5. Horton, R. (1973) 'Lévy-Bruhl, Durkheim and the scientific revolution', in Horton, R. and Finnegan, R., eds, *Modes of Thought*, London, Faber. For another un-masking of positivism, see Gouldner, Alvin W. (1970) *The Coming Crisis of Western Sociology*, London, especially ch. 4.

6. Rex, J. (1970) *Key Problems of Sociological Theory*, London, Routledge, pp. 164–6.

7. Myrdal, op. cit., 1958, p. 119.

8. Mannheim, K. (1936) *Ideology and Utopia*, London, especially chs 2 and 5. It is of course ironic that it is the introduction of ideological and social criteria into the interpretation of *natural* scientific theories, by Kuhn, Feyerabend, and others, that has played a large part in the revival of contemporary debate about sociology of knowledge.

9. Gouldner, op. cit., 1970, p. 483.

10. ibid., p. 484.

11. ibid., pp. 378–95.

12. ibid., pp. 31–2.

13. Another writer who makes explicit the choice of value goals for knowledge is Habermas; see especially the appendix to Habermas, J. (1972) *Knowledge and Human Interests*, London, Heinemann. Habermas there makes a threefold dis-tinction: the *technical* interest of the empirical sciences; the *practical* interest of the historical sciences, defined as 'the intersubjectivity of possible action-orienting mutual understanding' (p. 310), somewhat in the *Verstehen* tradition; and the *emancipatory* interest of the social sciences, whose function is *critique* of the established social order. In the light of examples such as are quoted in note 17 below, this is to put matters into a rather too restricted straitjacket.

14. Primarily in Myrdal, op. cit., 1970, pp. 55–6, where he supplements the positivist view of objectivity implied in *Value*, op. cit., 1958, p. 119, in the following terms: 'The only way in which we can strive for "objectivity" in theoretical analysis is to expose the valuations to full light, make them conscious, specific, and explicit, and permit them to determine the theoretical research.'

15. This objection was raised by participants in the Ross-on-Wye Conference, 26–28 September 1975.

16. For a discussion of this see Hesse, Mary (1975) 'Models of method in natural and social sciences', *Methodology and Science*, 8, 163.

17. There are some good (and some bad) examples in Blackburn, R., ed. (1972) *Ideology in Social Science*, London, Fontana. C. B. Macpherson describes the function of social theory as *justification* of a social system (ibid., pp. 19, 23 – cf. Gouldner's 'reduction of tension' quoted above); M. Shaw, on the other hand, in a critique of Gouldner, takes the goal to be the overcoming of academic sociology 'in the development of the revolutionary self-consciousness of the working class' (ibid., p. 44). In more moderate vein, in Horowitz, I. L., ed. (1964) *The New Sociology: Essays in Social Science and Social Theory in Honour of C. Wright Mills*, Oxford, S. W. Rousseas and J. Farganis assert that ideology (inseparable from social theory) 'must be concerned with the human condition and its betterment in an always imperfect world. Its justification for being is, in a word, progress' (p. 274).

18. It is significant that G. S. Jones, in an Althusserian piece in Blackburn, op. cit., denies that it is values or interpretations that are involved in theory choice, and holds that what is required is new concepts of structure (p. 114). In other words, the hard Marxist reverts to a view of the social sciences as theory-laden only, but of course the theory (and the values) are those of Marx.

19. I should like to express my thanks to those who commented on a first draft of this paper at the meeting of the Thyssen Philosophy Group at Ross-on-Wye in September 1975, and also to David Thomas for discussions on the general problem of values in social science.

Name index

Subject index